How to Create

Sustainable Hospitality

A handbook for guest participation

T0376190

What they are saying about this book

Anna Pollock - Independent strategist for regenerative tourism

Christopher Warren's *How to Create Sustainable Hospitality* closes any gaps in motivation that have existed between host and guest. All too often hosts have delayed adopting sustainable practices until there was proof of demand and guests have found it difficult to know what else they can do after hanging up their used towels. This book is an invaluable source for all hoteliers smart enough to see their guests as partners not consumers and provides a wealth of practical advice as how to make that partnership serve the business, the guest and the planet. The book is original, based on experience, well researched, very readable, convincing and deserves widespread circulation.

Bob Garner – Founder of EnviroRental and Owner of Casal dei Fichi

What a superb resource this is! Christopher draws on extensive research and experience to give us a master class in what to do to be a sustainable host. But importantly the focus is very much on the vital piece of the puzzle – how to communicate with guests and persuade them to be active participants. As Christopher says "guest participation should be deeply woven into service delivery". Active in this field for 15 years I felt I knew this topic, I learnt so much.

Nicole Ouimet – Previously Environmental Manager Disneyland Paris

Actively involving our guests is essential now to protect nature and to take part in this time of *great transitions*. Christopher's book is practical and innovative. Apply these ideas and you will see guests enjoying helping your business by interacting with employees in a new way, making significant savings and reducing the destruction of our natural resources.

Don Morris AO – Previously Chair of the Australian Tourism Commission, founding director of the Tourism and Transport Forum

The primal urge to escape the humdrum of daily life and to plunge into exotic new experiences and cultures – *wanderlust* – is indelibly imprinted in human DNA. Tourism is by far the globe's largest discretionary mass consumer activity. But, as Christopher Warren's fascinatingly clever and readable book makes crystal clear, authentic action on climate change and environmental sustainability are today's non-negotiable 'must have' values at the core of tourism demand, particularly for engaging with the dominant and influential Millennial and Generation Z cohorts. An absorbing and timely read for the entire tourism and hospitality sector.

Rodney Payne – CEO Destination Think!

Christopher's book is exceptional both educational and filled with opportunity. Nearly every tourism professional I know is woefully unprepared for the climate crisis. Even the most advanced sustainability professionals in our industry has trained for a very different world than the one we've now created.

The thinking in this book goes right to the heart of the type of behavioural psychology needed to catalyze transformational change among both guests and hotel staff. It is anything but a generic sustainability textbook; exposing the depth and complexity of the problems with a method of critical analysis that avoids the typical generalization.

My own reckoning of the true severity and pace of the climate emergency was a brutal awakening. The magnitude of disruption is staggering. This piece will be an important primer the hotel industry leaders of tomorrow. When you're ready to unbury their heads from the sand and grapple with an entirely new worldview, this book will help you to be part of creating a more prosperous world by bringing green tourism into the mainstream.

John Swarbrooke – Professor at Plymouth University

This unique book provides an invaluable practical guide to how hospitality businesses can encourage consumers to behave more responsibly. Based on the real-world experiences of the author, an acknowledged expert in the field of sustainable tourism, it also has a strong theoretical underpinning. This important text deserves to be read by practitioners as well as students and researchers in tourism and hospitality, marketing, and consumer behaviour

Harald Friedl – Associate Professor for Sustainability and Ethics in Tourism, University of Applied Sciences

This book is a refreshing source in the desert of sustainability guidebooks: where the mainstream spreads top-down advice with moral undertones, this author manages to address everyday needs of hoteliers and guests. Here, sustainability in tourism turns from an arduous challenge into a gain in quality, credibility and joie de vivre.

Alexandra Coghlan – Associate Professor Department of Tourism, Sport and Hotel Management, Griffith University

An enormous amount of experience, research, reflection, and conversations with other experts has delivered an insightful, engaging and practical handbook. His strengths are to show how stressors will and are compounding each other, through their direct and indirect interactions. Christopher's lived experience of the sector allows him to paint the system in an engaging and compelling way.

His step by step process, arguments and questions all serve to reduce the fear around inviting the guest to be part of the process of sustainability, leading to a deeper transformation in the direction needed. And while there is no sugar coating of the scale of the issue and the challenges we face, he quietly dispels myth after myth of what is and isn't possible in greening the hospitality sector and brings it home with concrete examples through clear images and explanations. And he consistently reminds us of the importance of true hospitality, not merely a series of transactions and trade-offs, and good old fashioned "waste not, want not", which in my view is an excellent creed to live by…

This is a book for anyone serious about greening their business, and who wants to move beyond the low hanging fruit and/or hit and miss technological solutions, to a deep, ongoing, adaptable and context-driven approach to sustainability.

Glenn Mandziuk, CEO, Sustainable Hospitality Alliance

Due to its reliance on the natural environment and its position in communities all around the world, the tourism industry has perhaps more reason than many other industries to manage and mitigate its impacts. However, this global presence and its interaction with thousands of travellers each year gives it a unique opportunity to be a huge force for good.

By connecting guests to local communities around the world, particularly those that will be most affected by climate change, accommodations can help spread awareness of key sustainability issues and what role individuals can play. This can also help them engage guests in their own sustainability efforts and amplify what they're doing.

Guests are increasingly looking for authentic experiences which enable them to connect with the world around them and are increasingly keen to take steps to be more environmental when they travel.

This book explains the business case for engaging guests in your environmental efforts and outlines five easy-to-follow steps to engage guests in a meaningful way, encouraging them to support your environmental efforts and, potentially, increasing their loyalty at the same time.

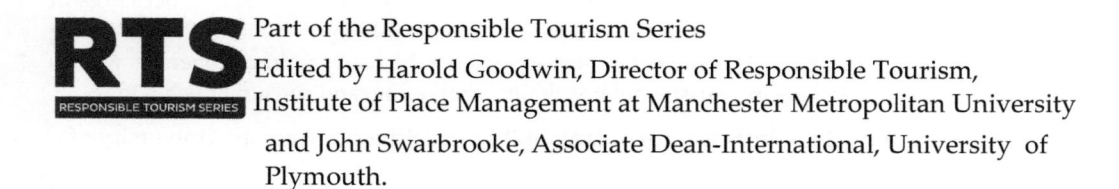

Part of the Responsible Tourism Series
Edited by Harold Goodwin, Director of Responsible Tourism, Institute of Place Management at Manchester Metropolitan University and John Swarbrooke, Associate Dean-International, University of Plymouth.

Sustainability is a necessity, climate change, biodiversity loss, the loss of cultural heritage and local economic development are challenges for the tourism sector. Too often sustainability is used as 'greenwashing'. Responsible Tourism requires transparency in reporting and respect for local people and their cultural and natural heritage. We need to leave more than footprints, to fund conservation and to compensate local communities for the opportunity cost of maintaining their heritage for our enjoyment. Too often tourism has just used destinations and this needs to be reversed. Responsible Tourism is about using tourism to make better places to live in and better places to visit, in that order.

How to Create

Sustainable Hospitality

A handbook for guest participation

Christopher Warren

(G) **Goodfellow Publishers Ltd**

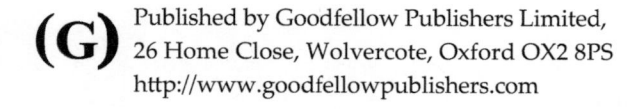 Published by Goodfellow Publishers Limited,
26 Home Close, Wolvercote, Oxford OX2 8PS
http://www.goodfellowpublishers.com

British Library Cataloguing in Publication Data: a catalogue record for this title is available from the British Library.

Library of Congress Catalog Card Number: on file.

ISBN: 978-1-911635-66-6

DOI: 10.23912/9781911635659-5276

Copyright © Christopher Warren, 2023

All rights reserved. The text of this publication, or any part thereof, may not be reproduced or transmitted in any form or by any means, electronic or mechanical, including photocopying, recording, storage in an information retrieval system, or otherwise, without prior permission of the publisher or under licence from the Copyright Licensing Agency Limited. Further details of such licences (for reprographic reproduction) may be obtained from the Copyright Licensing Agency Limited, of Saffron House, 6–10 Kirby Street, London EC1N 8TS.

All trademarks used herein are the property of their repective owners. The use of trademarks or brand names in this text does not imply any affiliation with or endorsement of this book by such owners.

 Design and typesetting by P.K. McBride, www.macbride.org.uk

Cover design by Cylinder

Contents

Foreword: Xavier Font

Professor Xavier Font, University of Surrey, United Kingdom, and UiT The Arctic University of Norway, Norway.

There are many tourism and hospitality businesses that already protect their environment and create meaningful jobs, purchase locally and promote the sense of place of where they belong. It's part of who they are, and they do many of these things naturally. These businesses may not be making the most of their sustainability practices because they are implemented in an instinctive way, without a systematic approach to reflect on their current practices, to set out plans to make continuous improvements, and to experiment with pro-sustainability changes. The book is very helpful to these and also to those businesses that have already made significant progress, and now want to scale up their work.

Christopher Warren has found the way to explain sustainability as a business opportunity, not a cost, in a way that will make sense to small and large hospitality firms alike. Few understand what is required to design sustainable experiences, and how to communicate persuasively with consumers to change their behaviour. The advice in this book is practical and evidence based. The examples used are current and wide-ranging. There isn't another book with a step by step, tried and tested process, that distils years of experience and the many reality checks of looking at a business owner eye-to-eye when you suggest how they can use sustainability to remain commercially viable.

The term sustainability is multifaceted, it will mean different things to different guests. Rather than expecting them to understand and appreciate every aspect of it, it's important to break it down into its many components that gives you 100 communication touch points rather than just one. This book shows how to unpack the S word into a wide range of aspects, and first focus on those that will mean something to your customer, and will not require a great effort. These customers will appreciate your knowledge if you are generous with it and not judgemental and transparent.

We often see guest participation in sustainability as punitive – reducing the quality of service offered. Sustainable luxury needs to be redefined, in the context of how the meaning of sustainable prosperity, wellbeing and quality of life are being redefined. A customer who demands a wasteful consumption environment is unlikely to leave satisficed for long, whereas a genuinely wholesome and fulfilling experience can create a sense of wellbeing that we sorely need these days. Multi-sensory sustainable guest experiences are positive, empowering, and satisfying. Christopher's many examples demonstrate clearly that businesses of every size and target market can improve their business models to provide lasting customer satisfaction by introducing sustainability-informed experiences.

Christopher advises that you do not shy away from sharing your sustainability practices since the media suggest that everyone exaggerates their claims and that customers are sceptical about what they hear. While *greenwashing* may be more common amongst large firms, we have seen that many tourism firms *greenhush* instead – they deliberately under-communicate their sustainability efforts, for fear of coming across as having compromised on customer service. The lack of knowledge and understanding of everyday things like electricity use of different appliances means that owners/staff like you can be scared to discuss what they are actually doing or answer questions. This book will help you understand the many different aspects of sustainability so you can feel more confident discussing the property's actions, as Christopher guides you on how to assess your impacts by looking more intently at everyday things and redesigning the guest experience.

We are a risk-adverse industry, and anything that may threaten our current business model is looked at with suspicion. But changing our business models is no less than what Christopher suggests, with his 20 years of experience owning a boutique accommodation and meeting guests himself. Host-guest engagement needs to go beyond contractual requirements and service level agreements, to create fulfilling, transforming opportunities. At home, most of our behaviours are routine-based, and a truly hospitable experience is a chance not only to refresh yourself, but also an opportunity to reflect on your daily behaviours and to break some of those bad habits and learn from experience. Environmental psychologists will call this spillover effect, Christopher makes it part of his mission.

The book encourages owners by accepting that though some guests are not interested in savings, they will do better if the owner has implemented changes that reduce wasteful behaviours. For those customers that are not ready to embrace change, at the very least you ought to provide "frictionless sustainability". This involves making sustainability behaviours be the default, easiest to choose offer, either by editing unsustainable options, or requiring guests to actively require them. While this book does not speak about behavioural economics in such terms, it does implicitly propose actions to nudge consumers, and to create a social identity of being a caring customer, aligned with this discipline. Not only are the solutions based on science/research, but Christopher has applied them himself to thousands of guests over the years. I am reassured by that unusual combination of research and evidence-based practice.

Co-created experience delivers competitive advantage, and this co-creation involves us all. It goes without saying that staff engagement will be essential to create the conditions for guest engagement. Guests will only truly participate if they can feel that staff live by the sustainability values that their organisation stands for. Staff design and deliver the experience context and mechanisms that then condition the impacts, positive and negative, that the guests will have. Few books have considered the design and delivery aspects of hospitality experiences, and here's where Christopher's hands-on experience provides a multitude of ideas on how managers can engage their teams, and in doing so make their business more competitive.

I appreciate a book that is not descriptive of concepts, but that is action oriented. The advice given helps you design a sustainability management system (it is less daunting than it sounds!) that helps you reduce your operating costs (and your impacts), as well as attract more customers, improve their satisfaction, increase their expenditure, promote customer loyalty and reduce seasonality. The breadth of ideas provided show you the multitude of opportunities to fine tune your current business model. There are many low-hanging fruit that are manageable, with a little budget and time, and a can-do approach. Before long, you will realise that both your mastery and self-efficacy have improved. This will fuel your ambition to do more, and you will re-read the book looking for higher targets. You will be encouraged by the positive response of your colleagues, friends and indeed customers, to keep going and progress further.

At a personal level, I find it hugely satisfying to read a book from Christopher, and I can hear his voice as I read every sentence, reflecting the many conversations we've had over the years on how to change the business models of our industry to do good.

Foreword: Susanne Becken

Professor Susanne Becken, Griffith University, Australia and University of Surry, UK

This handbook is an extremely useful resource for anyone involved in tourism and hospitality. The book addresses an important gap, indeed several gaps, in that it bridges theory and practice, and in that it finally tackles the most important dimension of the sustainability transition – the people. All too often, attempts to become more sustainable – and to use less energy and water as aspects of this – seem to almost purposefully and clinically dehumanise the process so to not 'inconvenience' anyone, be it the visitors or staff. The predominant focus on technology and higher level 'managerial solutions' has robbed us of an important opportunity to put the people at the centre of the solution. As Christopher Warren points out in his book, every guest can be a green guest and become part of a greater movement to 'do good'. I agree with the underlying assumption of this book that nobody travels to be a bad tourist... But all too often, the structures around us simply do not allow to make sensible choices. Or guests just don't know enough about their impacts. By including them in sustainability initiatives, we harness an important opportunity of positive learning. Holiday experiences (or even business travel) that are novel and intriguing are rewarding, exactly because they do not provide cookie cutter solutions that just don't deliver sustainable outcomes.

The text is based on a vast array of personal experiences and stories from across the world. This makes the book very readable, but also provides a sense of authenticity that few experts in this sector can deliver like Christopher. The depth and authority with which pertinent examples are shared and analysed leaves little doubt that the key arguments presented in this book are 'worth thinking about'. Many of the (nonsense) examples from real-world accommodation experiences will resonate with readers as they clearly expose the lack of thought that has gone into room design and service delivery in many places. Who hasn't arrived at a hotel room with all lights on and the air conditioner blasting at 18 degrees Celsius. And who hasn't wondered about the one milk container in the fridge, and the heat it generated in the cupboard behind it. And the lack of opening windows in many hotel rooms, I am sure, has driven to frustration many who would like to breathe some fresh air.

The book is usefully structured into two parts. I read it in two parts and that worked very well as it allowed me to digest the information presented in Part I, before engaging on how this would work in practice as outlined in Part II. The first part makes a clear case of why sustainability is important, and also why involving guests is a win-win for everyone. The text is soundly anchored in scientific theory and evidence, yet readable for a wide audience. Part II then sets out a 'course of action' with plenty of examples, graphs and tables to assess one own's situation. What came across to me is that if one followed the five steps from the first audit to a well rounded integrated business ethos of 'conserving together with the guest', one will not only achieve a major benefit for the environment, but a much better business as a whole.

And herein lies the challenge of the book! The call to action is not for hospitality providers to go out and change lightbulbs. It goes much deeper than that – encouraging owners/managers to take progressive steps to transform their business. The book actually is about spending considerable thought on every aspect of the business. The building design and infrastructure (the proverbial 'canvas to paint on'); the existing set up of service delivery and experiences (is human interaction minimised? Is the uniqueness of the location conveyed to the guest?); the staff and their empowerment to be part of this journey (have they been trained? Are they rallied around the purpose of the company?). And of course, finally the guest who arrives at the premise, eager to have a good time or relax, but a bit disoriented and grateful for sound advice that makes their stay more enjoyable without it costing the Earth. Commitment to understanding all of the above, and accepting that this will take a long time ('Iterate, iterate, iterate' as advised in the book), is part and parcel of a successful transition. I am convinced that the journey will be a rewarding one.

In summary, this is an excellent read that will help everyone in hospitality seeking to make a difference – including researchers who study this subject. Engaging with practical opportunities and challenges in our research designs is crucial to generating new knowledge that can help our collective endeavour of service-oriented innovation. Enjoy the read.

Limitations

Much of my research and project experience is within developed or developing economies, where most tourism occurs. There are therefore limitations in research and practical examples that represent a truly global perspective. However, I believe this book has relevance to all types of tourist accommodation where host-to-guest hospitality is provided. The examples used can in many cases be conceptually applied or even reversed (from hot to cold climates) and the guest's engagement methods adapted to different cultural contexts.

New technologies are providing contactless host-to-guest communication, the principles of which can be applied similarly to new automated systems, though they have not been detailed here because of the evolving nature of digital and sensory communication. For updates of the use of new technology please visit my website, www.mygreenbutler.com.

Messaging, using signs, cards, and leaflets has also only been summarised in this book. This is because research suggests it is contextual issues that matter most rather than the intricacies of the wording. Therefore, a significant proposition of this book focuses on contextual factors (the level of comfort, the sustainability story, the property's own integrity, the staff commitment) and how to redesign the experience to help guests consume your hospitality experience more sustainably, rather than how to write sentences that are more persuasive. What matters most is what the actual offer is and the integrity of the host.

Thanks

This book would not have been possible without Sophie, who courageously allowed me to conduct experiments at our own business – I am deeply indebted. To Harold and Xavier, who taught and inspired me. To Susanne and Alexandra for your advice and friendship. Thanks to Becky, David, Edward, Fred, Laurence and Sarah for your manuscript advice. And finally, to Maxwell, the next generation, who honourably stands by me to deliver these solutions to help others' transition.

For

All our guests, thank you for your enthusiasm to try the new.
My children, there is a brighter future.

About the book

Guests directly account for over 50% of resource use in hotels and as much as +90% in self-catering accommodation, while also delivering all the revenue. They are quite simply the most significant factor in hospitality's ongoing high resource costs, pollution and, waste. Given the targets to reduce carbon emissions by 66% by 2030, it is imperative that practical solutions for the sector are created and applied fast. *How to Create Sustainable Hospitality* is the first text to demonstrate how to persuade guests to participate in the accommodation's sustainability quest, while increasing customer satisfaction and building a competitive advantage.

Based on 16 years delivering sustainable hospitality experiences face to face with guests, and conducting hard research on guest engagement at sites in Australia and Europe (from 1000-bedroom hotels to self-contained holiday homes and timeshare lodges), the author presents a tried and tested five step methodology on how to directly, effectively and successfully involve guests to conserve resources. This presents a new paradigm for tourism. *How to Create Sustainable Hospitality* presents a clearly written, jargon-free, practical solution which:

- Demonstrates, using a triple bottom line balance sheet, why guests' participation in sustainability makes good business;

- Sees guests as an active and critical component in sustainable consumption and production at their holiday accommodation;

- Introduces a five-step methodology on how to directly and effectively involve guests in saving energy and water, reducing food waste and cutting carbon;

- Delivers a practical solution that has been successfully applied to achieve a fast ROI with scientifically measured savings;

- Uses persuasive theory to explain how to communicate with guests and by so doing increase stay satisfaction, 'delight' and brand reputation;

- Includes many case examples and scientific research to illustrate how the theories works in practice.

About the author

Christopher Warren, PhD, MSc, Dip Ad, Trainer & Assessor (Cert IV), Founder of My Green Butler, Director of the International Centre for Responsible Tourism Australia, was co-proprietor of multi-award winning Crystal Creek Meadows for nearly 20 years. As a Research Fellow at Griffith University, he was a member of the Australian Research Council's grant winning team researching conserving behaviours at tourist accommodation. He is also a partner in the UN Environmental Programme's One Planet network. Ecotourism Australia awarded Christopher the EcoTourism Medal for his contribution to tourism and nature, after founding one of the world's first destination carbon calculators, the 'Green Kangaroo' in 2006, and for voluntary work conducting audits to help tourism businesses.

Prologue

3rd January, 2020 - Kangaroo Valley, New South Wales

The air is becoming suffocating, hot, dense, as if an enormous oven door is open, fanning you with blistering dry heat from which there is no escape. It is an overwhelming force. Everything is wilting, yellowed grass splinters underfoot. All life shrinks away from this fierce force.

I look at my mobile phone. It is blank. The tech has failed with the temperature +50°C. I am outside putting the rest of the branches and leaf matter on another green waste pile, one of nine we built during 14 days of preparing our property in the face of a bushfire that creeps closer each day. I am the co-owner of a tourist accommodation business just two hours from Sydney and Canberra that would normally be buzzing with visitors during this time of the year. Now it is empty. All guests sent home days before and none in prospect, revenue has dried up overnight.

In desperation, I recheck pumps and hoses then continue clearing up more green waste that could ignite and turn our little patch of paradise into an inferno. My wife and youngest child have left for safety. News reports tell us the wind is picking up and will fan the fire. It has been burning since August. It started over 150 km away and is now consuming the forest on the other side of our mountain.

I plan to stay and protect what we have built up over 18 years: the nature conservation zone; the 4 ½ star cottages; all our pension and income reinvested into creating a multi-award-winning property …our dreams and our souls. As the sky goes orange and grey, deep and moody clouds appear on the horizon above the mountain to the southwest. My two remaining adult children say, "This is it, we must leave". I can't bear to go. I refuse. Their screams urge me to leave. I give in.

We drive out of the valley, a harrowing journey as the now gale force wind blasts in ahead of the fire front. Winds are able to drop a widow maker* on us at any moment, so we have to slowly snake up the tight bends of the eastern mountain pass. At the top we dash to safety and stop. I sit in my sweat stained clothes and cannot move for three hours. I say nothing. I am nothing as my business was me. The news suggests the fire is at our door. My mind is blank.

4th January, 2020

I wake at 6am and worry for our 15-acre property, our buildings, the habitats we created, the creatures that live there. Has it been destroyed, are we safe? Jumping out of bed I reach for a computer, tap in my password to My Green Butler, the sustainability tech solution I developed, and am overjoyed to see I have readings from my cottages. The inside temperatures had reached 45°C, but I am getting

---

* Australian eucalyptus trees will drop branches in severe weather conditions so the rest of the tree can survive. The branches are so heavy they will lay a man flat dead in a second.

readings. That means the buildings are standing. Dashing for the car I drive back up and over the mountain pass avoiding fallen branches to check if our livelihood is intact.

This was our experience of the Black Summer that wiped out over 3 billion native animals and forested areas larger than the size of Switzerland. We dodged a bullet that day. The fire had reached 4 km from our business and home, with embers travelling up to 12 km, and at the last minute the wind changed direction, redirecting the fire. The wind fanned that fire, it sped up and made an almighty charge as a firestorm taking a due north course up and across the neighbouring mountain. At what cost?

Friends own a similar tourism business down the road from us. Their buildings, olive grove, and natural habitats were wiped out. The firestorm intensity reached 1600°C, melting their basketball court surface to glass, forcing a parked tractor and truck, originally parked 10 meters apart, to be welded together as one metal block.

What remained of the lodges after the fire (Courtesy of Paul Williams & Alison Baker)

After two years of insurance claims and wading through new planning regulations, they are slowly regrouping and reforming their business. Two years of no income, two years of living on a charred and wiped-out site, two years of once magnificent views that had become blackened and dead, as though the world had become festooned with over-sized burnt matchsticks… everywhere.

Then came the floods, Covid, and again floods in 2022, which saw a year's rainfall within weeks and eroded the mountain pass of that destination, cutting off main road connections for months and with repairs lasting a year. A flooding downpour dumps over 390 mm in 72 hours, further demonstrating our weather has changed dramatically (on the mountain top they received 4000 mm January-June 2022 compared to an average annual fall of 1500 mm). A further economic blow as tourist numbers again plummet. This is tourism in a changing climate. This is why I have written this book.

Part I:
Where we are now

The need for action

In this first part, we discuss the business case for creating sustainable hospitality – highlighting the risks and advantages of innovation during recessionary times and crises, and then detailing how guest participation adds to your triple bottom line and overall business performance.

We then discuss if there really is such a thing as a *green* guest. Using research evidence from a wide range of sources, we uncover the reality of functioning in our modern world and the opportunity of targeting guests for more sustainable outcomes.

While cleaner technologies and renewables are a critical part of our de-carbonisng journey, we find that conserving is actually more important to start with. Start with a Plan C (for conserving) before going to the expense of over-engineering efficiencies and renewables.

We look into the psychological impacts of relying on technology alone and the threats of greater consumption

Finally, we identify the cost of inaction, the risk of weak action, and action and the benefits of strong action, including customer service and staff productivity.

1 The business case for guest participation

This book is a guide to achieving your most important sustainability initiative – achieving guest participation. Guests are key. They make the purchase decision and deliver revenue. They use most of the resources, contributing heavily to our environment footprint. They can act either responsibily or irresponsibly in what they see and do, and where they spend their money in the destination. A negative review can be very harmful to sales; their purchases during their stay can provide much needed additional revenue; and their return visits are very economic from a marketing sense. Yet until now, for some strange reason, we seem to have excluded them in our quest to become more sustainable. Let us address this key challenge now.

Throughout this book I am going to ask you to reassess the old hospitality adage that we should not bother guests about sustainability. This mantra that, "The guest is King. Long live the guest!" is out of date. Those times have changed through global necessity. I encourage you now to consider inviting your guests to be true sustainability partners. Through this invitation you will create a more successful business, become a sustainability leader, and build a distinctive brand reinforced by shared values of owners, managers, staff, guests, and suppliers (Figure 1.1).

It is a wasted opportunity to simply 'add on' sustainability as a marketing *feature*. It should be at the *core* of your business. From a guest perspective, you create a distinctive brand by combining a set of differences covering design, style, facilities, amenities, costs, quality standards, and service delivery to forge a distinctive experience your customers want. Everything is focused on generating that special experience to fit a customer profile. As a business you also seek to deliver the commercial returns the owners want and to progress the company's values that are beyond profit. These values are an important catalyst for progressing social and environmental actions for your sustainability programme.

Applying sustainability correctly should help create a distinct brand, strengthen your offer, and defend your business against competition. Implementing sustainability is a catalyst for innovation. Sustainability gives you greater distinctiveness as you should draw on core competencies, location, culture, and vision to flow through the brand experience and build a more resilient competitive advantage. Your commercial strategies and sustainability actions must therefore reinforce each other, work together, and be embedded throughout to broadcast brand values – not contradict them.

Recent events have whipped up plenty of examples of why creating sustainable hospitality has never been more needed, more commercially sound, and more desirable for your shareholders, managers, guests, and staff. Pressures like pandemics, wildfires, droughts, stifling heat and soaking rains, rising costs, carbon-energy legislation, over-tourism and price-cutting all appear to be constricting tourism. But there is a flip side. Yes, owners and managers are under acute pressure dealing with day-to-day challenges, but choosing to apply more sustainable practices can set the wheels in motion to change your trajectory, rejuvenate your business, and enable everyone to flourish. By recognising guests as your sustainability partners, you release massive potential to deliver sustainable hospitality in a positive, delightful manner that fortifies your brand and business.

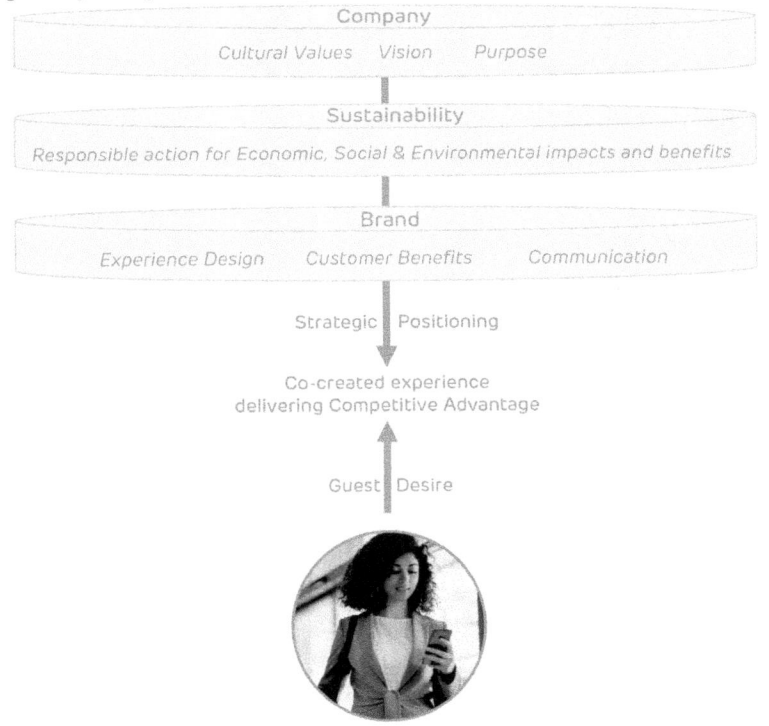

Figure 1.1: Foundations for a sustainable competitive advantage. Company values, vision and purpose reflect what you want to achieve. By identifying your environmental, social and economic impacts and benefits you take responsibility for the way you deliver the service. Your brand communicates the resulting distinctive solutions through an experience design that promotes guests' benefits. Guests co-create this experience meeting their needs more meaningfully.

Defining key terms

For clarity I also want to define some of the terms used so that we are aligned.

Sustainability is a concept. It requires a tourist accommodation operation to:

- identify its environmental, social and economic issues;
- through the responsible decisions of the owners, managers, staff, and guests, take actions that minimise those identified negative impacts and maximise those positive benefits when producing and consuming the service;
- ensure resources are not depleted, nor wasted, for the benefit of future generations of all life on the planet.

The principle of **hospitality** is delivered when accommodation is offered as overnight facilities for tourists (business, leisure, events). Where there is a *ritual* exchange between the host and guest that involves:

- a friendly welcome without prejudice;
- the desire to make the traveller feel comfortable;
- ensuring the guests' safety;
- having guests' needs and wants met by the host;
- service provided with generosity;
- guests responding to the hospitality ritual with courtesy because they know the host and follow 'house rules' (Chapter 9)

Hospitality is a cultural value where the level of generosity to strangers reflects the hosts' beliefs. In some accommodation the business of hospitality leads to a greater emphasis on selling services to meet the needs of the guest, as a commercial transaction expressed through a company culture and brand. This means that in some accommodation the hospitality experience is deeper, warmer, and less commercially focused than others.

With modern technology we see the hospitality role transferring from human hosts to technologies like robots and apps. The degree of warmth, cultural value and generosity these technologies offer will similarly affect whether the guests see them as part of the hospitality experience or merely functional services. Technology has an important contribution to make hospitality more sustainable and is explored in this book with references to my invention *My Green Butler*.

This book concentrates on guest participation. It therefore excludes or lightly covers certain fields of sustainability because they are less directly relevant to the aim of explaining why, how, and when to achieve guests' participation in creating sustainable hospitality.

1

Much of this book concentrates on dealing with our current challenges of climate change and biodiversity loss as these are 'red alert' challenges (United Nations, 2021) and therefore our collective priority, but the principles and methods I describe can be applied to a wider range of sustainability issues which may be of greater relevance in some locations.

My argument for change

In this first chapter of the book I have three sections in which I outline the business case for sustainable hospitality and why guests should be sustainability partners.

- **Section 1** summarises key threats and risks to hospitality firms. Many of these are climate change related.
- **Section 2** makes the case of taking an innovative approach in time of economic crisis, energy crisis and high competition.
- **Section 3** presents the argument for applying a sustainability focus. As sustainability is expressed as the triple bottom line (environment, social, and economic), the business case is set out as a balance sheet with pros and cons discussed from the perspective of assets, liabilities and equity.

A business case is essential. Being keen on progressing sustainability does not mean ignoring the realities of running a commercial business. Shareholders with profit-making interests can have a +8% return on their investment as their goal. You ignore them at your peril. Your business case is the justification for implementing a project for commercial benefit.

Throughout a specific emphasis is given to justifying why guest participation is so strategically important. My aim is to show you that applying Sustainable Hospitality is a smarter way to do business for the future.

1: Adapting to a climate-conscious world

Climate change related

Accelerating extreme weather events

Climate change is a 'red alert' threat to mankind and all life on the planet (IPCC, 2022), yet its far-off 2° or 3°C temperature rises sound so innocuous. That is because these incremental numbers are an average annual forecast temperature rise. The weather reality of course is very different. Five days of plus 42°C (14°C above the average summer temperature) is a different matter, and the devastating consequences through extreme weather events can destroy tourism and your livelihood – as described in the Prologue. Seemingly small increments in temperature rises hide a big threat to our businesses.

Extreme weather events impact consumption. Higher temperatures cause guests to use more energy to keep cool. My friend Dr Christian Werner is a climatologist and expert adviser to energy companies, and he regularly reminds me that during extreme weather events energy consumption can rise more than 25% above normal usage. The threat of climate change is therefore a threat to all our efforts to save energy. The longer we have these extreme weather events, the higher the consumption.

It is not just high temperatures we should be concerned about. Your property might be in a region that receives its annual average rainfall in a month (the fate that occurred in Kangaroo Valley two years after the drought and fires). That too can affect consumption simply because your guests are having to stay inside for longer, leading to more baths, watching TV, and leaving lights on.

Reports and research indicate that tourists are already succumbing to the impacts of heat stress when on holiday (Vanovac, 2018; Fortington, 2022) and summer heat is impacting local populations (BBC, 2019). In British Columbia's summer of 2021, 231 people died in a single day either in their own homes or hotels (Schmunk, 2021). Those in the most vulnerable age and accessibility categories (Climate Just, 2017) may be our regular guests. Do you have a heat stress strategy for older visitors, those with mobility needs, and your staff?

The impact of extreme weather can last a long time. A few days of high temperature is one thing, but an extended drought changes a destination's appeal. Some areas of South Africa, for example, are facing a significant threat to their tourism economy and biodiversity – the very magnet that draws the visitors in the first place (Smith & Fitchett, 2020). On the flipside, warming and lack of snow is terminally affecting the ski industry (NIDIS, n.d.) with operators having to change focus to summer activities (Pickering & Buckley, 2010). Some destinations see the erosion of their natural assets disappear each year. In Quintana Roo, Mexico, up to 4.9 metres of beach are disappearing every year (Jong, 2022).

Finally, not only is the increase in extreme heat waves likely to double, but also the size of the affected areas is likely to increase by 80%, which will put more strain on energy supply as demand rises over several days (Lyon et al., 2019) and could increase risk of power cuts (Komiya & Lies, 2022; Reuters, 2018) and drive electricity prices higher (Almeida, 2021).

When you assess the climate change threats to your business, review how many days of extreme weather you are regularly experiencing. Have you noticed how your energy use changes during extreme weather events? If you do not know, then now is the time to start monitoring. The risk is that if you have not avoided wasteful practices, energy consumption will accelerate during extreme events – times when staff productivity falls and guests' health can suffer. The risk of not being prepared for extreme events and having insufficient adaptive measures may well make your property less attractive.

Guests adapt faster than hospitality can

The threat of extreme weather also affects visitor numbers around the world (Shaw, 2019; Ngxongo, 2021). If it is likely to rain heavily, or to have extended days of high temperature, people think twice about visiting. The attractions they want to enjoy are just not comfortable (3Keel, n.d.). But the risk lies deeper. Your demand will drop or stop when there are hazards in the destination. Heavy downpours that wash away roads or flood campsites, extended days of high temperature with yellowing countryside, water bans, or bush fires, make people think twice. All these factors we experienced at our own hospitality business in three years. You might think that's just life in the Australian bush, but we have now seen fires in the green belt around London (Salisbury & Burford, 2022). The Australian fires sent smoke and particles across to Sydney for weeks, affecting visitor numbers. In total the Black Summer fires (Davey & Sarre, 2020) caused AUS $ 4.5 billion loss of earnings for the Australian tourism industry (Thiessen, 2020).

Guests naturally do not want to visit places thought to be dangerous because their primary reason for a holiday is to relax. Many put safety first. This has been demonstrated with the impacts of wildfires in California, floods in the Southwest of England, or lack of drinking water in South Africa. Even if the fires, shown on TV news, are more than 120kms away, guests' fear can stop your online bookings at a stroke. As climate change effects grow, guests will increasingly make changes – sometimes last-minute – to avoid visiting and may stay away for a long time. This threat to hospitality firms is not veiled. Guests, even loyal customers, will avoid you if hazards appear likely to ruin their dream holiday or disrupt their event. And they will do this with increasing promptness as the speed of environmental changes gathers pace, and holiday firms and insurance terms permit, and the internet gives them options to switch.

Tourist accommodation, on the other hand, cannot move. Our property is rooted to the spot. It is not easy to minimise risk from the threat of extreme events. You must now plan ahead to improve guest communication to pre-empt cancellations and have examples that justify your recovery messaging. While you manage the impacts of climate change, your guests can choose to holiday elsewhere (The Week, 2018). For my business, we assessed our risk of guests demand change as 'Very Likely', its impact 'Significant' and the threat level 'High', following 17 years of the escalating droughts, multiple high rain events, and the fires.

More legislation

Tourist accommodation buildings now face increasing compliance pressure to reduce energy. The Paris Agreement of 2015 was a major milestone that not only achieved a declaration with 196 parties (United Nations, 2015), but has become the spark for new government legislation that tackles climate change with buildings centre stage, because they are responsible for 40% of emissions in Europe (European Commission, 2020).

The relevance for hospitality is that tourist accommodation consumes a great deal of energy. Hotels, for example, will use considerably more energy than an equivalent office building and are one of the most energy intensive building types after hospitals. From my site visits I can also confidently state that it is not the size of building that indicates its energy intensity, nor occupancy levels. I have found multiple instances where day spa facilities will consume over 60% of the energy (mostly gas) at quite small properties. Or one can find swimming pools, sometimes individual pools for each accommodation unit, consuming vast amounts of energy resulting in a modest sized property consuming a similar amount of energy one would expect at a much larger hotel. These hot water dependent 'enhancers' (Lockyer & Roberts, 2009) may attract visitors to stay longer, but may become environmental liabilities unless sustainability practices are applied now.

The road to zero carbon

In December 2021 the European Union commission set out its ambitious plan to achieve zero emissions and fully decarbonise buildings by 2050 by linking policy with the European Green Deal Package, which will lead to grants for new systems to reduce greenhouse gas emissions (Directorate-General for Climate Action, 2021). The EU requires member states to establish verification systems with documentation completed by independent parties (Article 7.A5) including detailed monitoring and verification systems (Annex V.5.j) (European Union, 2018b). In particular, commercial buildings that are in the low classes of Energy Performance Criteria (G or F) must be renovated to improve their performance. This will cover 15% of the worst performing buildings in Europe. Commercial buildings will have to improve to at least performance level F by 2027 and to level E by 2030. Meanwhile the UK Government's Sixth Carbon Budget (UK Government, 2021), aligned to the European Union's Green Deal, sets in law a mandatory emissions reduction target for buildings by 78% by 2035. Using standards like EPC ratings (UK Government, 2009), buildings in the UK will have to make strenuous efforts to reduce emissions.

Experts believe that only 10% of hotel properties meet minimum 2030 carbon efficiency standards, which will lead to a decline in property valuation (Mosquera, 2022). Simply complying with regulations is therefore not going to be enough to protect future value and yields or avoid obsolescence. (See 'How the EU Directive on Energy Performance in Buildings affects tourist accommodation' in resources.)

Greater caution by insurers

Do not expect your insurance to tick along as it once did. Insurance companies are actively protecting their risk. Many were likely listening when Sir John Bevan, the chief executive of the Environment Agency at the annual conference of the Association of British Insurers said: "Much more extreme weather will kill more people through drought, flooding, wildfires and heatwaves than most wars have." He went on to say, "The net effects will collapse ecosystems, slash crop yields, take out the infrastructure that our civilisation depends on, and destroy the basis of the modern economy and modern society" (Taylor, 2021).

The insurance sector certainly had a rethink after the Black Summer fires in Australia, with insurers refusing to cover 100-year-old pubs close to national parks, doubling the insurance premiums and leaving hospitality providers to operate without insurance (Libatique, 2021). For my own business, insurance grew to over 4% of total expenditure.

A seismic change in financing and reporting

The threat of financial institutions minimising their risks will have a knock-on effect to your ability to raise capital. At some point in the future, you may want to raise capital for innovations. This can either be taken from surplus revenues/ cash flow or will require approaching third parties or stakeholders. The financial markets, be they banks, shareholders, investors, private equity firms, or crowd-funding, are critical for a hospitality firm's valuation and potential to raise funds to pursue sustainability progress.

To be successful in raising capital, you need to be sure you fit with the lender's aims like a "lock and key" (Vance, 2005). You need to be aware of the seismic change that is occurring in the financial markets in order to successfully secure funds. Otherwise, you risk finding it harder to raise capital, which could lead to being surpassed by innovative competitors, becoming less attractive to investors, partners, customers, and suppliers, and weakening your long-term durability.

Becoming an ethical investment

Companies who want to raise significant capital will have to meet ever increasing governance standards beyond climate action. The latest United Nations Environmental Report clearly shows a link between biodiversity, the health of the planet and human health. We cannot afford to continue to deplete natural resources at the expense of the environment or future generations, and we have so far failed to achieve the Brundtland 1987 sustainable development aim. If we want to avoid further global health crises like Covid, then we must reinvigorate efforts to rejuvenate nature. Wasteful use of resources is, therefore, a key consideration for hospitality firms. Environmental Social Governance (ESG) reporting will be expected to report far reaching challenges, not solely decarbonisation.

The seismic change in the financial markets can be demonstrated by ethical investment funds no longer being seen as a niche market, and billionaire investors looking for only substantive returns. Sustainability has become mainstream. Investors concerned about climate change can now radically change a company's sustainability trajectory. In 2015 there was a reported $5 billion contributed to sustainability investing, which grew to $51.1 by 2022 through middle aged millennials choosing value driven investing (Adamczyk, 2021). Take the example of AGL, Australia's largest electricity producer, responsible for 8% of the country's total carbon emissions. Mike Cannon-Brookes' Grok Ventures became AGL's largest investor in order to stop the proposed splitting of the energy generation arm, so that he could drive the company to decarbonisation much faster and speed up the transition to clean energy. This challenge forced out sensor management, cancelled the demerger, and drove a fresh, entirely new strategy (McKay & Stringer, 2022).

Investors now are looking for companies with a purpose that see decarbonisation, for example, as a competitive advantage. Larry Fink, Chairman, and CEO of Black Rock, the world's largest multinational investment corporation (with US$10 trillion under management), describes it as a tectonic shift in capital to more sustainable investments that has now reached US$4 trillion. "Every company and every industry will be transformed by the transition to a net-zero world. The question is, will you lead or be led?" he argued in his annual letter to CEOs (Fink, 2022). Fink's organisation sees decarbonising the world economy as the "greatest investment opportunity of our lifetime". Your sustainability reporting is therefore critical. Companies' sustainability performance is being watched. A report by the New Climate Institute assessed leading corporations responsible for 5% of the world emissions, finding that they were failing to meet their own targets (Rannard, 2022).

It is not only NGOs who are reporting. The G20 leading global economies want clear information on the risks and impacts of climate change on the financial performance of markets. Through the Financial Stability Board, they have established the Task Force on Climate-related Financial Disclosures (TCFD) to recommend company climate-related disclosures so investors can better assess their risks. As Michael Bloomberg says, climate change "has cost the industry trillions of dollars this year alone" (TCFD, 2022). Consistency is important because different banks assess a company's ESG performance differently with "the correlations ... astonishingly low" (Credit Suisse, 2020). That desire for consistency is being pursued by the International Sustainability Standards Board (Daubeney, 2021).

There is a flip side in the drive for standardised reporting. It might lead to competitive pressures on businesses (Mullan et al. 2021). Banks themselves are having to reassess their risks. The European Central Bank (ECB) saw the need to complete an economy-wide stress test over a 30-year horizon involving four million companies worldwide and 2,000 banks to examine the risk of climate change on the financial markets and the transition risk to carbon-intensive industries (Guindos, 2021). The ECB has acknowledged that current capital buffers for banks do not reflect the full extent of climate-related risk, and to fill regulatory gaps, fundamental changes are necessary to protect banks (Baranovic et al., 2022).

Are you at risk from outside pressures?

Tourism companies are feeling the most pressure to act compared to other sectors of the European economy, with 76% of CFOs under pressure from clients/customers, and 64% from government regulation according to a Deloitte report (Coppola et al., 2019). It also found 52% of tourism CFOs feel under direct pressure to act on climate change from their investors/shareholders. Yet only 16% of tourism businesses confirmed they had an emissions reduction target in line with the Paris Agreement, and 32% had just set their own targets. This suggests that less than half of tourism businesses have considered a carbon reduction target.

To drive sustainability in your business, consider these questions:

- Have you set a target and calculated what emissions reduction and adaptation will cost?
- Have you identified your key sustainability issues, including staffing, community, water use, and nature regeneration?
- How will you finance this?
- If you want to raise capital, consider how attractive your business is. Does it have a clear vision/purpose and how is sustainability fully integrated within this?
- If your hospitality firm has building assets with poor energy performance ratings, high energy consumption, high waste outflows, and buys unseasonal produce from afar, is it possible you would be rated poorly?
- If your business is in a high-risk region for flooding, fires, or sea level rise, how will you mitigate and adapt?
- Are your competitors able to showcase how well they are doing by benchmarking against others? (UNWTO, 2021).
- How will you show continuous progress in the above measures?

Other key other factors in developed economies

Rising costs for hospitality

In the past many hospitality firms found that their properties used a great deal of energy, but only limited actions were taken, often with the replacement of old equipment for new more efficient systems. Now the pain of not taking stronger action is coming home to roost.

It has been decades since the hospitality sector been confronted with such a large escalation in costs. These are mostly driven by higher energy prices, which have seen electricity and gas prices soar, putting businesses under enormous pressure (Scottish Television, 2022). My own clients have seen in some cases electricity prices double and gas prices triple, leaving energy 10% of their expenditure. Even 21.8% has been recorded previously (Coles et al., 2016). It is not for the want of trying to get a better-fixed rate, with a quarter of hospitality providers in the UK for example, unable to negotiate better terms (Thomsen, 2022). These energy price rises affect your staff too, especially the lower paid (Shearing, 2022).

The cost of water is also increasing (O'Beirne, 2022). One pays twice there, once for the mains supply and again for treated wastewater, which carries an especially high carbon emission rate. Water has been identified as a major challenge for sustainability. Increasing population growth, economic development, and climate change are leading to water scarcity, putting pressure on authorities to regulate consumption through price and monitoring as demand grows 20% to 30% over the next few decades (Maxwell, 2010; Patterson et al., 2022; Boretti, & Rosa, 2019). Learning from the sky rocketing price rises of energy gives us warning that rising water costs are also a threat. Both energy and water prices also affect laundry services and their costs which will be passed on. Choosing to not save on energy and water will mean equipment is running at full throttle, increasing maintenance costs.

These expenses are often described as variable costs; they adjust to the ebb and flow of occupancy. However, energy is not as variable as some might think. A great deal of energy can be used for heating/cooling public spaces, lighting the exterior and gardens, or heating spa facilities even when there is only one person in the hot tub. If you analyse your meter readings, you will find the significant share of energy is actually a fixed cost (depending on the characteristics of your tourist accommodation). Recessionary trends and lower revenues mean that energy price rises can strongly affect the bottom line.

Inflationary pressures are on the rise for food and beverage supplies as well, making any food waste all the more expensive as you are not just paying for the disposal of the waste but the costs of wasted ingredients.

Cut down on staff turnover

Cost of hiring, training, and the learning curve (lost productivity) for new staff is a significant amount of money per individual, running into the thousands (Hinkin & Tracey, 2000). It becomes wasteful investment if staff constantly leave (discussed further below). For example, hotels in the USA have been found to save over 21% of their food waste following the investment in new monitoring equipment and staff training (Simon, 2018). But if your staff are constantly changing, how will you manage to maintain attention to detail and correct control of the new equipment? After decades of reasonably stable costs, we are running into a period of inflation (at the time of writing). Continuing to focus primarily on revenue per guest night is a risk – for economically sustainable hospitality, operational and variable costs need to be closely monitored and wasteful practices stopped.

1

Since Covid there has been a seismic change in the way people view job opportunities in hospitality in developed economies. They are largely viewed as poorly paid with unsocial hours, where one has to succumb to difficult working relationships and inefficient communications (CABI, 2005). These barriers are very real and not solved by tempting people with more money (Town Square, 2021). Salary levels are low – 50% of staff in the UK are paid below the minimum wage (TUC, 2019) – though they still represent between 25-40% of total revenue, a big expense. But it is the overall working conditions that made people re-think even before Covid. Some properties experience a 150% turnover of staff per year (Harver, 2022). A general manager I know in New South Wales confided he simply could not implement his sustainability programme because "it's a revolving door…new staff are joining one month and leaving the next". Without consistency, you cannot build superior performance.

The risk is simply that we cannot deliver service without our staff. In fact, after Covid managers told me they could not sell all their available rooms simply because they did not have team in place – it affected their bottom line immediately. The risk is also that if we do not make working in hospitality more attractive, then we simply will not attract the right people and deliver the service standards expected. Good service is the prerequisite of high guest satisfaction (Padma & Ahn, 2020). Happy guests lead to great reviews. If your review rates are in the doldrums, then demand and revenue will be seriously affected. If your staff are unhappy, they also will not be listening intently to guests' feedback and organisational results will suffer (Lee et al., 2021). Conversely, responsible business practices do attract and maintain staff loyalty and improve market performance (Rhou & Singal, 2020).

More scrutiny on staff practices

There is a growing awareness that hospitality's desire for good returns to pay back investors might lead to irresponsible staffing practices, which can lead to revolt – something that has been further exposed during the Covid pandemic as subcontracted staff have been left out of welfare support and left to survive on food banks. An example of this is Las Kelly's (Spanish Chambermaids Trade Union) who have gained crowd funding support for their booking app that only lists responsible accommodation that cares for its staff (Burgen, 2021). The risk of weak action to staffing can lead to erosion of reputation.

Decent pay, training and working conditions strongly affect staff satisfaction, which is essential in providing quality customer service (these are a focus of the Sustainable Development Goal 8). For example, researchers found that in Spain and Greece where working conditions were poorest, staff satisfaction levels were the lowest in Europe. In counties with the highest conditions – Denmark, Finland, Sweden, and France – staff satisfaction was the highest (Diaz-Carrion et al., 2020). Social policies play a fundamental role in your brand's appeal and demand.

2: Why some thrive during recessions and economic crises

It is during recessions and recovery periods that businesses either go bust, are acquired, or cling on to survive. However, many thrive to become stronger and more competitive. The multiple crises over the last three decades show us how companies can respond positively. Having a vision which maximises guest appeal through sustainability practices wins through.

Cutting costs or surgical removal of existing wastage?

Cost reduction is the most popular strategy. Cost is cut by delaying maintenance, checking budgets to find cuts, using unpaid vacation to reduce the labour force, and replacing highly paid employees for lower-paid staff (Pappas, 2014). This is because the initial response to a recession is to improve cash flow (Lowth et al. 2020). Such tactics, while necessary, may not help you build a competitive advantage for the long term. Once these cuts are made you still need to build profits. Which can be difficult if your competition responds in a similar manner and/or a lengthy recession constricts demand further. Note that successful businesses that thrive cut costs and at the same time reinvigorate their service.

Recommendation: Hospitality firms are more likely to improve profitability during recessions from effective use of fixed assets than any other means. An example is to increase output from the same level of resource use or maintaining the same level of service using reduced resources (Patel & Guedes, 2017). Using smart technologies can help you make surgical removal of wasteful operations (Chapter 10), and improve the guests' experience.

Motivation and productivity

Reducing staffing levels is another early response as wages are a high proportion of hospitality operating costs, but there are repercussions. When staff leave so does their knowledge, as well as the investment that firms have spent in sourcing, hiring, and training. The remaining staff face an increase in workload and strain which can result in a drop in productivity (Phillipson et al., 2004), making the firm less able to steer out of the recession. Thriving companies, on the other hand, may cut staff or hours, but not at the expense of losing human resource capabilities. They see the importance of creating a collective sense of purpose and alignment which delivers better service to their guests.

Recommendation: High performing companies have been found to cut less. They increase the quality of their employees and motivate them. They see an increase in productivity with the impetus of change representing a motivation.

Motivated staff have been found to be a key factor in attracting more guests (Chapter 7), which in turn leads to improved market share and cash flow (Nickell et al., 2013). In contrast, employee resistance is a barrier for growth (Lowth et al., 2020) and may lead to lower levels of hospitality.

> A key motivation is expressing and sharing the business' commitment to socio-environmental actions as staff feel their job is more fulfilling: 51% employees don't want to work for a company that doesn't have a strong Corporate Social Responsibility commitment and 74% say their job is more fulfilling when they are provided with opportunities to make a positive impact at work (Cone, 2016).

Discounting should be avoided

How should a hospitality firm set prices post an economic crisis? A company might already be saddled with debts and operating structures like labour and energy costs. A decline in demand and external competitiveness makes it much harder for firms to compete on price when operating structures and costs remain. Discounting might bring short term cash-flow but does not suddenly ignite a thriving hospitality business because you still have to meet operational cost. Use of 'dynamic' pricing, 'competitor based' pricing, or 'cost-plus' approaches perpetuate commodified accommodation stock.

Recommendation: Aim in hard times to create a sustainable hospitality experience that attracts a discerning guest. Firms who thrive implement a customer-centric revenue model (Dholakia, 2016), where managers select the best value to price ratio. Properties that correctly identify the distinctive advantages which stem from their sustainability practices (Chapter 6), can place a value on these competitive factors, focus on internal quality control to optimise them, and build marketing and communication strategies which promote these attributes. A unique product is not comparable and thus less susceptible to discounting. This would enable your tourism business to sell its product at a price which allows you to offer quality and positively assist cash flow.

Creating shared value

In the past, some tended to focus solely on the drive for profit 'at all costs' and ignoring the wellbeing of their guests, health of their staff, and the improved use of resources by cutting waste with everyone's help (guests and staff).

Recommendation: Interweave into the core of your business, guests' health, staff needs, and positive resource management to drive business success (Chapter 4). It becomes a collaboration, which during recessions is seen as a key to thriving (Piercy et al., 2010).

Innovation

Businesses that thrive through improved profit, sales growth, market share, and cash flow have been found to use recessions as an opportunity to innovate by meeting the changing needs of their market.

Recommendation: In the service sector – a people intensive service – innovation does not have to be considered solely as hard technology. It can be new ways staff collaborate with guests (service), preventing waste (process), changing housekeeping structure (organisation), or applying a value-based proposition (marketing). From a motivational perspective this could be creating a more relevant collective sense of purpose and alignment within your business to implement a new business model (McKinsey & Co, 2020) that perpetuates sustainability progress – which most of your guests actually want to see and enjoy (Chapter 2).

There are numerous examples of tourist accommodation niche concepts. Take for example New Forest Escapes in England who have been applying a range of innovative steps involving their vacation home owners and guests to reduce energy costs, increase local expenditure and promoting the distinctive features of the local identity. These companies create a strong product/market fit to become highly competitive in times of recession and economic crisis.

3: Triple Bottom Line sustainability balance sheet

Sustainable hospitality business case pitch

By placing sustainability at your company's core and striving for continuous progress at every business layer you will ignite a powerful competitive advantage, a more resilient business, build a reputation as a market leader, and be more attractive to capital investors/lenders/insurers. You will achieve this by:

- Cutting costs more effectively than your competition,
- Cutting carbon to contribute to national goals,
- Reducing your climate risks,
- Adapting to extreme weather for the benefit of your guests and staff,
- Maintaining higher levels of service quality and enthusiasm from your loyal team.

You will achieve these while others who maintain a business-as-usual approach mount up liabilities. You will also achieve far more durable outcomes than those who pay lip service using the camouflage of eco-labels, generalised reports, and tokenistic projects that carry the risk of greenwashing.

The foundation to sustainable hospitality is to design your sustainability programme around creating an outstanding guest experience, where guests (and staff) can touch, smell, see, hear, and taste sustainability's benefits. These should emphasise the unique characteristics of your property, including your vision, the staff, local geography, and culture.

Sustainability is not a one size fits all approach but a neatly crafted focused plan that answers your specific sustainability issues. It should build distinctive guest experiences using sustainability led solutions that run throughout the veins of your business, reaching all facets, to produce a holistic balance of economic, social, and environmental benefits.

To demonstrate this business case, I will now summarise the application of sustainability through the triple bottom line of economic, social, and environmental measures applied to a balance sheet of assets, liabilities, and equity. The strategic relevance of guest participation and why it is your guiding focus to deliver stronger performance is highlighted. A balance sheet approach has been chosen because it is a recognised framework to evaluate a company and therefore helps us assess the benefit of the business case. My proposal (summarised in the following table) enables you to compare your assets (advantages) with liabilities (disadvantages of taking no action), leaving the sum balance as stakeholder equity.

Assets

Economic assets

The more we standardise hospitality service delivery through controlling systems in an effort to control cost, the harder it may become for hosts to personalise and create distinctive experiences. This makes hospitality vulnerable because human adaptive behaviours are limited, and it is human behaviour that is at the heart of hospitality. Value may come from volume and location, but one can be exposed to commodification and discounting. Alternatively, sustainability can grow the economic value of your assets by building a strong competitive advantage. This is achieved through the reciprocal process of offering your hospitality service in a way that enables guests to co-create their experience (Vargo & Lusch, 2004, 2016).

Economic sustainability can come from drawing on your strengths and hospitality competencies, and the contextual differentiations that set your property apart, then building on these factors to create benefits that establish marketing differentiation. Target guests who appreciate these benefits so they will want to co-create the experience for themselves. Develop host-guest relationship opportunities that deliver value propositions around the benefits to better meet the guests' needs (Chapter 9). Guests can then be invited to co-create their experience, which can be integrated with the property's sustainability drive (Chapter 7). The effect of applying sustainability propels continuous refinement, the guest experience is improved, and the skill of the host is further enhanced. The effect meets the pleasure-seeking needs of your guests, and growing success motivates staff. The co-created experience becomes a defining asset of your business.

	Triple Bottom Line Analysis for Sustainable Hospitality	Strategic relevance of guest participating as sustainability partners
ASSETS		
Economic	Drive sustainability through competitive advantages. Build brand value. Lower cost of production. Higher revenue per guest night.	Key source of revenue. Guests responsible for consuming +50% of resources.
Social	Staff loyalty. High staff sustainability literacy (training). Community support. Charitable programme supporting social causes. Staff able to persuade guests to participate in sustainability actions	Good service is a key determinant of guest satisfaction. Guests want to know they have made a good choice. Positive emotions from stay experience. Contribution to social programme. Enjoy participating in sustainability actions. WOM referral & return.
Environmental	Utilisation of solar energy. Rainfall harvesting. Waste prevention. Local and seasonal procurement. Strategic alliance with nature conservation partner. Strong ability to adapt to extreme weather events.	Guests are interested in eco innovations. Guests want to know they have made a good choice. New acquired knowledge transferrable to homes increasing wider benefits and building brand reputation. WOM referral & return.
LIABILITIES		
Economic	Cost of energy, water, waste, food & beverages, laundry. Cost of insurance. Cost or rehiring staff and training. Lack of preparedness for threats and commercial risks.	Loss of revenue – guests choosing alternative property with strong sustainability benefits.
Social	Level of reputation for working conditions, gender equality and terms. Accessibility limitations. Capabilities of staff to care for and apply sustainability practices. Lack of community support.	Dissuaded to write a review. Share WOM dissatisfaction as guests dislike modern slavery issues. Cognitive dissidence when comparing quality of life for local communities. Corporate clients expect social governance reporting.
Environmental	Scale of carbon emissions. Dependence on fossil fuels. Water consumption. Vulnerability to extreme weather events. Dependence on unsustainable procurement. Site impacts and use of chemicals. Lack of evidence.	Guests use more resources in hot/cold/wet weather, this jumps in extreme weather events. Guests want peace of mind that their choice of accommodation is not harming the environment. Dissuaded to save if they feel sustainability claims are greenwashing.
EQUITY		
Economic	Level of equity dependent on long term revenue/earnings trends – how vulnerable are these to changes in resource costs, cost of compliance and improved margins of competitors.	Dependent on ability for guests to co-create their sustainability experience with their own unique interpretation and values that justify a profitable tariff.
Social	Level of equity dependent on reputation meeting and reporting social responsible practices, licence to operate staff loyalty, training outcomes.	Dependent on increased stay satisfaction through culturally stimulating experience, or sharing of positive social values. Prepared to pay a premium for culturally stimulating experience
Environmental	Level of equity dependent on environmental performance compared to competitors, environmental codes of practice. Improved biodiversity	Dependent on increased stay satisfaction from enjoying eco-innovations, application of skills to conserve, or learning/contributing to the regeneration.

Figure 1.2: Triple Bottom Line Balance Sheet Analysis

Track your progress by systematically monitoring:

1. Guest satisfaction ratings internally.
2. Positive reviews.
3. Revenue per guest night compared to your competitors.

The more satisfied the guests the more likely you are to drive high demand, enabling you to raise tariffs (Chapter 6). This approach can build on the technology trend that is accelerating personalised guest experience. For my business, I was able to increase my tariffs by 10% and at the same time involve my guests in co-created experiences that saved +20% of our resources. The result was a positive increase in reviews, increase in forward bookings, and higher profits.

Better environmental and cost management also drives down the expenditure of producing hospitality. You can achieve savings as high as 38% (Warren et al, 2018) by encouraging guests to save through better advice and feedback (Chapter 10). Measure this by monitoring the use of resources and third-party services: per guest night, room night, by day, time of day, season, and temperature.

You need to apply a comprehensive matrix for your KPIs. Reliance on occupancy alone does not always reveal savings potential as you might have considerable resources used in public areas, leisure areas and restaurants, or be positively/negatively affected by the weather (Chapter 6).

Relevance of economic factors for guest participation

Guests are relevant economically because they are responsible for the majority of consumption – 50% in a hotel (City of Melbourne, 2007) and over 90% in self-contained lodges. Involve your guests and you directly positively impact your bottom line. Guests are the central source of revenue for your tourist accommodation. Without them you do not have a business. Make them your sustainability partner and you have a competitive advantage that saves costs and builds reputation.

Social assets

The revolving door of staff hirings and departures totally undermines the potential contribution the team can make to your sustainability drive. Your staff are responsible for producing and delivering hospitality. If they are motivated, they can be encouraged to save a great deal of resources, prevent waste, apply progressive procurement choices, take preventative actions in extreme weather events, and set and maintain rules. The degree of your sustainability success lies with staffs' level of carbon literacy (Coles et al., 2016), attitudes and behaviours towards impacts (Yao-Fen, 2016), and agility to take adaptive actions (Dosa & Rosemary, 2019). Staff therefore can make or break your sustainability ambitions.

Consider combining all your social sustainability initiatives (training, community and charities) into a single powerful integrated programme. In gamification terms this is called an 'epic meaning' (Chapter 11) where the synergy between each initiative builds shared value for all and makes it easier for you to drive it forward. A strong social programme can be the glue that holds teams together so you can drive improvement.

The effect of a social sustainability programme can reduce significant amounts of wastage. For example, I have saved one client 1.5 million of litres of water in three months (by identifying maintenance issues and cutting housekeeping hot water use) just by showing them how much they actually were using when accommodation was unoccupied. We motivated staff to make savings by offering them a day off to visit charitable projects that the resort supported.

By integrating strong cultural values, you help to fuse relevant local context – what matters in your destination – with your sustainability goals (Moscardo & Hughes, 2018). Design the programme to include charitable partners that reflect local values, to build staff motivation through a shared sense of purpose (Warren, 2022) and to be inclusive so you build team spirit (Lemon Tree Hotels, 2021). Apply gamification to motivate staff when faced with challenges, tedium, or anxiety. Making the initiative fun, maintains team interaction and comradery – essential glue for loyalty (Apostolopoulos, 2019). Gamification can reward staff through recognition, and build an individual's own sense of achievement (Groening & Binnewues, 2019). The benefits grow if you attract candidates with strong green attitudes who can become more receptive to your vision (Chan et al., 2014). Remember that hospitality attracts a high proportion of younger staff members. Today these individuals have very high levels of interest, concern about social injustices and a sense of inheriting a colossal environmental challenge, with 48% of Generation Z and 43% of millennials putting pressure on their employers to take climate action (Deloitte, 2022).

Your performance indicators can be: i) staff length of service; ii) involvement in the charitable programme; iii) competency levels from your literacy training; iv) guest satisfaction; and v) resource and cost savings.

Relevance of social factors for guest participation

The Covid pandemic emphasised how important good customer care is for reputation management (Song et al., 2022), and it remains a leading factor for guests desiring personalised, comfortable, and beautiful experiences (Padma & Ahn, 2020). Using your customer service team to communicate your social sustainability programme (Chapter 8) directly to guests has the triple benefit of:

- Reinforcing to guests they made a good choice in accommodation,
- Inviting them to participate in that social programme also offers co-created opportunities which enhance the stay,
- Demonstrating brand integrity which can help temper guests' complaints by increasing tolerance of service delivery failings.

I heard one general manager tell me that 75% of their staff were locals but did not go on to say they could recommend local places to visit that met my interests. A missed opportunity because most guests love to see the special places that locals know are best. This feeling was only heightened following months of lockdowns when there was a boom in hobby activities and increased sense of environmental concern (Westbrook & Angus, 2021). Being able to delight guests with recommendations is a very effective asset to stimulate greater participation and help your sustainability drive (Butcher & Chomvilailuk, 2021), maximising the benefits of the programme and encouraging guests to spread the word (Huang, 2017; Anantara, 2020).

Environmental assets

Decarbonising accommodation through the installation of new equipment is a primary focus for most building owners. However, this has be considered carefully. If you buy before conserving, there is a high risk the new equipment will be oversized for your actual consumption (meaning you have wasteful consumption *locked in* if you invest in larger solutions than you actually needed). Intelligent assessment and investment in greener operating systems is a powerful environmental asset if you follow this logical order.

1. It is essential to reduce consumption. Tourist accommodation buildings consume high levels of energy and water, and produce corresponding high levels of waste and emissions. Conserving resources through mindful operational adjustments with responsible staff practice changes will make savings immediately (Chapter 4). Conserving has been strongly encouraged by governments to manage the energy crisis in 2022 (France 24, 2022). Conserving is a normal historic practice humans have applied for centuries, which maybe we had forgotten, but companies must now live with.

2. Retrofit with biomimicry design solutions and or better methods to apply adaptive behaviour (Chapter 6), minimise use and maximise the behaviours of people that occupy the building **before** you look at buying high-cost cleaner technologies.

3. Build your capacity to take preventative action in advance of extreme weather events and adapt to ensure guest and staff comfort and health through maximisation of biomimicry solutions and adaptive amenities (Chapter 7).

4. Widen the scope of your business by contributing to the restoration of biodiversity on your property and within your destination, to improve the health of the environment and maintain its attractiveness. This provides staff and guests with positive regenerative signs that are emotionally uplifting. Select seasonal and locally sourced foods.

5. Consume wisely and install renewable technologies to minimise reliance on network supplies and costs. Guide staff to consume within the provision of renewables.

The effect of taking these steps in the right order is an invaluable asset demonstrating success. It builds your credibility as an expert with your guests (Chapter 7), which is essential in persuading people to adjust their wasteful behaviours. It is also an asset in tempering consumption to within what you have set as acceptable consumption limits.

Your performance indicators can be: i) baseline versus consumption by hour/day; ii) carbon per guest night/room night; iii) average inside temperature versus outside temperature by hour by season; iv) change in wildlife sightings/planet specific, insects weekly; v) share of total energy and water provided by renewables

Relevance of environmental factors for guest participation

Guests will help you reduce your environmental footprint through the adaptive amenities and advice to save resources (Chapter 10) without the need of monetary incentives (Dharmesti et al. 2020). We have the opportunity of reaching out to millions of households who want positive change (Taylor et al., 2019). By sharing our use of renewables and explaining adaptive actions (in advance of extreme weather events that guests can apply at home), we can protect guests' health and help to reduce global emissions on a wider scale.

It will not cost you the earth to involve guests as research shows that guests can apply responsible actions in hotels without the need for fiscal incentives (Warren & Warren, 2022). The more innovative the green practices, the more positively guests feel – choosing to opt out of towel and linen replacements is considered basic (Yu et al., 2017; Dharmesti et al. 2020). They will feel emotionally uplifted by learning and seeing the positive impacts you have made to improve biodiversity. The backstage use of renewable energies and water will be interesting for them to learn (Koch et al., 2020). The total benefit increases guests' assessment of your professionalism and leads to a positive cascade of good reviews and WOM referrals (Chapter 8).

In short, do not keep your eco innovations hidden under a stone – use your KPIs to illustrate progress. Involve your guests. They are an extra pair of willing hands, as shown at Conscious Hotels in Amsterdam (www.conscioushotels.com) and Mockingbird Hill in Jamaica (villamockingbirdhill.com/sustainability).

Liabilities

Economic

Poor cost control and inaction to conserve will leave you with high on-going financial liabilities. The continued inflationary pressures are caused from the multiple events of Covid pandemic, the war in Ukraine, utility price rises, demographic changes, and decline in the globalisation of trade (Coggan, 2022). Properties have seen massive price rises from suppliers as they negotiated new contracts.

1

Failure to take steps to conserve therefore leaves those bills super high with no reductions in sight. Over time these higher costs affect competitiveness. Failure to take action reduces the energy performance of your building and could reduce its value. Failure to record ESG progress could potentially reduce businesses access to capital expenditure loans. Inaction or weak action escalates economic sustainability liabilities. It also reflects on management capabilities.

Your costs affect your net operating income (NOI). When costs of staffing, energy, water, waste and food goes up, and sales revenue does not keep pace, your NOI is weaker. A NOI of less than 15% is not good. This is a measure banks will use to consider if your business is sound. Losing control of your costs and resource use affects your Cap rate (the return on a property investment). Investors will consider the Cap rate by dividing the net operating income (NOI) by the current value of the property – a good Cap rate can be between 7.5-10.5% (Kerrigan, 2020). If the building's value goes down due to its classified sustainability performance (e.g., energy rating) you are left with a weaker commercial position. All businesses from time to time want to raise capital. If you want to renovate and make your business a super green success, then you need to watch you Cap rate and your NOI (Avana Capita, 2022). Delaying action increases your liability to progress. Where do you stand now? Consider these questions:

- Have you done an energy audit; carbon audit?
- How have you used the information; have you a clean technology plan?
- Have you considered the mid-term consequences of taking no action?
- Have you established a baseline of how you are performing pre Covid and post Covid with the energy rises?

If you have not done these, please take a look at the audits later in this book (Chapter 5).

Energy is just one area to focus on, but what about other services? For example, laundry and housekeeping. It might contribute less than 0.5% of your total environmental footprint, but laundry and housekeeping wages can cost four times the amount you are spending on energy, water, and waste. Failure to audit your guests choosing to 'opt out' for room service linen and towel change could cost you as much as your electricity costs (based on $30 per hour for housekeepers, and $20 per room supplies and allowance for upgrade x occupied rooms – 'opt out' room x 365 days), which is why we introduced the housekeeping auditing service at My Green Butler.

Likewise with food. There are plenty of examples of zero carbon claims from food digesters or composting food waste, but what is the cost of the food that has been wasted, the labour costs of preparing it, and the energy and water to cook it? Moving food waste into zero carbon reporting solutions is ignoring the financial liability of having the waste in the first place. Food costs can represent 30% of your F&B costs, as prices rise, this waste reduces the bottom line. A further liability is that food waste is already being fined in some countries (Frost, 2022).

Cost liabilities also extend to failures in keeping staff, as the cost of hiring, training and low productivity impacts financial performance. As does a failure to take extreme weather events into consideration, which could impact your insurance premiums. This means keeping up with fire and flood regulation, as a lack of preparedness for threats and commercial risks increases your liability. We often overlook these factors as a cost burden. If we had integrated them into revitalising the guest experience and service delivery, we could have seen them as assets in being ready and ahead of the game.

Relevance of guest participation

I have noticed that as costs have risen many managers have automatically turned to finding ways to raise revenue. Eyes have been focused on mini bar sales, selling packages, offering group discounts, and overall trying to stimulate volume through deals. Almost no one has considered how to use sustainability as a mechanism to improve the per guest night margin – how can we sell our accommodation at a higher price and higher margin? Very few managers are assessing if they are losing revenue because they are not offering sustainability. I would argue this lack of information (feedback from their team, guest surveys and corporate clients) is a liability from not being aware of the potential to earn more.

In times of market downturn guests look for greater value from what they are buying. They may choose fewer holidays or business events, but the ones they do have are all the more important and they may pay a premium to enjoy quality. Failure to see how sustainability can be turned around in people's minds from being something about preachy messages to crafting a better experience customers want, is a liability – a failure in not grasping the opportunity that a values-driven sales mindset can offer your business.

If you focus on simply selling on price you can end up ignoring the desires of your guests and smoothly resolving the pains they can have when staying in an unfamiliar place. In the end this makes you less competitive. Turning this into an asset would have been redesigning the guests' experience to being one they enjoy more (Chapter 6).

Social

The concerns for workers' conditions, training, decent pay, protection of vulnerable people, and freedom of movement to change jobs has led many nations to forge laws to protect people from what is termed 'modern slavery' (Monash Business School, 2018). Modern slavery is a growing problem, even in developed countries like Australia, where there are an estimated 15,000 victims (Global

Slavery Index, 2018). There is a growing awareness that hospitality's tight cost control can lead to irresponsible staffing practices and this appears to be on a large scale in outsourced roles like cleaning. Even if you maintain good practices internally, do your suppliers? The impact from one news story can paint brands like Claridges, Hilton and Park Plaza Hotel County Hall with the same brush of contracting outside suppliers who pay contract staff below the minimum wage and bully them with unreasonable work pressure. (Roberts, 2015). An ill-considered business decision to save money can cost dearly in undermining your brand. It becomes a major liability for the whole industry, as who would want to work in such a role, or work for a company that treats others so poorly.

The recognition that poor staff care is a problem in the UK has led the hospitality sector to create the Stop Slavery Hotel Industry Network (Stop Slavery Hotel Industry Network, 2018), providing a framework for owners/managers to check their business' liabilities. There is a raft of new labour laws that also protect gender equality in many countries. And while the hospitality sector has been singled out for its high level of food waste (Eversham, 2021), their local communities are surviving off food banks (Halliday, 2022), sometimes donated by hospitality. Irresponsible social policies also lead to the exclusion of physically or mentally disadvantaged people seeking work (Rääbus, n.d.).

The effects of poor care for staff are numerous and can deeply erode any investment made into technical efficiencies (Chapter 4). Waste is going to result from poor training and monitoring because the staff do not have the capabilities to apply your sustainability ambitions, which leads to friction and frustration harming reputation (Roberts, 2015). For cost reasons, third party contractors have been hired for housekeeping, stewards, chefs, or bar staff and there has been no careful checking of their terms against the supplier code of conduct (Meliã Hotels International, 2018). Social sustainability impacts can therefore be a reputational and productivity liability.

Relevance of guest participation

Modern Slavery is now centre stage in ESG reporting for leading companies like Intrepid (Intrepid, 2022) and will lead to corporate clients and travel operators benchmarking your performance against competitors (Dyson, 2021). Since customer service is a prerequisite for guests' satisfaction, ignoring sustainability training erodes reputation (or builds a bad one). This is a particular problem for small and independent accommodations which usually do not have the same scale of resources compared to chain hotels. Decent pay, training, and working conditions strongly affect staff satisfaction, which affects customer service quality and guest satisfaction (Son et al., 2021), and service matters not just in the expensive hotels but budget accommodation too (Ngelambong al. 2016).

Likewise, guests requiring adequate accessibility facilities will warn others. There are 14.6 million people with disabilities in the UK – 9% of children, 21% of working age adults and 42% of pension age adults (Scope, 2022). The demographics in developed nations lean towards an ageing population (Haub, 2008). Weak implementation of accessible experiences becomes a hindrance when you are seeking to boost revenues in a recession, and short sighted if you want to appeal to wealthy older guests. Take the USA, where people in their sixties are the wealthiest category (DQYDJ, 2022). In Germany and Italy older households are three times richer than younger households (Bartels & Morelli, 2020). A failure to welcome guests with accessibility needs limits revenue opportunities.

The pandemic created havoc for our sector and exposed us all to the precarious nature of retaining great staff. Caring for our staff is a responsibility we cannot ignore. It is a factor guests care about but might wish to turn a blind eye to. It is not pleasant to stay in a five-star hotel knowing that most contract staff are paid a fraction of the legal wage (Walk Free, 2019). Treating staff this way truncates your ability to persuade guests to participate in conserving as you have demotivated staff, with limited sustainability training, who make errors in service delivery (the famous replacing all towels routine – even though you hung the towels up to reuse) and expose some to irresponsible business practice. As a guest why should I help such a property?

Environmental

One of the most critical catalysts for change this century is taking climate action. The changes to global temperatures will affect wildlife, plants, crops, the health of humans, and as we delay cutting emissions, our capacity to redress emissions goes down. This is globally accepted by scientists and governments. Now leading corporations are pledging to take action (Climate Action 100+, 2002).

Failure to act in reducing your emissions will leave you liable to future carbon taxes and a legacy of inaction, which will set you behind the innovators and early adopters of sustainable hospitality. They can use their pedigree for competitive advance. High levels of chemical use onsite, whether requiring housekeeping to use out-of-date toxic materials to clean rooms, or the application of chemicals on the soil, or the removal of habitat, are all liabilities that carry dangers for the future. The massive decline in global biodiversity might be out of sight, but it affects your procurement, long term cost of food and beverages (Zurich, 2022) and puts another pandemic at high risk (Heileman, 2020). Unsustainable procurement, like flying in shellfish from another continent, symbolises irresponsible practices.

Liabilities also come in the form of actions you have taken, like installing renewable energy before making serious inroads in cutting consumption. If you have chosen to offset your carbon emissions without trying to save carbon, then you have a liability in proving the effectiveness of all those trees planted. Do you have annual reports with images that verify the plantations? Are they a monoculture and therefore prone to disease? Have they taken land for food production?

The effect of not taking action to continue a business-as-usual approach or paying lip service could leave your business considered as a laggard, with a mounting carbon liability, out of step with government procurement and corporate clients' preferred supplier listing. Already leading destinations like Dubai are recording partner accommodation's carbon footprints, water use and waste (Dubai Sustainable Tourism, 2022). The UNWTO is benchmarking properties and able to demonstrate progress, albeit small – 10% carbon reduction between 2015 and 2018 (UNWTO, 2021) , while the City of Sydney has recorded a 23% reduction between 2018 and 2021 (City of Sydney, 2022).

Taking insufficient action erodes your licence to operate within the community, for example, when authorities note that on a per person basis tourist accommodation can use up to eight times more water than the local community (countries like Fiji, India, Sri Lanka) and individually properties can be consuming over 2000 litres per guest in affluent dessert countries (Becken, 2014). The effect of the liability is cranked up if you are not taking any precaution over extreme weather events, which leaves you at high risk of turbocharging consumption – high use of energy to keep cool for example – as you become at the mercy of the elements.

Relevance of guest participation

You will have to show your compliance report to corporate clients, guests, the media, government, the International Sustainability Standards Board (ISSB, 2021) and stakeholders, but the real moment of truth will be to show *continuous progress over time*. The whistle is being blown on those that promise (Ambrose, 2019) or make exaggerated claims. Only three of the 25 multinationals monitored by New Climate Institute were committed to removing 90% of carbon emissions from their production and supply chains (Rannard, 2022). Experts like Eric Ricaute and Professor Harold Goodwin will pull apart carbon reduction claims when they primarily rely on offsetting, a cheap device that avoids the challenge to genuinely decarbonising the sector (Ricaute & Goodwin, 2021). Public opinion is driving change, as demonstrated by Hilton which has pledged to cut carbon emissions by 61% and water by 50% (Touryalai, 2018). Your liability could be the gap between claims and under-delivering, or offsetting only to find the forest has gone (Welch, 2022) or to have made no progress at all.

Remaining dependent on fossil fuels leaves you exposed to the claims of greenwashing when you promote your single-use plastic campaign or highlight the beehive on the roof but continue to use electricity generated by coal. Good intentions cannot hide the pollution from the energy, the waste from food. While it is super that Google is identifying greener properties (USA Today, 2021) we cannot hide behind the leaf of their logo. The failure to act as a collective and help promote a relevant low-carbon sector is affecting us all when corporations like Microsoft change their business travel policies by charging staff an internal carbon fee for business travel. This fee has been increased for $15 to $100 per metric tonne. (Skift, 2022).

Equity

For this sustainability balance sheet model, equity is the value of success that is returned to the owner, managers, staff, guests, community, and nature after liabilities have been deducted from assets.

Economic

The strength of your assets will be dependent on how well you have:

- Driven sustainability to be a competitive advantage,
- Built brand value and relevance whilst lowering costs,
- Increased revenue per guest night by willing guests paying more for the experience.

Minus inaction:

- Ignoring the amount of resources and waste,
- Failing to audit laundry and other services to keep a real tally on how much is being used,
- Accepting insurance premiums and ignoring extreme weather event precautions,
- Accepting the current cost or rehiring and retraining as 'normal'.

The value of your economic success will be dependent on how well you have invested in your assets and reduced your liabilities leading to:

+/- revenue

+/- operating costs

+/- cost of compliance and building value

+/- performance compared to competitors.

Relevance of guest participation

The strength of your assets will be dependent on how well you have:

- Acknowledged how much guests consume when they come from different climate zones, during different seasons (Chapter 5),
- Adjusted the experience design to help guests save resources during different seasons (Chapter 6),
- Translated sustainability initiatives into tangible and experiential guest benefits (Chapter 7).

Minus inaction:

- Ignoring guests' desire to select sustainable accommodation,
- Ignoring the loss in revenue from guests booking elsewhere because another property offers a more attractive sustainability experience.

The value of your economic success with guests will be dependent on how well you have invested in your assets and reduced your liabilities leading to:

+/- degree guests can co-create their sustainability experience

+/- preparedness to pay a premium for a genuinely differentiated experience

Social

The strength of your assets will be dependent on how well you have:

- Built staff loyalty,
- Educated staff on energy and carbon literacy,
- Created an 'epic meaning' integrating into your social sustainability programme(s) which are genuinely motivating meaning to everyone.

Minus inaction:

- Avoiding creating a truly desirable place to work with positive work culture,
- Neglecting to build a reputation of responsible management,
- Ignoring accessibility access,
- Limiting staff empowerment to apply sustainability practices and to understand why,
- Ignoring how the business could work with community needs making the destination desirable for both the community to live in and guests to enjoy.

The value of your social success will be dependent on how well you have invested in your assets and reduced your liabilities leading to:

+/- licence to operate within the community

+/- length of employee employment

+/- degree of staff applying greener practices.

Relevance of guest participation

The strength of your assets will be dependent on how well you have:

- Built and maintained staff satisfaction,
- Encouraged guests to participate in social programme,
- Persuaded guests to make sustainability choices (Chapter 9),
- Stimulated guests WOM referrals and return stays.

Minus inaction:

- Permitting a bland experience that does not inspire strong positive reviews,
- Unable to demonstrate a positive employee culture to guests,
- Ignoring unpleasant disparity between community living standards and wasteful property service delivery,
- Shortfall in ESG reporting to corporate clients.

The value of your social success with guests will be dependent on how well you have invested in your assets and reduced your liabilities leading to:

+/- guests stay satisfaction

+/- degree guests can co-create their sustainability experience leading to a high sense of value and product differentiation

+/- preparedness to pay a premium for a genuinely differentiated experience reflecting local culture and heritage.

Environmental

The strength of your assets will be dependent on how well you have:

- Applied renewable energy and water systems and waste prevention,
- Minimised fossil fuels, auditing carbon,
- Researching and applying local procurement policies,
- Forged strategic alliance with nature conservation partners,
- Devised adaptive actions in event of extreme weather events.

Minus inaction:

- Remaining unaware of your carbon footprint and what are the main courses,
- Dependence on fossil fuels,
- Avoiding strategies to reduce hot water consumption and water leaks,
- Ignoring the need for operations to adapt to extreme weather events,
- Ignoring irresponsible purchasing that leads to high water use, high food miles, high packaging or food waste,
- Unaware of environmental impacts of the site including use of chemical,
- Ignorant of the business' impacts.

The value of your environmental success will be dependent on how well you have invested in your assets and reduced your liabilities leading to:

+/- environmental performance compared to competitors

+/- land regeneration with resulting changes to biodiversity health

+/- capacity to apply biomimicry actions that save using energy

+/- identification of the most effective eco investments that generate highest long-term returns

Relevance of guest participation

The strength of your environmental success with guests will be dependent on how well you have:

- Enhanced guests' stay experience by sharing eco-innovation technologies
- Demonstrated positive eco results (Chapter 10)
- Established ways for guests to positively contribute to local biodiversity building 'pleasure' from their stay experience

Minus inaction:

- Hiding true performance increasing vulnerability to claims of 'greenwashing'
- Avoiding guest guidance on how to best use the amenities and facilities, especially in extreme weather events

- Preventing guests learning the true impact of their stay and how to minimise

The value of your environmental success with guests will be dependent on how well you have invested in your assets and reduced your liabilities leading to:

+/- Reputation by transparently showing environmental actions and results

+/- Using eco-innovations as a differentiation that build demand

+/- Turning sustainability into direct guest benefits helping build a competitive advantage, including transferring adaptive skills to guests

Sustainability is not an add-on but a fundamental foundation to your company that boosts business performance. If you weld together your business values, sustainability goals, and brand attributes, you will create strong market differentiation, increase the value of your business, and protect it for the long term.

A guest-centric vision translated through sustainability led benefits will make your business an outstanding success. I know because I personally delivered this with my own property with outstanding results that have been independently verified, as I demonstrate through this book. Everything I am sharing I have personally applied in the real world. Now let us get to work developing your solution.

References

3Keel (n.d.). Assessing the impact of climate change on UK tourism. Case Study National Trust. [Accessed 29 June 2022]

Adamczyk, A. (2021). Millennials spurred growth in sustainable investing for years. Now, all generations are interested in ESG options. CNBC Make it. www.cnbc.com/2021/05/21/millennials-spurred-growth-in-esg-investing-now-all-ages-are-on-board.html [Accessed: 23 July 2022]

Almeida I. (2021) . Heat wave sends European power prices surging from UK to Spain. Bloomberg. www.bloomberg.com/news/articles/2021-07-20/heat-wave-sends-european-power-prices-surging-from-u-k-to-spain#xj4y7vzkg [Accessed 30 June 2022]

Ambrose, J. (2019). Major global firms accused of concealing their environmental impact. *The Guardian.* www.theguardian.com/environment/2019/jun/16/major-global-firms-accused-of-concealing-their-environmental-impact [Accessed 12 July 2022]

Anantara. (2020). Join hands with us as we preserve the world's most beautiful destinations. www.anantara. com/en/social-responsibility

Apostolopoulos, A. (2019). The 2019 gamification at work survey. Talent LMS. www.talentlms. com/blog/gamification-survey-results/ [Accessed 4 July 2022]

Avana Capita (2022). How to increase hotel revenue: Understanding hotel NOI. avanacapital.com/hospitality-lending/how-to-increase-revenue-in-hotel/ [Accessed 11 September 2022]

Baranovic, I., Busies, I., Coussens, W. Grill, M. & Hempell, H. (2022). The challenge of capturing claims risk in the banking regulatory framework: is there a need for macroprudential responses? European Central Bank. www.ecb.europa.eu/pub/financial-stability/macroprudential-bulletin/html/ecb.mpbu202110_1~5323a5baa8.en.html [Accessed 2 July 2022]

Bartels, C. & Morelli, S. (2020). A tale of two countries: The long shadow of the crisis on income and wealth in Germany and Italy. *Journal of Modern European History*, 1-7

BBC (2019). Summer heat killed nearly 1,500 in France, officials say. www.bbc.com/news/world-europe-49628275 [Accessed 29 June 2022]

Becken, S. (2014). Water equity – Contrasting tourism water use with that of the lcoal community. *Water Resources and Industry*, 7-8, 9-22

Boretti, A. & Rosa, L. (2019). Reassessing the projections of the World Water Development Report. www.nature.com/articles/s41545-019-0039-9.pdf [Accessed 16 June 2022]

Burgen, S. (2021). Spanish hotel booking app to show working conditions of staff. *The Guardian*. www.theguardian.com/world/2021/sep/01/five-stars-for-staff-working-conditions-on-new-hotel-booking-app [Accessed 5 September 2021]

Butcher, K. & Chomvilailuk, R. (2021). Guest benefits of hedonic value and perceived community value drive hotel CSR participation, *Journal of Sustainable Tourism*, DOI: 10.1080/09669582.2021.1931255

CABI (2005). "Low pay, won't stay" troubles of hotel staff. www.cabi.org/leisuretourism/news/5636 [Accessed 17 June 2022]

Chan, E., Hon, A., Chan, W. & Okumus. (2014). What drives employees' intentions to implement green practices in hotel? The role of knowledge, awareness, concern and ecological behaviour. *International Journal of Hospitality Management*, 40, 20-28

City of Melbourne (2007). Energy wise hotels toolkit. Melbourne: City of Melbourne

City of Sydney (2022). The 2021 achievements of the Sustainable Destination Partnership. www.cityofsydney.nsw.gov.au/environmental-support-funding/sustainable-destination-partnership [Accessed 23 September 2022]

Climate Action 100+. (2002) Companies. www.climateaction100.org/whos-involved/companies/ [Accessed 23 September 2022]

Climate Just. (2017). Socially vulnerable groups sensitive to climate impacts. www.climatejust.org.uk/socially-vulnerable-groups-sensitive-climate-impacts [Accessed 30 June 2022]

Coggan, P. (2022). Analysis. Beyond the cost of living. BBC Radio 4.

Coles, T., Dinan, C. & Warren, N. (2016) Energy practices among small and medium sized tourism enterprises. A case of misdirected effort. *Journal of Cleaner Production*, 111, 399-408

Cone. (2016). 2016 Cone communications employee engagement study. www.conecomm.com/research-blog/2016-employee-engagement-study

Coppola, M., Krick, T. & Blohmke, J. (2019). Feeling the heat? The Deloitte Sustainability Services

Credit Suisse (2020). Credit Suisse Global Investment returns yearbook 2020. www.credit-suisse.com/about-us-news/en/articles/media-releases/credit-suisse-global-investment-returns-yearbook-2020-202002.html [Accessed 2 July 2022]

Daubeney, D. (2021). Sustainability reporting for the future. PricewaterhouseCoopers, London. www.pwc.com/gx/en/issues/esg/publications/sustainability-reporting-for-the-future.html [Accessed 30 December 2021]

Davey, S. & Sarre, A. (2020). The 2019/20 Black Summer bushfires. *Australian Forestry*, 83(2), 47-51

Dharmesti, M., Merrilees, B. & Winta, L. (2020). "I'm mindfully green": examining the determinants of guest pro-environmental behaviours (PEB) in hotels. *Journal of Hospitality Marketing & Management*, 29(7), 830-847

Deloitte. (2022) The Deloitte Global 2022 Gen Z and Millennial Survey. www2.deloitte.com/global/en/pages/about-deloitte/articles/genzmillennialsurvey.html [Accessed 23 September 2022]

Dholakia, U. (2016). A quick guide to Value-based Pricing. *Harvard Business Review.*

Diaz-Carrion, R., Navajas-Romero, V. & Casas-Rosal, J. (2020). Comparing working conditions and job satisfaction in hospitality workers across Europe. *International Journal of Hospitality Management*, 90, 102631

Directorate-General for Climate Action (2021). Delivering the European Green Deal, European Union.https://ec.europa.eu/clima/news-your-voice/news/delivering-european-green-deal-2021-07-14_en [Accessed 1 January 2022]

Dosa, K. & Rosemary, R. (2019) Making sense of carbon footprint: how carbon literacy and quantitative literacy affects information gathering and decisions-making. *Environmental Education Research*, 26(3)

DQYDJ (2022). Average Net Worth by age plus median, top 1% and all percentiles. www.prb.org/resources/global-aging-and-the-demographic-divide/ [Accessed 23 September 2022]

Dubai Sustainable Tourism (2022). Welcome to Dubai Sustainable Tourism. https://dst.dubaitourism.ae/ [Accessed 30 July 2022]

Dyson. M. (2021). BTA to benchmark business travel's sustainability position. Business Travel News Europe. www.businesstravelnewseurope.com/Management/BTA-to-benchmark-business-travel-s-sustainability-position [Accessed 23 September 2022]

European Commission (2020). Energy efficiency in buildings. https://ec.europa.eu/info/news/focus-energy-efficiency-buildings-2020-lut-17_en [Accessed 30 June 2022]

European Union (2018b). EU Directive 2012/27/EU on energy efficiency. European Union Law. https://eur-lex.europa.eu/legal-content/EN/TXT/?uri=uriserv:OJ.L_.2018.328.01.0210.01. ENG&toc=OJ:L:2018:328:TOC [Accessed 1 January 2022]

Eversham, E. (2021). Hospitality food waste bill could reach 3 buillion pounds by 2016, warns WRAP. Big HospitalityInternet; www.bighospitality.co.uk/Article/2013/11/21/Hospitality-food-waste-bill-could-reach-3bn-by-2016-warns-WRAP.

Fink, L. (2022). The power of capitalism. BlackRock. www.blackrock.com/corporate/investor-relations/larry-fink-ceo-letter [Accessed 1 July 2022]

Fortington, L. (2022). Study reveals summer bush walk danger. Edith Cowan University. www.ecu.edu.au/newsroom/articles/research/study-reveals-summer-bush-walk-danger [Accessed 29 June 2022]

France 24 (2022). France unveils plans for avoiding winter power cuts due to Ukraine war. France 24, www.france24.com/en/france/20221006-france-launches-energy-savings-push-to-avoid-winter-power-cuts [Accessed 8 October 2022]

Frost, R. (2022). Supermarkets and restaurants in Spain could face fines of up to €60,000 for wasting food. www.euronews.com/green/2022/06/08/supermarkets-and-restaurants-in-spain-could-face-fines-of-up-to-60-000-for-wasting-food [Accessed 30 July 2022]

Global Slavery Index (2018) – Australian Human Rights Commission. www.globalslaveryindex.org/2018/findings/country-studies/australia/ [Accessed 23 September 2022]

Groening, C. & Binnewues, C. (2019). "Achievement unlocked!" – The impact of digital achievement as a gamification element on motivation and performance. *Computers in Human Behaviour*, 97, 151-166

Guindos, L. (2021). Shining a light on climate risk: the ECB's economy-wide climate stress test. www.ecb.europa.eu/press/blog/date/2021/html/ecb.blog210318~3bbc68ffc5.en.html#short [Accessed 2 July 2022]

Halliday, J. (2022). "There's nothing else to give them: Liverpool food banks confront rising hunger. *The Guardian*. www.theguardian.com/society/2022/jul/22/liverpool-food-banks-confront-rising-hunger [Accessed 23 September 2022]

Haub, C. (2008). Global aging and demographic divide. PRB. https://dqydj.com/average-median-top-net-worth-percentiles-by-age/

Harver (2022). 8 Causes of employee turnover in hospitality. https://harver.com/blog/causes-of-employee-turnover-in-hospitality/#Communication [Accessed 17 June 2022]

Heileman, L. (2020). Celebrating and safeguarding biodivesity to prevent the next pandemic. United Nations. www.un.org/en/un-chronicle/celebrating-and-safeguarding-biodiversity-prevent-next-pandemic-0 [Accessed 23 September 2022]

Hinkin, T. & Tracey, J. (2000). The cost of turnover. *Cornell Hotel and Restaurant Administration Quarterly*.

Huang, N. (2017). 5 remarkable hotels involved in social responsibility. *Pegasus*, 2 February. www.pegs.com/blog/5-remarkable-hotels-innovating-in-social-responsibility/

Intrepid (2022). 2021 Statement on Modern Slavery. www.intrepidtravel.com/au/2021-statement-modern-slavery [Accessed 23 September 2022]

IPCC (2022). Climate Change 2022 Impacts, Adaption and Vulnerability.

ISSB (2021) International Sustainability Standards Board, Deloitte. www.iasplus.com/en/resources/ifrsf/issb [Accessed 31 December 2021]

Jong, F. (2022). Sun set on Mexico's paradise beaches as climate crisis hits home. *The Guardian*. www.theguardian.com/environment/2022/mar/14/mexico-cancun-beaches-tourism-sea-levels-climate-crisis-quintana-roo

Kerrigan, A (2020). Hotel and Hospitality Cap rates Explained. Multifamily Refinance. https://multifamilyrefinance.com/apartment-investing-blog/what-is-a-good-cap-rate-for-a-hotel [Accessed 11 September 2022]

Koch, J., Gerdt, S. & Schewe, G. (2020) Determinants of sustainable behaviour of firms and the consequences for customer satisfaction in hospitality. *International Journal of Hospitality Management*, 89, 102515

Komiya, K. & Lies, E. (2022). Tokyo June heatwave worst since 1875 as power supply creaks under strain. Reuters, 29 June. www.dw.com/en/japan-warns-of-possible-power-cuts-amid-record-high-heatwave/a-62293565 [Accessed 30 June 2022]

Lee, C., Che-Ha, N. & Alwi, S. (2021). Service customer orientation and social sustainability: The case of small medium enterprises. *Journal of Business Research*, 122, 751-760

Lemon Tree Hotels (2021). Lemon Tree Hotels Ltd. Release first report on environmental, social and governance performance. https://amazingworkplaces.co/lemon-tree-hotels-ltd-releases-first-report-on-environmental-social-and-governance-esg-performance/ [Accessed 1 July 2022]

Libatique, R. (2021). Tourism businesses in Australia face underinsurance woes. Insurance Business Australia. www.insurancebusinessmag.com/au/news/environmental/tourism-businesses-in-australia-face-underinsurance-woes-256570.aspx [Accessed 2 July 2022]

Lockyer, T. & Roberts, L. (2009). Motel accommodation: trigger points to guest accommodation selection. *International Journal of Contemporary Hospitality Management*, 21(1), 24-37

Lowth, G., Prowle, M. & Zhang, M. (2020). The impact of economic recession on business strategy planning in UK companies. Chartered Institute of Management Accountants, London.

Lyon, B., Barnston, A., Coffel, E. & Horton, R. (2019). Projected increase in the spatial extend of continuous US summer heat weaves and associated attributes. *Environmental Research, Letters*, 14, 114029

Maxwell, S. (2010). Historical water price trends. Journal AWWA, April. www.sullivanlaw.com/assets/htmldocuments/Historical-Water-Price-Trends-B1406911.pdf [Accessed 16 June 2022]

McKay, G. & Stringer, D. (2022). Australia's biggest greenhouse-gas emitter AGL shelves demerger plans in win for billionaire's climate push. Bloomberg. www.bloomberg.com/news/articles/2022-05-29/agl-shelves-demerger-plans-in-win-for-billionaire-s-climate-push#xj4y7vzkg [Accessed 1 July 2022]

McKinsey & Company (2020). A leader's guide: Communicating with teams, stakeholders, and communities during Covid.

Meliã Hotels International. (2018). Code of ethics for suppliers. www.meliahotelsinternational.com/EthicalDocs/C%C3%B3digo%20%C3%A9tico%20proveedores%20EN/mhi_codigo_etico_a5_suppliers_jul18_en.pdf [Accessed 30 July 2022]

Monash Business school (2018). What Australia's impending modern slavery reporting means for business. www2.monash.edu/impact/articles/labour-market/what-australias-new-modern-slavery-reporting-means-for-business/ [Accessed 12 September 2021]

Moscardo, G., & Hughes, K. (2018). All aboard! Strategies for engaging guests in corporate responsibility programmes. *Journal of Sustainable Tourism*, 26(7), 1257–1272. https://doi.org/10.1080/09669582.2018.1428333

Mosquera, L. (2022). LinkedIn, 22 July.

Mullan, H., Cheetham-West, R. & Braithwaite, M. (2021). Banking, climate and competition. Financial Conduct Authority. www.fca.org.uk/insight/banking-climate-and-competition [2 July 2022]

Ngelambong,A., Kibat, S., Azmi, A, Nor, N. & Saien. (2016). An examination of guest dissatisfaction in budget hotel: a content analysis of guest review on TripAdvisor. The 7th International Research Symposium in Service Management

Ngxongo, N. (2021). The impact of climate change on visitor destination selection: A case study of the Centra Drakensberg Region of KwaZulu-Natal. JAMBA *Journal of Disaster Risk Studies*, 13(1), 1161

Nickell, D. & Rollins, M. & Hellman, K. (2013). How to not only survive but thrive during recession: a multi-wave, discovery-oriented study. *Journal of Business & Marketing*, 28(5), 255-461

NIDIS (n.d.). Recreation and Tourism. National Integrated Drought Information System. www.drought.gov/sectors/recreation-and-tourism [Accessed 29 June 2022]

O'Beirne, S. (2022) Commercial water rates to increase in April 2022 – how this affects your business. Facilities Management Journal. www.fmj.co.uk/commercial-water-rates-to-increase-in-april-2022-how-this-affects-your-business. [Accessed 16 June 2022]

Padma, P & Ahn J. (2020). Guest satisfaction & dissatisfaction in luxury hotel: An application of big data. *International Journal of Hospitality Management*, 84, 102318

Pappas, N. (2014). Achieving competitiveness in Greek accommodation establihsments during recession. *International Journal of Tourism Research*, https://doi.org/10.1002/jtr.1995

Patel, P. & Guedes, M. (2017). Surviving the recessions with efficiency improvements: The case of hospitality firms in Portugal. *International Journal of Tourism Research* 19, 594-604.

Patterson, L., McLaughlin, A. & Doule, M. (2022). Customer assistance programs and water affordability, *Journal - American Water Works Association* 114.

Phillipson, J., Bennett, K., Lowe, P., & Raley, M. (2004). Adaptive responses and asset strategies: the experience of rural micro-firms and Foot and Mouth Disease. *Journal of Rural Studies*, 20, 227-243.

Pickering, C. & Buckley R. (2010). Climate response by the ski industry: the shortcomings of snowmaking for Australian resorts. *AMBIO*, 39, 430-438. [Accessed 15 March 2022]

Piercy, N., Cravens, D. & Lane, N. (2010). Marketing out of the recession: recorvery is coming, but things will never be the same again. *The Marketing Review*, 10(1) 3-23

Rääbus, C. (n.d.) Everyday ABC. www.abc.net.au/everyday/struggle-to-get-and-keep-work-when-you-have-a-disability/11141692 [Accessed 23 September 2022]

Rannard, G. (2022). Climate change: Top companies exaggerating their progress – study. BBC News. www.bbc.com/news/science-environment-60248830 [Accessed 12 July 2022]

Reuters (2018). Heat wave leaves thousands of Australian homes without power. 29 January. www.reuters.com/article/uk-australia-power-idUKKBN1FI0CX [Accessed 30 June 2022]

Rhou, Y. & Singal, M. (2020). A review of the business case for CSR in the hospitality industry. *International Journal of Hospitality Management*, 84, 1023300

Ricaute, E. & Goodwin, H. (2021). Responsible Tourism Partnership. www.youtube.com/watch?v=B0oyWJrUDyY&list=PLxurWwfJqy7ZFEwzpXUONRDV2qgOk4CKm [Accessed 2 January 2022]

Roberts, Y. (2015).Britain's hotel workers – bullied, underpaid and with few rights. *The Observer*. www.theguardian.com/business/2015/may/30/hotel-workers-bullied-underpaid-few-rights-uk [Accessed 23 September 2022]

Sailsbury, J. & Burford, R. (2022). London fires: Scores of homes destroyed by devastating blazes as firefighter tells of 'absolute hell'. *Evening Standard*, 21 July. www.standard.co.uk/news/london/fires-london-brigade-heatwave-weather-latest-met-office-warnings-wennington-b1013474.html [Accessed 23 July 2022]

Schmunk, R. (2021). 595 people were killed by heat in B.B. this summer, new figures from coroner show. CBC. www.cbc.ca/news/canada/british-columbia/bc-heat-dome-sudden-deaths-revised-2021-1.6232758 [Accessed 29 June 2022]

Scope (2022) Disability facts and figures. Scope. www.scope.org.uk/media/disability-facts-figures/ [Accessed 23 September 2022]

Scottish Television (2022). Hotel faces £400,000 energy bill as living costs soar. www.youtube.com/watch?v=Q3sjYuw1ZsA [Accessed 15 June 2022]

Shaw, N. (2019). Tourist attractions see drop in numbers thanks to weather. *Cornwall News*, 27 March. www.cornwalllive.com/news/cornwall-news/tourist-attractions-see-drop-numbers-2689608 [Accessed 29 June 2022]

Shearing, N. (2022). How policymakers should tackle energy price inflation. Chatham House. www.chathamhouse.org/2022/02/how-policymakers-should-tackle-energy-price-inflation [Accessed 15 June 2022]

Simon, E. (2018). Study quantified cost savings of reducing food waste. Hotel Management. www. hotelmanagement.net/food-beverage/study-quantifies-cost-savings-reducing-food-waste [Accessed 17 June 2022]

Skift (2022). Microsoft discourages corporate travel by raising own carbon feed 600%. https:// skift.com/2022/03/14/microsoft-discourages-corporate-travel-by-raising-own-carbon-fee-600-percent/ [Accessed 10 May 2022]

Smith, T. & Fitchett, J. (2020). Drought challenges for nature tourism in the Sabi Sands Game Reserve in the eastern region of South Africa. *African Journal of Range & Forage Science*, 37(1), 107-117

Son, J., Kim, J. & Kim, G. (2021). Does employee satisfaction influence customer satisfaction? Assessing coffee shops through the service profit chain model. *International Journal of Hospitality Management*, 94, 102866

Song, Y., Liu, K., Guo, L., Yang, Z. & Jin M. (2022). Does hotel customer satisfaction change during the Covid -19? A perspective from online reviews. *Journal of Hospitality and Tourism Management*, 51, 132-138

Stop Slavery Hotel industry Network (2018). Framework for working with suppliers. Mitigating risk of modern slavery. www.stopslaverynetwork.org/wp-ontent/uploads/2018/03/SF17_ SHIN_framework_dec17-11-links-RGB-min-1.pdf [Accessed 12 September 2021]

Taylor M. (2021). Climate crisis hits 'worst case scenario' levels – Environmental Agency head. *The Guardian*. https://www.theguardian.com/environment/2021/feb/23/climate-crisis-hitting-worst-case-scenarios-warns-environment-agency-head [Accessed 24 June 2022]

Taylor, M & Watts, M., Bartlett (2019) Climate crisis: 6 million people join the latest wave of global protests. *The Guardian*. (accessed 9th November 2020) www.theguardian.com/environment/2019/sep/27/climate-crisis-6-million-people-join-latest-wave-of-worldwide-protests

TCFD (2022). Task Force on Climate-Related Financial Disclosures. www.fsb-tcfd.org/ [Accessed 30 June 2022]

The Week (2018). Heat wave lures in tourists as economy shakes off winter gloom, 12 July. www. theweek.co.uk/94947/heat-wave-lures-in-tourists-as-economy-shakes-off-winter-gloom [Accessed 29 June 2022]

Thiessen, T. (2020). Australia bushfire burns tourism industry: $4.5 billion as holidayers cancel. Forbes, 20 January. www.forbes.com/sites/tamarathiessen/2020/01/20/australia-bushfires-hit-tourism-industry-as-holidayers-cancel/

Thomsen, P. (2022).Skyrocketing energy costs force hospitality businesses to raise prices and cut opening hours. UK Hospitality. www.ukhospitality.org.uk/news/599740/Skyrocketing-energy-costs-force-hospitality-businesses-to-raise-prices-and-cut-opening-hours.htm [Accessed 15 June 2-22]

Touryalai, H. (2018). Sustainable Travel: Young travellers drive Hilton's latest effort to cut carbon footprint in half. Forbes. www.forbes.com/sites/halahtouryalai/2018/12/10/hilton-hotels-sustainability-environment/ [Accessed: 30 December 2020]

Town Square (2021). The reasons why it's so hard to hire in hospitality right now. Beanbox. https://beambox.com/the-reasons-why-its-so-hard-to-hire-in-hospitality-right-now [Accessed 17 June 2022]

TUC (2019). Low pay in the hotel and accommodation sector. TUC. www.tuc.org.uk/research-analysis/reports/low-pay-hotel-and-accommodation-sector [Accessed 17 June 2022]

UK Government (2009). Energy Performance Certificate https://assets.publishing.service.gov.uk/government/uploads/system/uploads/attachment_data/file/5996/2116821.pdf [Accessed 30 June 2022]

UK Government (2021). The Sixth Carbon Budget. www.theccc.org.uk/publication/sixth-carbon-budget/ [Accessed 30 June 2022]

United Nations (2015). The Paris Agreement. https://unfccc.int/process-and-meetings/the-paris-agreement/the-paris-agreement [Accessed 30 June 2022]

United Nations. (2021) Climate Action. www.un.org/en/climate-action/un-issues-red-alert

UNWTO (2021). The Cornell Hotel sustainability benchmarking index allows hotels to benchmark their environmental performance against peers, www.unwto.org/Covid-oneplanet-responsible-recovery-initiatives/chsb-index-allows-hotels-to-benchmark-their-environmental-performance-against-peers [Accessed 3 January 2022]

USA Today (2021) www.usatoday.com/story/travel/2021/09/27/google-launches-sustainable-hotel-options-eco-friendly-travelers/5880683001/

Vance, D. (2005). *Raising Capital.* Springer, p.2

Vanovac, N. (2018). German tourist wandering 17 km off Central Australia hiking track before dying of dehydration, heat stress. ABC. www.abc.net.au/news/2018-11-26/german-tourists-died-central-australia-walked-17km-heat-stress/10554408 [Accessed 29 June 2022]

Vargo, S. & Lusch, R. (2004). Evolving to a new dominant logic for marketing. *Journal of Marketing,* 68(1), 1–17.

Vargo, S. & Lusch, R. (2016). Institutions and axioms: An extension and update of service-dominant logic. *Journal of the Academy of Marketing Science,* 44(1), 5–23.

Walk Free. (2019). Hotel sector failing to protect workers ahead of Australian MSA anniversary. [Accessed 12 September 2019]

Warren, M (2022). Designing gamification for responsible tourism: Giving people a purpose. My Green Butler. https://mygreenbutler.com/designing-gamification-for-responsible-tourism/ [Accessed 10 July 2022]

Warren, C. & Warren, M. (2023). 'Incentivising guests to save resources?', in W. Legrand, H., Kuokkanen, & J. Day (eds). *Critical Questions in Sustainability and Hospitality.* Routledge

Warren, C., Becken, S., Nguyen, K. & Stewart, R. (2018). Transitioning to smart sustainable tourist accommodation: Service innovation results. *Journal of Cleaner Production,* 201, 599-608

Welch, C. (2022). Polluters are using forests as 'carbon offsets'. Climate change has other plans. National Geographic. www.nationalgeographic.com/environment/article/forests-as-carbon-offsets-climate-change-has-other-plans [Accessed 12 July 2022]

Westbrook, G. & Angus, A. (2021). Top 10 global consumer trends 2021. https://go.euromonitor.com/webinar-video-ec-210223-gct.html [Accessed 10 January 2022]

Yao-Fen, W. (2016) Development and Validation of the green food and beverage literacy scale. *Asia Pacific Journal of Tourism Research,* 26(1), 20-56

Yu, Y., Li, X. & Jai, T. (2017). The impact of green experience on customer satisfaction: evidence from TripAdvisor. *International Journal of Contemporary Hospitality Management,* 29(5), 17

Zurich (2022). How biodiversity loss threatens food production. www.zurich.com/en/media/magazine/2021/food-for-thought-what-biodiversity-means-to-you [Accessed 23 September 2022]

2 Re-imagining the Green Guest

The key points of this chapter:

- **Knowledge gaps lead to bad practice.** The hospitality sector is hamstrung by a dearth of information and first hand experience. New technology and research can empower us to make smarter long-term choices

- **Tourism can – and should – flip the status quo**, creating market demand rather than waiting for it. Sustainable behaviour can enrich guest experience

- **The most valuable research focuses on real-life case studies**. What people say and what people do does not always match. The beating heart of sustainable tourism is real-world behaviours

- **All guests are potential green guests**. Typecasting people is counterproductive, leading to faulty assumptions and a false sense that 'green' guests are a niche market

Flashback

It was another extended drought in Kangaroo Valley, New South Wales. The normally lush green farms were parched, with deep cracks running across the land. Even the surrounding forests looked fatigued, everything wilting from successive days of +45°C heat. Hard times for an area the National Trust reveres for its 'outstanding natural beauty', and especially tough for tourist accommodation providers surviving on harvested rainfall. It was in such situations that Margaret, owner of tourist accommodation Valley Park, would resort to removing taps from all her guest bathrooms to prevent too much water being used. She did not trust her guests not to waste water.

Margaret's business had faced the challenges of drought and extreme heat on and off for years, but the occurrences were becoming more frequent and were lasting longer. Her desperate measure was the only practical solution she thought existed to avoid paying heavily for water to be carted to her property. Asking guests to be mindful of water didn't seem enough. In 2003, nobody felt that paying guests would voluntarily reduce their water use. Despite climate change news and government water restrictions, a holiday was just that, a holiday.

Knowledge vacuum

There is a vacuum in understanding how guests behave 'behind closed doors', particularly during times of scarcity. Some accommodation providers use signs, and most install water and/or energy saving appliances, but there is still a general distrust of guest attitudes to 'green' behaviour. With continued harsh conditions will Margaret's extreme actions become normal for hospitality?

The year I met Margaret, Sophie and I bought Valley Park and commenced our journey to renovate, extend the accommodation, and ultimately introduce a higher level of self-sufficiency. We renamed the business Crystal Creek Meadows. We kept the bathroom taps and actually offered our guests *more* access to resources. Despite this we use less water and energy, and reduced our waste even though the business has grown tenfold in the years since we bought the original property.

And yet I really felt for Margaret and still sense her worry. It is incredibly stressful to go through droughts and power blackouts – as I, Sophie, and our staff have experienced. Like so many in the industry, Margaret's decision was based on what she knew and felt was right at that time, even though it contradicts the concept of hospitality.

Flipping the status quo

During our journey, I have come to realise hospitality is seriously held back by a lack of scientific information and practical solutions. This is preventing us from evolving, which is now so obviously required for the future.

Our solution meant reversing the status quo, directly involving our guests in consuming and wasting less. But it goes much further than this. The solution has transformed our business and significantly improved our productivity. The lessons learned from our research and invention we share globally to help large and small hospitality providers save millions of kilowatts of energy, millions of litres of water, and cut thousands of tonnes of carbon emissions.

Central to our approach is that guests and staff can be persuaded to *participate* and *conserve*, positively enjoying this process.

Market disruption

The status quo says we cannot disrupt the guests' experience when saving energy, water, and food waste because they will not accept change. In this book I challenge that belief, as well as the idea that hospitality must evolve *in response to* strong market demand from 'green minded' guests.

Instead, I'm going to illustrate a market disruption that is not just positive but revolutionary. This disruption means flipping how we provide services so that we empower guests to participate directly. It means instead of inconveniencing them, we make them happier. It means instead of putting people at the bottom of a list of environmental solutions, they sit at the top.

Let us start by examining the truth of the so-called 'green guest' and 'green host.' Then, together, we are going to reshape the hospitality paradigm.

Why guests are key for sustainable hospitality

Tourist accommodation uses a lot of resources, and most of this can be attributed to guests' behaviour. Which of these directly involve the guests?

- **Energy:** Air conditioning, heating, hot water heating, recreational areas, laundry, lighting, cooking, pumps, and refrigeration.
- **Water:** Showers, cooking/cleaning, taps, toilets, and cleaning; and in those air conditioning systems with cooling towers.
- **Food waste:** Preparation, buffet display, and plate waste.

Guests can be directly responsible for around half of the energy and water use in hotels and resorts. In self-contained (self-catering) accommodation it is more than this, as cooking and other daily chores increase use, as do the size of the living spaces. Therefore, guests' behaviour greatly influences a tourist accommodation's amount of energy and water use, number of linen/towels used, and the quantity of food wasted. If we keep sustainability at arm's length, guest behaviour is unlikely to change. Involve guests and you have a powerful lever that controls the majority of consumption.

Sustainable tourism guest engagement

Hospitality firms generally take on one of four approaches to reducing environmental impacts and involving guests:

1. Not bother the guests at all and optimise the efficiency of their systems behind the scenes using technology;
2. Tell guests that the firms are making great efforts to reduce the property's environmental footprint and provide the evidence, so they can relax in the knowledge everything is taken care of, and they have made a good choice;
3. Focus on a few areas like inviting guests to choose a reduced level of service (reusing linen and towels) and sweeten by offering loyalty points or drinks at the bar;
4. Strive for guest participation by showing guests how to minimise their use of resources and encourage them to participate in creating a more sustainable hospitality experience.

Most accommodation providers choose options one or two. The first is not confrontational and is often led by a strong Return On Investment (ROI) focused on newly installed equipment. The second seeks to build a reputational advantage without disrupting guests' behaviour. Increasingly firms are applying the third approach, which does involve guests, but may rely on costly incentives. Few try the fourth, an option that appears to suggest significant extra work while narrowing the property's appeal to just green guests.

The conundrum of guest involvement

Guests account for most resource usage and waste at tourist accommodation. By ignoring the potential for guest involvement we therefore limit saving potential. There are, however, different barriers for hospitality firms depending on the approach:

- If we shield guests and take on all responsibility, we set a limit of what can be achieved, locking ourselves into the tried and tested traditional exchange of service delivery.

- If we tempt guests to make savings while failing to walk the talk, we open ourselves up to recriminations for not doing more to address the issues ourselves.

- If we take on more sustainable practices we fear compromising our quality service and losing loyal guests, all for a seemingly niche market of green travellers.

It ultimately feels like a straight up Hobson's choice – a choice between full punitive green policies or keeping quiet and hoping no one will notice. Lexico (2021) describe Hobson's Choice as "a choice of taking what is available or nothing at all". At best, some hospitality tends to choose the half measure, skirting around the edges to avoid being typecast as a green hotel, while a few businesses celebrate their holistic *greenness*.

But what if making transformational changes made you *more* competitive? Maybe it is less about being 'green' and more about being responsible, resourceful, adaptable, creative, and enjoyable? Maybe we are too stuck on typecasting green guests. Who are they anyway?

Re-imagining the green guest opportunity

As a sector, we tend to believe a large majority of guests are not environmentally-minded. We group green guests together as an isolated segment with characteristics quite different from everyone else.

Some managers have told me that their guests' minds are too focused on other things – like their holiday or business meetings – to be troubled with eco-friendly matters. Others think confronting guests with preachy messaging seems inappropriate, and too risky for their business.

These views tend to assume that offering more sustainable hospitality, that directly involves the guests, is somehow already well defined and limited to a specific course of action, i.e. signage with planet-saving claims.

But it might be that we just have not thought it was possible to offer an alternative approach to green messaging. For example, do staff know **what** to show guests to help them save within the existing facility? Are they sure **how** to show guests in a sufficiently persuasive manner? Do the staff actually **apply** these methods themselves backstage? How can these actions make the guest experience better?

To create solutions, we will now unpack the various research approaches that have dominated tourism in the last 20 years. This will shed light on opportunities and illustrate that answers are easier to come by when we better understand the mirage of green guests.

The green guest mirage

We are not certain if our guests are green. Being sure would require measuring the consequences of each guest party's individual stay. We would then need to compare this to a baseline, consider each guest's personal circumstances and other variables (like health, age, dependent children), make adjustments for this, and then be able to make a reasonable definition with parameters.

What's more, we are not sure what terms to use to define what 'green' and 'greenness' actually mean; for example, is a guest green because they choose to recycle or have solar panels? Does a real green guest live in a house made with recycled materials, use no grid electricity, and grow their own food? Or do they have an electric car, choose only ethical investments and live in a new high tech Leadership in Energy and Environmental Design (LEED) certified apartment? Or somewhere in between… or both? When we take a step back, the sensible answer is that we should not stereotype people.

The truth is we might, on occasion, be applying too narrow a research focus that hides the full picture. It is important to recognise that one's individual green activities occur in a bubble of acceptable social behaviour that ignores the wider complexities within our human world. For example, complying with the socially acceptable option to fly to a Pacific island for a holiday which you have chosen for its green credentials. Research might judge your green participation at this eco-resort but ignore the wider consequences of travelling to the destinations.

Our thinking process

A starting point for much research has been to assess people's attitudes. These exist in a broader context of values, beliefs, attitudes, behaviour, and choice. Our values and beliefs are established from family, social circle, and cultural influences. These are strong constructs that guide our decision making from childhood. Attitudes are a blend of emotions and the values we have grown up with (Cherry, 2010), and evolve through experiences, social circumstances, and our life journey.

An example of how social circumstances influence our attitudes would be the Covid-19 pandemic. Before it started I might have considered wearing a mask in public unacceptably restrictive and thought my hygiene practices were sufficient for disease prevention. But our everyday attitudes towards hygiene might have changed due to experiencing a family tragedy, following a community leader's advice, or by learning more about transmission. For my part I drew on my own values of doing the right thing to protect my elderly neighbours.

These kinds of experiences could well spill over into how you notice a hotel guest room when you first enter, or how clean the cutlery and glasses are on your table. Just as the crisis taught us to think again, as consumers learn more about climate change their attitudes are changing. Now more than ever, people around the world want urgent responses and are prepared to change their behaviour, from fashion to diet (UNDP, 2021).

What we say, meet what we do

A great deal of research time and energy has examined people's attitudes towards the environment and compared this with their actions. Many tourism studies have found an inconsistency between what people say they care about and what they actually do. This has come to be known as the Attitude Action Gap or Attitude Behaviour Gap (Miller et al., 2010) where holidaymakers might claim to care for the environment but strongly argue that their right to fly should be upheld (Barr et al., 2010). This has led to the conclusion that we do not do what we say (Blake, 1999).

Changing attitudes does not always lead to new behaviour. Behaviour is what we do; choice is the options available. In the example of the Covid-19 crisis, masks and hand gel were available and government lockdown policy mandated. Our choices were clear and behaviour followed. With climate change, things are more complex. The dynamics of the outside world and the choices it offers can limit pro-environmental behaviour as people appear locked into unsustainable behaviour (DEFRA, 2005). This can leave us to appear to contradict our evolving attitudes towards pollution and biodiversity loss by often behaving in the opposite manner. For example, believing one should cut fossil fuel consumption but having no alternative other than to drive to work.

But Covid permitted us to work from home and use video conferencing. This change of workplace was not possible for many before Covid, yet the virus lockdown dislodged 'normal' behaviour and released a new and, for many, a more enjoyable way of working (Boland et al., 2020). It is often social innovations that can unlock us from unsustainable consumption, enabling progress away from limited choices to new ways of living (Shove, 2010).

2

Insight: The reasons for contradictions

The restrictions of available choices affect how people can apply more pro-environmental behaviours. They can be one of the reasons behind the gap. I have put a number of the foundation research studies into four groups: **motivations**, **information**, **facilities**, and the **slow progress** found within society. Do the summarised research findings below ring any bells for you?

Table 2.1: Why we might behave differently to our pro-environmental attitudes

Motivations
Denial of responsibility, distrust government Want to see the same action from others Feeling powerless Not prepared to sacrifice comfort (Stoll-Kleemann et al., 2001)
Shift responsibility: Expect technological solutions to be implemented by 'management' Support limited restrictions so enabling continued consumption (Becken, 2007).
Find it hard to view environmental choices in a wider context Manage self-identity conflict by accepting eco taxes, but would continue to fly (Barr et al., 2010).
To protect themselves, visitors tend to maintain a positive self-view and believe they are more pro-environmental than other tourists (Doran & Larsen, 2013).
Basic human need (comfort, security) present multiple motives that become the main drivers of action. They can be more powerful goals, meaning individuals can make decisions that pursue hedonistic goals that appear to contradict their environmental values (Lindenberg & Steg, 2007)
Joint decision making may also influence pro-environmental action, as achieving consensus can be an important responsibility (Kennedy et al., 2009)
Expect leadership from political/society figures Believe flying is a well-earned break (Miller et al., 2010)
Individuals appear to weigh up their options and look around at the consensus choosing to maintain their self–identity. They may take calculated actions that best preserve their opportunities in the face of continued conspicuous consumption (Young, n.d.).
Lack of pro-environmental information
Unfamiliar about impacts Unaware of different impacts from components of their holiday and underestimate accommodation's impact Only 4% of tourists have used a carbon calculator (Juvan & Dolnicar, 2014b).

Unclear what action to take in accommodation
Expect more information and to be told what the accommodation provider is doing (Warren, 2012).
Lack of standardised information so visitors cannot compare (Young et al., 2010)
Having environmental knowledge can positively contribute to proactive behaviour (Cottrell, 2003).
People's carbon literacy can be low and is affected by the context from which they make decisions. So key personal goals can trump other concerns if they can see impacts (Dosa & Rosemary, 2019).
Insufficient pro-environmental infrastructure
Lack of infrastructure in destinations to support eco-friendly behaviour (Dolnicar & Grun, 2008)
Lack of infrastructure can also be an excuse for alternative action even by environmental activists (Juvan & Dolnicar, 2014a).
Individuals comply with expected social practices and use readily available systems (Shove, 2010).
Slow institutional progress
Policy barriers that prevent people from living more sustainable lifestyles prevent voluntary action The permitted consumerist society locks individuals in a strangle-hold (Lorenzoni et al., 2007)

What's wrong with the science?

Some scientific research might not be relevant to 'real world' behaviour as often used theories catalogue people's *intended* behaviour. One of the most popular is the Theory of Planned Behaviour, which determines what research participants believe they are likely to do under certain conditions, but it has been described as 'suboptimal' by academics who recommend focusing on actual behaviour (Ganglmair-Wooliscroft & Wooliscroft, 2016).

If your survey asked me what is my intention to book a green hotel on my next trip? I might score "very likely". But the reality is that when booking I might also have to consider many other factors. Does this accommodation have a baby's cot, an accessible bathroom for grandma, a quiet room for my tired wife, and last-minute availability? These might be priorities for me.

Another way to consider this is through Goal Framing. This was a concept which Siegwart Lindenberg and Linda Steg introduced that combined three goals (Lindenberg & Steg, 2007). These describe how our environmental behaviour is influenced by what we think is appropriate behaviour (normative), as well as feeling better right now (hedonic), and our desire to guard and improve one's resources (gain). In everyday life our motivations can combine a mixture of goals. When these conflict, it is likely the hedonic gaols will take the lead. Feeling better right now can be achieved by selecting the hotel that will make my family happiest, and frankly, that is going to be a clear winner when we are on holiday together for two weeks to enjoy our "well-earned rest". It does not mean that the environment is unimportant to me, just that my initial decision to take a holiday was to have a happy time with my family and they need a cot, an accessible bathroom, a quiet bedroom and availability at the last minute, achieving this makes me feel better to achieve their main goal. There was no 'green' search option on the major online travel agent sites, and it would have taken me hours to work my way through the listings, compare them and run an analysis on my footprint choice. (Booking.com is experimenting with this now to see if it makes a discernable difference to visitor site activity.)

Planned intentions do not necessarily reflect how we live day to day. Nor do they indicate how I might behave in green accommodation, which is different from my home. Intention to do something pro-environment has been found to account for only 27% of the reasons to enact a pro-environment behaviour (Warren & Coghlan, 2016) .

Insight: A dearth of real world insights

There are hundreds, perhaps thousands, of research papers on green tourism and hospitality following high standards of research rigour. Unfortunately, only a fraction of them have had access to 'real world' behavioural data. For example, by 2017, social psychologist Claudia Nisa and colleagues (Nisa et al., 2017) could only find 12 papers (from a carefully selected sample of 6,229) that reported using data collected from the field, and only nine of them provided evidence of individual guest behaviour change in hotels.

The research my colleagues and I have undertaken adds to this sample and considers self-contained accommodation (Warren et al., 2017). There have been further studies since 2017, mostly on towel reuse and plate waste in hotels, which I include later in the book. But overall, it is a meagre amount of research evidence for the world's largest industry.

Green messages are not enough

The narrow focus of pro-environmental behaviour research leaves us ignorant of multiple factors influencing guest activities. Relying on what we have could lead to poorly constructed guest engagement programmes, resulting in disappointment and renewed belief that we cannot involve guests. Insights from other research fields indicate that a holistic approach is required.

There are genuine dangers to promoting pro-environmental messages without advisory information. For example, suppose you provide signs to guests explaining you have taken steps to reduce your property's footprint by using new technology. This could reverse the desired effect. Individuals consume more energy for greater comfort when they know they are using energy-saving infrastructure (Gram-Hanssen, 2014) – an example of the Rebound Effect (Sorrell, 2007).

Messaging responsible use of materials without alerting individuals to consequences can lead to greater use: the provision of a paper towel recycling bin actually was found to increase paper usage (Catlin, & Wang, 2012).

Ad hoc approaches run the risk of failure because they do not involve the guests in a deeper experience that includes more information persuasively presented. In short, green messaging needs follow up and exposition.

Can guests make informed green accommodation choices?

Green accommodation is a relatively new concept, so naturally some people are cagey about choosing it. This makes researching attitudes complex. Surveys can collect negative responses to a perfectly possible scenario because it is not something people have actually experienced. Similarly, people tend to respond to open questions about social responsibility with a degree of moral obligation, which might inflate the positive response rate.

Asking broad green questions does not give people a clear idea of what is being proposed.

Close your eyes and imagine a green guest room at my accommodation. What will you find inside? Will it be more or less comfortable than a regular accommodation or your own home? Will it sacrifice luxuries and if so, which? It is possible your answers will not be accurate, but you will put forward suggestions that you expect to meet the idea of being green.

To make a positive choice, we need to assess if new ideas are going to be a good or bad experience, hear views from friends and family, and see how easy it will be to achieve. The scope of our decision-making processes is complex and the public is sceptical about claims (Nimri et al., 2017). We generally do not possess sufficient life experience or knowledge to weigh our options up.

To get a sense of what I mean, try answering the following questions.

Quiz

1. Rank the following guest activities from highest to lowest energy use
   - ■ Sleeping
   - ■ Morning shower
   - ■ Having your towels replaced every other day
   - ■ Watching TV
   - ■ Ordering room service
   - ■ Brushing teeth
   - ■ Using the hairdryer
   - ■ Asking to have your sheets changed every day
   - ■ Day spa treatments and sauna

Answer: Aha, if only it were that simple!

When considering the impacts, did you think of how much energy is used to heat water? From our tests we found that guests' hot water usage is similar to the total electricity they use for the rest of the amenities in their room during their stay. Do you know how much energy the hotel's washing machine uses? Typically a single sheet will require 4.32 Wh of electricity and a large towel 3.96Wh. If you selected the sauna you could be right (6 kW system, so 6000Wh) but sharing the sauna means you split the energy use. If the sauna is left on all day for just a single guest visit that amounts to a great deal of energy; is that the guest's responsibility?

Why add sleeping? What temperature do you like at night? Can the bedroom windows open? Is it too noisy outside? Are you acclimatising to the local weather? These factors can influence your energy use of an a/c or heating system (more on this later in the book).

Cooking can use considerable amounts of energy. If you have chosen lobster flown from Canada to your hotel in Germany, that choice's energy and carbon intensity will be high.

In truth the answer is, it all depends. It depends on so many hidden factors people find it hard to judge and make greener decision. In the absence of that knowledge, they make assumptions.

---

2. While on holiday, what is the most eco-friendly way to drink bottled water?
   a) Refillable aluminium bottle with screw cap;
   b) Refillable plastic bottle with screw cap and straw;
   c) Buy new individual bottled water;
   d) Take a cup you already own.

Answer: D. The most eco-friendly way to drink water is to drink tap water, if it is safe to do so. Not only is it less harmful to the environment, it is also more economic! Buying water in a bottle is only a recent phenomenon in many destinations, where city water quality is of a high standard e.g. Sydney, London and Paris (Sydney Water, 2022). Taking your own cup and rinsing it out to avoid machine washing saves water, energy and chemicals. There is a footprint to buying a new water bottle and plastic water bottles have a huge footprint in the production process. But it is inconvenient to walk around with a cup!

---

3. Rank these five-holiday scenarios from the highest to lowest daily water footprint, assuming you were flying from the UK
   a) Luxury golf holiday in Paphos, Cyprus in a 5-star hotel using a medium sized car and a meat-rich diet for seven nights;
   b) Walking/hiking in Polis in Cyprus, camping using a small car eating vegan diet and staying nine nights;
   c) Taking a budget beach holiday in Bodrum Turkey staying in a 2-star apartment, eating a Western diet for nine nights;

d) Relaxing beach holiday in Mykonos Greece in a 4-star hotel, with a holiday diet for 12 nights;

e) Backpacking in the Levant, staying in local houses, using public transport and eating a local diet for 28 nights.

Answer: It is surprising how much water is involved in each day of our holidays (Hadjika-kou et al., 2013). The relaxing beach holiday in Mykonos used the least water at 5460 litres per day compared to the budget holiday (5790), walking holiday (7080), backpacking (8290) and golfing (8940). The beach holiday had a low meat diet, so that helped keep down its overall water consumption. The walking holiday with camping involved the lowest overall local water footprint. So the type of accommodation is the second most important contribution to water consumption. Note it is the embedded water that comes with all our choices, including the fuel for flying that is the biggest factor.

6. If you were planning a holiday from London to Marseilles in the South fo France for seven nights, rank the carbon footprints from lowest to highest for the following scenarios? Staying seven nights and:

a) Driving by car and staying an extra night en-route

b) Flying direct

c) Taking the train

d) Taking a coach and staying an extra night en-route

e) Taking a connecting flight in Paris

Answer: Taking the train has the lowest carbon footprint per tourist (21.1 kg CO2), then coach (25.9), Car (50.9), Flight (52.8 and connecting flights 77.1) (Filimonau et al., 2014). Accommodation accounted for the largest share of carbon for both the train and coach options and accounted for over a third in the car option.

Insight: Can tourists easily choose a low carbon holiday?

- Seventy-three carbon calculators examined using the same itinerary showed a sixfold difference between the highest to lowest estimated carbon footprints.

- A study asked 261 people to calculate the carbon footprint of one of six-holiday itin-eraries using carbon calculators. On average, it took participants 50 minutes to do the calculation because there were unfamiliar with such systems and they found it difficult to match the elements of their trip with the categories in the calculator.

- A second study of 126 participants found it hard to estimate the carbon intensity of different parts of their trip. Even though they knew travel to be an important source of carbon, only 40% identified it as a major contributor to a holiday's footprint. While 9% thought that not keeping your towels for reuse at accommodation was the most important impact. (Juvan, & Dolnicar, 2014b)

People have the desire but lack the knowledge to make green decisions

A whopping 82% of people say they would like to invest in an environmentally positive way. But half of the private pension investors don't know where their funds are placed, leaving a third investing in oil and gas companies according to Investec. Their survey of 2,000 individuals demonstrated that it was pension fund complexities that prevented people from really understanding where their funds were going. By informing the public of their sustainable investment options there is likely to be a greater propensity for them to select investments in low-carbon environmentally positive funds (Investec, 2019).

Knowledge gaps fuel tension

Often it feels as though the public get more standoffish the more research drills down to deeper questions. People might care for the environment, but equally, they feel deserving of the holiday's promise of 'me time'. Inevitably in focus groups, people get defensive when challenged to assess their lifestyle (Barr et al., 2010). This leads to denial about consequences.

The social value of holidays enables hard-working people to spend time with loved ones, the key for the well-being of the family. It introduces exciting new worlds to us all. Likewise, hospitality helps firms to stage networking, team building, and incentivising events that are key for business. However, these values and benefits are compromised by a corresponding lack of consumer awareness about environmental impacts.

There is no going back. The industry acknowledges its shared environmental and social challenges (WTTC, 2019). We should not want to be singled out as a negative contributor to pollution and waste. Rather than waiting, hospitality has the opportunity to turn a lack of knowledge into educational and inspiring experiences that provide a competitive advantage.

We are in the driving seat

A startling programme in Australia called 'The War on Waste' is credited to have changed the views of many adults there. It starred Craig Reucassel, a quick-witted young Australian satirist, who showed his audience the scale of waste and the social complexities that created it. In one memorable scene, Reucassel travelled through Melbourne on a tram filled with single-use coffee cups. At every stop, he told peak time commuters they could not get on as the tram was already too full with the quantity of cups Melbourne throws out daily.

Research clearly shows people care for the environment. That sense is evolving and strengthening through social media, donation appeal campaigns, voluntary time, and school projects, such as establishing vegetable gardens. They all build greater awareness and lead the public to question governments over environmental policy (the survival of the Great Barrier Reef is just one example).

Research also points out that guests expect us to resolve the pollution, depletion of resources, and waste problems from their stays. Importantly, it also suggests people are willing to try new ideas if they think it helps.

We are clearly in the driving seat to deliver change, the problem is, our passengers are not clear where and how to sit.

Insight: Concern for the environment is growing around the world

- In the Netherlands, 55% of adults in 2017 believed pollution is getting worse (40%, 2012), and 75% said nature had been seriously damaged (59%, 2012) (Netherlands Bureau of Statistics, 2018)

- Gallup (2019) compared US citizens over a twenty year period and found that people who believe "the seriousness of global warming is generally correct" dropped from 35% (1999) to 25% (2019) while those who felt it to be "underestimated" has risen from 27% (1989) to 42% (2019), i.e. people had increasingly recognised the challenges have grown. This is supported by the recent GlobalScan survey of 18 countries that found most people wanted leaders to set ambitious climate change targets (43% in 2015 and 58% in 2021) (McGrath, 2021).

- The greatest anxiety can be found in emerging economies like India, where 61.4% of National Geographic's (2014) sample are strongly concerned about the environment.

Concern for the environment is a global phenomenon. But the concern is not translated into sufficient action (Coughlin, 2018).

Mass consumption

While people express concern for the environment, as a society we are consuming more than ever. This is partly because escalating standards of living merge with resource use in complex manners in developed and developing economies. If we take personal hygiene as an example, earlier generations had weekly baths, then society progressed to showers, and their frequency increased to daily, and then twice daily.

New products normalise this transition through the improvement in instant hot water systems, use of integrating shower units, and easy dispensed shower gels. Each of these innovative steps helps to self-perpetuate the 'normal' behaviour. Each has environmental consequences that interrelate with the original personal hygiene desire.

Bathrooms have to be renovated, new equipment installed, bricks, mortar and old fittings put into landfill. Increased water and chemicals are used to clean the shower and launder towels. This escalation directly affects tourist accommodation, which must comply with social trends to avoid being seen as old fashioned or passé.

New ways of shopping have created hollow experiences where we might buy more but increasingly do not use what we buy (Farber, 2016) or choose items with low durability which frequently have to be replaced, adding further to waste. (Semuels, 2018)

Such 'normal' behaviours are in direct contradiction to increasing environmental concern.

Insight: Facts on 'normal' consumption

- Domestic energy use has increased despite more efficient technologies. Look at your country's domestic electricity use in the last 60 years; it has risen from just running lights to powering a kaleidoscope of systems.

- In the 1950s, 97% of household electricity was used to just power light, by 2006 that represented just 11% of total use as we now use washing machines, heating, and cooling systems.

- Energy-saving light bulbs averted our eyes to what else we were consuming; our overall use has skyrocketed by the huge increase in TV and computers which can account for 20% of total home use – think what is happening at your own accommodation! (Røpke, et al., 2009)

- The same can be said for food waste, which in the USA has increased by 50% since 1974 to 1,400 kcal per person per day. This food waste accounts for a quarter of total water consumption and 300 million barrels of oil per year. (Hall et al., 2009)

Don't make assumptions

This escalating level of consumption is not uniform, just as the level of environmental concern and knowledge about the impact is not uniform. At home, we do not all use the same amount of energy, water, and food as other households. This can lead to incorrect assumptions about whether others will save resources, thinking there are clues in people's appearances.

I have found that it is very easy for hospitality staff and management to make assumptions about people's likely consumption levels, making superficial judgements based on guests' appearances, the cars they drive, or where they live. My research has shown such judgements were not accurate when it comes to their consumption behaviour at tourist accommodation.

Take for example Mr. B and his wife. They arrived at our accommodation in a Ford Selby (a huge 4x4), and when they were shown into their accommodation

I told them what our energy use was per accommodation. Mr. B remarked on our energy use being lower than his household. This was because he had three TVs, two dishwashers, and hundreds of LEDs in a seven-bedroom house. His household bill was more substantial than our entire business!

Naturally, one might have expected them to consume a high amount of energy during their stay. In truth they made every effort to conserve their electricity and water use, and during their stay beat the targets set for them. I will explain more about how we do this towards the end of this chapter.

Insight: The fallacy of Mr & Mrs. Average

Some guests use more than 14 times more resources per hour than others staying in the same room at the same time of year!

Using a specially adapted monitoring system I recorded guests' electricity, gas, water, and room temperature in real time. Per hour the lowest consuming guests recorded significantly less resource use and in-room cottage temperatures

		Lowest	Mr & Mrs. Average	Highest
Electricity	Wh	83.9	243	1100
Gas	m3	0.00033	0.00732	0.03
Water	Litres	1.84	6.46	27.4
Temperature	°C	22.6	24	31

If we just added up our bills and divided the totals by a number of guests, we would have arrived at an hourly Mr & Mrs. Average consumption. As you can see Mr & Mrs. Average are a fallacy, just like green guests are a mirage.

We are in danger of oversimplifying, and in doing so missing real opportunities. People are not aware of their consumption. They apply 'normal' routines using resources that emit carbon and are invisible, often consuming on autopilot (Warren, 2015).

Different dreams, different holidays

Often at industry events, I hear people make generalisations about guests which tends to limit our creativity to find solutions. My favourite is how people hold opposing ideas of what green guests and luxury guests look like and want.

People choose different types of holidays and will consume differently on such occasions. Research that asks general questions using words like 'holidays' without acknowledging that we may enjoy different *types* of holidays can lead us to make assumptions and obscure reality.

A middle class North European couple can leave their eco-smart home to enjoy a simple stone built gite in France, with its mismatched wooden furniture and simple appliances. They ride bicycles all day and in the evening dress casually while enjoying a rustic meal of bread and cheese with characterful cheap local wine, while admiring the view. It's their annual escape.

They could also stay at a magnificent Singapore hotel, dressed in their best, sipping French champagne, and eating strawberries flown in from California. It's their anniversary. If you met them here would you assume they like rustic rural life too? People have lots of different dreams, which manifest as lots of different holidays.

Generalisation diminishes green market potential

By generalising we tend to oversimplify green solutions. Management's focus may simply be to change light bulbs and shower heads because they perceive that's the accepted method and a demonstration of greenness to guests. This still doesn't get to the heart of the matter, which is that people's routines and understanding will lead them unknowingly to wasteful behaviour wherever they stay. I discuss this further in Chapter 3.

There is also the argument that holidays are hedonistic, a word that is often applied to the tourism industry as a whole. In turn, this makes holidays appear sacrosanct and impenetrable to responsible tourism practices, leaving managers believing that asking individuals to moderate their consumption is untenable.

Equally there are occasions when tourists are described as being altruistic because they selected a perceived 'greener' experience. In so doing we can over-simplify. This leads to missed marketing opportunities because people's motivations are far more complex than this neat titling implies. We are not selling fast moving consumer goods where market segments are clearly defined; we are offering a service which is co-created and consumed using the customer's expertise in managing available resources.

Within a holiday there are multiple opportunities for consumption to be modified without reducing customer satisfaction. These go far beyond changing a few fixtures (I explore this more in Chapter 6). Thinking that sustainability can only apply to altruistically-minded people leads to false pictures of a niche market when there are actually mass market opportunities and sector-wide challenges.

Greener tourism must be a mainstream service. Generalising solutions that solely focus on 'low hanging fruit' are missing golden commercial opportunities. We need to look deeper into how and why consumption occurs. With these insights we can design better services throughout the guest experience journey. This will help people to conserve, make your business more resilient, and create a sustainable tourism sector.

Insight: It is how we use things that matter

- A study of 22,400 detached houses in Denmark found that their use of heating was influenced most strongly by the "everyday habits of the families", which were not socio-economic related, and was less influenced by the size of house and age of construction. (Gram-Hanssen, 2014)

- In another study of 32 households near Copenhagen, people who thought they used a small amount of energy and liked cool rooms were in fact, some of the highest energy users with the highest internal temperatures. People's efforts to use natural ventilation were found not to be because they were trying to save energy, but as a preference for "enjoying lots of fresh air."

- While monitoring 100 Danish homes, it was found that some families used 50 kWh for washing per year and others were using 750kWh. In another example, one household used 0kWh for appliance stand-by power while another used 1,300 kWh per year. In the same urban areas, there was no consistency in use, only remarkable individual home differences.

A new approach to research

Investors might prefer to wait and see strong demand from a growing and sizable segment of genuine green guests (those who are both highly committed to the environment and highly skilled at minimising their footprint) before justifying the investment.

Had Margaret known how much water guests were really using she might have chosen a different method to save. Had she applied this all year round, she might have had more water available. Likewise, had the individual guests known about their own use they might have changed their consumption – something a persuasive approach from Margaret could have enhanced.

How much of the resources people actually consume is obviously a far better indication of their impact at accommodation than any researched intention to purchase green holidays. The established benchmark (people's concern for the environment) does not always equate to active greener consumption.

All guests are potential green guests

We need a radical research approach to fill the knowledge vacuum and move towards more sustainable behaviour. Today's consumption complexities must be understood and tested first-hand on site. This is a crucial missing link for your hospitality service. As a small hotelier, examining my business in more detail, enabled me to formulate solutions from what appeared, at first sight, to be opposing ideas for green and luxury. (This applies an integrated thinking approach discussed in Chapter 6.)

We are in the driving seat. The alternative to waiting for green guests to arrive, is to flip our perspective. We can *create* market demand by delivering excellent hospitality experiences which embed far greater guest involvement. This way, guests understand the idea of being a green guest and their expectations are exceeded, leading them to enjoy their break more.

Our focus should be on improving our understanding of how to help all guests consume more wisely. As the example of Mr & Mrs. Average shows, there is considerable scope to encourage high consumers to match the levels of those more frugal.

Insight : Eco-friendly attitudes don't translate into savings

I asked Australian travellers if they "took environmentally friendly tourism considerations into account when making a decision about where to stay". They could select either: "Strongly Disagree, "Disagree", "Undecided", "Agree", or "Strongly Agree". I found 67% said that they "strongly agree/agreed" to taking eco-friendly considerations with 22% "undecided" and 11% "disagreeing/strongly disagreeing" from a sample of 259 telephone interviews.

When these same participants were monitored as guests staying at the same accommodation, their actual consumption use was surprising. There was little difference between those who had said they took environmental considerations into account and those that did not. You can see in the following three charts there were some outliers that did use more, but the overall average mean is similar for each of the three resources.

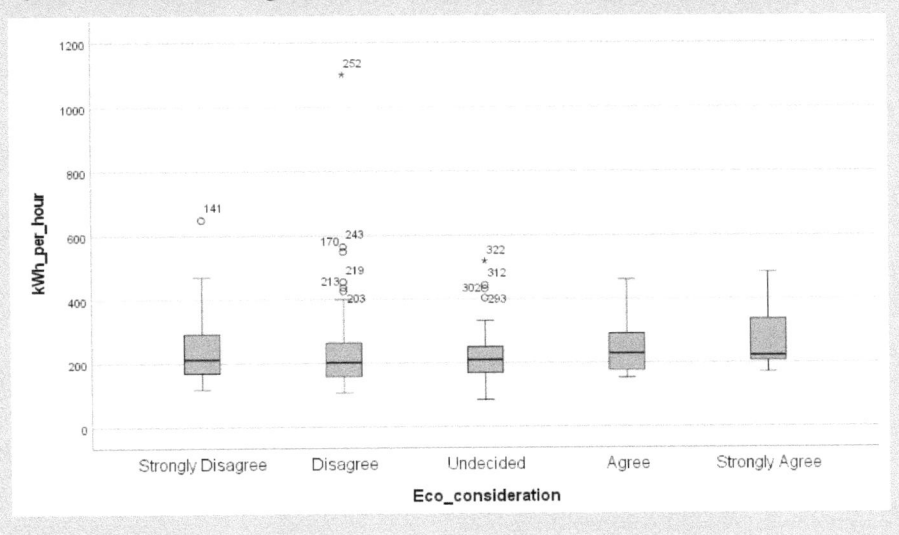

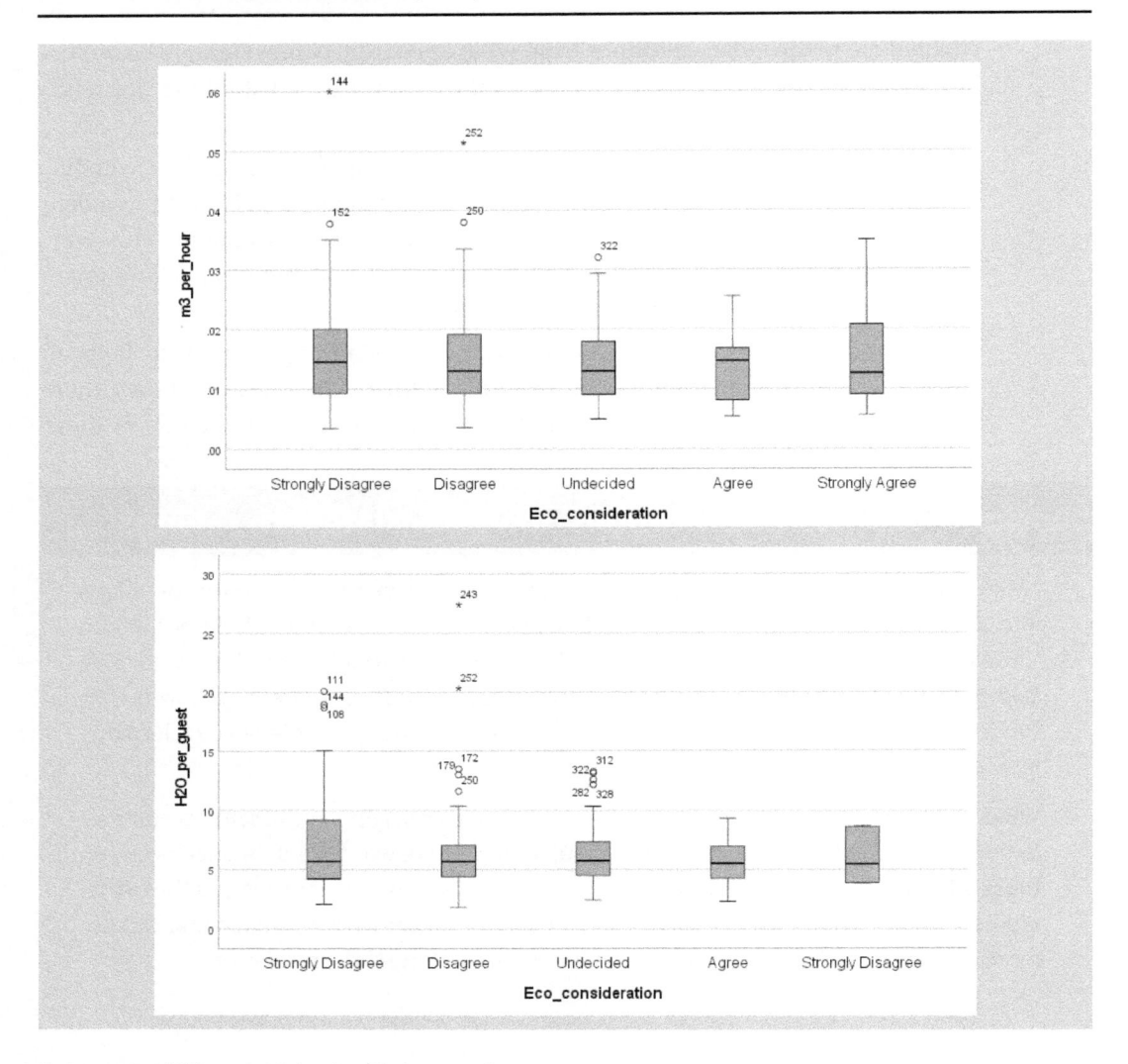

Story: A different kind of innovation

Not long after establishing our business, when margins were tight and expectations high, I was a little stressed. One summer evening I strode home to my wife and exclaimed in a tone rather too similar to Basil Fawlty (of the famous TV series *Fawlty Towers*) that, "The guests have gone out but left the lights on, I don't believe it!"

After similar episodes, where I observed guests not behaving as I would wish, wasting energy, using lots of water, and putting the wrong things in bins, something began to dawn on me. I realised that the problem was not necessarily that guests were out of control. True, they may have brought their lavish home routines with them, but quite often that was because they did not understand a better way of doing something.

Innovation has always been the domain of manufacturing, where new products come from technical inventions. Innovation for services is different to manufacturing. Unlike manufactured products, a service's customers are part of the consumption and production process. As guests use the majority of hospitality's resources it should make them central to innovations that seek to save resources, cut costs, and reduces pollution.

Many years after that summer evening, following our research and my Ph.D. we launched 'My Green Butler', a service innovation for all guests which is now shared through the UNEP's One Planet Programme, City of Sydney Sustainable Destination Partnership, at sites including the World Heritage Lake District National Park, a major theme park accommodation in France, and more......

Insight: Time for action

Scientific experts say we should be consuming less. The global population is skyrocketing past 7.3 billion and we have devoured more resources in the last 50 years than the whole of humanity before us (Dovers & Butler, 2019). The impact we humans have made has been called by scientists the 'Anthropocene epoch'. Unlike divisions of time in the past caused by geological or climate processes, this is one that we are wholly responsible for.

Next steps

1. Conduct observational research. Monitor guest behaviour using the available systems you have in place. Look in detail at how they leave their room: did they leave the lights on, what did they place in the bins, where did they leave their towels, have they been watching TV, did they prepare any food, did they do any washing, did they turn the appliances off at the wall plug? Check with reservations what types of guest, how long are they staying, what was the booking source?

2. Write your observations down on paper and allow yourself to prepare notes in an informal creative way, i.e. draw arrows, emphasise words, create mind maps to explore the dynamics and reasons 'why'.

3. Over time see what similarities you find between different guest party observations.

4. Talk to your guests informally, without a survey, get their opinion on social trends, e.g. new technology, carbon footprints and waste. Make notes.

5. Write up your findings in a short 400-word report to yourself answering four key questions:
   a) How do our guests use the facilities we offer to save effectively?
   b) How do we explain how to use facilities to save resources and cut waste?
   c) Are we missing facilities such as a recycle bin, and what are they?
   d) Overall, what are the gaps between what we offer and how guests behave, to substantially save resources?

References

Barr, S., Shaw, G. & Coles, T. (2011) Times for (Un) sustainability? Challenges and opportunities for developing behaviour change policy. A case study of consumer at home and away. *Global Environmental Change*, 21, 1234-1244

Barr, S., Shaw, G., Coles, T., & Prillwitz, J. (2010). 'A holiday is a holiday': practicing sustainability, home and away. *Journal of Transport Geography*, 18(3), 474-481.

Becken, S. (2007). Tourists' perception of international air travel's impact on the global climate and potential climate change policies. *Journal of Sustainable Tourism*, 15(4), 351-368.

Blake J, 1999, Overcoming the 'value-action gap' in environmental policy: tensions between national policy and local experience. *Local Environment*, 4, 257-278

Boland,B., De Smet, A., Palter, R. & Sanghvi, A. (2020) Reimagining the office and work life after Covid-19. McKinsey & Co. www.mckinsey.com/business-functions/organization/our-insights/reimagining-the-office-and-work-life-after-covid-19

Catlin, J. & Wang, Y, (2012). Recycling gone bad: When the option to recycle increases resource consumption. *Journal of Consumer Psychology*, 23(1), 122-127.

Cherry, K. (2010) *The Everything Psychology Book*. F & W Media Inc.,Avon MA, USA.

Cottrell, S. P. (2003). Influence of sociodemographics and environmental attitudes on general responsible environmental behavior among recreational boaters. *Environment & Behavior*, 35(3), 347-375

Coughlin, J. (May 2018) Greener Than You! Boomers, Gen X & Millennials score themselves on the environment. sheffi.mit.edu/sites/sheffi.mit.edu/files/2018-05/Greener%20Than%20You.pdf

DEFRA (Department for Environment, Food and Rural Affairs) (2005) *Changing Behaviour Through Policy Making*, The Stationery Office, London

Doran, R., & Larsen, S. (2013). Are we all environmental tourists now? The role of biases in social comparison across and within tourists, and their implications. *Journal of Sustainable Tourism*, 1-14

Dosa, K. & Rosemary, R. (2019) Making sense of carbon footprint: how carbon literacy and quantitative literacy affects information gathering and decisions-making. *Environmental Education Research*, 26(3)

Dolnicar, S. & Grun, B. (2008). Environmentally friendly behavior: can heterogeneity among individuals and contexts/ environments be harvested for improved sustainable management? *Environment and Behavior*, 41(5), 693-714

Dovers,S.andButler,C.,(2019).Populationandenvironment:aglobalchallenge.AustralianAcademy of Science. www.science.org.au/curious/earth-environment/population-environment

Farber, M. (2016) Consumers are now doing most of their shopping online. www.fortune.com

Filimonau, V., Dickson, J. & Robbins (2014). The carbon impact of short-haul tourism: a case study of UK travel to Southern France using life cycle analysis. *Journal of Cleaner Production*, 64 (1) 628-638

Ganglmair-Wooliscroft, A. & Wooliscroft, B. (2016) Ethical holiday behavior, wellbeing and orientations to happiness. *Applied Research Quality Life*, 11, 83-103

Gram-Hanssen, K. (2014). New needs for better understanding of household's energy consumption – behaviour, lifestyle or practices? *Architectural Engineering and Design Management*, 10(1-2), 91-107

Hadjikakou, M., Chenoweth, J. & Miller, G. (2013). Estimating the direct and indirect water use of tourism in the eastern Mediterranean. *Journal of Environmental Management*, 114, 548-556

Hall, K., Guo, J. & C+Chow, C. (2009). The progressive increase of food waste in America and its environmental impact. *Plos One*. https://doi.org/10.1371/journal.pone.0007940

Investec (2019) Interviewed by Webb, J. Today, BBC Radio 4, 15 October, www.bbc.co.uk/programmes/m0009b2p

Juvan, E. Dolnicar, S. (2014a). The attitude-behaviour gap in sustainble tourism. *Annals of Tourism Research*, 48, 76-95

Juvan, E. Dolnicar., S. (2014b). Can tourists easily choose a low carbon footprint vacation? *Journal of Sustainable Tourism, 22*(2), 175-194

Kennedy, E., Beckley, T., McFarlane, B. & Nadeau, S. (2009). Why we don't "walk the talk": understanding the environmental values/behaviour gap in Canada. *Human Ecology Review*, 16(2), 151-160.

Lexico (2021) Hobson's Choice. www.lexico.com/definition/hobson%27s_choice

Lindenberg, S. & Steg, L. (2007). Normative, gain and hedonic goal frames guiding environmental behaviour. *Journal of Social Issues*, 63(1), 117-137

Lorenzoni, I., Nicholson-Cole, S., & Whitmarsh, L. (2007). Barriers perceived to engaging with climate change among the UK public and their policy implications. *Global Environmental Change*, 17(3-4), 445-459

McGrath, M. (2021). Climate change: Polls show rising demand for government action. BBC News, 29 October: www.bbc.com/news/science-environment-59067471 [Accessed 31st October 2021]

Miller, G., Rathouse, K., Scarles, C., Holmes, K., & Tribe, J. (2010). Public understanding of sustainable tourism. *Annals of Tourism Research*, 37(3), 627-645.

National Geographic (2014). National Geographic/GlobeScan study reveals increased concern about environment. EurekAlert! AAAS. https://www.eurekalert.org/news-releases/820033

Netherlands Bureau of Statistics (2018) More people find the environmental highly polluted. www.cbs.nl/en-gb/news/2018/37/more-people-find-the-environment-highly-polluted

Nimri, R., Patiar, A. & Kensbrock, S. (2017) A green step forward: Eliciting consumers' purchasing decisions regarding green hotel accommodation in Australia. *Journal of Hospitality and Tourism Management*, 33, 43-50

Nisa, C., Varum C. & Botelho, A. (2017) Promoting sustainable hotel guest behavior: a systematic review and meta-analysis. *Cornell Hospitality Quarterly*, 58(4), 354-363

Røpke, I., Christensen, T. & Jensen, J. (2010). Information and communication technologies – A new round of household electrification. *Energy Policy*, 38(4), 1764-1773

Saad, L. (2019). Americans as concerned as ever about global warming. Gallup, 25 March. https://news.gallup.com/poll/248027/americans-concerned-ever-global-warming.aspx

Shove, E. (2010). Beyond the ABC: climate change policy and theories of social change. Environment and Planning A, 42(6), 1273-1285

Sorrell, S. (2007). *The Rebound Effect:* UK Energy Research Centre.

Semuels, A. (2018) We are all accumulating mountains of things. *The Atlantic*. www.theatlantic.com/technology/archive/2018/08/online-shopping-and-accumulation-of-junk/567985/

Stoll-Kleemann, S., O'Riordan,T. & Jaeger, C. (2001) The psychology of denial concerning climate mitigation measures: evidence from Swiss focus groups. *Global Environmental Change*, 11, 107-117

2

Sydney Water (2022). Safe drinking water. www.sydneywater.com.au/water-the-environment/how-we-manage-sydneys-water/safe-drinking-water.html

UNDP (2021). The People's Cliamte Vote. www.undp.org/content/undp/en/home/librarypage/climate-and-disaster-resilience-/The-Peoples-Climate-Vote-Results.html

Warren, C. (2012). Positive Aspirers. A test study of Sydney resident' level of aspiration to select responsible accommodation. International Centre for Responsible Tourism. Leeds Metropolitan Unversity.

Warren,C. (2015) Resource use of guests. H. Goodwin (Ed). *Responsible Tourism*. World Travel Market, London. 6th November.

Warren, C., & Coghlan, A. (2016). Using character-based activities to design pro-environmental behaviours into the tourist experience. *Anatolia*, 1–13. doi:10.1080/13032917.2016.1217893

Warren, C., Becken & Coghlan, A. (2017) Accommodation in Australia. *Journal of Hospitality and Tourism Management*, 33, 43-50

World Travel & Tourism Council (2019). WTTC calls for commitment to sector-wide climate neutrality by 2050. wttc.org/news-article/wttc-calls-for-commitment-to-sector-wide-climate-neutrality-by-2050

Young, A. (n.d.). Game theory: prisoners' dilemma. LabSpace. Retrieved 6th March 2014, from http://labspace.open.ac.uk/mod/oucontent/view.php?id=426560&section=1.1.1

3 Beyond efficiency and renewables

It is tempting to think improved energy efficiency and the occasional solar panel will take care of our environmental targets, but it's not that simple. In fact, that kind of complacency can lead to more consumption. In this chapter I show the 'green ceiling' of efficiency and renewables, and identify a third, crucial piece in the sustainability puzzle.

These are the key points at a glance:

- Efficiency and renewables are not silver bullet solutions. They are essential to green hospitality, but they have their own costs and complexities that deserve our informed attention. Hospitality businesses must go further to meet their environmental targets.

- Rebounds and backfires often undo our savings gains. The complacency of 'job done' attitudes can dismantle all the gains of green initiatives. Savings don't mean as much when people take them as license to waste.

- Carbon offsetting programmes do not absolve us of the responsibility to reduce emissions. Planting trees may feel good (and it is good!) but reducing carbon emissions demands a little more elbow grease than that. Carbon offsetting programmes should be but one piece in a broader green strategy.

- Any plan worth its salt must be shaped around a site's unique context. Beware the one-size-fits-all quick fixes. Every site is different and requires personalised sustainable solutions. Putting in the research reaps rich rewards.

- Resource conserving is the crucial third piece in the puzzle. Behaviour should not just be included in sustainability strategies – it should be central. Staff and guests alike can transform green tourism; we just need to trust them.

- This chapter will get you thinking differently about the foundations of sustainable hospitality, shining light on nuances we all need to understand and embrace. Only with that mindset can we hope to revolutionise the sector.

Question

Are we limiting our options to save? Many of us have turned to eco-efficient technologies or renewable energy to become greener. Both are worthy, but they are not enough. Their results are not going to deliver the savings we need in time. I will explain in this chapter a third way forward that complements the others and helps us achieve sustainable hospitality.

In this chapter I compare the benefits of efficiency and renewable energy/water, drawing your attention to the elephant in the room - our consumption and waste. Hospitality's escalating consumption and waste never goes away despite the benefits of new equipment, photovoltaics, heat pumps, and other green technologies. This consumption is compounded through business expansion and population growth. But it is also strongly affected by our need to maintain healthy environments in extreme weather conditions when we consume even more resources to cope. We must do more than simply rely on efficiency and renewables.

I have avoided doomsday data and have not gone into details on climate and carbon emissions because, first, there are many excellent sources of information (See, for example, the reports published by the Intergovernmental Panel on Climate Change at www.ipcc.ch). Second, my purpose is not to lament, but to help us take strategic action that draws on our strengths as managers of large, medium, and small hospitality businesses, to make us more commercially successful and truly environmentally responsible.

What is energy and water efficiency?

There are several types of savings: efficiency, renewable resources (energy and water), and conserving. We should use these terms precisely to understand their scope and to maximise our benefits.

Efficiency is a popular method. It means using equipment that provides you with the same or improved performance while using fewer resources. For example, a five-minute shower using 15 litres of hot water a minute amounts to 75 litres. Using a new water saving shower head, you still enjoy the five-minute shower but now use only 45 litres of water. The equipment is 40% more efficient and you haven't had to change your behaviour. This is how the costs work out at current rates in Sydney. The cost of the shower head is $47, over 12 months the cost of the water saved (10,950 litres assuming one shower per day) is $23 (Sydney Water rates), and energy saved (kWh 385.5) to heat the hot water is $96.34, so you have a ROI of six months (Elements of Heating, n.d.). What do your think might be a weakness with this scenario?

Arguments for efficiency tend to revolve around saving money, which is why it is a popular method with sales of energy-efficient appliances projected to almost triple (Alsop, 2020). It can cover energy analytics, company energy auditing, advances in processing, waste heat recovery, smart plug, and LED lighting. My shower example saves both water and energy to reduce carbon. Many energy processes have a nexus effect where they involve other factors, so there can be multiple benefits.

Types of renewable energy

Renewables are a second option that can cut carbon emissions, cut costs, avoid using fossil fuels, and make you more self-sufficient.

You can collect energy from the planet's four elements: earth, wind, fire, and water. From the earth, bioenergy using harvested trees (trees are processed into wood pellets to become bioenergy fuel, which is a fast-growing global market); from the atmospheric processes causing wind; using the sun's fiery radiation for heating and lighting; and hydroelectric power from water turbines (other forms of renewable energy include tidal and geothermal).

The benefits of renewable energy are that it is not depleted by continuous use, does not produce significant pollution, and generally does not cause health hazards. As with efficiency, the strong business case for renewables has led to wide acceptance by both businesses and the public. However, there are impacts, such as bioenergy, where the production of wood pellets and their burning emit pollutants (Quinterio et al., 2019).

The recognised solar industry way to calculate the ROI is to divide your annual electricity costs into the price of the solar equipment. Solar equipment costing $30,000 / $10,000 annual electricity bills = ROI three years. What do your think might be a weakness with this scenario?

Cleaner technologies are often included within renewables as they reduce or eliminate waste, seek to utilise renewable resources, and reduce carbon emissions. Biogas is considered a cleaner technology because processes collect the gases from the breakdown of organic matter, and methane is used as a fuel to heat water. Research has also proposed that it is feasible to convert organic waste from guests into biogas cooking fuel at individual hotels and restaurants using a bio digester (Dhital, 2018). Cleantech solutions are a popular option, as demonstrated by their escalating share price, e.g. Tesla up +1070% (Pernick, n.d.), and are now being retrofitted into tourist accommodation (Deveau, 2019).

Renewable water for hospitality

I also include renewable water – something we don't talk about as much as we should. Water scarcity is arguably our biggest immediate challenge (as Margaret from Chapter 1 would testify). Renewable water offers promise for growing tourism destinations like Aqaba in Jordan and Gulf states.

You can collect rainwater from the sky, reuse blackwater after processing to drink, or collect greywater for selected amenities and garden irrigation. Collecting rainwater might sound low cost but there are important health standards to meet and maintain. Cleaning and processing water is also expensive and requires checks. All these options I mention here need to be managed by people, which of course means time and money.

There has been growing confidence in the tourism sector to use clean technologies which process seawater using desalination plants. This technology can reduce pressure on local community water supply and has made some construction projects more feasible (Kuredu Resort, 2014). Desalination water production powered by solar has been assessed as a secure sustainable combination for water-scarce regions (Trieb & Muller-Steinhagen, 2008). Do such investments have any consequences?

Story: The Green Ceiling

For a long time I had no idea about the climate emergency or the impacts of energy generation because I had lived (before the explosion of the internet) in a geographic bubble, beyond the reach of regular news and social media for 17 years. When I finally heard about the devastating consequences of human behaviour on the environment, I was greatly saddened. It put much of my life into question, but the shocking details also gave me resolve.

We started measuring our business's carbon footprint in 2006, covering all the Scope 3 emissions categories.* Every quarter, I would account for energy, waste, and travel to build an annual picture. We managed over the years to cut carbon emissions from 50 tonnes CO_2 to 16, without offsetting. But then we couldn't see how we were going to cut it much further with our financial and practical limitations.

While we have planted over 3,000 trees on our property, we did not claim carbon offsetting as it can take 80 years to realise the carbon/oxygen benefits from each tree (Koberstein & Applegate, 2019). This does not sound like a debt I want to pass on to my children. We had reached a 'green ceiling'.

We had solar panels, rainwater collection, instantaneous gas hot water, a heat pump, new light bulbs, and so on. How were we, a fully committed company with grant

* Scope 1 = direct emissions from your property, e.g. gas, diesel and vehicles; Scope 2 = purchased electricity or district heating/cooling; Scope 3 = business travel, waste, supply chain, franchises.

opportunities, helpful equipment suppliers, and accreditation labels, going to get to Zero Net Emissions (the target world scientists, governments, and UN had set) or science-based targets set by tourism?

You may also be in a similar position thinking 'what can we do next'? There is another step which I will come to shortly.

Insight: What are science-based targets?

In 2017, the Sustainable Hospitality Alliance (formerly the International Tourism Partnership) commissioned Greenview to report on meaningful and measurable carbon reduction goals. Science-based targets were calculated using data from UNWTO, Cornell Hotel Sustainability Benchmarking Index, median carbon intensity per room, and each country's electricity emissions factor (Sustainable Hospitality Alliance, 2017).

The report shows that hotels need to reduce their absolute carbon emissions by 66% by 2030 and 90% by 2050 against a 2010 per-room baseline. This has been calculated based on the assumption that hotel numbers will triple by 2050.

Further it states it is "no longer credible to set simple efficiency targets" because per occupied room or per guest night calculations disguise the true picture from the sector's overall growth. (Sustainable Hospitality Alliance, 2017)

Left to a 'business as usual' scenario, accumulated carbon emissions will jump from 663,291,576 (MT) in 2014 to 3,684,095,566 (MT) by 2030, and 8,247,108,036 (MT) by 2050.

To achieve this, hotels are urged by Fran Hughes (former International Tourism Partnership director) to use science-based targets to "support an evolution of thought and approach" (ITP, 2017). Eric Ricaurte (founder of Greenview and author of the report) emphasises that "an entire new mindset is needed to even contemplate" reaching these targets.

Eric tells me there are further factors that may influence the science-based targets if applied to the overall accommodation sector:

- Domestic tourism trends are not included but in some parts of Asia, domestic tourism is now growing faster than international arrivals;

- Absence of shared economy accommodation (or called peer to peer accommodation) from the calculations;

- UNWTO report faster tourism growth than originally forecast (pre-COVID);

- Calculations use energy intensity per room per country on historical data rather than future levels (implications I will discuss further in "The impacts of extreme weather');
and

- Overtourism may constrain some destinations with capacity ceilings.

Net Zero and carbon offsetting are more work than you might think

Carbon offsetting does not absolve us of the responsibility to reduce emissions. Offsetting has failed to reduce emissions (Carbon Market Watch, 2017), has questionable management reporting accuracy (Becken & Mackey, 2017), and can even be seen by the public as cheating (Cheat Neutral, 2012) because it appears as a form of medieval pardon (Goodwin, 2009). There will be some factors contributing to your accommodation's footprint that are tricky to remove completely (e.g. waste water). While you resolve these to reach Net Zero, conservation work like tree planting can be a positive action, but it is not a permanent solution for our pollution.

Offsetting carbon is complicated. The idea of regenerating nature using native tree species from the specific land area you are restoring is a good ambition and one that can reap numerous rewards for the local environment and tourism. It requires careful consideration to make your hospitality business more sustainable. Forty-one scientists stated (Climate Home News, 2020):

- Be careful where you plant trees. Choosing tree plantations in tropical areas because they grow faster "threatens the rights, culture and food security of Indigenous Peoples", plus they can destabilise the delicate biodiversity balance.

- Assuming carbon emissions can be interchangeable with offsets, with immediate effect is not accurate; it takes trees a long time to compensate.

- Claiming "carbon neutral" or even "climate positive" are false and these marketing claims could even lead to increased consumption. We contribute more to climate solutions by consuming and travelling less.

Carbon offsetting programmes, therefore, need to:

1. Accurately explain the carbon offsetting scientific reality;
2. Acknowledge consumption now is not negated, that it still has consequences;
3. Target renewable projects and forest protection in developing countries which has broader social benefits for those communities;
4. Monitor their offsetting programme, providing details of the total volume of greenhouse gasses avoided or reduced, and to explain the calculation method;
5. Have carbon credits audited by third parties and explain the quality for the credit.

Breaking things down to rebuild

Science-based targets are useful for getting a broader picture of the sector. They illustrate how 'high we have to jump' to manage our carbon, energy, and supply chain impacts. However, these targets are not intended to show us how to achieve savings. A plan still has to be devised to identify what resources are the major contributing factors.

Similarly, while the Sustainable Hospitality Alliance decarbonising report does stress the value of improving efficiency to cut emissions and costs, where we apply such methods effectively depends on the nature of your property. Rather than replacing equipment, can you improve upon the way it is used? Or can you redesign the service delivery that uses that equipment? Or resolve the unique characteristics of your own property's context? Does this alter your initial choice? For example, rather than replace light bulbs, consider fibre optic cable solar lights. Although initially more expensive, they demonstrate an inventive solution that also helps show your commitment to sustainability.

To determine the best strategy to reduce carbon emissions, costs, and waste is to break down their sources. In Chapter 1 we saw that people's resource use is not in nice, neat, simple, equally distributed sums. It is highly complex, unique to each case, and shows generally rising consumption.

The nature of your property's amenities, equipment, climate, location, aspect to the sun, and the types of guests will affect production (service delivery) and consumption (what the guests use) and the corresponding carbon footprint. Solutions therefore require unique approaches for each property. We have a tendency to reach for the standard solution (e.g. light bulbs) but ignore how alternatives could help create a distinctive experience – more about this later in the book.

Is efficiency a fallacy?

Efficiency has shortcomings. It is not a panacea.

Recently I saw an advertisement about a new power drill being the "the world's most energy efficient". Being an electric drill from a famous company I didn't doubt it. Then I reflected, it wasn't so long ago my father would reach into his DIY box to get his hand drill. Wasn't that more efficient?

Homes used to have a wood or coal fire for a few rooms, then we got moveable gas and electric heaters, and when central heating came along we could heat the entire house. I write this in January having recently noticed a poster advertising an efficient central heating system. The picture draws me into a beautifully efficient warm living room with a view of a snow covered garden. Yet the picture shows models all wearing light clothing, even T-shirts. Fashion leads us to use more energy.

Changes in our expectations have seen indoor levels of comfort rise. Rather than putting on jumpers, our living environment is adapted to suit what used to be summer clothing and is now worn in winter – inside temperatures in British homes are getting warmer in winter with the advent of central heating (Mavrogianni et al., 2013).

Technology being unclear or inaccessible can also lead us to waste energy. We might accept temperatures that are too hot or too cold from heating/cooling systems because we find the controls too hard to understand. Confusion can lead us to accept energy waste in public buildings like offices, as we are not personally responsible for the cost of inefficiency (Karjalainen, 2009). On the flipside, when smart controls empower people, we are prone to 'tweaking' the heating system to suit our ad hoc needs, taking away any energy efficiency benefits from improved heating scheduling (Miu et al., 2019).

Efficiency is about using technology, but this can exclude people, making them feel applying their own adaptive behaviour to be redundant. Efficiency savings can become a fallacy in the modern world if we spend those savings in another form of consumption elsewhere.

Growth devours savings

Efficiency should not be taken in isolation of other consequential behaviour, otherwise we mislead ourselves. Take Peter, a long-standing friend I have known from my time working in Dubai. He is now proprietor of a private hotel in Cannes and worked hard to achieve greater building efficiency. He even bought green energy to cut overall carbon emissions by 34% from 47 to 31 tonnes a year.

He shared his success of saving money and carbon and was delighted to tell me his story. He then said that he had also just received permission to build an extension that would increase the hotel's floor size by more than 30%.

Unmanaged growth can devour the savings you may achieve. Portfolio growth is the number one challenge for hotel groups who need to curb environment impacts from both their individual properties and the collective impact from a greater number of franchised properties they launch. It is a challenge for everyone in hospitality because our sector had, until Covid-19, been expanding at a higher level than original projections (UNWTO, 2019). Despite the pandemic's impacts, our collective sector targets have just got higher to account for growth, despite investments in efficiency!

Laboratories are not the 'real world'

Efficient technologies are developed in labs, not in the real world. There is sometimes a disparity between laboratory research findings and the results from actual application in the field.

You would expect the highest environmental building grades to perform best in energy efficiency, right? Wrong. The Australian Government's CSIRO compared Grade 5 house efficiency standards compared with lower-grade properties. They found that Grade 5 houses in Melbourne and Brisbane used MORE energy for cooling in summer than lower efficiency graded houses. Also, people with higher grade houses in cooler parts of the country, like Melbourne, choose higher indoor temperatures in winter, reducing potential energy savings. No winter savings were found in warmer areas like Brisbane (Ambrose et al., 2013).

I experienced this myself when I went to meet a European energy monitoring company that claimed its equipment would save users 30% of their energy. At the end of my meeting, I asked what research they had done. Their answer was amazing. They had done no research themselves, just read other people's research data. "We noted that monitoring would achieve up to 15% savings; we also read research that suggests that by telling people which appliance is turned 'on' there would be a further 15% saved". They had simply added them together!

We cannot take for granted that equipment and processes tested in laboratories will perform the same ways in the real world. There is a key element missing from the equation: the humans involved in everyday life.

Insight: Research limitations

- A wind-hydrogen energy system test chose not to consider the electrical load factor of air conditioning in its modelling for a Greek Island hotel, because the average temperature from May to September is 26°C (Bechrakis et al., 2005). What happens if the property needs to add air conditioning because Greece is forecast to succumb to extreme weather events that will increasingly push the average daily temperature higher to extreme levels (Giannakopoulos et al., 2011)?

- Some technologies may work better in practice than expected. For example, water-saving devices installed at a Premium Inn in England were more successful, while the solar heat exchange system did not meet expectations (Hawkins & Bohdanowicz, 2012).

- Processes can be designed to optimise a person's experience, but people have a habit of taking their own route to a solution that does not necessarily match the procedure conducted in a laboratory setting (Turpin & Hersh, 2001). Real-world scenarios could also involve an individual's own objectives and skills, which may not be consistent with theoretical concepts used to devise strategies (Coleman, 2014).

Rebound effect...

Human nature is a further challenge. If I buy a more energy efficient car, might the cost savings encourage me to drive further and more often? In this way increased efficiency may not save resources. It's partly because we don't appear to be able to help ourselves when buying something more efficient, as we can also tend to then think we can afford to buy something larger or more advanced.

This phenomenon is called the *Rebound Effect* and there is a great deal of scientific evidence to support it (Walnum et al, 2014; Sorrell, 2007). Rebound is defined as to "recover in value, amount, or strength after a decrease or decline", or to "have an unexpected adverse consequence" for someone (Oxford English Dictionary, n.d.). Put simply, we often use the same or more energy after choosing more efficient energy solutions. There are many ways this can occur and five are listed below that are most relevant to this book:

- **Direct rebound:** when improvement in energy efficiency increases use of products. You might choose a more energy efficient heater, saving money compared to your older system, that then makes one feel comfortable using it for longer than before.

- **Indirect rebound:** when money you have saved on reducing electricity is spent on other energy intensive goods. A hotel owner might save money from a new hotel heating system, and pours these funds into installing large TVs in a sports bar.

- **Embodied rebound:** where more energy intensive items are ordered. The savings from the new heating system are directed to offering guests free salted almonds at the sports bar (almonds have a high water footprint requiring electric pump irrigation).

- **Service/quality rebound:** the accommodation upgrades airport transport from mini bus to electric cars offering improved private transport, but use grid-supplied energy.

- **Transformational rebound:** when a hotel installs outdoor spa pools in its lodges to remain competitive, effectively locking in additional energy and water use.

But it can be worse… you can have 'backfire'!

While rebound implies returning to a similar level of consumption, 'backfire' leads to consumption increasing *above* the original amount.

The argument goes that energy-efficiency can increase energy consumption because of improved profitability, new inventions, and consumer behaviour (some of these factors already explained above). It is not a recent phenomenon; it was first observed by William Stanley Jevons in 1865 in his book *The Coal Question* when describing England's rising use of coal (and the environmental consequences). The Jevons Paradox, as it is known, poses a severe challenge to sustainability because we seem to be trusting that more efficient technologies will clear up the mounting carbon emissions.

When we replace one method with a new, more efficient model, consumption actually increases!

What is the evidence? Jevons suggested that the improved efficiency of steam engines in the 1800s (used originally in coal mines) led to the wider use of this technology, which caused a subsequent escalation in using this fossil fuel. This we have seen. Today the rise in air conditioner sales in France might be considered as backfire. Traditionally a country with a low penetration of air conditioners units in homes (compared to the USA), France now sees sales boom (BSRIA, 2021).

Could this be simply because of increased efficiency of the air conditioner units? We have to be careful about claiming backfire. In the example of air-conditioners this could also be due to many changing factors like the equipment's improving efficiency, discounting or the changing climate (Noack & Hassan, 2019), or just the greater diffusion of air conditioners. It is hard to nail down.

An expert in this field is Steve Sorrell, who concluded that the most likely cause of backfire was a wider energy supply that stimulates economic growth, which in turn increases energy use, rather than one invention being responsible (Sorrell, 2009).

Trying to prove backfire is hard because of society's complexities that make a baseline "not meaningful, or at least only so in particular and narrowly defined terms" (Marsden, 2019). And that's the key point. Without establishing a very focused baseline, you cannot identify if the new energy-efficient equipment you have installed actually has saved, caused a rebound, or backfired.

What does history show us about rebound and backfire?

Artificial light was a wondrous invention. Before the 1700s people lived in darkness save for day and moonlight. The introduction of new ways to see at night changed the way our forefathers lived. The price of energy dropped as more and more people used it and began to depend on light.

Roger Fouquet and Peter Pearson examined the pricing of candles, whale oil, gas, petroleum, and electricity over the centuries, comparing price and consumption of energy used for lighting in the UK. They found by 2000, while the Gross Domestic Product per person had risen by 15 times compared to 1800, lighting was less expensive by a staggering 1/300th of the comparative cost over the 200 years. Over this period, people's use of lighting was 6,500 greater, and total lighting consumption was 25,000 higher. Lighting consumption grew faster than GDP, due in part to the drop in the cost of lighting. This was due to improved lighting efficiency (becoming 1,000 times more efficient) and reductions in energy costs (dropping by 180th of the original price). Efficiency played a more import role in creating greater consumption (Fouquet & Pearson, 2006).

Table 3.1: Key lighting variables 1300-2000

Year	Price of lighting	Lighting efficiency	Price of lighting service	Consumption of light per capita	Total consumption of light	Real GDP per capita
1300	1.5	0.5	3	-	-	0.25
1700	1.5	0.75	2	0.17	0.1	0.75
1750	1.65	0.79	2.1	0.22	0.15	0.83
1800	1	1	1	1	1	1
1850	0.4	4.4	0.27	3.9	7	1.17
1900	0.26	14.5	0.042	84.7	220	2.9
1950	0.4	340	0.002	1528	5000	3.92
2000	0.18	1000	0.0003	6566	25630	15

Note: 1800 = 1.0 for all indices

Insight: More efficient to less efficient and back again

- A four-year engineering study of 24 hotels in Sri Lanka showed that, as a group, energy and waste efficiency grew but water efficiency declined. Individually only ten of the hotels were considered to be efficient.(Kularatne et al., 2019)

- This study reveals that between 2010 to 2012 efficiency rose from 55% to 68%, then dropped in 2013, then rose again in 2014 to 65%. Performance is not stable and can be affected by human behaviour. Measuring efficiency on a year-to-year basis can be fraught with complications.

More efficient but poor performance

Poorly implemented efficiency measures negatively affect guest satisfaction. Analysis of 3,273 guest reviews was undertaken from Booking.com, Tripadvisor, hrs.de, and Holidaycheck, generated from 53 German hotels which participate in a sustainability certification programme and 53 conventional hotels of a similar type in Germany (Gerdt et al., 2019). Critical factors for guests were sustainability measures that affected their experience of water-saving, energy-saving, and greenhouse gas reduction. Designed solutions were not guest-centred:

- Water – 19% of negative guest reviews. An example could be poor water flow from the water-saving shower head

  "What really bothered me was this annoying water-saving shower head. You had to actively search for the water to get wet"

- Carbon – 22% of negative guest reviews. An example could be failing to link comfort options

  "No air conditioning and not possible to open the windows on the hottest day of the year – probably the price we have to pay for sustainable living?"

- Energy – represent 19% of negative guest reviews. An example could be failing to consider usability, like energy-saving lamps being a source of (dis)satisfaction, since they are usually less bright.

Where's the evidence of efficiency savings?

At the time of writing, only 17 scientific studies have measured energy and water efficiency saving for tourist accommodation. Twelve used only laboratory modelling. No study has assessed 'rebound' or 'backfire'. The five real world studies were done only in hotels in three countries (UK, Greece, and China). This is a very small source of evidence for one of the world's largest commercial markets. It also shows that collectively we are still short of the science-based targets we need to reach. The clock is ticking.

You can see the savings data at www.mygreenbutler.com/ resources.

We need more science

Before committing to any significant capital expenditure it's essential to have the right facts. Spending time with fast-talking sales people trying to get to the bottom of product claims can be wearying. Relying on just five real world studies on energy and water efficiency leaves us short of evidence. Can we afford our knowledge be so slender?

I spent the best part of three months interrogating several scientific search engines to find evidence. I found hundreds of papers from engineering, architectural, tourism, and energy scholarly journals which focused on resource use. I read over 500,000 words from them (my wife will testify to finding me surrounded by columns of scientific papers). Only 17 papers generated comparative findings that showed actual savings (at the time of writing). We also need to study if savings have been achieved and not resulted in rebound or backfire.

Renewable energy and water have limitations too

Renewables are a great way to reduce the use of fossil fuels or mains water, but be aware they have limitations:

- **Solar supply is not guaranteed**. If you have a series of cloudy days, you can find production plummets significantly. If in summer you have several days of rainy weather after warm sunny weather, guests will likely stay inside and use more electricity, outstripping supply and battery storage
- **Rainwater supply is not guaranteed**. No clouds, no rain for months can dramatically cut your storage, leading to shortages
- **Dayime solar energy production is limited** to periods when guests are away from the property, so you need storage. How much?

- **Telling everyone you have renewable energy doesn't change behaviours**, in fact it can encourage people to enjoy guilt free consumption, i.e. rebound.

- **Renewable resources must be maintained**. Panels washed, gutters cleaned, water tanks inspected and tested – and this all means more work.

- **Longevity of equipment.** How soon will it be out of date, past its guarantee period and selected for an earlier replacement? This can lead to increased footprint and decreased ROI.

- **Irregular demand.** Your occupancy may not be consistent; you need to design the system to match the ebb and flow of guest numbers and time of year. This requires data.

- **You must be sure of supply governance** and plan for price difference when you buy green energy. Otherwise energy costs could increase.

- **Desalination has serious drawbacks.** I have attended several scientific conferences in the Gulf which report on algae blooms, fish depletion, and loss of habitat. Though there are 213 active sea water desalination plants in the Persian Gulf and a further 51 are planned, which is equal to half the global production (Sharifinia et al., 2019), reusing black water (which is permitted under Islamic codes) and reducing consumption is critical.

Insight: Consumption does not match solar production or rainfall

It sounds obvious, but just to remind us, guests use electricity at completely different times from when we can generate it from solar panels. Occupancy changes across the year put into question exactly how much battery capacity we should invest in. I have studied our guests' use and solar generation and still been left with the option it is better to reduce the baseload, for example from fridges, than to buy batteries which have to be replaced every ten years.

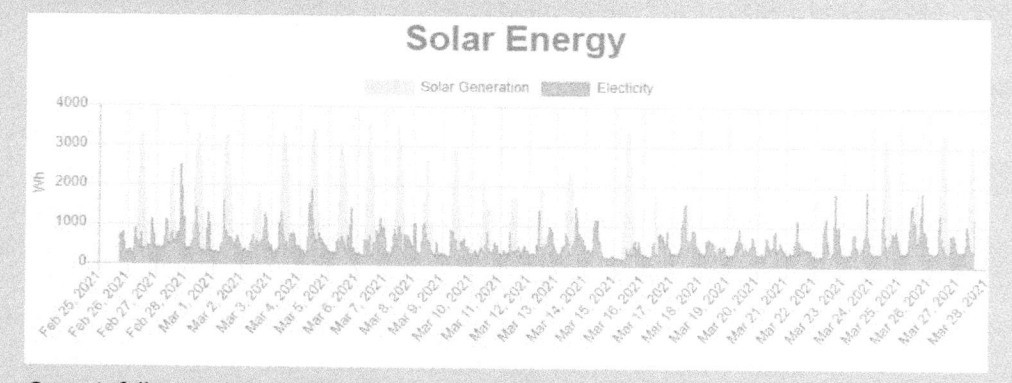

Our rainfall is inconsistent too. At our property rainwater harvesting was our only source of water, but we could have years with less than 30% of the precipitation that fell in the previous 12 months. Again, adjusting human consumption is a better solution than buying and installing more tanks, which have to be kept hygienically secure for public water consumption in a warm climate.

The tables of our solar production and energy use can be seen on our resources page: www.mygreenbutler.com/resources

Evidence of renewable's energy viability

Investing in your own renewable energy infrastructure requires serious site assessment because of seasonality, variable weather conditions, occupancy and costs. Given that running accommodation requires high levels of energy to maintain expected services, it is surprising that there have been only seven studies calculating the specific saving benefits for renewable energy, with only one using real-world sites (Dalton et al., 2009).

That study proposed a combination of wind, solar power, hydrogen cells, and analysed data using HOMER software. The properties were small to medium-sized accommodation, each in a markedly different location (South Australia, Victoria, and Queensland) and they already had a level of renewable energy facilities supported by diesel generation.

The researchers found significant differences between each site, the effectiveness of the technology and, therefore, its economic viability. A key factor was the environment the properties were located on. That alone resulted in wide power generation variations, which affected payback periods.

Wind power achieved a far higher level of payback than solar panels as photovoltaics have to be replaced after 20 years (claimed by the study). The hydrogen fuel cells, whilst technically feasible, were not economically viable at that time. Of particular interest was the significant differences between maximum and average wind speeds, strongest in summer and winter and lower in spring and autumn. Likewise, solar irradiance was markedly different between winter and summer. The Queensland site could maintain a fourfold winter power generation advantage over the site in Victoria, for example.

Because of the cost of the hydrogen fuel cells there was no cost disadvantage to maintaining a diesel generator, which would be essential to enable the accommodation to provide consistent services over low power generating periods of the day/night/season.

The study shows that an off-grid strategy requires a unique plan to fit your site's specific characteristics and not an off-the-shelf solution. The study also shows marked differences between the properties' different kwh load factor. But the authors make no suggestion of changing operations to reduce the amount of energy being used, nor adjusting the consumption to the fluctuating availability of renewable energy…. and nor most likely would the renewable equipment salesperson.

Another example of renewable technology shows how improvements have boosted renewable efficiencies, like the Cape Town Radisson Park Inn's new thermal energy and photovoltaic system. This is claimed to "deliver about three times more energy on the same surface area" and save water and energy from the grid (Building and Décor, 2018).

The continued improvements to renewable technologies appear to sideline the question of can we reduce our consumption in the first place. Are we monitoring renewable power/water and ensuring there is no rebound? Are we planning expansions that require more energy and water? Have we forgotten the inevitable cost of replacing equipment after time?

Case study: Making a renewable power judgement in a high solar potential country

Tunisia is a tourist destination offering holidaymakers sunshine and warmth for much of the year (March to November), and it is a country with high renewable energy potential from solar power (Zafar, 2020). If you were a hotel owner, then renewable energy might appear a sound investment that could save money and offer a positive environmental story for guests. But how many panels do you need? What size battery capacity would you require? To progress a site assessment is required.

Over 12 months, a Tunisian hotel's electricity consumption was monitored to reveal that the property in July used two and a half times more electricity than March, and September more than twice November (Khemiri & Hassairi, 2005). In another study Tunisia's solar radiation count was calculated over three years, showing that July's solar radiation performance was only half as much again than March, and September less than half that of November (Ouderni et al., 2013).

Therefore there would be a gap between consumption and production unless additional panels were introduced. If this was the case it would either result in energy being sent back to the grid, lost, or consumed through rebound. Consumption of energy in hotels is generally higher during breakfast and the evening, with a higher baseload for air conditioning during warmer months (or left on throughout the year). This adds to the complexity of choosing battery size.

The solar study used multiple modelling methods to predict solar radiation. While there was a small margin of error in the summer days of 4.1%, during cloudy periods the error rose to 14.26%. Therefore, not only would additional solar panels be required to cover the disparity between summer and spring/autumn, battery capacity would also have to be increased beyond the original calculation to cover for weaker power generation during cloudy days.

Renewables are not a simply 'plug-in and play' solution, they require careful site assessment.

The tables for this summary can be seen on our resources page: www.mygreenbutler. com/resources

Table 3.2: Monthly Tunis hotel electricity consumption (2020)

Month	Total kWh	Electricity cost (DT)
January	32,331	2605
February	23,374	1925
March	24,920	2043
April	27,745	2257
May	33,864	2721
June	41,316	3287
July	62,014	4857
August	52,138	4128
September	48,175	3807
October	37,262	2979
November	22,536	1802
December	26,717	2136

Graph 3.1: Variation in total solar radiation

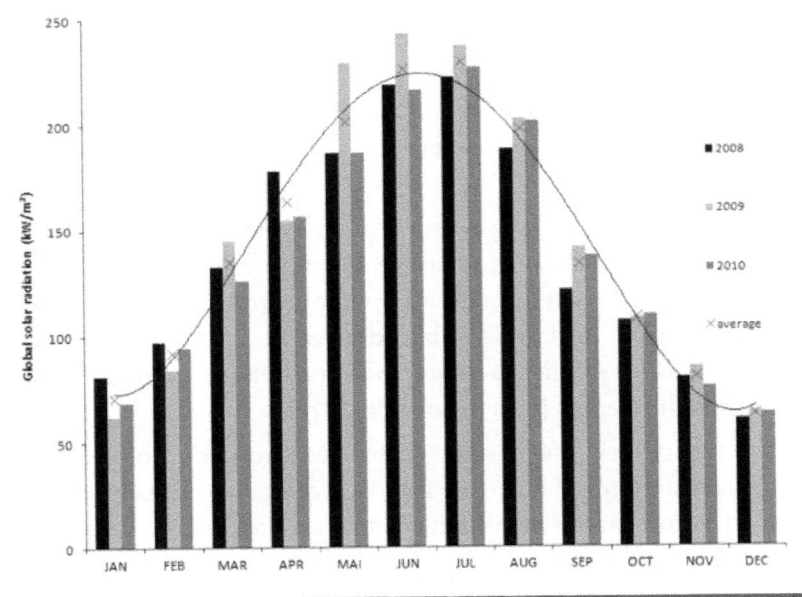

Insight: Cleaner technologies can also have consequences

There have been positive studies testing the feasibility of running water desalination plants using solar power. They demonstrate significant cost savings and fuel savings, and provide drinking water to water-scarce regions of the world like North Africa and the Middle East (Hamed et al., 2016; Trieb & Muller-Steinhagen, 2008).

However, while this cleaner technology is progressive, we still have severe consequences from desalination plants damaging the underwater environment, affecting habitat and fish populations (Roberts et al., 2016). Disposing of concentrated brine and warm water in sensitive marine environments requires further work to reduce impacts (Root, 2019).

Be aware of social impacts

There are further consequences with energy storage. While it seems a logical thing to choose, be aware that lithium batteries require cobalt. At the time of writing, there are only a few suppliers of cobalt and they use child labour in appalling conditions (Kara, 2018). There has been a UN drive to ensure child labour in cobalt mining is stopped, but contacts between mining companies and battery makers are still unresolved.

Review the EU's environmental assessment of batteries (EU Directive 2006/66/EC) to see there are high environmental impacts from choosing lithium. For example, in Australia, lithium mining involves high levels of energy and mining waste. Sulphuric acid has to be carefully processed to avoid it contaminating the surrounding area. The other method of lithium extraction is from salt lakes involving high levels of water (evaporation ponds) with consequential environmental impacts.

The consequences of escalating lithium consumption is that it can put sensitive places under increasing pressure. For example, at Salar de Uyuni in Bolivia, the world's largest salt flat and a popular tourist attraction, the world's largest lithium deposit is beginning to be extracted at a contested natural heritage site (Stahl et al., 2018) placing pressure upon and between nature, local communities, and outside influences (Sanchez-Lopez, 2019).

Batteries, which use non-renewable resources, do not solve our long-term energy consumption challenges. They do not change our behaviour, and can help sustain routines and systems that actually escalate energy consumption.

What have I done?

Of course awards are good to win, but when they come with prizes they can help make change happen. On one warm November night in Hobart we were particularly indebted to QANTAS, who sponsored the sustainability category of the national tourism award. We won $25,000. Such a sizeable cash prize made us focus our attention of what we needed to do next that would justify such an investment. It could not be frivolous, it had to be meaningful and quantifiable.

The sum allowed us to create an integrated solution for renewable resources that met our specific needs. It's a 3 in 1 system that combines photovoltaics, rainwater harvesting, and storage for firewood seasoning.

Learning about solar energy and getting good advice meant we purpose-built a roof structure so the 5 kW system faces the sun at the right angle in the right direction. Corrugated roofing lets us collect water, feeding a 10,000 litre tank that supplements storage. We planted 2,000 trees, selecting local varieties of eucalyptus and wattle native to our area. Random coppicing allows us to continually harvest from the same tree whilst conserving the habitat. Logs are stored under the panels. I wonder what Margaret would have thought?

For our small business the solar energy production accounts for 33% of total property usage. Some years later, I looked into installing a replacement system using the same space. 19 kW, with batteries, for the same price as my original system and using the same space. I did not go ahead because the batteries would be lithium, if I used traditional batteries they would only last half as long, and both types still have waste recycling problems. If I replaced the panels, in under a third of their claimed lifespan, then their carbon footprint would have increased from a 30:1 equivalent to fossil fuel to 10:1.

Neither of the reputable solar consultants who visited the site could determine the appropriate number of panels versus battery size for our fluctuating occupancy level. There would have been significant storage over-capacity at some periods, or unprofitable supply back into the grid.

The lack of insight from the contractors worried me. By this stage we were monitoring all our accommodation's energy use by the minute, the contractors had never seen data from a small business and did not use it to help them plan. They simply tried to sell a plug-and-play system. There was no fine-tuning to optimise. So we choose to conserve and look after what we already had, and continue to drive down our energy demand.

Having read this far, you might think I am against efficiency and renewable electricity and water. Far from it, but my own experience shows they are not a panacea. They cannot, in the time frame we have, help us reach the science-based targets alone. We need a new mindset.

Insight: Hard technology is only half the story

Having more efficient equipment tends to allow us to avoid questions that challenge consumption habits in the first place. Take the La Perouse Hotel in Nantes, for example, which went further than relying on technological efficiency by informing guests on "good housekeeping practices", which include recommended temperature levels of 19°C in the winter and 26°C in the summer, as it is "also essential to communicate the non-visible efforts we make, such as purchasing electricity from renewable sources". (UNTWO, 2011)

We can involve guests in conservation

There is a third way to save, which I have only alluded to so far. It is arguably the most powerful method to significantly reduce consumption. It will not only save cost but requires limited capital investment. It's so obvious, perhaps that's why we tend to close our eyes to its potential. To recommend this solution I have:

- Undertaken more than ten years of intensive scientific research based on 'real world' situations;
- Noted thousands of observations;
- Visited sites around the world, from the Palm in Dubai, to the wet mountains of Cumbria, to the open plains of Botswana and the city of Sydney;
- Interviewed thousands of guests to understand and identify the technique's potential.

To check my findings:

- I had two of the world-leading professors interrogate my data;
- Then had their findings vetted by leading engineers from Griffith University.

To ratify my approach, my research findings have:

- Been blind peer-reviewed and published in the world's leading tourism and clean technology scientific publications;
- Been examined and passed the rigours of a doctoral thesis.

Perhaps most telling is that the method has walked the walk in the real world:

- I have applied this knowledge to my own business with excellent results;
- My peers have willingly trialled my invention 'My Green Butler';
- My case study has won multiple international awards;
- We have successfully passed the scrutiny of several different government grant programmes.

In short, this is the real deal.

Sustainability in hospitality has never been so transparent or economical to achieve

I am introducing the concept of resource conserving rather than efficiency and renewable energy and water. Resource conserving is where you, the staff, guests, and suppliers apply knowledge to consciously cut resource consumption to optimise performance. For many this is a new mindset and encourages an "evolution of thought and approach" to transform the way we do business. It can achieve outstanding savings for a very reasonable level of time and effort. Conserving has now been re-introduced following the energy crisis in Europe (Lowen & Maishman, 2022).

Resource conserving seeks to save energy and water, cut food waste, and reduce laundry by:

- choosing to use less,
- not wasting;
- or avoiding usage altogether.

I am sure you have been applying this principle with your staff, perhaps behind the scenes, now I am suggesting you put it out front and involve your guests.

Conserving increases guest satisfaction and builds staff loyalty. Why? Because most people recognise the human race now faces global challenges, and collectively we are in the same boat assessing our values. By applying the old adage that problems are opportunities, hospitality firms can face these challenges. We can play our part, creating shared values with guests and staff. It can lead to innovation and improve productivity, while at the same time exceeding guest expectations.

As we have seen, not all guests consume the same amount. In fact, no two households use the same amount of energy or water or create the same amount of waste. Their individual routines and habits, using similar materials, are applied with different levels of skills and meaning. The resulting comparison shows extraordinary differences. Capture this, and you have enormous conserving potential – watch this video.

Video link - https://www.youtube.com/watch?v=XLk4M0lp9sU

Case study: The Science Innovation Food District

The scale of food waste brought Whirlpool to collaborate with 16 other companies in Italy to prevent waste in a programme called Science Innovation Food District (Alberti & Belfanti, 2017). This was inspired by the following realities:

- One third of food ($750 billion at 2009 prices) is wasted each year
- 54% of the loss is in post-harvest handling
- 46% is wasted in processing, distribution and consumption
- 31-39% of total waste can be at the consumption level in high income regions, 4-16% in low income regions.

SIFooD chose to rationalise purchasing and better manage expiry date labelling. The way to make this happen with multiple partners was to use the shared values. The steps for successful collaboration were:

1. **Find a common agenda by establishing the agreed 'rules of the game'**. In the case study it involved establishing identified scientific guidelines that all members could apply.

2. **Agree on a measurement system**. This enabled all parties to monitor progress and identify what adjustments were necessary.

3. **Apply a mutually reinforcing system** that enabled collaborators to support one another to fill the gaps and deliver more as a cohesive group and as individuals.

4. **Maintain constant communication** because they realised the important of providing continuous support and that their individual behaviours influenced others to reduce waste.

5. **Establish a collaborative hub** which acts as a dedicated 'backbone' structure.

Could we not think of staff and guest participation in a similar way? It is the same process of requiring a common agenda to save, measuring progress, supporting individuals, filling the gaps in knowledge and skills, maintaining a dialogue so people feel connected, and running the programme in an efficient, integrated manner.

Evidence of conserving

There are now several 'real world' studies that demonstrate that behaviour, when adjusted, can make significant savings in tourist accommodation. My own research shows guests are prepared to contribute to helping hospitality cut energy, water, waste, and laundry. There have also been seven towel reuse studies that find guests will participate (six papers do not indicate the amount of water, chemical and energy saved, so are not included here) other studies show the benefits of key tags and the like. Interestingly there have been no laboratory or modelling studies.

You can see the savings achieved in the online resources:

www.mygreenbutler.com/resources

Innovation in the way we consume

Imagine you are putting forward the idea that guests should actively participate in a conserving programme at your business. Do you think it is likely that colleagues will respond with:

- "How can we offer less, we are in hospitality!"
- "Luxury and indulgence are at the very heart of what we stand for!"
- "We can't have dissatisfied guests!"
- "Think of the reviews!"
- "We are already eco, everything possible has been done, and we don't need to involve the guests!"

Am I right?

These are predictable reactions. Hotel managers must all respond to guest satisfaction, the key KPI, and no one wants to deal with a series of complaints that reduce morale and distract from one's positive online review tally.

There is quite often a misunderstanding between what I am suggesting (to encourage guests to participate in your responsible, sustainable hospitality programme) and what colleagues think they hear (telling guests to participate and preachy messaging with the installation of eco-efficient technologies that restrict enjoyment/comfort). These are two entirely different approaches. The former is the ethos of this book, and supported by research.

Asking guests to save electricity and reduce their towel use to "save the planet" is not adequate. In a study of 10,461 guests at a 96 room hotel in Slovenia, guests were asked to save, but findings revealed they felt that the messages made them feel guilty, annoyed, and bad (Dolnicar et al., 2017).

A German study of 974 hotel managers and 62,766 online reviews found that high sustainability behaviours by hotels were noticed and appreciated by guests because "thoughtful implementation and communication of sustainable behaviourists (that) increases customers' satisfaction" (Koch et al., 2020).

These examples demonstrate that we must introduce a cascade of thoughtful, well-planned information to guests that does not promote a single isolated message. We should share sustainability efforts that:

- **Do not affect guests directly** but are appreciated (e.g. social conditions of staff) – if they are visible, showcase them;
- **Do involve guests directly** and are personally desired (e.g. fresh organic produce) – emphasising your attention to detail for them;
- **Let guests choose to participate** (e.g. conserve resources) while explaining the tangible benefit that emotionally rewards them for making an effort – and show that others do the same.

Achieving such a cascade of communications requires service innovation. We should not treat sustainability efforts in isolation to one another; they should come together as a holistic approach that emotionally involves guests and creates a competitive brand positioning for your property.

I am also not suggesting that sustainable behaviour must be mandatory for guests, only that we clearly articulate the outcomes from taking sustainable actions. Efficiency and renewables have an essential role in convincing staff and guests, but as explained, they have limitations. To convince colleagues, one needs to take steps that build their knowledge and confidence through a clear demonstration that those early steps have made a genuine, tangible difference.

The impact of extreme weather conditions

We can't avoid one key factor – the increasing impact from extreme weather events, which affect performance of efficiencies and renewable energy and water. This requires us to learn adaptive skills to conserve.

Extended periods of high temperature put enormous pressure on equipment, beyond its original design and purpose. The summer of 2018 in Europe required systems to work in overload as many accommodation providers tried to keep buildings cool.

In Australia we have now have regular threats of blackouts in our major cities each summer, as high temperatures are maintained over many days and nights. As temperatures rise, so the intensity of energy usage for accommodation is likely to rise too, putting pressure on our targets. This is a rising threat to carbon reduction and energy saving across regions with high temperature and humidity (Bureau of Meteorology, 2019).

We can't ignore this. The climate affects energy consumption more than your occupancy (Wang, 2012) and I have verified this with My Green Butler research on sites over time.

Renewable energy is affected by heat too. High temperatures make power generation less efficient. Extended droughts lead to mains water shortages in cities (e.g. Cape Town) and states (e.g. New South Wales, Queensland)

Conserving resources will be a critical factor in helping us maintain comfortable, safe, and healthy environments for our guests. In the following chapter I examine the cost of not taking action, and explain the enormous benefits from positively embracing guest participation. Afterwards we commence the 5-steps process that will guide you to revolutionise your hospitality business.

Next steps

1. Have you completed a carbon audit? If not, you can complete one here.

2. Have you completed an energy, water, laundry and food waste audit?

3. List the new eco-efficient technologies and renewable projects you have implemented at your property in the last five years, for energy, water, laundry and food waste. Put a date by each.

4. Have you measured your savings and carbon reductions? Are they clearly attributable to your projects?

5. Have you implemented any projects where you have deliberately sought to conserve using behavioural methods with staff, suppliers and guests? Put a date by each.

6. Have you measured savings and carbon reductions attributed to these actions?

References

Alberti, F. & Belfanti, F. (2017). Creating shared value and clusters. *Competitiveness Review*, 29(1), 39-60

Alsop, T. (2020). Global energy efficient products market size by type 2015-2022. www.statista.com/statistics/785514/global-energy-efficient-products-market-size-by-type/ [Accessed 27 March 2021]

Ambrose, M., James, M., Law, A., Osman, P. & White, S. (2013). *The Evaluation of the 5-star Energy Efficiency Standard for Residential Buildings*. CSIRO, Australia.

Bechrakis, D., McKeogh, E. & Gallagher, P. (2005) Simulation and operational assessment for a small autonomous wind-hydrogen energy system. *Energy Conservation and Management*, 47, 46-59.

Becken, S. & Mackey, B. (2017). What role for offsetting aviation greenhouse gas emissions in a deep-cut carbon world? *Journal of Air Transport Management*, 63, 71-83

BSRIA (2021) French air-conditoning market due to soar to new levels. Designing Buildings WiKi. www.designningbuildings.co.uk/wiki/French_air-conditioning_market_due_to_soar_to_new_levels [accessed 12th March, 2021]

Building and Décor. (2018). Thermal and solar energy for Cape Town hotel. www.buildingand-decor.co.za/thermal-and-solar-energy-for-cape-town-hotel/ [Accessed 16th March, 2021]

Bureau of Meteorology (2019) Tracking Australia's climate through 2019. www.bom.gov.au/climate/updates/articles/a036.shtml

Carbon Market Watch (2017) New study adds urgency to end UN carbon offsetting scheme. https://carbonmarketwatch.org/2017/04/18/press-statement/

Cheat Neutral (2012). Green TV. www.youtube.com/watch?v=I6zpnVW134k [accessed 27th March 2012]

Climate Home News (2020). 10 Myths about net zero targets and carbon offsetting, busted. www.climatechangenews.com/2020/12/11/10-myths-net-zero-targets-carbon-offsetting-busted/

Coleman, L. (2014). Why finance theory fails to survive contact with the real world: A fund manager perspective. *Critical Perspectives on Accountancy*, 25, 226-236.

Dalton, G., Lockington, D. & Baldock, T. (2009). Case study feasibility analysis of renewable energy supply options for small to medium-size tourist accommodations. *Renewable Energy*, 34, 1134-1144.

Deveau, D. (2019). Inn at Laurel Point goes hydrothermal 2.0. Mechanical Business, 6th December. https://mechanicalbusiness.com/2019/12/06/inn-at-laurel-point-goes-hydrothermal-2-0/

Dhital, A. (2018). *Opportunities for Small-Scale Anaerobic Digesters for Hotels and Restaurants in Kathmandu, Nepal*. KTH School of Industrial Engineering and Management, Stockholm.

Dolnicar, S., Cvelbar, L. & Grun, B. (2017). Do pro-environmental appeals trigger pro-environmental behavior in hotel guests? *Journal of Travel Research*, 56(8), 988-997.

Elements of Heating (n.d.). How to calculate the kW required to heat a volume of water in a particular time. https://elementsofheating.wordpress.com/2012/09/26/how-to-calculate-the-kw-required-to-heat-a-volume-of-water-in-a-particular-time/

Fouquet, R. & Pearson, P. (2006). Seven centuries of energy service: the price and use of light in the United Kingdom (1300-2000). *The Energy Journal*, 27(1), 139-177.

Gerdt, S., Wagner, E. & Schewe, G. (2019) The relationship between sustainability and customer satisfaction in hospitality: An explorative investigation using eWOM as a data source. *Tourism Management*, 74, 155-172

Giannakopoulos, C., Kostopoulou, E., Varotsos, K., Tziotziou, K. & Plitharas, A. (2011) An integrated assessment of climate change impacts for Greece in the near future. *Regional Environmental Change*, 11, 829-843

Goodwin, H. (2009) Carbon offsetting a dangerous distraction. https://haroldgoodwin.info/carbon-offsetting-%EF%BF%BD-a-dangerous-distraction/ [Accessed 27th march 2021]

Hamed, O., Kosaka, H., Bamardouf, K., Al-Shail, K. & Al-Ghamdi, A. (2016). Concentrating solar power for seawater thermal desalination. *Desalination*, 396, 70-87

Hawkins, R. & Bohdanowicz, P. (2012). *Responsible Hospitality: Theory and Practice*. Goodfellow, Oxford

Kara, S. (2018). Is your phone tainted by the misery of the 35,000 children in Congo's mines? *The Guardian*. www.theguardian.com/global-development/2018/oct/12/phone-misery-children-congo-cobalt-mines-drc [accessed 17th March 2021)

Karjalainen, S. (2009) Thermal comfort and use of thermostats in Finnish homes and offices. *Building and Environment*, 44, 1237-1245.

Khemiri, A. & Hassairi, M. (2005). Development of energy efficiency improvements in the Tunisian hotel sector: a case study. *Renewable Energy*, 30, 903-911.

Koberstein, P. & Applegate, J. (2019). Tall and old or dense and young: Which kind of forest is better or the climate? Mongabay. https://news.mongabay.com/2019/05/tall-and-old-or-dense-and-young-which-kind-of-forest-is-better-for-the-climate/

Koch, J., Gerdt, S. & Schewe, G. (2020). Determinatings of sustainable behavior of firms and the consequences for customer satisfaction in hospitality. *Interntional Journal of Hospitality Management*, 89, 102515.

Kularatne, T., Wilson, C., Mansson, J., Hoang, V. & Lee, B. (2019). Do environmentally sustainable practices make hotels more efficient? A study of major hotels in Sri Lanka. *Tourism Management*, 71, 213-225.

Kuredu Resort. (2014). From seawater to fresh water: Kuredu's desalination plant. Kuredu Resort Maldives. www.kuredu.com/desalination-plant/

Lowen, M. & Maishman, E. (2022). Europe energy crisis: Italians told to turn thermostats down. BBC News. https://www.bbc.com/news/world-europe-63173533 [Accessed 8 October 2022]

Marsden, G. (2019) Rebound, in Rinkinen, J., Shove, E. & Torriti, J. (eds.) *Energy Fables*, Taylor & Francis.

Mavrogianni, A., Johnson, F., Ucci, M., Marmot, A., Wardle, J., Oreszczyn, T. & Summerfield,A. (2013). Historic variations in winter indoor domestic temperatures and potential implications for body weight gain. *Indoor and Built Environment*, 22(2), 360-375.

Miu, L., Mazur, C., van Dam, K., Lambert, R., Hawkes, A. & Shah, N. (2019). Going smart, staying confused: Perceptions and use of smart thermostats in British homes. *Energy Research & Social Science*, 57, 101228

Noack, R. & Hassan, J. (2019). Europe never understood America's love affair of air conditioning – until now. *Washington Post*, 25th July. www.washingtonpost.com/world/2019/06/28/europes-record-heatwave-is-changing-stubborn-minds-about-value-air-conditioning/ [Accessed 12th March, 2021]

Ouderni, A., Maatalla, T., Alimi, S. & Nassrallah, S. (2013). Experimental assessment of the solar energy potential in the gulf of Tunis, Tunisia. *Renewable and Sustainable Energy Reviews*, 20, 155-168.

Oxford English Dictionary (n.d.) 'rebound'. www.lexico.com/definition/rebound [Accessed 12 March 2020]

Pernick. R. (n.d.) Q4 2020 Review. Clean Edge. https://cleanedge.com/views/latest

Quinterio, P., Tarelho, L., Marques, P., Martin-Gamboa, M., Freire, F., Arroja, L. & Dias, C. (2019). Lifecycle assessment of wood pellets and wood split logs of residential heating. *Science of the Total Environment*, 689, 580-589.

Roberts, D., Johnston, E. & Knott, N. (2010). Impacts of desalination plant discharges on the marine environment: A critical review of published studies. *Water Research*, 44(18), 5117-5128

Root, T. (2019). Desalination plants produce more waste brine than thought. National Geographic, 15 January. www.nationalgeographic.com/environment/article/desalination-plants-produce-twice-as-much-waste-brine-as-thought [Accessed 27 March 2021]

Sanchez-Lopez, M. (2019). From a white desert to the largest world deposit of lithium: Symbolic meanings and materialities for the Uyuni Salt Flat in Bolivia. *Antipode*, 51(4), 1318-1339

Sharifinia, M., Bahmanbeigloo, Z., Smith Jr, W., Yap, C. & Keshavarzifard, M. (2019). Prevention is better than cure: Persian Gulf biodiversity vulnerability to the impacts of desalination plants. *Global Change Biology*, 25, 4022-4033.

Sorrell, S. (2007) *The Rebound Effect: An assessment of the evidence for economy-wide energy saving from improved energy efficiency*. London: UK Energy Research Centre

Sorrell, S. (2009) Jevon's Paradox revisited: The evidence for backfire from improved efficiency. *Energy Policy*, 37, 1456-1469.

Stahl, H., Baron, Y., Hay, D., Hermann, A., Mehlhart, G., Baroni, L., Rademaekers,K., Wiliams, R. & Pahal, S. (2018). Study in support of evaluation of the Directive 2006/66/EC on batteries and accumulators and waste batteries and accumulators. European Union.

Sustainable Hospitality Alliance (2017) Global Hotel Decarbonisation Report. https://sustainable-hospitalityalliance.org/resource/global-hotel-decarbonisation-report/

Trieb, F. & Muller-Steinhagen, H. (2008). Concentrating solar power for seawater desalination in the Middle East and North Africa. *Desalination*, 220, 165-183.

Turpin, A. & Hersh, W. (2001).Why batch and user evaluations do not give the same results. SIGIR'01, September 9-12 2001, New Orleans, USA

UNTWO (2011). Hotel Energy Solutions. www.unwto.org/fr/hotel-energy-solution

UNWTO. (2019) World Tourism Barometer. UNWTO, 17(3), September

Walnum, H., Aall, C. & Lokke, S. (2014). Can rebound effects explain why sustainable mobility has not been achieved? *Sustainability*, 6(12), 9510-9537

Wang, J., (2012). A study on the energy performance of hotel buildings in Taiwan. *Energy and Buildings*, 49, 268-275

Zafar, S. (2020). Solar energy prospets in Tunisia. EcoMENA. https://www.ecomena.org/solar-tunisia [accessed 17 March, 2021]

4   The costs of inaction

A lot of people in hospitality don't believe they can afford to take action on sustainability. The real question is, can you afford not to? Here I show the costs of inaction when it comes to conservation, using real-life examples from around the globe.

This is what you're missing out on when you don't conserve:

- Conserving can cut energy costs by up to 50%. Sustainable behaviour isn't a financial hit you have to take in the name of a good cause. Be it water usage or equipment repair, inaction costs you a huge amount of money.
- Guests and staff alike want brands who share their values, and live them. Inaction costs you the loyalty of those you need most to succeed. From retention rates to user reviews, the doers become leaders.
- Sustainable hospitality earns the right to charge higher premiums. The numbers are in and guests will happily pay more for an incredible green experience. Those who choose inaction have no business charging more.
- Your local community benefits. Conserving is good for you, and it's good for the causes you choose to support as well. Plus, guests love knowing they've been a part of it.

Piecemeal steps may seem like the 'sensible' option, but part of the paradigm shift this book argues for means looking at green behaviour differently. The costs of doing nothing are damaging; the rewards of taking action are life-changing.

A horrifying surprise

As a small hotelier, when I first came to assess the facts – the amount of resources we were using, the level of waste and scale of carbon emissions – they horrified me. This can be a bitter pill to swallow, but sometimes we need to take medicine to make us better. I felt that beneath the facade of our tourist accommodation with high quality linen, stylish furnishings and tranquil gardens, I was actually *offering a dirty business*. Our waste was just conveniently out of view.

It seemed totally contradictory to the ideal I was offering guests – almost a lie. Just because much of the resource use, waste, and pollution is invisible doesn't mean it does not exist. The more I knew, the bigger the lie felt.

Consuming better

This is the chapter in which I introduce a brave new world. It is also where I show why it makes good business sense to conserve. We can all dream about a better world, but to deliver it requires open minds and actionable knowledge.

I will introduce the risks of inaction, sharing surprising details and eye-watering facts backed by proven scientific research. My aim is to draw attention to what can erode or enhance your value proposition, and undermine or strengthen your value architecture, to deliver an exemplary hospitality service for the 21st Century.

The premise is simple: we must conserve more, so we consume less. Only by doing this will we maximise the capital investments we have made in efficiency and renewable energy and water. We can prevent 'rebound' and 'backfire' not by leaving these technologies on autopilot, but by working with them to improve our adaptive skills.

Insight: Conserving saves money

An in-depth study of 15 accommodation businesses in New Zealand found owners claimed they had a good understanding of energy efficiency. Only five said they could reduce their energy use – the others believed they were already running efficiently. An audit of each business found further opportunities, missed by most managers, to save an average of 20% and up to 40% of energy use. Notably, 37.7% of the measures identified to save energy were behavioural, requiring no capital investment (Becken, 2013). These exclusively behavioural factors included policies and practices for staff to avoid wastage.

Conserving is a very cost-effective approach. Note that guests' direct electricity use was not considered in this study. Since our paying customers are responsible for 50% of the resources used in hotels and almost all in other types of accommodation (like extended stay suites and apartments, cottages, timeshare lodges, villas, and holiday homes) then one might expect overall behavioural savings involving both staff and guests could have a substantial saving for almost no capital cost.

The hard truth

What I have talked about so far is all well and good, and you might even think it's a worthy good cause, but you might also be wondering, "How much?" "What's the cost to my business?" "Will it really benefit me?" You might even be asking yourself, "Should I bother with this at all?".

Amazon founder Jeff Bezos believes that a successful leader is someone who is able to face hard truths. This sounds simple but is difficult to do. Many of today's hospitality owners and managers are aware of climate change, biodiversity loss, overpopulation, and tourism's impact on the local community. They are also aware of forthcoming legislative changes, social trends, and risks as a result of these challenges. Yet every day at the front of their mind are the pressing needs to meet KPIs and remove complexities to keep the business running smoothly. Hospitality is fast-paced and involves a great deal of human interaction, and the human brain is attending to the here and now.

On balance, a manager might feel they cannot tell staff and business partners hard truths if they don't offer responsible solutions. Changing shower heads and light bulbs (all reasonable actions) do show progress, but they also deflect attention away from long term sustainability truths. It is difficult to come up with more substantive solutions when one is time-poor. This is hospitality's hard truth.... we find it hard to allocate sufficient time to think more deeply about global challenges and our local responsibilities.

After 14 years of research, testing, applying, and trialling, I wish to share with you a substantive solution: *conserving*. Conserving can inspire colleagues, motivate staff, and bring joy to guests, which, as a manager, is what you require if a solution is to work. Conserving saves costs; it reduces maintenance, equipment wear and tear. Conserving empowers you to redesign your guest experience and restructure how you operate positively. It provides a consistent vision, guiding you and your team on how to adapt. It increases profits, decreases risks, and demonstrates a progressive, positive hospitality business that attracts investors.

I write this not to sell you an ideology, but to share evidence of a way forward, because we are all in this together. I have conserved at my own business with great success, as well as in multiple properties around the world. Conserving offers opportunities at every resource and waste touchpoint in your business. It applies to every level of your business, like training housekeeping staff to place bed rugs attractively on the beds in cooler weather, or offering menus indicating the carbon footprint of meals, or filling guests rooms a floor at a time rather than scattering them over a skyscraper, or directing guest donations and financial savings to help protect the local environment.

In the next chapter, I explain how, by taking my five steps, you can achieve realistic targets and advance sustainable hospitality so it becomes a truly beneficial commercial advantage. It has transformed hospitality firms both large and small around the world, and can transform yours as well.

The risk of inaction

A business needs a long term vision to survive and thrive. Avoiding challenges won't resolve factors like being poorly prepared for extreme weather events and consequential dissatisfaction of guests uncomfortable in their rooms.

The public discontent over hospitality's food waste weakens our appeal. Poorly communicated green efforts make guests suspicious. If we avoid acknowledging the status quo, we risk standing meekly against competitors who step up to embrace challenges with solutions that transparently report progress, build confidence, and cut costs.

A leading challenge is staff retention and quality service delivery. Inaction puts us in the same square as indistinct brands, which may not signal career opportunities or job satisfaction. Young people starting their careers want to choose a firm that has a meeting of minds and positively tackles the situation they are inheriting. They seek leadership and choose brands with shared values.

Ignoring the potential that an innovative step can achieve is to risk further unnecessary costs from staff loss, retraining new staff, and wasteful loss of expensive resources. To not recognise the science-based targets as a goal is to extinguish potential inspirational conserving solutions. Ignoring suppliers' capacity to help create shared values to conserve may limit innovation opportunities (consider the Whirlpool example earlier) and make it harder to control costs.

'Inaction' is a disastrous mindset in today's fast-changing world.

Case studies: The cost of inaction

Here are two examples when I have monitored energy and temperatures.

Hotel A is a five-star property located in a large international city with a similar climate to Buenos Aires. It was built in 1999 with 37 floors and 430 guest rooms. I found that the top tier floors (13 floors = +135 rooms and executive lounge) run at 5 °C higher corridor temperature than the middle floors (13 floors = +150 rooms). The corridors provide the only fresh air through the HVAC system and therefore affect inside humidity, which touches our sense of thermal comfort. The hotel has a building management system but did not pay attention to the variations, not thinking them significant to guest comfort.

This setup means that during winter the upper corridors use approximately 40% more energy than the mid floors, by calculations based on EU best practice (Styles et al., 2013). In summer, the top floor guests rooms would be using potentially more energy to counteract the higher corridor temperatures. The guests only had one control for the a/c with no visually available alternative to reduce temperature other than a curtain which would have darkened the room during the day (three sides of the building received full sunshine during the day). There was a screen but so well integrated many guests did not appear to notice. Leaving the windows unscreened when unoccupied increased room temperatures. At night when guests might have wished for warmth, there was no sign of an alternative to the a/c, though there was a bed rug 'hidden' in the top cupboard at the back out of sight. Therefore, guests on the different floor levels in the same building are working to adjust their room temperatures differently on account of the variation in temperature. The limited options did not take into account the aspect of the room, guest knowledge of amenities, or corridor temperatures.

Hotel B is a three-star property located in a large international city, with a similar climate to Vancouver. It was built in 1991 and has eight floors with nearly 900 rooms surrounded by parkland. This property allows the guests to open one window, but only by 7.5 cm for security reasons. The inside corridor temperatures were held between 24/25°C during cooler months, yet the guest room average was 20°C. The management had assumed guests wanted to be warm and had never measured guests' in-room temperature preference. Most people prefer to have a lower sleeping temperature, with an average of 18.3°C (Pacheco, 2020).

Upon observation, I found that 25% of the room windows were open at 7:15 am (indicating they had been open all night) during March. The outside temperature was 7°C at that time of the morning but well below 5°C overnight. This signified guests had been trying to get their room temperatures down, but the corridor temperatures were continuously heating the rooms. If they had run the internal temperatures at 19°C they would have saved money and cut their carbon pollution (saving 6°C × 8% = 48% of energy use). The room temperature controller was set to not go below 18°C, and occupants were given only a sliver of the window opening to moderate their comfort.

What is the cost of conserving?

1. The wastage of energy and increase in carbon liability. Hotel HVAC can consume as much as 70% of the building's electricity use, but the cost can be greater if the system is working hard during peak tariff periods in mornings and evenings (City of Melbourne, 2007). This is a considerable amount, for Hotel A which was spending $607,188 on electricity per annum.

2. The cost is also guest frustration making them less willing to act pro-environmentally.

3. Extreme weather events exacerbate these costs.

Global temperature rise will increase electricity consumption

Global temperature rises will be the primary factor for increased electricity consumption. A 1 °C temperature rise in Hong Kong was found to increase electricity consumption by 9.2% in domestic buildings – and hospitality services are more energy-intensive. This would have a HK$1.74 billion (2004 prices) cost impact every year, rising to HK$ 3.67 billion for a 2°C temperature rise (Fung et al., 2006). There is a benefit. As gas is used to heat water, rising temperatures would mean gas use would drop by 2.4%. So how can we maximise this?

Award winning hotel's carbon reduction strategy still leaves a gap

A leading 5-star hotel in Hong Kong set about a series of efficiency measures that reduced carbon emissions by 1,900 tonnes. These included lighting, air conditioning, waste, solar energy and transport. These measures have seen savings over five years grow from 84,000 kWh to 826,000 kWh. This accounts for 10% of its total electricity consumption and 8% of its total carbon emissions (Cheung & Fan, 2013). While good results, they are still far below the 66% science-based targets we have to reach by 2030.

Too hot to handle

City accommodation faces heat rises in warmer months, where building materials and road surfaces trap warm air and prevent overnight cooling effects. This is made worse by the age of the building and climate zone. Global temperature rises will enhance this effect, but not equally across all cities. The increase in electricity use for each additional 1°C temperature rise was found to rise from 0.5% up to 8.5% in Maryland (Santamouris et al., 2015).

Figure 4.1: Increase in electricity demand per degree of temperature rise

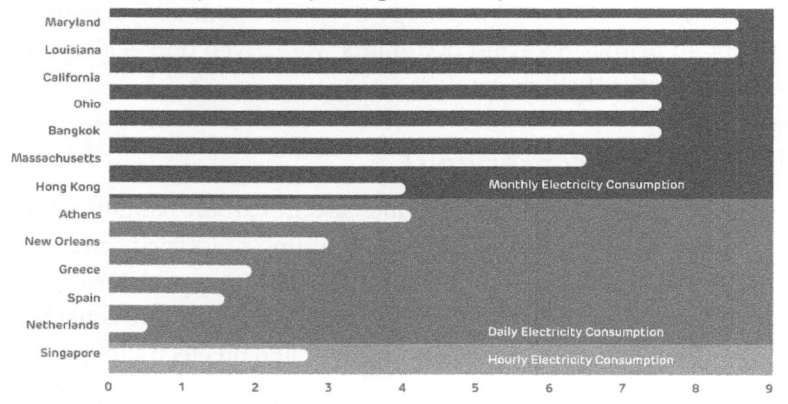

City/Country	% increase of base electricity	Inflection point°C
Louisiana, USA	8.5	20
Maryland, USA	8.5	15.6
California, USA	7.7	17
Ohio, USA	7.5	16
Bangkok, Thailand	7.49	n/a
Massachusetts, USA	3-6.5	12.8-15.5
Athens, Greece	4.1	22
Hong Kong, China	4	18
New Orleans, USA	3	22
Greece	1.1-1.9	18.5
Spain	1.6	18
Singapore	1-2.5	n/a
Netherlands	0.5	18

Note: Inflection point is the threshold temperature over which the electricity consumption starts to increase.

The increasing number of days cities have extreme temperatures (over 35°C) is likely to rise by as much as 50% over the next 70 years in Australia (Australian Commonweath Government, 2016). The number of hot days recorded in Australia has doubled since the 1960s (Steffen et al., 2013). Therefore future climate trends would indicate significant increases in energy use to keep us cool and healthy during extended periods of extreme heat when cities can not easily cool down overnight. This will likely wipe out efficiency and clean technology savings. We have to do more.

Implications for buildings in a changing climate

Both gradual climate change and extreme weather events will have multiple impacts on buildings (De Wilde & Coley, 2012):

- **Shift in energy use**: decrease in heating, increasing in cooling means further emissions.
- **Shift in thermal operations**: risk that passive or natural systems don't function effectively = discomfort.
- **Overstretched Heating and Ventilating Air Conditioning (HVAC)**: could lead to reduced building performance with subsequent impacts on people's health and wellbeing; high temperatures cause fatalities (BBC, 2021).
- **Increase in rain**: insufficient drainage capacity and storage means potential stoppage of operations.
- **Increase in wind**: peak structural loads means potential stoppage.
- **Flooding**: building structure and content could lead to potential stoppage or permanent close-down.

Many existing building standards are based on historical climate data. Building performance will need to be reconsidered based on guests' need for comfort in a changing climate. Maintenance, renovation, and repair will play an increasingly important role in adapting buildings for climate change impacts.

The risk of weak action

Some have been willing to take tentative steps because they think this minimises risks. There is an inherent danger in this strategy. You risk being misunderstood, or underachieving, or failing to establish yourself as a market leader.

Some reasons for, and examples of, weak action:

- *Monitoring your monthly bills is cheap to do but offers you trends and the ability to benchmark progress only.* This does not deal with the root cause – what equipment and what social practices do your staff and guests perform that uses the most?

- *Insufficient funds, so choose the lowest cost utility provider and offset carbon.* This does not deal with the root cause and leaves you exposed to calls of greenwashing from those educated guests and media who do not believe offsetting is a valid route (until all options have been investigated) – as prices rise you still have not dealt with the wasting of resources.

- *Conduct sustainability training with your staff but not include any communication methods to approach guests,* because you do not feel you have progressed enough and or do not want to interrupt your guests' sense of relaxation or luxury. The risk here is that while you train your staff to avoid wastage, they continue to see guests being wasteful, which demotivates them. Moreover, as guests consume over half of the resources and create waste, how are you going to reach Net Zero?

- *Change your electricity to renewable power but do not conduct an energy audit to identify what systems and behaviours waste.* This does not deal with total consumption. While you can claim green power to staff and guests, you will continue to waste this precious resource, could well pay more for the privilege and draw power from battery sources which are finite when savings could have been achieved, thus sharing renewable power with others.

- *Build an extension but do not consider biomimicry design, natural materials, methods of insulation and waste prevention* because of cost. These omissions leave you still with the footprint of the construction and the ongoing operations, which will be less effective. In addition, by choosing only price as a metric, you lose the opportunity of turning your extension into a Net Zero project with lifelong energy reduction built-in, losing long term marketing and cost advantages.

You might understandably think that it is easy for me to suggest grand plans from my safe position as an outsider. Let me reassure you here. My background is in new product development, forged at Craton Lodge & Knight in London. This was a pioneering innovation consultancy that used projective techniques, originated by the talented Creenagh Lodge, that gave the agency's clients a 1:2 success rate for product launches rather than the 1:10 market norm. My appreciation of research grew from those early days attending focus groups that, unknown to the participants, were assessing my creative work. It left an indelible impression and fostered a strong appreciation for qualitative methods.

You may feel it is better to take cautious steps so as to not destabilise your business. When asking colleagues, staff, and guests what they expect from a green hotel, they will only be able to express attitudes using their personal sense of reality, drawn from their knowledge and experience. Each is different. You can be reduced to the lowest common denominator and risk weak action. Use research to devise solutions and test them by projecting ideas in sufficient detail that others can grasp fully (Chapter 6).

Insight: Meeting and surpassing guests' expectation

- TripAdvisor reviews show that guests don't take kindly to poor implementation of green practices and will write negative comments if there are problems. Likewise, they will not write green reviews if you do not showcase your green efforts. Guests are strongly influenced by certain experiences like "guest training", "energy", "water", "purchasing", and "education and innovation". Guests expect towel and linen reuse programmes, so they are not necessarily strong influencers for positive reviews; however, poor application of recycling, guest training, energy, water, and purchasing rankle guests and lead to negative reviews (Yu et al., 2016).

- Meanwhile, at least 30% of guests are fearful of 'greenwashing' and avoid hotels that make green claims. Poorly conceived green claims are a "major dilemma in the hotel industry". An integrated, holistic approach to green hospitality is required throughout the hotel to avoid (justified) consumer scepticism, and guests are expecting a strong link between the hotel's actions and wider environmental protection (Nimri et al., 2017).

- One study of 30 smaller hotels in Germany suggests that managers appear to only communicate what they think guests want to learn about the hotel's green and social efforts, rather than what guests actually want to know. Overall, communication is very limited. Guests mainly notice aspects of sustainability they are familiar with (Gerdt et al., 2019). As consumers become more aware of sustainability, their knowledge is likely to increase and apply to the broader hospitality issues they see.

Guests want you to go the extra mile

Accommodation must move beyond basic eco-friendly initiatives – just emphasising such features on their own will not be a strong reason to switch between hotels. If the guests evaluate them unfavourably, they negatively affect satisfaction, but they do not have a positive effect if they are evaluated favourably. Where the green initiative comes into its own is when it is considered innovative.

Case study: Human behaviour

Hotel C is a 396 room city centre property in Australasia. Its clients are a mix of corporate business and leisure. Monthly water bill monitoring and replacement of shower heads were considered the primary step to control water use by guests.

Upon careful examination I found a strong correlation (47%) levels of water use and weekdays or weekends. Occupancy and water use only showed a small (2%) correlation. Examining the water consumption by the hour it became apparent that Sundays saw water usage climb to 485 litres per guest night compared to Mondays at 320 litres per guest night. Occupancy would be tracking at 68% on a Sunday and as much as 99.7% on Mondays.

The showerheads do not change by days of week. Many of the guests who stayed on Sunday also stayed on Mondays. The cause was behavioural. On Sundays, people take a longer shower, they visit the pool and take a second or third shower. It is a day to relax.

The missed savings of conserving

Water might not seem like a high cost, but in shower use, energy is used to heat the water. As much as half of the energy used by guests in their room can be attributed to heating water (identified in my other studies). The hotel was paying $191,734 for water per year and $91,540 for gas to heat it for showers. The 51.6% of extra water use on Sundays accounted for over $20,871 cost and 21,562.5 kg CO_2 per year. Managing guests' Sunday water use better was a missed opportunity. Simply putting in improved shower heads does not necessarily change behaviour, our behaviour also changes based on the day of the week.

Poorly planned green practices

There is also the cost of not reaching for the highest standards, as you risk not satisfying guests living in societies where green initiatives are so common they are normal. Smugly tell an Australian guest you have a water saving shower, and they may just look at it blankly thinking, "Of course mate, we have one at home". Proudly show a Frenchman freshly grown herbs from the kitchen garden and they may silently murmur, "We've being growing herbs at home for centuries".

These activities are not standard around the world, so you should reflect the best in the world because we are open to the world.

My friend Xavier Font, a professor at Surrey University, has done a tremendous amount of tourism research and coined the term 'greenhushing'. He defines this as the reverse of greenwashing, where committed green firms can be morally mute. That is, they don't explain their green actions, silently appearing to maintain tourism's status quo, so that visitors have the comfort of selecting a green business without hearing inconvenient truths.

Greenhushing doesn't change guests' behaviours. Xavier Font says that some firms do not disclose to guests up to 70% of their green actions (Font et al., 2017). This is because hosts don't know how to balance their message, something we will cover in Chapters 6, 7, and 8.

The limit of green accommodation online

A hotel's efforts can also be invisible online. Researchers examined 54 online travel Agents and 27 Meta Search Engines' web metrics and compared them with 10 award-winning sustainability hotels' own content, and found they did not match. In the words of the researchers, "We find a massive lack of transparency for the growing number of tourists using these channels to obtain online information about and/or to book accommodation". To compound this, they found that previous guests had no review categories in the formats to signal an approval rating for good green or social practices.

Strive for excellence

Appreciation of green services varies by nationality. A studying of Mexican, American, and other tourists visiting the same upmarket destination found that Mexicans rated energy-saving light bulbs significantly higher than Americans and other nationalities. Mexicans rated a towel and bed linen reuse policy, dispensers higher than Americans but lower than other nationalities. Americans rated the use of key cards, occupancy sensors, and water-saving practices higher than Mexicans, while other nations were less impressed than the Mexicans and other nationalities. All of the tourists were less satisfied with the idea of recycling (Berezan et al., 2013). If you run a hospitality business with many different guest nationalities, you will need to strive for excellence across a wide range of sustainability initiatives to meet different cultural expectations.

Reputation management

We live in fast-changing times. What we feel is impossible today becomes normal tomorrow. I grew up in England, known for its grey clouds and rain. Never would my friends and family have ever thought we would hear these words from the chief executive of the Environmental Agency: "We need water wastage to be as socially unacceptable as blowing smoke in the face of a baby or throwing your plastic bags into the sea. We need everyone to take responsibility for their own water usage" (Taylor, 2019). England now requires water conserving behaviour. This sort of message from neutral officials can help tip the balance. What's the cost of weak action in the future if your guests think you squander water, the basic necessity for life?

As we have learnt, efficiency and renewable energy and water are not enough. Therefore our plans must include conserving resources with the help of those who use most – our guests. Tentatively waiting for a sizeable green market segment to appear is not going to be sufficient. As covered in Chapter 1, the green guest is a mirage. Instead, we need to learn how to help *all* our guests conserve persuasively. This calls for well-crafted plans that redesign the way we deliver our service.

The cost of ignoring water waste

A study compared local community water consumption to 720 certified hotels in 21 countries. The water disparity between visitors and community can be strongest in developing economies. In some countries (e.g. China) water use in hotels can be nine times higher than the local community's consumption, per person per day. It's eight times in Fiji and Sri Lanka, and similarly high in Egypt, India, Jamaica, Indonesia, Malaysia, Mexico, and the Philippines. Hotels also had enormous variations in water use, from 371 litres per person per night in a property in Fiji, to 2,461 litres per person per night in the Gulf (Becken, 2014).

Research found that guests considered water the most important resource when visiting less developed countries. Yet 60% had not noticed any attempts by the hotels or tourist destinations to conserve water. Many wanted to see ways for tourists to pay to improve local water supplies – by taxes (70%), voluntary donations (65%), or higher price of holidays (41%), and were prepared to accept reduced laundry use (79%), reduced availability of swimming pools (73%), and restrictions on baths and showers (57%). With the increasing threats from climate change, water equality issues will "escalate future conflict" between tourism and local communities (Page et al., 2014).

The cost of ignoring food waste

Around 85% of an accommodation's water use is embedded water (water that has been used to grow the food, used in production making mattresses, in the plastic for the water bottle). So food waste is not only financially costly, but it also wastes water. If you are based in a water-scarce region and source local food, the impacts from food waste have community impacts. Water is perhaps our biggest challenge. An incredible 2.8 billion people live in areas of high water stress, compared to 2.5 billion who have unreliable or no access to electricity.

Food waste also wastes energy used to pump water, grow, process and transport food. The food we waste that goes to landfills emits methane which is 22 times more polluting than CO^2 when buried in landfill waste (World Bank, 2016).

The commercial benefits of conserving

Tourist accommodation, whether hotels, resorts, extended-stay suites, apartments, timeshare lodges, or self-contained cabins/cottages, all face serious profitability challenges. These are in the main, rising costs of resources, high fixed costs, seasonality/demand fluctuation, and dynamic tariff pricing squeezing margins – typically profit growth was already hard before Covid-19 (Mandelbaum, 2018). If you are an independent hospitality business, then you also face the challenges from international chains, mainly if you are in a destination unfamiliar to foreign travellers or offer a lower service level (Ribaudo et al., 2020).

In addition to these 'regular' pressures, we have all been hit hard during Covid-19 pandemic, with Income Before Non-Operating Expenses dropping by -80.9% (Mandlebaum, 2020), leaving RevPAR (revenue per available room) weak, draining cash flow. And as we have found, restarting hospitality, whether it is due to a pandemic, bush fires, or floods, is expensive and involves the time-consuming process of hiring and retraining staff. A way forward is to build cash flow and to maximise our means for long term profitability (Dimitric et al., 2019).

Sustainable hospitality solutions depend on your internal means, and your business' unique abilities to innovate. Means is defined as the intangible and tangible factors we identify as strengths and weaknesses within a business (Wernerfelt, 1984). Here I group 'means' to cover staff knowledge and skills, brand, service delivery, loyalty club, amenities, recreational services, business, and event facilities, nature-based on-site activities, cultural heritage values, design and atmosphere, technologies, and capital.

For those of you who do not own the building, the intangible assets are even more important. It is what we do inventively with these means that gives us a competitive advantage to build profits by cutting costs, improving cash flow, increasing customer loyalty, and I argue here that they are the very same factors that cut our environmental footprint and deliver returns to the community and nature. If you are the first and or best at conserving by truly integrating it within your business then it is entirely possible to command a premium.

It is arguable, under current circumstances, if investing in capital expenditure like renewables and cleaner, more efficient technologies, to save operational costs will place further pressures on your business. Such readily available technologies are often excellent, but you also need to be assured that resource use does not suffer from 'rebound' or 'backfire'. You also should consider if they deliver a competitive advantage from a guest perspective. Better initally to first stamp out wastage and pollution through conserving, to improve cash flow and through this create a better service experience (discussed in the following chapters).

One of your strengths lies with the skills and knowledge of your staff and how they deliver excellent service. Improving their sustainability knowledge, guiding those sustainability skills when applying services, and applying a holistic conserving strategy can therefore improve cash flow and increase profits. This is a cost-effective way out from the pandemic/fire/flood and a great strategy to increase your competitive edge.

Remember, conserving requires minimal capital expenditure. It is straightforward to start and offers immediate results. In my case study examples so far you can see staff attention to detail to manage heating and cooling and communicating with guests on their water usage can have direct, immediate benefits to your bottom line because these are the scenarios where you are leaking money.

Placing conserving at the heart of your sustainable hospitality business plan allows you to extend staff knowledge and skills, which builds their loyalty. It adds to your brand value by demonstrating responsible business practice. You integrate conserving into your service delivery, rewarding guests through your loyalty club. By maximising use of no- or low-carbon amenities, better managing recreational and event facilities and directing fiscal support to your nature-based on-site activities, you tangibly demonstrate brand values. You build the guest experience by celebrating cultural values, design, and atmosphere to emphasise attributes of conserving. You use capital to utilise responsible technologies that maximises the saving from the advanced actions you have taken rather than wallpaper over cracks.

The costs are minimal, because you are first changing how you use your existing business' means, through creative organisational innovation. Invest as you build confidence. Focus on ways to generate long term profit, as costs and risk are lower, and reputation and premium positioning command market leadership.

The benefits of strong action

What distinguishes a successful service business is the effective implementation of a clear and coherent mission that involves management and all staff on a daily basis. The core values should be clear to guests. Everything the business does should feed its core values.

The staff work hard towards delivering those values, with smiles on their faces because they know they are working for a good business.

The presentation is distinctive, polished and immerses us in the promise.

The supplies are specific and discernible from standardised alternatives.

If you were taken there with your eyes closed, and you opened them in the middle of the premises, you would know where you are because it is distinctive.

As a guest you consume a perfectly presented service that is consistent, convenient, and personalised. You co-produce this by using effective, well explained, and easy to use systems. Some offer frictionless tech solutions, others manual. You know when and how to use them. Personalised or customised services are clearly promoted before you arrive and throughout your experience.

Guests leave happy that their expectations have been exceeded and want to return again, telling their friends what a marvellous time they had.

This is achieved only by a service business that has taken strong, decisive action in the first place. Such an experience can be truly greener, as we will find out.

Case studies: The rewards of strong action

Resort A is a large complex in the Northern Hemisphere's cooler regions. It invites guests to conserve their resources. The lodges are 5-star with multiple bathrooms, cooking facilities, and gas central heating, similar to a well fitted contemporary home for six to eight persons.

Guests were invited to conserve, following the principles described in the following chapters. As it is a popular timeshare, we were able to gather guests' past seven-year electricity, gas, and water usage from the same holidays periods they had previously stayed. We set them a saving target from the average seven-year mean and provided persuasive information via My Green Butler.

Guests voluntarily saved 23% of their gas and 15% of the electricity usage. Gas is used for central heating and hot water, so savings were a personal choice to cut down on heating by turning off radiators, using curtains and rugs, and taking shorter showers or fewer baths. Electricity baseload was high due to the number of appliances and the kitchen facilities being exclusively electric, so conserving was directed to turning off lights and mindful use of cooktop oven. There was no rejection of the idea of conserving by any guest party.

Resort B is a large nature-based complex in Europe with electricity used for all domestic appliances, heating/cooling, and hot water. Guests were invited to strive to match a savings target following a similar guest persuasion approach to Resort A (as described later in this book) and using My Green Butler. Voluntarily guests saved 34% water and 24% electricity. Guests mainly saved through reduced hot water usage and mindful use of the reversed cycle air conditioner, and applying advice to close curtains and use bed rugs. Only three parties choose not to participate, representing only 0.6% of the guest bookings.

Conserving pays for itself in months

In these two examples, it only required one day of staff training and five minutes of staff-guest introduction to the conservation programme. The capital cost of hardware was paid off within six months, though actual savings were higher when staff monitoring was also integrated, showing operational savings which are described below. Combining guest and staff resource-conserving in these rooms led to a ROI in three months.

The savings of strong action

Let's first look at how conserving impacts our Triple Bottom Line account.

	Costs	Savings
Economic		
Revenue	Raised tariff	
Staff	Invest in guest relations staff	Reduce staff recruitment time
Monitoring & Training	Invest in systems	
Energy, water, waste		Reduced resource use
Food		Reduced resource use
Maintenance		Reduced equipment use
Carbon tax		Reduced emissions

Social		
Staff retention	Loyalty of staff	
Competency	Staff skills	
Guest satisfaction	Reviews WOM	
Environment		
Carbon		Reduction in emissions
Non-renewable resources		Reduced depletion
Biodiversity conservation Measured programme		
Air quality		Reduced GHG emissions

The numbers don't lie:

Higher Revenue + Less Expenditure = Improved margins

Higher staff performance + Guest satisfaction = Increased performance

Reduced impacts + Monitoring + Measuring = Tangible savings

I will now summarise these Triple-Bottom-Line factors through the rest of the chapter then explain how to achieve this advantage through the 5 Step process.

Improved customer service

Can inviting guests to participate in conserving resources actually increase their satisfaction? The answer is a resounding "yes!"

To deliver resource-conserving successfully you must deliver an anticipatory service that exceeds guests' expectations. Does your guest accommodation have multiple methods to keep warm or cool, and are they explained? Do you know what dietary requirements guests have, and what they would like to see and do before they arrive?

To deliver an anticipatory conserving experience, the staff should inform guests that they can help the property by conserving, and the equipment/facilities/amenities should work effectively. Both these key factors must work in tandem through a guest experience that has been designed to avoid the flaws that prevent people from conserving in the first place. This means tackling ineffective amenities and improving staff knowledge. We'll cover the experience design in Chapter 6.

One of my clients in Europe, with several large hotels and cabins located at their theme park, fully embraced the staff's role in delivering conservation messages. We worked together to add a *theatrical* element that families love as they discover useful information in a fun way. Our approach adds to the guests' stay experience rather than reducing it, as it helps to create greater comfort and better memories. The client's accommodation is almost 100% full throughout the year.

Service is king, where do we take it from here...

- A study of 63,026 positive and 11,406 negative reviews from 442 hotels in Switzerland found 'service' to be the highest recorded reason for writing a good review, followed by 'room', 'location', and 'food and beverages'. Conversely, 'room' and 'food and beverages' were the most frequent reason for writing a negative review. The research emphasised that price is no longer the sole consideration when choosing a property – reviews and rating inform their purchase too. What they found was that 'positive voice' (positive guest reviews and ratings) had the greatest impact on hotel demand (occupancy) and revenue (RevPAR). (Phillips et al., 2017)

- Customer service is the most important factor in guest satisfaction in hotels – more important than price. Whilst rewards programmes are important, the emotional attachment guests have to the hotel and its amenities are also reasons for selection. (Tanford et al., 2012)

- We should go one better and raise the bar to make service a strong competitive advantage. Nine out of ten people want more meaningful relationships with the brands they buy. A study of 15,000 consumers in 12 countries found that seven out of ten thought brands were self-centred and simply interested in increasing profit. People want the business to be conducted in a way that aligns with their values. (Edleman, 2013)

4

Case study: What guests say about conserving

I conducted research with guests following their stay by handing them a self-completion questionnaire. 40% of the sample were a control group and had not been directly asked to conserve, while 60% had received a holistic approach (as discussed in Chapters 6-8). Both samples were asked if they had tried to reduce their resource use, with 59.5% of the control group stating that they had indeed tried to reduce while 85.5% of the intervention group said they had made conservation efforts. When the intervention group were asked, "What reasons made you try and reduce your energy and water during your stay?" they said:

Because they had learnt:

- "Education and understanding that these ideas may save energy and cost."
- "After reading the information folder and eco-feedback, wanted to help make a difference."
- "The clearly eco-friendly accommodation makes people aware."

Because they want to reciprocate the efforts made by the property:

- "To continue the effort made by the resort in reducing the impact on the environment during our stay."

■ "The general commitment to sustainable practices made here."

■ "Seeing and reading about the commitment of the staff motivated us to continue the philosophy during our stay."

Because of their own knowledge and values:

■ "Being aware of Climate Change and trying to contribute to a green-friendly environment."

■ "We wish to be mindful of not wasting energy."

■ "Awareness of the property's commitment to the environment, and we take these types of actions generally as part of our lifestyle."

While some guests found the invitation to conserve surprising as they had not come across this idea before at tourist accommodation, the vast majority of the intervention group responded positively due to the educational information, the commitments already made and explained by the properties, and because it met their own values.

Longer lasting equipment/reduced servicing

Applying conserving strategies means you've looked at the functionality of your property, identified where alternative systems could be offered, and introduced them to complement existing equipment. This process is about taking the strain off the systems you do have and providing alternatives which use fewer resources, providing guests with alternative options. Reduction of maintenance costs is frequently underestimated as a strategy to conserve. Simply by using equipment less, you can save significant sums.

We introduced several new features to our guest rooms, like ceiling fans as an alternative to existing air conditioning systems. As a result, running time of the a/c systems has been cut dramatically, with some guests now not using the a/c at all. Each year we maintain the a/c, cleaning the intake filter so it runs efficiently. We are yet to need to buy replacement parts.

Less repair and replacement means less cost.

Insight: Conserving helps cut maintenance costs

■ By conserving energy you could save between 18-50% of your energy costs, extend the life of equipment and reduce the need for maintenance (Woodroof et al., 2008).

■ A breakdown of maintenance activities at 41 hotels (3 to 5 star properties) found that 21% of work was preventative, 31% was corrective, and 11% emergency, but without a strategic maintenance plan the 37% of time spent on routine maintenance was likely to be wasted (Chan, 2008).

Increased productivity and profits

Many hospitality managers tell me they face reduced productivity from rising resource costs and dynamic pricing pressures that eat into their margins and profit. They also share their battles to increase direct bookings using high-cost tech solutions and expensive loyalty schemes.

Let me share with you one outstanding feature of introducing a conserving plan: it helps *raise* your tariff, not cut it. By changing your guests' ability to conserve through a revolutionary approach to hospitality, they respond with genuine satisfaction, which can improve WOM promotion and your guest review profile.

Conserving focuses on energy, water, and waste, which combine to be a big cost for hospitality. Add laundry and the cost of unnecessarily wasted food and you will be covering some of your main operational expenses. The likelihood of carbon tax (already operating in Scandinavia) will only add further pressure. Failure to take control of consumption means we are always on the back foot, firefighting rising costs.

As a small hotelier, I cannot expand my property, so must work more effectively and focus on operations to increase productivity. By introducing My Green Butler we have the highest Tripadvisor ranking in the region, and command one of the top tariffs, whilst still cutting the cost of electricity, gas, water, and waste to just 2.5% of revenue.

There is an alternative to the growth and commodification of accommodation properties. Your hospitality growth can come from improved productivity and the skilful application of conserving strategies. Put simply, if guests are delighted by conserving strategies applied by staff, you can command a price premium... and save costs.

Insight: Investing in a better guest experience pays dividends

- Guest reviews which score staff highly are able to achieve a higher price level. Following an analysis of Booking.com hotels in Paris (758), London (610), and Barcelona (316), researchers found that an increase in guest scores for 'staff' resulted in higher advertised prices and the property was seen to have a higher reputation (Yacouel & Fleischer, 2012).

- Using Travel Click data from 178 US hotels, researchers found that Tripadvisor ratings and the number of reviews correlated to higher valued transactions. The greater number of reviews can suggest a more popular property, and increasing the number of reviews might also increase guest evaluation (Torres et al., 2015).

- Research in Spain found that hotels holding first place in Tripadvisor's Popularity Index in a given region sell their accommodation at a 22.26% price premium compared with the competition in the same region (Diana-Jens & Ruibal, 2015).

Increased environmental benefits

Do your environmental initiatives delight guests? Do they exceed their expectations and make them feel good about their stay experience from the moment they enter their accommodation?

Everyone talks about *minimising impacts* which, as we have learnt, only generates a neutral response, but what about the environmental *benefit* you create? Search Google with "What are the environmental benefits of a hotel?" Did you find any relevant search results? Sure, there are a lot of results (199 million) but the overwhelming focus is on minimising impacts, rather than examples of how hospitality can benefit the environment. This got me thinking that we only see the environment as a negative problem, not a positive. As I've told you, I don't want my business to be considered part of a *dirty industry* – I want it to be a *clean service* which enhances the place where we are located. Your conserving strategies should do good, beyond simply saving. A different mindset, right?

We tell guests before they arrive that fiscal savings go to two local wildlife causes. This is a unique factor of My Green Butler that demonstrates it is a positive, responsible technology for regenerative tourism. From the moment guests arrive we shine a light on the benefits of their stay. They see their conserving efforts going to a greater good. It unleashes a powerful feel-good factor.

Insight: Guest reviews benefit the writer

When writing a guest review on social media, the writer takes part in a form of self-presentation reflecting how they wish to be seen. As most people want to be seen in a positive light, the review reflects better on them than the hotel. Guests want to see and write about green innovations, rather than the expected standards of shower head and light bulbs.

The service innovation that My Green Butler offers is to bring the apparent contradiction of green and luxury together, offering a superior experience.

Guests must see environmental benefits, not just hear about efficiency

Guests understand their actions have environmental consequences, and by staying in green accommodation they may contribute to protecting the planet, leaving the environment better for future generations, and meeting their obligations. Environmental initiatives must be visible to guests, with educational content that expresses the positive benefits, verified by independent bodies.

Such accommodation is seen to offer a healthier environment to stay in, and green restaurants are seen to provide healthier food. Therefore managers should highlight how they positively contribute to environmental protection at the time guests are selecting accommodation, and explain the overall quality of the visitors' experience, because guests believe that staying in green accommodation delivers stronger environmental benefits than personal benefits. This would deliver long term commercial success particularly because younger generations appear motivated to stay at greener accommodation.

Reduced cost of staff retention

Staff are vital in our aim to offer exceptional service, so we should be paying more attention to retain them, but how?

My friend Caroline, a responsible travel consultant, became frustrated with a hotel when she asked for another way to keep warm: "The engineers couldn't get the air conditioning to provide more hot air, so I called and asked the attendant at reception if they had spare blankets. They replied that they weren't sure and would check. Ten minutes later, up came an electric fan heater. No blanket! It took me a further 10 minutes of calls before someone found a blanket. How can I keep my carbon footprint low when this happens? Would other guests bother to keep pushing?"

Sad but true, a tiny number of our employees choose to work in hospitality for career reasons (just 3% in the UK, 2018). Poor pay, working conditions, and career prospects are the areas that need to be tackled. Following Covid we have seen severe staff shortages, challenges retaining staff and hospitality's long-term weakness in attracting top talent. The cost of retaining staff is a major consideration for many of us. So introducing a guest participation programme should also seek to retain staff by:

- Showing they are valued.
- Providing personal development training.
- Involving them in product development and service changes to deliver conserving strategies.
- Involving them in selecting charitable partners.
- As a diverse cultural service sector, encouraging staff to draw on their roots to help generate seeds for new innovative concepts, which also gives employees a sense of self-respect.
- Redirect some savings to reward staff.

My Green Butler research

How can I be so confident about conserving? Because over the last ten years I have run multiple experiments at my own business (and now others) testing ways to engage guests – from just using signs and gentle remarks to the full scale programme I now run and share, called My Green Butler.

Clearly, stronger conserving action delivers remarkable results. You get to a tipping point where all your previous efforts combine and prove to staff and guests that this is really worthwhile. Guests' usage of energy and water has dropped significantly. My doctoral research recorded guest consumption savings:

- 38% less firewood (men aren't as good at making fires as they tend to think they are!),
- 33% less electricity (guests choose less energy-intensive amenities),
- 21% less water (choosing to use less),
- 20% less gas (choosing to use less hot water and alternative cooking methods)
- Guests generate less waste by separating materials, including food scraps, helping to cut our landfill by 85%.

We have rolled out the scheme and 80% of guests feel the new service adds greatly to their stay experience and are twice as active as previous guests in using resource-saving methods. To top it off, we are able to command a premium price and have some of the best guest review results in our category. We exceed guests' expectations, not at a cost, but at a profit!

Following the study in 2018, I raised our prices by 10%, no discounting, promoted the My Green Butler service as a dedicated page on our website and introduced the service to all paying guests. Since then, we have see our positive reviews double on TripAdvisor and Google and now claim, according to Reviewpro, the best positive review position for our category in our region, second in the state, and fourth in Australia.

"The eco-friendly approach in the planning and running ... is unobtrusively woven through the whole experience of staying there. We found [it] perfect in every way."

Guest from Canberra / TripAdvisor - Excellent

"The cabin was "smart" so we received a notice of how much energy we used each day - it was great to know that what we saved will be donated to wildlife."

Guest from Bulli / Trip Advisor - Excellent

"We loved the 'green' focus and environmental commitment. The information and tracking of our energy and resource usage is such a great idea."

Guest from Sydney Trip Advisor - Excellent

"We eagerly awaited the morning sustainability report trying to better ourselves from yesterday! We will bring these tips home with us."

Guest from Sydney / Google reviews - 5/5

"The emphasis on sustainability was evident everywhere and never felt put on or preachy. The hosts walk their talk."

Guest from Sydney / Google Reviews - 5/5

Next steps

1. Do you have a strategic maintenance plan? If not, this needs to be prepared with your conserving strategies included

2. Compare your pricing, guest review numbers and rating by OTAs, and review sites with competitors.

3. Have you monitored energy, water, waste and food costs over the last five years? Do you have projections of their costs in the next five years?

4. Review your staff retention levels, the cost of rehiring and retraining. Compare this to the green programme training you conduct for all your staff.

References

Australian Commonweath Government (2016) Increased extreme weather events. https://soe.environment.gov.au/theme/built-environment/topic/2016/increased-extreme-weather-events [Accessed 29 march 2021]

BBC (2021). Canada weather: Donzens dead as heatwave shatters records, 30 June. www.bbc.com/news/world-us-canada-57654133 [Accessed 31 st October 2021]

Becken, S. (2014). Water equity – Contrasting tourism water use with that of the local community. *Water Resources and Industry*, 7-8, 9-22

Berezan, O., Raab, C., Yoo, M. & Love, C. (2013). Sustainable hotel practices and nationality: The impact on guest satisfaction and guest intention to return. *International Journal of Hospitality Management*, 34, 227-233

Chan, K. (2008). An empirical study of maintenance cost for hotels in Hong Kong. *Journal of Retail & Leisure Property*, 7(1), 35-52

Cheung, M. & Fan, J. (2013) Carbon reduction in a high-density city: A case study of Langham Place Hotel Mongkok Hong Kong. *Renewable Energy*, 50,433-440.

De Wilde, P. & Coley, D. (2012). The implications of a changing climate for buildings. *Building and Environment*, 55, 1-7

Diana-Jens, P. & Ruibal, A. (2015). Online reputation and its impact on hotel pricing strategies. *Cuadernos de Turismo University of Murcia*, 36, 453-456

Dimitric, M., Zikovic, I. & Blecich, A. (2019) Profitability determinates of hotel companies in selected Mediterranean countries. *Economic Research*, 31(1), 1977-1993.

Edleman. (2013) Consumer attitudes towards brand connections. www.marketingcharts.com/customer-centric/customer-engagement-37199) [Accessed: 12 April 2021]

Font, X., Elgammal, I. & Lamond, I. (2017). Greenhushing: The deliberate under communicating of sustainability practices by tourism businesses. *Journal of Sustainable Tourism*, 25(7), 1007-1023.

Fung, W., Lam, K., Hung, W., Pang, S. & Lee, Y. (2006) Impact of urban temperature on energy consumption of Hong Kong. *Energy*, 31, 2623-2637

Gerdt, S., Wagner, E. & Schewe, G. (2019). The relationship between sustainability and customer satisfaction in hospitality: An exploration investigation using eWOM as a data source. *Tourism Management*, 74, 155-172

Mandelbaum, R. (2018). Profit growth presents enormous challenge for hotel industry. *Hotel Management*.   www.hotelmanagement.net/operate/cost-controls-perpetuate-u-s-hotel-profit-growth-2017

Mandlebaum, R. (2020). Hotel operators adapt and survive in 2020. CBRE. www.cbrehotels.com/en/research/articles/hotel-operators-adapt-and-survive-in-2020. [Accessed 5th April 2021]

City of Melbourne (2007) Energy Wise Tool Kit

Nimri R., Patiar, A. & Kensbock, S. (2017). A green step forward: Eliciting consumers' purchasing decisions regarding green hotel accommodation in Australia. *Journal of Hospitality and Tourism Management, 33*, 43-50.

Page, S., Essex, S. & Causevic, S. (2014). Tourist attitudes towards water use in the developing world: A comparative analysis. *Tourism Management Perspectives, 10*, 57-67.p66.

Phillips, P., Barnes, S., Zigan, K. & Schegg, R. (2017) Understanding the impact of online reviews on hotel performance: An empirical analysis. *Journal of Travel Research, 56*(2), 235-249.

Ribaudo, G. Moccia, S., Orero-Blat M. & Palacios-Marques, D. (2020). Comparing chains versus independent hotels based on international sales: an exploratory study. *Economic Research, 33*(1), 2286-2304

Santamouris, M., Cartalis, C., Synnefa, A. & Kolokotsa, D. (2015). On the impact of uran heat island and global warming on the power domain and electricity consumption of buildings – A review. *Energy and Buildings, 98*, 119-124

Steffen, W., Hughes, L. & Karoly, D. (2013). *The critical decade*. Climate Commission. http://www.climatecouncil.org.au/uploads/94e1a6db30ac7520d3bbb421322b4dfb.pdf [Accessed 29 March 2021]

Styles, D., Schoenberger, H. & Galvez Martos, J. (2013). *Best Environmental Management Practice in the Tourism Sector*. Joint Research Centre . European Union.

Pacheco, D. (2020). The best temperature for sleep. Sleep Foundation. www.sleepfoundation.org/bedroom-environment/best-temperature-for-sleep.[Accessed: 11th April 2021]

Tanford, S., Raab, C. & Kim, Y. (2012). Determinants of customer loyalty and purchase behaviour for full-service and limited-service hotels. *International Journal of Hospitality Management, 31*, 319-329.

Taylor, L. (2019). England faces 'jaws of death' as taps set to run dry in 25 years. Reuters. https://www.reuters.com/article/instant-article/idUKL8N2162N2. [Accessed: 12 April 2021]

Torres, E., Singh, D. & Robertson-Ring, A. (2015). Consumer reviews and the creation of booking traction value: Lessons from the hotel industry. *International Journal of Hospitality Management, 50*, 77-83

Woodroof, E., Turner, W. & Heinz, S. (2008). The 'Secret Benefits' from energy conservation. *Strategic Planning for Energy and the Environment, 28*(1)1-10.

Yacouel, N. & Fleischer, A. (2012). The role of cybermediaries in reputation building and price premiums in the online hotel market. *Journal of Travel Research, 51*(2), 219-226.

Wernerfelt, B. (1984). A resource-based view of the firm. *Strategic Management Journal, 5*(2), 171-180.

World Bank (2016). International Workshop on Food Loss and Food Waste. Washington D.C. 7-9 November 2016.

Yu, Y., Li, X. & Jai, T. (2016). The impact of green experience on customer satisfaction: evidence from Trip Advisor. *International Journal of Contemporary Hospitality Management, 29*(5), 1340-1361

Part II:
What to do about it

The 5-Step Process

In the first part of this book we covered where we are now in terms of demand, efficiency, and the cost of inaction.

In the second part we will discuss where we want to go and how we get there.

By following my 5 Step Process you will:

- Identify the factors preventing guests from conserving resources
- Design saving experiences
- Master how to involve staff
- Master how to persuade guests
- Understand the value of eco-feedback and how to apply it

At the end of each step I give you a set of recommended next actions.

By the end of this book, you will have developed your own strategy for guest participation that will revolutionise your hospitality business.

THANKS
FOR MY
GREENER
STAY

5 | Step 1: A Green Audit

Introduction

Knowledge is power. To make transformative changes to your business you first need to understand it back to front. You need to untangle the web of often conflicting decisions that help your hospitality business to operate. A thorough green audit is a first step that makes the steps that follow far easier.

- **Untangle the web**. The consequences of your decisions do not play out in a vacuum. To have the different pieces of a hospitality business working in harmony it is essential to spot when they are working against each other.

- **Embrace individuality**. One-size-fits-all standards will only get businesses so far. Every site is unique and deserves personalised plans. Anything less will lead to waste.

- **Technology is your tool, not your master**. Smart systems can be superb allies, but only if you take the time to learn to use them. The buck always stops with you.

We begin by looking at the complexity within accommodation, using both large and small examples, including the increasing use of technology. Next, I introduce social practice theory – helpful in unravelling this complexity. Finally, I provide you with tools to identify issues that will help you to establish a plan of action.

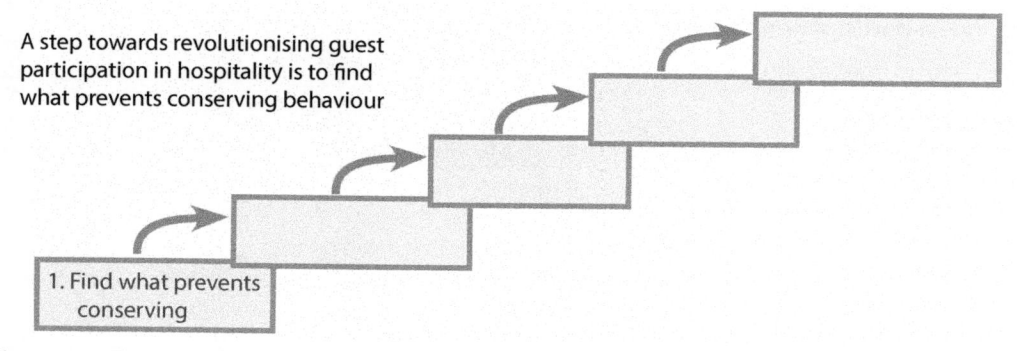

Figure 5.1: The 5 Step Method to create transformative guest participation

The size of the cup vs. the size of the kettle

How can a hotel chain claim to be a leader in environmental hospitality when their teacups are just 100ml and the minimum water level in the kettle is 600ml? This mismatch means I had to boil water for six cups just to enjoy one during my stay at that Canberra hotel. I can understand why guests do not bother to save, why they complain, and attempts to reduce consumption backfire.

A second example: Recently I stayed in a London Kings Cross hotel which truly went to town with its breakfast buffet. They used a large array of heat lamps in the hope of warming bacon and eggs, had three toasting machines running full-time, two individual coffee makers strategically placed, and all down lights turned on. The windows could not be opened so the air conditioning, on a mild autumn day, was running at top speed to counteract the heat from all these devices.

This scene, for what is described in the hotel's lift posters as a *quick breakfast*, lasts from 6:30 till 10:30, 365 days a year. This means that for 16.7% of the 24 hour day, many energy-hungry devices are running in conflict with each other in order to provide a constant supply of bacon, eggs, and toast under what felt like full stage lighting (even though there were floor-to-ceiling windows). The ebb and flow of guests meant toasters were running empty for most of the time, coffee makers were set for continuous action, and the Himalayan mound of bacon and eggs was held in purgatory as no one wants lukewarm cooked food. As a guest how are you going to convince me to participate and save if you don't yourselves?

Entangled web

There are many factors that affect resource use at tourist accommodation, including hundreds of individual devices (at large resorts, there might be millions!).

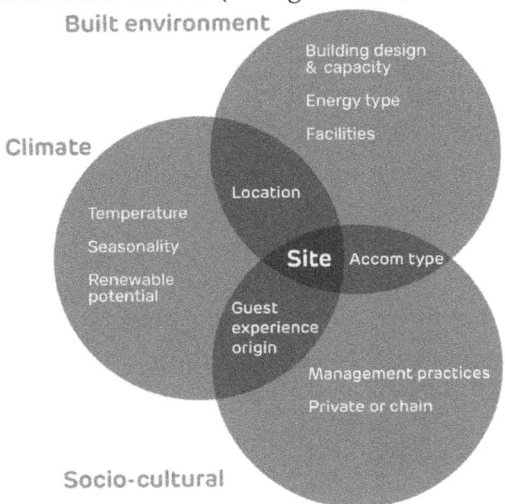

Figure 5.2: Factors affecting resource use at tourist accommodation

These factors include guests, staff, management, the outside temperature, season, supply of resources such as renewables, age and type of facilities, as well as the size and type of accommodation. Each of these can in various ways obstruct or encourage the progress on another factor. (Warren & Becken, 2017)

Outside influences

Throughout an accommodation building there are competing systems visible to guests which magnify resource use and waste. Unless these are conscientiously streamlined, and working in harmony with other factors, they will remain tangled. The more guests become aware of green issues, the more these entanglements frustrate, reducing guests' motivation to save. As we have seen from research, it is the ineffective green initiatives that are detected and highlighted in social media and by word-of-mouth.

Tourist accommodation has machines, physical structures, and people operating around the clock. Even on the micro- or small business scale, there will be systems running when your accommodation is not occupied (e.g. fridges). It is no surprise that accommodation is second only to hospitals as the most energy-intensive building type. But this could change if we become less wasteful.

Competing agendas

From a wider perspective, much of the excellent construction science and resource advice does not always get translated into the 'real world' of accommodation buildings because of the competing agendas of building production and use.

Investors have different goals to the architects and the local council. Things change when building contractors actually come to break ground. And for big hotel chains, they only have a management contract that results in limited capacity to change infrastructure. And for heritage buildings, of which we have many in hospitality, there are regulation complexities when introducing concepts like solar window film, double glazing, or roof solar panels.

There very positive initiatives to produce Net Zero buildings (UNEP's One Planet initiative, for example) and these are already significantly cutting emissions (British Land, 2021) as they focus on the construction and use of materials to reduce the embedded footprint, yet we still need to ensure that future renovations are also low carbon, and that staff and guests operate the building effectively.

Waste can become a tangled web further complicated by the differing goals of the actors involved.

Standards standardise

Our need to save makes using benchmarks and accreditation seem a failsafe option. Certainly I learnt a great deal from complying with certification myself, but is it really enough to help us achieve that paradigm shift? In my community we have conducted carbon auditing for micro and small businesses since 2007. I found no similarity between the businesses and their carbon footprint.

When consulting for a Gulf state, studying the carbon footprint of 600 large and medium hotels, I found an enormous variation in results even though many of the buildings were constructed in a similar way to similar standards during the last 15 years using similarly efficient technologies. There are other reasons why we need more than standards; we should include excellent training to maintain high levels of resource conservation awareness within the maintenance team, as well as management consciousness of the positive impact of high service standards.

Likewise, I found, from studying seven accredited resorts over a four-year period located in the same holiday destination, that there was no similarity in their level of resource use (energy, water and waste), nor achieved savings.

There is an inherent danger with setting benchmarks and sharing them with a number of businesses, where there can be a rebound effect of those who are below the average mean. I explain more about this in Chapter 9.

Insight: Evaluations of LEED and Energy Star buildings

5

The Leadership in Energy and Environmental Design certification (LEED) is an often-cited green hotel accreditation, but there are conflicting views as to its benefits. Investors are advised that operating costs can be reduced by 8-9%, in part achieved through energy savings of up to 30% (Nelson et al., 2010).

However, academic research differs on whether LEED actually offers energy saving potential; Scofield challenges research, which suggests LEED certification helps achieve 18-39% savings (Newsham et al., 2009), because of the calculation method (Scofield, 2009). Further research by Scofield directly compares LEED and non-LEED buildings in New York and identifies only the Gold rated LEED buildings as outperforming non LEED buildings by 20%, while the Silver and Certified LEED buildings underperformed (Scofield, 2013).

There have been lead challenges that bring into question the criteria of how one determines savings from an unbuilt structure (Messinger, 2015).

Researchers warn that building certification can only change a limited range of factors (Hawkins & Bohdanowicz, 2012) and that there is no ceiling on resource use.

Benefits include the ability for investors to charge a higher price premium for their buildings – 18% to 35% (Fuerst & McAllister, 2011).

Let's get to the details

A big and frequent misconception I have found when talking with hospitality managers is that they question if guests will really save at all. Remember there can be a limited number of visible examples that the guests can see. If we don't manage the obvious, we erode reciprocal behaviour from the guests, and they are also less likely to believe the bigger corporate social responsibility story your business is trying to promote.

The tangled web also extends to small things, like offering tea bags in sealed paper sachets but not providing recycle bins. Or seeing bolts securing the window to the frame that prevent opening it for fresh air (yes, I have seen this countless times).

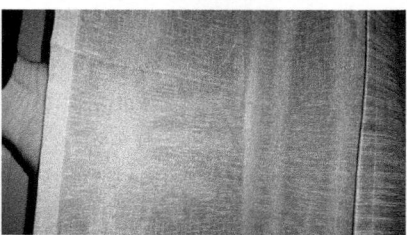

This is the main curtain in a Berlin Hotel. Waifer thin! We are losing energy just trying to heat the room or prevent summer heat entering through the window

Spot the mistake...the marked hot tap is actually the cold tap! This is a danger to guests from scolding, but also how much water is wasted trying to set the right bath temperature?

In so many places I have seen the radiator located behind a full length curtain. Style is important, but not at the expense of wasted energy.

The radiator is turned 'off' but the light clearly shows it is still 'on'. Beware of aged equipment where knobs and switches are not effective anymore.

The instructions on extending this window to allow more air flow are displayed at an angle in tiny script, very hard for a guest to notice let alone apply.

Figure 5.3: Lack of attention to detail can undermine your efforts.

These examples show that your guests are not going to be keep warm and save energy if curtains are decorative but too thin, as in the case of this German hotel. Or when the taps are incorrectly labeled, as in this London hotel, so you then waste energy. Or when the curtains trap the heat, as in this English property. Or when you turn off the electric radiator but the switch is old and the system continues to run, as in the case of this Belgium cabin. Or the hotel windows that are hard to operate because the instructions are written in a tiny script on a side bar, at a property in northern England.

Wasting even at the simplest level

Example A

How many cups of tea required, how much wasted water boiled?

To boil 1 litre of water takes 0.225kWh

If only 100 ml was required this wastes 900 ml of boiled water or 0.2025 kWh

We do this twice a day = 0.405 kWh x 160 rooms (80% occupancy 200 room hotel) = 64.8 kWh per day or 23,652 kWh per year = € 6,665 or US$ 7,805. That is how much we might be wasting from just one example of poor design integration!

Example B

A 47 litre minibar fridge may use 248 kWh per year x 200 rooms, that is 49,600 kWh per year = 13,888 euros or US$ 16,368. That's how much we are wasting by putting a noisy fridge in the room!

For a hotel client in Sydney we calculated they would save 6% of their total electricity cost by inventively replacing the minibar fridges and kettles with a totally new hospitality concept – using corridor space on the floors to offer a café style facility, with one fridge and vending machine, all linked to the key card – with the social benefits of meeting others. Plus integrated waste management, using a three-in-one bin for organic waste, landfill, and recycling.

Running day and night

Ten percent of electricity in homes is wasted on standby power. How does tourist accommodation compare? When researchers checked 10 top hotels in Harrisonburg, Virginia, USA, and spot checked 50 guest rooms, they found 468 appliances were plugged in, and 233 used standby power (4.66 per room!) – 53 TV sets, 50 alarm clocks, 50 hair dryers, 40 fridges, 35 microwaves, and 5 DVD players (Quinn & Schrier, 2011).

In self-contained apartments or villas, the level of standby power used is likely to be much higher because of the number of kitchen appliances. A study in New Zealand found that over 40% of home microwaves used more energy in standby mode than while cooking – would this be higher in tourist accommodation (EECA, 1999)?

Who has real control?

Solving the problem of this tangled web has led some to bypass staff and guests entirely, instead introducing innovative tech solutions. They prefer to rely on advanced sensor equipment and smart systems.

I am not against technology, far from it. I don't think I could survive well living in a cave and hunting bison! However, the hunters of the past made their own technology work for them. They crafted their own tools and tracked their performance. That is how they got better.

Advanced technology which runs resource-using tasks on autopilot can have inherent dangers, where staff, guests and managers do not learn by practical experience and become unaware of conserving opportunities. I discuss this in detail in Chapter 8.

How intelligent should a system be?

"Ultimately, the customer will determine what the hotel room of the future will look like. Hoteliers should try and keep it simple to use." These are the views of Deloitte (2015) who reported that in-room technology for its own sake can prove costly, and damage the brand as it might be seen as gimmicky.

While some technology systems do try to do the thinking for us by monitoring the environment and our behaviour (as an intelligent hotel room), given earlier examples this still leaves us with a danger of entanglement. Consider utilising the amazing intelligent feature already in your guests' rooms… the human being that knows their own needs best of all.

Humans have a unique system that tells us when we are too hot or cold (skin temperature) and this comfort level is unique to us all. We do not want to wrestle with Artificial Intelligence that thinks it knows our needs better. That does not mean removing AI, but instead recognising we can choose its level of intelligence. For staff and guest participation, I prefer to start with Level 3 – Inferring, which is what My Green Butler provides. The systems I have previously described use learning and anticipating, but life is complex and guest circumstances even more so when you are running accommodation.

Table 5.1: Levels of intelligent systems (Derzko, 2006)

Intelligence Level 1	Adapting - modifying behaviour to fit the place
Intelligence Level 2	Sensing – awareness of everyday factors
Intelligence Level 3	Inferring – draws conclusions from rules and observations
Intelligence Level 4	Learning – improving performance from experience
Intelligence Level 5	Anticipating - working out what to do next
Intelligence Level 6	Self – ability to self-create, self-organise, self-sustain

While Deloitte prophesised we will have technology in every hotel room, maybe we don't need to have HAL waiting for us (and all his cost and complexity).

Insight: You look great but you don't understand me

- A three week 'real world' study of an intelligent thermostat found that, while people loved its neat design, it did not understand the human intent behind certain behaviour. One user described the system as "arrogant" because it kept reverting the temperature back to a level it had memorised. Users did not feel it actually saved any energy. "It seems like it stays warmer longer than what we would have done if we left it purely manual..." *(respondent)* While the systems are helpful and very interactive (using tablet/mobile interfaces) in increasing user participation, this means that people actually pursue greater levels of comfort and therefore savings become questionable (Yang & Newman, 2012, 2013)

- Later studies by the Behaviour Insight Team have found energy savings of about 5% using the same equipment, partly achieved by using less energy when people were asleep. Further research found people use a similar amount of energy when setting the thermostat manually as programmable thermostats, when in cooling mode (Bailes, 2015).

- Therefore more focus should be placed on human behavioural factors, and providing timely feedback, rather than diverting attention to smart technologies (Darby, 2018).

Untangling

Human behaviour can make the web more complex.

A leading UK waste consultant told me some hotels found it cheaper to waste food from the buffet than to employ more staff to provide table service. Alternatively, in less developed economies, some hotels permit leftover food to go to staff and families. Where are the incentives to save food?

Behaviour can help us. The attentive owner of The Glen, a Cumbrian B&B I visit, asks exactly what you want for your English cooked breakfast, the number of juicy Cumberland Sausages and eggs, and if you want tomatoes. The fruit compote is in reasonable sized portion, and you can choose to have more tea or toast. The owner is delighted if you want a hearty breakfast, but it is easy for you to apply self-control, and she doesn't waste much food.

I have watched Chinese visitors to a 55-storey Gold Coast Meriton Apartment block be guided in the supermarket below on what to buy and how to use ingredients effectively. A thoughtful approach that could lead visitors to be less likely to buy and waste things.

People matter when it comes to untangling the web.

Making change stick

While people play a key persuasive communication role in conservation-aware behaviours (as you will find out in Chapter 6) we also need solutions which are easy to understand, provide a better experience, and are frictionless to apply. This way, conserving behaviour can become our new everyday routines. This requires us to better understand the dynamics of the social practice we are trying to influence, and allow us to devise a suitable service innovation.

Imagine you have just returned from work after a long day – think through the steps involved in washing for just such a typical day. Maybe this includes a shower, or a bath, shaving or washing and drying hair, and so on. Each of these activities is called a social practice. It involves **materials**, **skills**, and **meaning**.

When I say **materials** I mean the appliances and resources that we use in everyday activities – e.g. a hairdryer, a beach towel, a flat screen for a presentation. Behind each of these we have the supply of resources like electricity, water, and chemicals, which are invisible to the user, as is their carbon footprint.

Skills are the ability and competence to apply our knowledge to successfully perform the practice. This could mean your skills in using your new shower system to set the temperature you like or getting that flat screen to work for a presentation to the board.

What drives us is the **meaning** we give to these practices. That is to say what is our motivation, is the activity 'everyday' or 'special', how functional or how crafted it is to our personal choice. This could mean, as a good parent, one ensures the children are super clean and neatly presented when they are going to a family dinner in a classy restaurant. It is a social norm, it reflects on us and our pride as a parent.

These three elements, materials, skills, and meaning are linked together. To create a shift in social practice there must be changes at the same time to each of the elements to create a transition, one that significantly changes the way we do things, and which is sustainable.

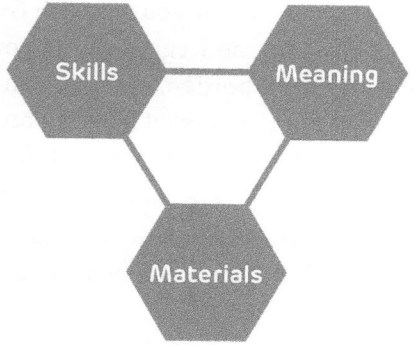

Figure 5.4: The three elements of social practice. (Adapted from Shove, Pantzar & Watson, 2012)

I will use these three terms – Materials, Skills, and Meaning – throughout the rest of the book, to help you focus on areas to change and explain how you can work to assist guest participation transitions.

To define these elements, by *Materials* I refer to the amenities and facilities available within your property, e.g. lighting, cookers, fridges, entertainment systems, switches, control systems and energy, water. By *Skills* I refer to the ability one has to operate the materials, meaning the competency to use the a/c controls, to operate window blinds and to judge when to draw those blinds. And *Meaning* represents the attitudes and emotions we hold to the actions we are doing, how important it is to wash, to watch TV, to eat breakfast, to ensure the children are warm or cool.

Reciprocate with the consumer

Importantly, social practice elements are not rigid in everyday activities in modern society. Elements are constantly evolving, creating new activities, routines, habits, and performances. They can be changed through consumers' own creativity and innovation – this is a realm no longer exclusive to manufacturers or service providers like us. Think of the shared economy.

This is an important social trend to observe. We are better educated, better informed, and with higher disposable income to pursue our passions than in the past. People are putting time into evolving their leisure pursuits and sharing their innovations with other manufacturers.

Likewise, businesses are offering more reciprocal relationships with consumers, forging a free flow of advice which historically has not been usual in the commercial world. With my earlier projects for consumer goods giants like Best Foods and Clorox, we sought to change consumption behaviour using multimedia education. As they were leading brands it was a necessity to evolve markets that could only be achieved with the willing participation of customers. It is an informal organisational innovation between producer and consumer.

My Green Butler

To convince guests to conserve, accommodation needs a green advisory service which educates, motivates, and rewards within the spirit of hospitality, while also respecting privacy. Which is why we named our invention 'My Green Butler' . It fuses materials (comfort appliances and building systems) with skills (personalised advisory support) and meaning (eco-feedback and nature conservation). Guests work with us to deliver a better all-round service experience. It untangles complexities and can revolutionise your service.

A new mindset

If we consciously focus on these elements by thinking: "what materials do we provide?", "how well do people understand them?", "what are the motivations to change and what are their benefits?"; then we can start to 'unstick' high resource using practices in favour of conserving ones .

This is the underlying ethos I share in this book. We should be helping everyone improve their skills rather than searching for green guests, we should be giving them better materials and avoid making bland 'green' claims.

Accommodation guests are part of the consumption and production process. Hospitality and tourism firms have increasingly encouraged co-creating guest experiences through customisation. We go even further in accommodation buildings, especially in self-contained ones, where guests are involved in the co-production (both guests and staff produce the experience) using resources to fulfil everyday life needs. By personalising experiences, this co-production can also include the agreed setting of rules (Chapter 7) and the reduction of wasteful consumption.

Applying a new mindset, one of creativity and monitoring, you can manipulate the elements of social practice and establish conservation-aware behaviours as a third option to reducing our footprint and positively help your move towards important environmental goals, as we will see through the 5-Step process.

Where to start

I have prepared a set of tools to make the sound assessment needed for your guest participation plan. These tools help assess the accommodation's environmental impacts, level of advisory information, guests' ability to take greener actions, and staff competence. From this you can identify the gaps preventing conserving.

1. **Conduct an audit of resource use**. This can be a painless task if you ask your accounts department to provide reports. You are assessing the resource use/ waste that results from the combination of social practice elements (Materials, Skills, and Meaning). I want you to review the figures on a quarterly basis. There could be striking seasonal variations, and we should examine these to see how consumption and waste varies.

2. **Conduct a Guest Green Experience Audit**. Go to the accommodation and assess what materials guests use to be comfortable, conduct their routines, prepare food, access entertainment, visit restaurants and outdoor activities. You are assessing how these materials help them conserve.

3. **Assess what information and advice you are offering the guests** so that they have the skills to conserve.

4. **Audit the level of conserving knowledge your team has** – formal, vocational or ad hoc training – and if they are incentivised or contracted to apply conserving skills.

I want you to consider these factors from a totally guest-centred perspective. That is, not from a production process that ends with the guests, but a holistic service experience which directly involves the guests and staff together.

Resource use audit – sample

Identify the resource and waste issues – what is the target we are trying to achieve? How much?

Go to www.mygreenbutler.com/resources to find charts to help you measure your resources or you can use the more comprehensive My Green Butler online Guest Experience Audit.

Year							
Resource	Q1	Q2	Q3	Q4	Sub total	X 000	CO2
Weather (days over 30°C)							
Electricity (kWh)							
Gas (m3)							
Fuel (L)							
Water (L)							
Waste Organic (L)							
Waste Plastic (L)							
Waste recycling (L)							
Waste landfill (L)							
3rd Party							
TOTAL							
Total cost							
Occupancy							
Carbon per guest							
Mean Tariff							
Revenue							
Total costs							
Ratio revenue to costs							

If you prefer, you can use my free carbon footprint audit, Carbon Detective, and add metering data so you can input different meter performance and identify which facilities account for the largest impact.. Then add them up. Compare your regular year with a Covid year, it will reveal where you are wasting resources. Go to www.carbondetective.com

5

Guest green experience audit – sample

Guest Room Type	Electricity	Gas	Water	Waste				
				organic	plastics	recycling	landfill	3rd party
Bedroom(s)								
Bathroom	Opening windows							
Kitchen								
Ironing								
Laundry								
Public area								
Restaurant 1								
Restaurant 2								
Gym								
Transport								
Grounds								

Guest information audit – sample

Guest Room Type	Electricity	Gas	Fuel	Water	Linen	Eco Benefit	Community Benefit	Carbon
Bedroom(s)								
Bathroom								
Kitchen								
Ironing								
Laundry								
Public area								
Restaurant 1								
Restaurant 2								
Gym								
Transport								
Grounds								
Partner								
Community								

Staff sustainability knowledge audit – sample

Staff	% in Green team	Do their contracts specify sustainability responsibilities with KPIs?	Specific training in conserving in last 6 months				Specific training in last 6 months to prevent	
			Electricity	Gas	Fuel	Water	Waste	CO²
Management								
Guest relations								
F&B								
Kitchen								
Maintenance								
Finance								
Procurement								
Housekeeping								
Gardens								
Gym/Pool								

Staff	Specific training in last six months on your CSR projects		% holding vocational training in sustainability	% holding sustainability degree
	Environment	Community		
Management				
Guest relations				
F&B				
Kitchen				
Maintenance				
Finance				
Procurement				
Housekeeping				
Gardens				
Gym/Pool				

If you prefer, you can use the more comprehensive My Green Butler online audit tool. Write to me for a copy, christopher@mygreenbutler.com

What you will learn

Your audits are the foundation for your guest participation programme. They are the basic asset from which to build and justify plans. They tell you where to focus efforts to reduce carbon emissions, which resource is most important, and, if you use my online version, which facilities are the largest culprits for electricity use.

By adding occupancy, tariffs and resource/waste/third party costs too, you can compare seasonally your revenue against costs and environmental impacts.

Tell me, is this daunting? Are the figures hard, even impossible to find? If the answer is yes, then believe me, this project will be illuminating. It is worth making the extra effort, don't give up!

When you compare the inflow of impacts against the actual practical physical delivery of service, you might see significant limitations, and areas will present themselves for redesigning experiences. This is a genuinely exciting moment. Enjoy!

Start with small projects and build. Remember that conserving will not be one big single solution, but the integration of many parts that will enable your staff and guests to transition.

In the next chapters I will explain how you can design guest experiences that enable both front and back of house to provide better, higher quality, and friction-less experiences, which are greener at the same time as offering superior comfort, enjoyment, and overall satisfaction.

Your solutions will be unique to your property and brand. I have never found two firms the same, all sites have different multiple factors that make their tangled web unique to them. The solutions must be too.

Next steps

1. Complete the resource audit and discuss with colleagues
2. Complete the guests' experience and audit yourself by visiting the facilities

You will be able to use your findings to help identify where things are entangled therefore preventing conserving strategies from being implemented.

References

Bailes, A. (2015). Does the Nest learning thermostat save energy? *Energy Vanguard*, May 20.

British Land (2021). Halving embodied carbon at scale – 100 Liverpool Street. www.british-land.com/sustainability/our-views/halving-embodied-carbon-scale-100-liverpool-street   [[Accessed: 7 November 2021]

Darby, S. (2018) Smart technology in the home: time for more clarity. *Building Research & Information*, 46(1), 140-147

Deloitte (2015) Hospitality 2015. Game changers or spectators? Deloitte LLP, London, England.

Derzko, W. (2006) Smart Technologies. *Proceedings of the World Future Society*, July 29.

Deuble, M. & de Dear, R. (2012) Green occupants for green buildings: The missing link? *Building and Environment*, 56, 21-27.

EECA. (1999). *Energy Use in New Zealand Households, Report on the Year Three Analysis for the Household Energy End Use Project (HEEP)*. Wellington (New Zealand): Energy Efficiency and Conservation Authority.

Fuerst, M., & McAllister, P. (2011). Eco-labelling in commercial office markets: Do LEED and Energy Star offices obtain multiple premiums? *Ecological Economics, 70, 1220-1230.*

Hawkins, R., & Bohdanowicz, P. (2012). *Responsible Hospitality: Theory and Practice*. Oxford, England: Goodfellow.

Messinger, L. (2015) One third of US construction market could be green by 2018 – report. *The Guardian*, September 18. www.theguardian.com/sustainable-business/2015/sep/18/green-building-leed-green-business-council-epa?CMP=share_btn_tw

Nelson, A., Rakau, O., & Dorrenberg, P. (2010). Green Buildings - A niche becomes mainstream. In T. Just (Ed.), *International topics: Current Issues*. Frankfurt: Deutsche Bank Research.

Newsham. G., Mancini, S. & Birt, B. (2009). Do LEED-certified buildings save energy? Yes, but…. *Energy and Buildings, 41,* 897-905

Quinn, M., & Schrier, T. (2011). Is there a vampire lurking in your hotel? An examination of standby power consumption in Virginia hotel rooms. http://scholarworks.umass.edu/grad-conf_ hospitality/2011/Poster/103/ [Accessed 20/10/2016]

Scofield, J. (2009). Do LEED-certified buildings save energy? Not really… *Energy and Buildings, 41,* 1386-1390.

Scofield, J. (2013). Efficacy of LEED-ceretification in reducing energy consumption and greenhouse gas emission for large New York City office buildings. *Energy and Buildings, 67,* 517-524.

Shove, E., Pantzar, M., Watson, M., (2012). *The Dynamics of Social Practice: Everyday Life and How it Changes*. Sage: London.

Warren, C. & Becken, S. (2017) Saving energy and water in tourist accommodation: A systematic literature review (1987-2015). *International Journal of Tourism Research*, 19(3), 289-303

Yang, R. & Newman, M. (2012) Living with an intelligent thermostat: Advanced control for heating and cooling systems. Proceedings of the UbiComp'12, 2012, September, 5-8,Pittsburg, USA

Yang, R. & Newman, M. (2013). Learning from a learning thermostat: Lessons for intelligent systems for the home. UBIComp'13, September 8-12, Zurich, Switzerland.

5

6 Step 2: Designing change in your accommodation (Materials)

This chapter explains the tensions between resource use and 'unrestricted' hospitality experiences. (I say unrestricted because most hospitality providers do not limit the facilities and amenities offered.) It shows how to reconcile seemingly opposing forces – like guest conserving versus guest satisfaction – and create transformational new approaches.

Some key points:

- **Integrated thinking** can transform your approach to problem solving. It is how to get the most out of your audits.

- **Be guest-centred**. Step away from one-size-fits-all approaches to hospitality and really try to put yourself in your guests' shoes. It is ultimately people who use resources, not buildings.

- **Call on altruistic values**. People want to help. They also want to see the benefits for themselves. Where possible, design experiences that make green benefits immediate and clear.

- **Look at the big picture**. Think holistically and embrace the complexities when they appear. It is an intimidating task, but the best solutions come when problems aren't isolated from one another.

- **Iterate, iterate, iterate**. There is no shame in not getting it perfect first time. Any plan worth its salt has a strong feedback loop, allowing you to refine designs over time.

The focus here is on Materials, because they consume the highest proportion of energy. The following chapters concentrate on Skills and the Meaning we have for social practices in hospitality.

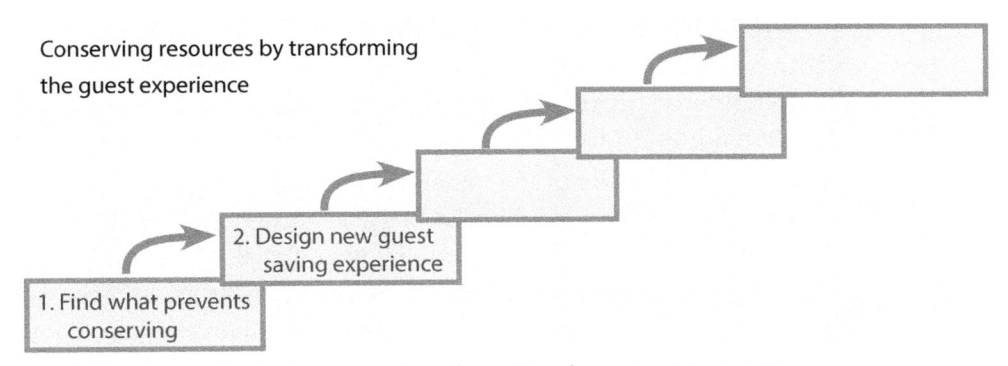

Figure 6.1: The 5-Step Method to create transformational guest engagement

Avoiding conflict

So far you may have been asking yourself questions like: How can you build a leaner more effective business that wastes less whilst offering guests a more satisfactory experience? How can you create a new accommodation concept that feels lavish to guests, yet is low carbon? How should you renovate bathrooms that use minimal hot water but are still enticing? How can you minimise peak rate energy use in summer when you have to offer guests a greater sense of cool comfort?

These questions bring up the conflict between taking responsibility for your hospitality's footprint and providing a guest experience that exceeds expectations. At first sight, they do appear to conflict, particularly if you wish to maintain a standard hospitality approach to service delivery. It can lead owners and managers to feel they must choose: either achieve a lower carbon footprint by sacrificing service, or keep things as they are and only make superficial carbon reduction. Choosing the 'or' option does not solve the problem – it still leaves your business vulnerable to future risks and legislative change. Choosing 'or' leaves the conflict unresolved.

Embracing conflict

Many good solutions come from the tension of opposites. The acclaimed business strategist Roger Martin calls resolving such tension 'Integrated Thinking' (Martin, 2007). As an example, he cites the creation of the Four Seasons Hotels and Resorts. He explains the blending of what was then the regular accommodation model of either a small scale motel or a large convention hotel. Instead of either/or, the strategy was to offer accommodation with both a personal touch and all the amenities a guest could want (Martin, 2009).

Martin's research found that integrated thinking was a natural skill applied by many highly successful business people. They do not choose 'either/or' options, or create a compromise between the two. They resolve the conflict by identifying innovative alternatives launched by the dynamics of opposing ideas.

Integrated thinking is one of the underlying themes of this book. Integrated thinking teaches us to create superior solutions using the tensions between opposing ideas and constraints. Martin believes that integrative thinkers relish business complexities because that is where valuable solutions come from. In other words, we should not avoid the knotty problems of making hospitality more sustainable, we should relish them. They are how we steer our businesses to greater success.

Is there a conflict between technology and the human touch?

An example of a conflict in hospitality is the divergence between technology used for building automation, check-in services, 'contactless' engagement, and relationship management verses the desire many guests have for human connection with a property and personal recognition delivered by hotel staff.

On the one hand, technologies that offer guests chatbots, voice controlled apps, and the personalisation of room amenities using the Internet of Things are described by Benoit-Etienne Domenget, CEO of the hospitality institution, Sommet Education, as transformational for hotels (Sommet Education, 2019).

On the other side, Mari-France Derderian of Glion Institute acknowledges human to human customer relationships are still key. "Human interaction remains core to the hospitality industry. In the luxury industry, this human service is vital for brands to deliver a bespoke experience, in which guests can feel both at ease and pleasantly surprised by service that surpasses expectations…these shared moments of personal service may turn out to be the real luxury that guests most value." (Sommet Education, 2019). The Covid-19 crisis created a surge in contactless technologies and strong commitments (Lane, 2021), but one wonders how long it will be before personalised service actually becomes a competitive advantage. It is Accor's raison d'être to become more sustainable (Accor, 2016).

Rapidly evolving technology has led many service firms to see only two models: embracing technology to optimise service, or focusing on a highly trained staff experience. Again, these either/or options do not have to be the case in sustainable hospitality, where we need both systematisation and ability for staff and guests to enact sustainability goals (Baker & Schaltegger, 2015).

Case study: **Technology with the human touch**

The integrated thinking behind My Green Butler was to mesh human-delivered hospitality with artificial intelligence to provide an entirely new level of service. While this invention does provide guests with a much higher level of control, information, and insight, we did not seek to replace staff with a robot or app.

Instead, we sought to embrace the value of human contact and project the sustainability consciousness of the owner, manager, and staff with a new human-like member of staff – the Green Butler. Rather than choosing between opposing ideas of technology and personal service, we embraced them both. Technology can make sustainability issues real, but it requires humans to enact the responsible goals, and staff to personally involve guests in the positive experience.

Rather than avoiding the complexity of reporting a property's footprint and asking guests to conserve, we have relished the challenge of finding a solution. Left to its own devices, technology can be cold and its data dull. What if you can humanise sustainability? What if you can build staff loyalty and reputation through the personal delivery of the service? The real-time reporting and advice is gamified to involve both staff and guests. Not only does this conserve resources, it builds reputation as well.

At my own property the service has enabled us to reap the benefits of cost cutting and carbon emission reduction, which the technology records, but it has also greatly boosted our independent guest reviews and feedback. This has in turn led to an increase in bookings.

Following My Green Butler's introduction, guest reviews changed. Visitors became more aware of our sustainability activities and enjoyed sharing their experience to conserve, recognising the behind-the-scenes personalised touches from staff and congratulating us on our environmental progress. The service enabled us to win awards (World Responsible Tourism Awards 2018 and Banksia Award 2018) and increase occupancy. Our early successes have now been replicated around the world (United Nations Environmental Programme, 2020).

Focus on the users

The human touch is important because it is humans – not buildings – who use energy and water. The built environment is a shell operated by the people who occupy the space, whether staff or guest. How we behave within these environments dictates the building's level of resource use and waste. While higher-rated 'green buildings' are perceived to be more energy-efficient, they still require humans to operate them effectively. Your focus should first be on the people who use and waste resources. Then, by applying innovative green solutions, you make your property a business leader that guest want to book.

This means you must be guest centred in your strategies. This begins with a deeper understanding of what will make their stay more relaxing, interesting, appealing to the senses, and achieve environmental goals in a frictionless way. Your integrated thinking can use technology – both IT and the 'social technology' of staff, guests, and suppliers.

Your overriding aim should be to move from the passive idea of guest engagement to real participation. You want them to *co-produce* their stay as effective as possible. I say co-produce because in hospitality, it is guests who use the majority of resources without awareness of the consequences. We also want to help them co-create their experiences, so they are memorable. Simply calling on people's eco-friendly values when on their holidays or while they are at an event has negligible results compared to designing an experience that increases pleasure while reducing environmental impacts (Dolnicar, 2020).

Most people are concerned about the environment, but knowing their stay benefits the local community can be a stronger lever. This can bring travellers pleasure, but be specific (Warren & Coghlan, 2016). We are all better educated than our forefathers and we are re-evaluating our lives to make better choices that render the old way of doing business obsolete. That includes what we define as pleasure, perhaps. Offering guests more pleasure does not have to be hedonistic but can be altruistic. People like knowing their stay contributes to positive local results (more on this in later chapters).

Case study: **Calling on pro-environmental values**

The Bohinj Eco Hotel in Slovenia ran a field experiment using several types of stickers in guests rooms to encourage towel reuse and electricity saving. The experiment was run over 81 days in 1,836 room nights from 784 guests parties. Four types of stickers were used to:

1. Remind guests to be pro-environmental (recycle symbol on a towel),
2. Remind them and amuse (piggy bank and towel),
3. Induce thoughts to counteract hedonistic enjoyment by presenting the consequences of the actions (polar bear on a small ice block on the towel),
4. Act as a control.

The stickers were visually-led in order to communicate to guests with different languages. Findings showed no significant difference across the experimental conditions to save electricity or reduce towel use and that pro-environment appeals, therefore, may not persuade guests to save in the hedonic context of their holiday (Dolnicar et al., 2017). The study authors argue that the pro-environmental triggers one might use to encourage people to save resources in their home may, therefore, not automatically be taken up in the same way in holiday places. We need to be more sophisticated in the way we persuade guests (and staff).

Calling on altruistic values

Hotels in the United States have raised considerable sums from guest donations. Ace Hotel raised $25,000 in six weeks to help three Chicago art-centric nonprofit organisations, and Omni Hotels has raised $3.3 million for non-profit organisations since 2002 (Silver, 2017).

Mainstream hotel group Accor found that their guests think it is "very important" that their hotel is protecting children and minors from prostitution (68%), promoting the local economy (48%), protecting the environment (48%), protecting local culture/heritage (42%), supporting local communities (36%), partnering with local NGOs (28%) and collecting money for charity purposes (20%)[5].

Linking wider sustainability efforts to your pro-environmental practices is a practical strategy.

Insight: Targeted message

During the summer of 2018, up to 361 guests in a four-star Italian hotel saw different messages every day at the salad bar. These ranged from:

1. Promoting the salad vegetables which were from a local farm next door
2. Emphasising the freshness of the ingredients
3. Highlighting organic qualities
4. Pointing out that the majority of guests preferred this food fresh
5. Natural food because it was not large scale commercially grown, and finally
6. A message that showed a picture of the farm where the vegetables were grown and invited guests to visit.

The final message was most effective in increasing the consumption of more sustainable food sourced by the hotel (Cozzio et al., 2020). Guests are motivated by the direct benefit to them, and if well crafted, the messages can add to the stay experience.

Why we should take this approach

Today people do not measure their level of satisfaction by the amount they consume but by enjoying a personalised experience that is more meaningful to them. This is a great place to start creating a true marketing advantage – rather than adding promotional messages to appliances that guests cannot understand and can invite claims of greenwashing. Too many miss this golden opportunity about their eco-friendly facilities by making bland generalisations.

Another concern is that it is easy to avoid the genuine opportunity of creating distinctive guest experiences by only adding *green fluff* around the edges of their businesses. Focusing on people and their needs then designing a service that delivers sustainability results in a revolutionary new way will mean your marketing campaigns almost write themselves. It will enhance your market competitiveness because people will feel part of positive change. It also promotes itself by offering an outstanding modern solution that guests love and write about.

Let us avoid the 'Business As Usual' scenarios and embrace the notion that if people – not buildings – use resources, we can design services that guide them to use less.

Designing food waste solutions

In a survey of 29 Californian restaurants, it was found only 38% proactively asked customers to take home left over food. Around 86% of chain restaurants had not designed their service to donate edible food (Sakaguchi et al., 2018). In Scotland, a campaign to offer guests a 'doggy bag' helped restaurants reduce their food waste by 40%. While customers were too embarrassed to ask for a container, they were happy to receive one. A specially created package was supplied branded "Good to go and enjoy later" with "Natural Scotland" and "Love Food" logos (Sheffield, 2016).

France has applied legislation for restaurants and supermarkets to avoid food waste (Chrisafis, 2016).

In Germany, a new law on packaging will require restaurants to provide reusable containers rather than single-use packaging from 2023 (Bundesministerium fur Umwelt, 2021).This is a long-overdue policy considering 85% of Germans support a deposit refund system for reusable containers (WWF, 2021).

Integrating management, equipment and guests

Designed solutions to prevent food waste can encompass eight elements as an elegantly integrated solution:

- **Legislation:** requirement for chefs to prepare and not throw away sample dishes,.

- **Dining concept:** because it is hard to predict the number of guest dinners when offering buffet-style, there is the danger that food may not be used at the expected rate leading to potential wastage, so implement a Chef's Special that uses ingredients that may be close to expiry.

- **Matching equipment and ingredient quality:** making batches of food and maintaining an attractive display at the buffet throughout.

- **Management practices:** how kitchen activities are controlled, deciding on the amount of food to be prepared, menu planning.

- **Professional skills:** employing trained motivated staff who apply common sense.
- **Guests:** poor taste and appearance of the food leads to food waste.
- **Competitors:** the attractiveness of another outlet's menu and food impacts on your food waste levels.
- **Communication:** make it easy for chefs, staff, suppliers, and guests to share information, e.g. complaints about food quality.

Effective solutions require a holistic design approach (Heikkila et al., 2016).

Looking in detail

When developing your vision for change, you should be reaching for the stars and thinking big. However, that does not mean ignoring the detail.

What is the number one critical service tourist accommodation hospitality providers should be offering? A really good night's sleep, I say. It is the single most important need for the guests... but do we really deliver this? I can't tell you how many times I have found synthetic fabrics, mattress protectors, or synthetic mattresses on a bed. This can make it too hot to sleep. In an accommodation where you cannot open the windows the matter becomes worse.

Synthetic materials can be long lasting and require less water to launder, but have you measured the extra energy used by the a/c to keep guests cool all night? As we covered in Chapter 5, looking at the details helps us untangle service delivery. If the bed was made with natural fibres with additional quality rugs, pillows, and ceiling fans, guests could better self-regulate and have a good night's sleep.

Sometimes when running a business we listen to the voice of efficiency rather than reason. If we want good reviews, it is essential that guests sleep better than when they are at home.

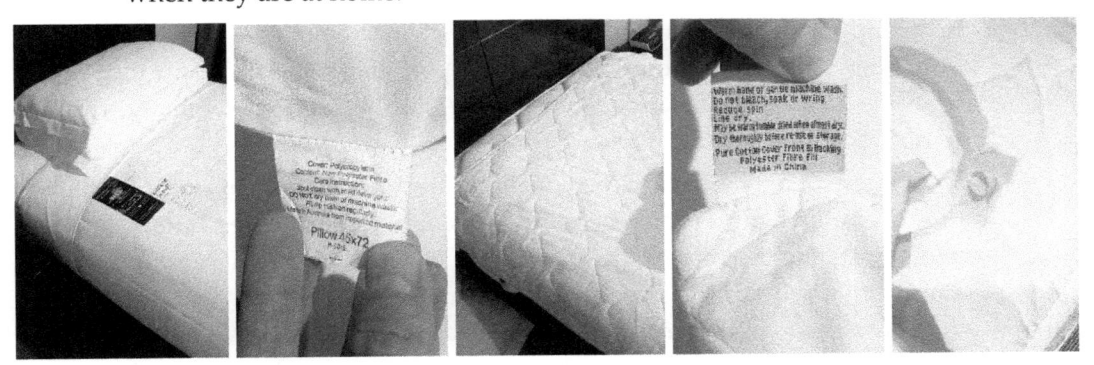

Figure 6.2: Each layer of the bedding is synthetic and the windows do not open in this Sydney hotel. In such a room guests might find their bodies increase in temperature and with no option of natural ventilation must revert to the a/c

Figure 6.3: Or there is the reverse where only the basics to keep warm in the Berlin spring were provided in this room – a top sheet and a small duvet and one pillow

Targeted solutions

In a 2015 study, 2,504 guests were asked about the sleep quality at hotels. On average, guests felt that they slept less well in hotels than at home. Generally, men reported better sleep than women and older guests. Factors that affected their sleep quality were poor pillows, high room temperatures, poor mattresses, poor duvets, noise from the street, poor indoor climate, too much daylight from the windows, and noise from the ventilation system. Only 50% of guests reported that their sleep tended to improve over their stay while 8.4% reported that it worsened, suggesting 46% endured the same level of sleep quality throughout their stay, not improving or worsening (Pallesen et al. 2019).

Designing for the bigger picture

In attempting to make our systems more efficient, we put too much faith into the technology. This in turn diminishes our responsibility and takes our focus away from the actual reason for our guests' stay. For business travel many trips can have a repetition in the itinerary, but not every trip is business.

One hospitality business personalises the room temperature according to pre-determined guest preference chosen the first time the guest enters the room and adjusts the thermostat. Let us take the example of arriving in London. The temperature would be set to 21°C. It is winter outside and the guest is cold so they push the temperature to 24°C as they are sitting in their work shirt and not moving; but when the same guest checks in at their Rio hotel, the temperature is now set at their perceived preferred temperature of 24°C. The reason for the trip determines temperature preference, the attire a guest would pack, different sleep patterns for leisure or business, and of course acclimatisation to the reversed winter/summer seasons. In Rio the guest might prefer 26°C compared to the warmer outside temperature of 30°C, or if they find the humidity too much, 21°C.

By giving control back to the guests, we make them responsible for creating their own comfort conditions. The creative part is which Materials we give them control of, how we encourage their Skills-set so that they use them efficiently, and how we generate a Meaning that motivates conservation-aware behaviour.

Design for the future

Structures planned as Net Zero Energy Buildings have been designed using historic weather data and will not meet their efficiency targets under the new changed climate scenarios. Net Zero classification means every building has the potential to eliminate carbon emissions from energy consumption through their own renewable generation or similar supplied (zero energy imported from the grid or exported to the grid annually).

However, designs have been found to rely on historic weather information covering 10 to 20 years and end up simulating the performance of the advanced building for an operation in 2030 based on data from periods back to the 1960s. Researchers applied forecasting weather conditions in the future based on Climate Change data and found that while more solar would be generated on site, it was not sufficient to negate the increase in energy consumption in warmer months (e.g. July + 26%) leaving a shortfall (Robert & Kummert, 2012).

There are further gaps in achieving more sustainable buildings. Saving can be an afterthought to the originally approved building design. Expensive and complex simulation tools to determine energy saving may be applied after a design and not consider the location, aspect, shape, and potential to generate renewable energy. Even the lifecycle for new buildings frameworks can be difficult to introduce as they require a complete transformation of the way designers, architects, builders, and contractors work.

Building codes do not always deliver the expected energy saving as regulations are checked at the design stage and when the building is completed, but do not take into consideration modelling performance (Dawood et al., 2013) or occupant behaviour factors (Ambrose et al., 2013.

People need more effective design solutions

The buildings we have in cities cannot cope with the increasing extreme temperatures, they are becoming dangerous for people's health, including our guests (Purtill, 2021).

From a study of 252 homes in the UK during summertime, building design and occupant behaviour accounted for higher inside home temperatures. Elderly residents used their heating at night to compensate for the drop in temperature after a warm summer's day. Inside temperatures rose in some cases to reach around 30°C at night which is unsuitable for health reasons. Heating bedrooms in this way preloads the buildings thermal mass for the following day. Researchers found that flats held higher internal temperatures in summer than free standing or semi-detached houses. Top floor flats are particularly at risk of high inside temperatures (Lomas & Kane, 2013).

Designing alternative adaptive measures for people to adjust from day-time to night-time temperatures could save energy and improve guest health. Accommodations in multi-floor buildings need to take a more intensive adaptive design solutions.

Are we stopping guests from adapting?

Social science tells us we should re-examine the way we provide heating and cooling in our accommodation.

People are not passive recipients of the indoor temperature. Comfort is the goal they seek. So we should not look at buildings as *providing* comfort, but as a *means* for the building occupants to *achieve* their unique comfort goal. People will take adaptive measures to become comfortable using equipment and other non-electric methods in a rational way that makes sense to them.

Stopping them taking adaptive measures can be when the window is difficult to reach or open, or that it is too windy outside or too noisy, preventing them from using natural ventilation. Architects have to balance a whole range of subjects to produce their final concept, which may or may not consider the variety of needs (Nicol, 2011). We need to pay close attention to new systems that guests could use to optimise their own energy use.

Figure 6.4: This hotel in Tasmania that has an excellent design to permit air flow into the central public area with open windows. However, the guests' rooms do not self ventilate into the main building atrium, except through a small sliding vent, which due to painting was not possible to open. After 15 minutes of maintenance's time the newly opened vent was insufficient to function becasue the windows did not open sufficiently wide....leaving the a/c as the only practical option.

Details, details, details

Let us say you have changed the sheets and mattress in my room so I have natural fibres to sleep on. Are there any other factors in your control that would stop me sleeping?

I travel a great deal and what I regularly find is the entangled fight between me trying to sleep and the systems at war with each other. My favourite (most infamous) is the fridge. This machine is often inserted in a cupboard to disguise the fact it is there. The poor thing works hard all night while incarcerated with little ventilation, so all the hot air it generates to keep the contents cold just keeps raising the stakes for the machine.

In some apartments I have stayed in, I observed that the fridge is larger than the one I have in our family home, and yet it only houses four single-serve UHT milks (something that was translated to many properties over the Covid-19 crisis to reduce cross-infection, leaving accommodation fridges humming away for months with almost nothing inside)! Get these details right and you could persuade guests to save… now that they can sleep well.

Figure 6.5: The fridge is set at maximum '7' and the only content is a small UHT milk container.

Many ways to be comfortable and use no/low energy

I used to look at our guest accommodation to achieve two things: to comply with the Star Rating criteria and to look as unique and attractive as possible. My thinking was that by reaching 4.5 status on the rating scheme, we would meet all guest requirements and that images of our attractive rooms would keep website visitors engaged enough to book.

The functional elements like windows and a/c were secondary. If I am honest, I didn't look beyond noting that they existed, for I had never thought deeply about how people actually used different systems to be warm or cool. This narrow vision prevented me from seeing the room in its full complexity.

We redesigned our rooms by staying in them to apply integrated thinking, examining how we could make all areas more comfortable, and totally guest-centred. There are no TVs in the bedroom; they are in the lounges because we are trying to create an atmosphere that helps people sleep (we all know watching TV in bed does not). We now have couples returning with their young families.

A change in my awareness has driven improvements. Where before there were everyday features, there are now integrated systems. There are ten zero-carbon ways to be comfortable and an eleventh that is incredibly low carbon.

Figure 6.6: Example: Here we included 11 no or low carbon techniques to improve guest comfort. Internet: https://mygreenbutler.com/resources

We have exterior shading (3) reducing the sun's heat, which allows guests to sit outside when it is raining and warm. It even has transparent sections so daylight inside is not adversely affected. Floor coverings (5) are removable, they can be set out in cooler months and wrapped up in warmer months so that left bare the floor is cooler underfoot in summer. Wicker furniture (6) permits more airflow in summer and adding cushions makes them cosy and heat-sealed for winter. Attractive natural fibre rugs (7) let guests stay warm easily when there is only a slight chill. Thick glass windows (8) have higher insulation values, fitted with fly screens (9) that allow the natural fresh air in and nothing else. Natural fibre bed sheets and covers (10) aid comfortable sleeping and soft white dimmable lights (11) add a cosy feel to the room. We respond to such sensations, even the room colours have been selected to work well in all seasons. Lastly, we changed regular ceiling fans (1) for ones that use 1/3 of the energy (being DC).

Case study: **Hilton launched world's first 'Vegan Suite'**

Here is an example of an integrated design approach. At the Hilton London Bankside, guests can experience a vegan stay from the moment they step into the hotel, with a specially designed plant-based check-in desk, botanical artwork, and keycards and seating made from Pinatex (vegan-friendly leather made from Pineapple). The bed has a Pinatex headboard which is hand-embroidered by local artist Emily Potter. Pillow options include anti-bacterial, non-allergenic eco-friendly course materials. Stone-grey flooring is used and carpets are made from cotton. The mini bar contains locally sourced vegan treats, there is an in-room vegan menu, toiletries are made with recyclable packaging, and stationery is animal-free. Finally, the cleaning products are non-toxic and non-animal tested (Starostinetskaya, 2019).

Opportunities for better designed guest comfort

People will tolerate a wider spectrum of inside temperature if they feel they have control over their environment. Before reaching for the a/c button, guests can follow three forms of adaption:

- Behaviour – changing clothing or opening a window;
- Adjusting to the climate – the body adapts;
- Psychological – overcoming a repeated experience of a specific stressful indoor place (De Dear et al., 1997). This could be achieved by noticing, understanding and adapting to local lifestyle behaviours.

People have very different ideas about what constitutes a comfortable temperature. They actively engage with fixtures that allow them to adjust the temperatures of their homes. This often involves quite complex systems (Tweed et al., 2014). Research has found that new generation thermostats can be too complex for people, whilst usability might be improved with feedback and audible commands (Peffer et al., 2011).

A survey of 1,000 people using the same naturally ventilated building in two seasons showed a wide variety of responses even when occupants experienced the same weather conditions. Offering opportunities for air flow was found to be a significant factor in attaining an optimised comfort level, and they are able to sense quite low movement. "Our present findings demonstrate that it is clearly possible to design low energy, naturally ventilated … buildings that will be thermally acceptable to discerning occupants with experience of the fully air-conditioned alternatives" (Brager et al., 2004).

6

By designing a specific service to encourage guests to adapt their behaviour we saved electricity in spring (35%), summer (21%), autumn (22%) and winter (22%) by explaining to guests (Warren et al., 2018).

Five steps to design change at your accommodation

These five steps will help you apply integrated thinking to make your business offer excellent hospitality, significantly cut emissions and benefit the environment;

1. Review your auditing
2. Research your guests
3. Develop concepts
4. Test prototypes
5. Refine your prototype

I want you to think about times when you felt lethargic, like forming groups with strangers at a workshop to solve a problem you were not particularly interested in. It is hard to get motivated when you are uninspired. It is absolutely essential that you read these five steps with the word 'fun' revolving around in your mind. The interactions between your property's team and guests should be enjoyable, the design solutions should be exciting to try. They need not make every single guest smile, but they should be so well designed that people can feel positive and uplifted (Chapter 11). Fun is the secret to a greener future, not the idea of punitive insufficiency.

1. What do your audits tell you?

What is the plan? To start your project, use three of the audits we discussed in Chapter 9. These will allow you to focus on the key issues. You can assess them using my Innovation Focus shown below (you can get a fresh copy from www. mygreenbutler.com/resources).

First, focus on the resource audit.

- Which resource holds the highest share of your footprint? That could be the first area to focus on.
- What guest services make the greatest demands on the resource in question?
- What guest experience fixtures/amenities do you have/not have that can help reduce that impact?
- What levels of guest information do you have/not have that helps to use less of the resource?

Figure 6.7: Sustainability Focus

Concentrate on the materials that restrict/release conserving opportunities						
				Where is the focus?		
	Key learning	Insights	Organisation	Process	Product/ service	Marketing
Resource Use Audit (a) Which resource holds the highest share of your footprint?						
Resource Use Audit (b) Which guest service contributes most to resource use?						
Guest Green Experience Which fixtures/amenities do/do not help reduce impacts?						
Guest Information Audit Which level of information helps/does not help to reduce?						

What are the building, climate, destination, guest and staff limitations?

What are your key areas of weakness and strength?

Do the observations mainly apply to the:

- Way your team/guests interact to share responsibilities/use facilities?
- Equipment and systems used to deliver the service?
- Final product of service you offer?
- Way you market your hospitality business?

Tick the boxes which are more suited to the outcomes you have found.

Break down your areas of focus into:

- *Organisational* – What are the roles and responsibilities of staff and how can this include sustainability criteria?
- *Processes* – What methods report and provide a standard for quality control?
- *Product/service* – What is the service we are delivering? How critical is it to guests' satisfaction? What are its criteria for high quality?
- *Marketing* – How is the product/service communicated to customers?

Repeat with the other resources or waste that have high carbon and cost.

You can populate each of the areas on the canvas with ideas which you will research further as your concepts develop, are researched, and tested.

This process will start you on the journey of *sustainability-oriented innovation*. It is an innovation that meshes together organisational, process, product, and marketing solutions to deliver positive change.

You can strive to reach for the stars and think big, but you can also consider 'quick fixes' and 'low cost' solutions. This is because there are three levels of innovation:

- Short-term incremental innovations that add to your current service
- Really new innovations that stand out from a social technology/hard technology and marketing perspective
- Long-term innovations that are radical and disruptive to the market

Consider them all. You can build momentum and confidence to invest over time. But remember, just focusing on guests to reduce utility bills to save money is not going to be enough to survive in a competitive global lodging market (Vondrasek, 2011). Consider the broader aspects of service delivery and the systems in place that delivers them.

Story: The Green Kangaroo

In 2007 I set up the first carbon calculator, called the Green Kangaroo, for an Australian destination. It was applied to Kangaroo Valley, the small and beautiful location where I live. We introduced the idea to a 107-strong public meeting in our village (a third of the population), and were pleased to see 24 tourism businesses and 14 households signed a pledge to cut emissions then and there.

The carbon calculator has given me a valuable window into tracking small accommodation, restaurants, and activity providers for well over a decade. Emissions have been cut between 30-70%.

The carbon calculator lets you focus on the most impactful areas first, not simply picking low hanging fruit. You get to grips with what are the big factors causing significant pollution. Regularly measuring your carbon emissions allows you to see progress.

One restaurant owner told me, "I was going to take action to become greener, but the Green Kangaroo has helped me get started, continue to take action, and maintain that discipline to cut food waste and reduce energy use."

I designed the calculator specifically for Kangaroo Valley, including recording firewood and septic tanks waste because they are relevant local issues. It gets everyone to acknowledge there are different ways to source firewood and protect the river's water quality.

Users enter their quarterly bills' consumption for electricity, gas, firewood, waste (landfill), septic tank (by guest numbers), fuel, flying, and occupancy. It is essential to undertake carbon audits seasonally so you hone in on areas of significant waste and pollution. Monitoring by itself is passive; you want to identify factors that are increasing consumption. With the bills to hand audits are easy to do, taking just 5-10 minutes.

Such audits are good for an overview, but not helpful for product development and testing your design changes. For measuring individual product or service features the best way is to set up submetering. This lets you use resource/waste calculators, at higher resolution, to measure a large number of items and compare with key influencing factors. If you sub-meter to measure individual performance, you can test the impact of new design changes. We now sub-meter separate guest rooms and service areas in properties to test new concepts and retrofitting ideas before owners have to spend large sums.

2. Research your guests, its benefits

Researching the views of our customers is essential when creating participatory experiences. Currently, you may have many guest surveys. They can be useful, but the kind of guest research I am asking you to do is different. It requires your participation too.

You can find valuable nuggets of information by observing guests and holding informal chats with them. I thought I knew my guests, because for years I took bookings, managed check-ins, and met people during their stay. You see and hear all there is to know, right? Wrong. Throughout, I had been acting the proprietor, performing tasks without the mental space to reflect and observe. Likewise, the people who arrived acted as guest, not necessarily revealing what they needed for a happier, greener, more sustainable stay. Why should they? It is not their job. I just saw them "wasting resources". I now on occasion, go as far as reviewing the guest accommodation after their stay and look at what has been used, how it has been used, what is thrown out, and what state the room was left in. It gives me a fuller picture of their consumption and what needs to be improved.

When I gave more thought, empathised and applied a different mindset, the veneer cleared. I realised guests were unfamiliar with their building, its microclimate and our services, and had no time to plan what they were going to do to relax. In the case of international guests, these factors became even more extreme.

Conducting guest research

With your existing guests.....

Start by considering your guests' culture, better understand where they are from and what are 'normal' social practices for them. Consider their type of stay (leisure, business, bleisure) and type of experience.

Change your attire, be on holiday at your own place. Make mental notes on what guests are doing and why, specifically when it comes to consuming food, water, and energy. Examine how guests interact with systems you have applied and what level of interaction with staff exists. Could they have behaved in another way? How would you have handled that situation with your family? Best of all, also stay in your accommodation, try using the systems. Now try saving. Do you know how much you saved, did you use more or less than you guests? If you do not know, then you will realise why I invented My Green Butler.

Or if you want to target new guest types....

Can you observe them when staying at a competitor, or at public places at your destination? Meet with your Tourism Destination Manager and find out about their needs, their culture, and ways of consuming.

You should also have informal conversations with guests, where you discuss their stay, the things they liked and disliked, problems they have overcome and how the property could improve. Encourage their views, empathise. Now pitch an idea to your guests, just explain your concept in 30 seconds with a clear sustainability benefit and guests benefit. Then afterwards write down everything and anything you can.

Examples of some outputs

Here are ten areas you can focus on to pitch. These serve as examples, but each property is unique. What would you add?

1. Guests be better prepared before they arrive so you surpass their expectations (save energy/water)
2. Guests to have better thermal comfort satisfaction (save energy/water)
3. Encourage guests to visit better local places, quality local products, entertainments and heritage places (reduce carbon, increase local expenditure)
4. Guests stay longer, revitalise your public areas (increase expenditure)
5. Guests more satisfied, revitalise your dining and bar services (increase expenditure/cut food waste)
6. Guests avoid waste, effective use of leisure facilities (save water/energy)
7. Guests avoid waste, minimise laundry service (save water/energy/chemicals)
8. Guests enjoy stay more, maximise staff-guest interaction with customised stay experience (increase participation)
9. Guests delighted by new rooms, retrofit green materials and renovate rooms (saving energy/water/minimising waste)
10. Guests applaud new accommodation concept design with active cooling/heating low carbon comfort (reduce carbon footprint/minimising waste)

(Put your ideas here. Think about staff loyalty, environmental benefits...)

11. ....

12. ....

Consider using these resulting situations to target your plan. Be specific on the savings you want to achieve.

Research your staff

In a similar way to the guest research, you should also delve into the views of your managers and staff. Your team will have its own insights on what is practical and impractical for them to change in their duties. Informal conversations, walking tours with them to investigate and discuss in situ is helpful to generate more ideas. It will most likely also reveal complexities, which as an Integrated Thinker you will take on board identifying the tensions that must be resolved.

If you want to truly progress towards sustainable hospitality, it will most likely require transformational approaches to service delivery. Part of our industry's problem is how we have delegated roles and responsibilities over the years and how far we have integrated the responsibility to self manage wastage of resources. Researching staff will reveal both new ideas and weaknesses in the set up.

Often I find it can be that staff prioritise speed of delivery, the speed of cleaning rooms, speed in preparation tables/event rooms, and speed of preparing meals, that is the excuse of maintaining the status quo. The idea of introducing a new idea upsets their focus and is perceived to add workload. "But I am too busy preparing dishes to keep checking if the junior kitchen staff have properly closed the cold room door!"

The opportunity of implementing staff innovations must not be derailed. It requires a holistic approach to understand barriers. A key to introducing more sustainable practices is considering the staff's level of knowledge about the consequences of waste and careless use of equipment (like leaving on heat lamps for hours when not required).

People Power: Concentrate on the Meaning and Skills that restrict/release conserving opportunities

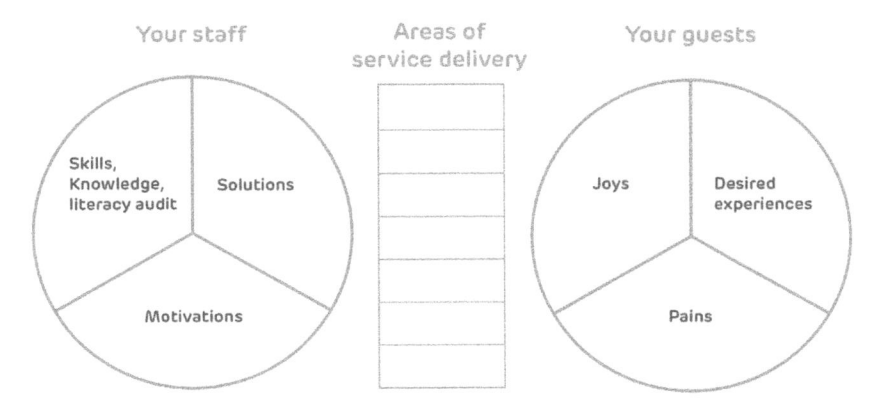

Use sticky notes to populate the fields in each of the guest staff frames.

Consider the areas of service delivery in which staff and guests most and least interact. What are the gaps/opportunities to improve skills, knowledge and competency? What are the ranges of meanings (motivations, experiences) that could influence adapting behaviour?

Figure 6.8: People Power

Insight: Are staff energy, water and carbon literate?

Many like to start staff research with a survey to measure their knowledge and attitudes towards resources and carbon. There have been various studies you can refer to when designing the survey. In particular, Jeou-Shyan Horng and her colleagues created a carbon literacy scale for staff; their paper gives details of the questions (Horng et al., 2013).

The survey will provide you with a baseline, showing a moderate level of care for the environment, knowledge of carbon and energy use, and preparedness to take action to reduce wasteful use of resources and carbon emissions. It is normal, when asked if you care about the environment, to say yes. However, when you conduct face to face informal conversations, you are most likely to discover that people tend to have a very low level of understanding for resource use and carbon literacy (Teng et al., 2014; Coles et al., 2016).

Literacy is a basic function of education. You have to learn individual letter shapes, pronounce them, read sentences, and understand the meaning to eventually read and enjoy Shakespeare. Literacy in the context of this book is about energy, water, waste, and carbon literacy. It is their understanding of the impacts of sourcing, using, and better managing resources (Moseley, 2000), so people have the capability of taking personal responsibility and action (Whitmarsh et al., 2009). From my experience, literacy is the key problem I find at all properties. We all have a much lower level than we realise.

It is highly likely your team (and guests) have a low resource/carbon literacy rate. Unlocking the potential of sustainable hospitality is about furnishing everyone with more practical knowledge.

Time to look at the big picture

Now you have your audits, guests and staff research, and completed sheets (Sustainability Focus & People Power) what do they tell you? Reflect on the findings. It is always tempting to jump in and narrow down a shortlist of points. This leads to standardised ideas of compromise. Use the research and thinking time to consider options.

Integrated Thinkers take a holistic view of problems. Use this time to expand your investigation and go beneath the surface of issues. The complexities are important and should not be avoided.

A way forward is to assess the details by breaking them down. For instance, by: thermal comfort, relaxation, food & beverage, personal hygiene, laundry. How easy is it to use the current systems to save energy, save water, reduce food, and other waste? What causes guests and staff to waste? What stands out as glaringly obvious, but what is also not so obvious? The resource audit will demonstrate the cost of inaction.

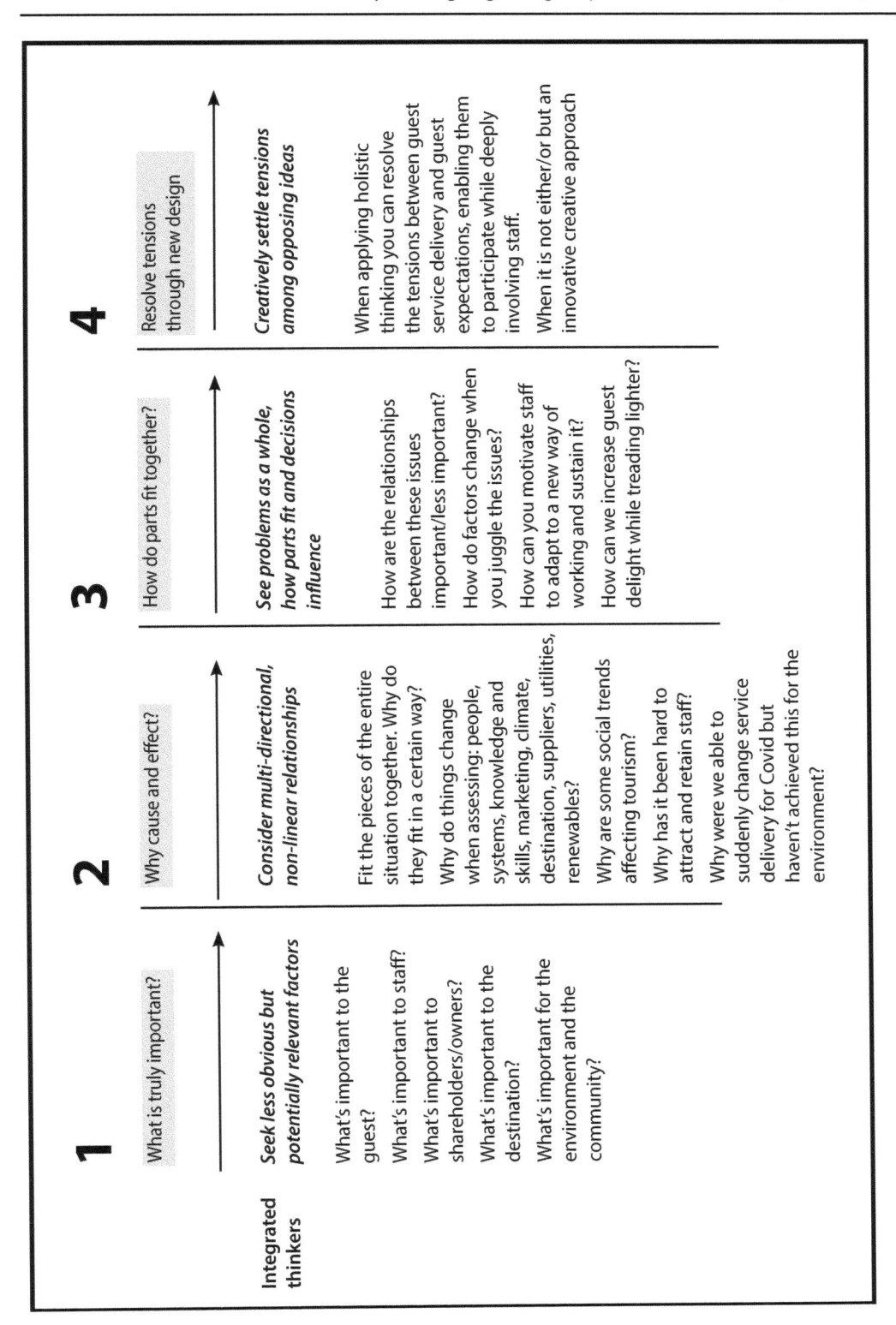

	1	2	3	4
	What is truly important?	Why cause and effect?	How do parts fit together?	Resolve tensions through new design
Integrated thinkers	***Seek less obvious but potentially relevant factors***	***Consider multi-directional, non-linear relationships***	***See problems as a whole, how parts fit and decisions influence***	***Creatively settle tensions among opposing ideas***
	What's important to the guest? What's important to staff? What's important to shareholders/owners? What's important to the destination? What's important for the environment and the community?	Fit the pieces of the entire situation together. Why do they fit in a certain way? Why do things change when assessing: people, systems, knowledge and skills, marketing, climate, destination, suppliers, utilities, renewables? Why are some social trends affecting tourism? Why has it been hard to attract and retain staff? Why were we able to suddenly change service delivery for Covid but haven't achieved this for the environment?	How are the relationships between these issues important/less important? How do factors change when you juggle the issues? How can you motivate staff to adapt to a new way of working and sustain it? How can we increase guest delight while treading lighter?	When applying holistic thinking you can resolve the tensions between guest service delivery and guest expectations, enabling them to participate while deeply involving staff. When it is not either/or but an innovative creative approach

Figure 6.9: The four stages of design thinking. Source: based on Martin (2007)

Another way to consider the information is from external to internal. Consider your destination, its regenerative needs, what part can your property play in donations, working bees, supply chain, conservation of nature and litter elimination? How can these be tied to the property's clientele, their stay experience, and staff loyalty through waste prevention or conservation in the property? I have found this method particularity helpful in creating levers to persuade guests and staff (more is explained in Chapters 6 and 7).

You might find Figure 6.9 helpful to assess and reflect on where the conflicts lie and how you can creatively resolve them using Integrated Thinking. I have adapted it from Roger Martin's breakthrough work in design thinking which identifies that successful leaders work through problems in four stages to 'craft innovative solutions' (Martin, 2007). Unlearn conventional thinking which focuses, narrows down, and gives you either/or choices. Open the problems up, experiment with ideas and design a solution which resolves the tensions that are restricting sustainable hospitality.

Time to complete the Sustainable Hospitality Innovation Canvas

This canvas will help you set responsible sustainable goals. Summarise where you are now and then write out projects that first tackle individual issues. These build and integrate over time to help you transform your business. List them as short-term incremental projects, really new innovations at your business and fundamentally radical steps that giving you a strong competitive advantage, reach Net Zero emissions and help rejuvenate nature/ regenerate your destination.

3. Developing concepts

Some people genuinely believe they are 'not creative', regarding their contribution to problem-solving to be limited. Perhaps it is more a cultural factor. In Western cultures, people are conditioned to problem solve in specific ways, narrowing down options to converge upon a single answer (which can be the best single option rather than the right holistic solution). They often only think in linear ways because it is quick.

Conversely, people from East Asia apply a more contextual approach, examining relationships from multiple perspectives. This can lead to very different results. As individuals we become used to following a conformed way of thinking (De Oliveira & Nisbett, 2017). Creative problem-solving is about applying divergent thinking that looks to *create* choices rather than divergent thinking to *make* a choice (Brown, 2009). It is learnt rather than pre-established.

Divergent thinking is essential for our sustainable hospitality topic because life and sustainability are both complex. They require us to integrate knowledge and behaviour change to successfully run a commercial business and achieve a net-zero footprint (Westley et al., 2011) and create real change by design.

Sustainable Hospitality Canvas

Integrate and evolve innovation concepts

		Innovation impact goals		
	Where you are now	1. Short term incremental	2. Really new social/hard technology/ marketing	3. Radical, long-term disruptive
Materials Which resources hold the highest share of the footprint of your equipment/systems, and how are you going to tackle them in the short, medium and long term?				
Meaning Which guest service contributes most to resource use and how will you draw on staff/guest motivations/experiences to engage them in innovate opportunities? Why will this be a competitive advantge?				
Skills What fixtures/amenities do/do not help reduce impacts? How will you improve staff/guests skills and knowledge to competently operate materials more effectively?				

Integrate your observations and conclusions to plan: i) straightforward improvements; ii) introduce new methods; iii) and plan radically positive change – to give you a market advantage, reduce GHG & improve nature. How can internal innovation be linked to positively regenerate your destination?

Figure 6.10: The Sustainable Hospitality Canvas

Being creative in some way is, therefore, a question of relaxing and letting go of the habitual way of approaching problems. While you will revert to your own knowledge and way of looking at life, try to look at things from other people's perspectives. Put yourself in their shoes. As previously mentioned, have you taken the time to experience your own hospitality service from the guest perspective?

Your experience and those of your team will vary, and this makes for rich interactions. Here are guidelines to follow when developing creative ideas:

- Criticism deflates people, avoid this.
- Kick around lots of ideas, but always return to the plan, do not get too distracted.
- Draw on the expertise of your team, work as an integrated group, not separate cells.
- Keep an open mind, look holistically.
- Do not worry about complexity; it is your friend, poor solutions stem from simplifying things and resorting to compromise.
- Do not rush to find a solution; let your knowledge and insight evolve.

Freewheeling thinking and synthesis

When I started out as a junior in advertising, I was amazed to see creative thinkers with feet on desks, munching on a pencil or chocolate bar, surrounded by what looked like chaos, and chatting. Perhaps that is what attracted to me to work in a creative environment. I think we all like to feel comfortable with one another to 'shoot the breeze'. While those creatives were 'sitting around', they were of course creating. Inspiration does not just flow out of a tap, you have to nurture it in a comfortable environment.

Everyone works differently, but the key to developing ideas is trust. It is essential to create an environment of trust, where everyone feels comfortable to share ideas, however crazy they may seem. As previously mentioned, it is critical to avoid criticism, remove barriers and maintain a relaxed setting.

At the same time, developing innovations also require structure. There have to be some parameters when resolving tensions in sustainable hospitality. Even creatives in an agency work to a brief; it is not just a freewheeling creative environment. The synthesis requires reviewing the information you have collected and finding patterns. It requires looking at the edge of the problem where it intercepts all related factors, rather than solely the problem itself.

Creatives will go back to their brief and then back to their ideas, going through continuous progress of refinement between their divergent and convergent thinking. It is a constant refinement process involving the full team, not an individual, to arrive at a synthesis.

Getting your ideas on paper

Here are two further approaches that can help you and your team

- First plan your strategic path by listing the objectives on one side, the guest needs on the other, and in the middle write in circular order (anti-clockwise) the insights you have learnt, what the issues and opportunities are, what impact this will make and what ideas you can come up with that resolve the design task.

- Next draw out the guest's experience journey. You can do this with post-it notes. Use a different colour for each area and put them on a large wall: the guest's behaviours/attitudes, front of house, then back of house Materials and Skills that are offered to fulfil the guests' behaviours. Add guests' needs.

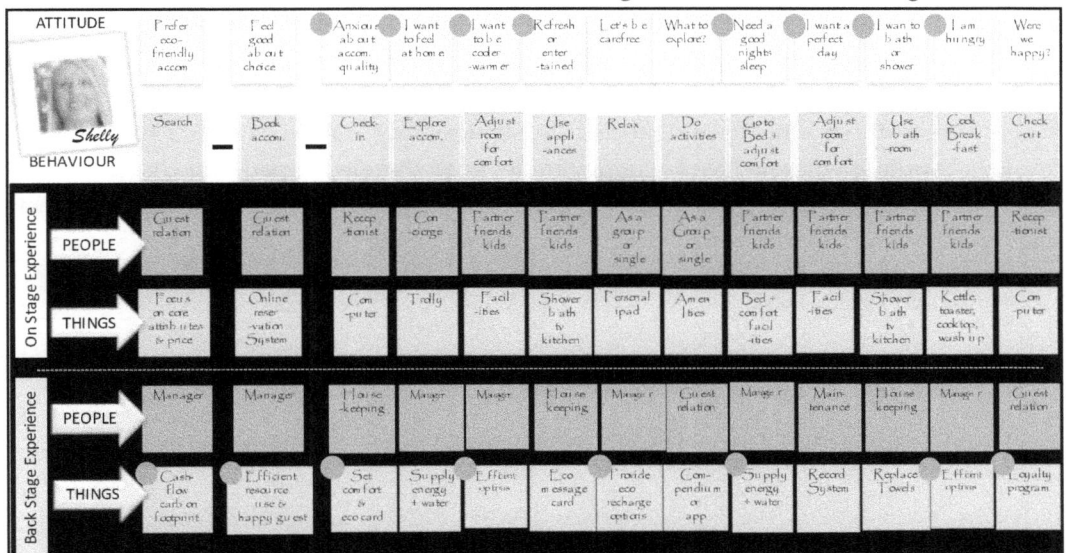

What you are seeking to do is understand and empathise with why guests are behaving the way they are. Look at the guest experience journey and find how you can reduce friction along that journey. (Think beyond energy-hungry techno gadgets that might make your accommodation appealing to new guests.)

How can you create new environments that use less energy and water, that waste less food and reduce laundry changes from the start. How can you get your guests to feel comfortable by using less energy? How can you use technology/ social technology to give your guests better control without using more resources?

Think about improving back end systems (this is where IT can be great) so more time can be spent assisting guests and offering customised experiences.

Remember that simplicity is still central to design change after you have resolved the complexity of tensions from opposing ideas and constraints. Your design solution should be clear enough for everyone to implement and follow.

Benefit of designing outdoor spaces

As an example of creative thinking, have your considered outdoor space?

Gardens can be one method to enable people to adapt to a cooler temperature without using air conditioning. Comfort in a garden setting is another way of interpreting what a comfortable environment can be. Many historic buildings used shade, water, and cooling techniques to provide relief, and inner courtyard gardens are culturally significant in Arabia. Enclosed areas (walls or shrubs) provide private spaces where people can escape from the building and are popular with the 1950s Californian garden offering a 'private realm'. Well placed plants, shady trees and water features have long been recognised as reducing the sun's impacts helping to keep a building cool. Modern garden design should provide a refreshing retreat and reduce air conditioning running costs (Cooper, 2008).

Urban deciduous tree planting can be a very successful way to reduce carbon emissions because of their benefits to offer shade to buildings in summer making them three times more effective in sequestering carbon than trees in a forest. Evaporation from trees in summer can keep the air temperature cooler with an estimated energy saving of 30%. Trees also help improve air quality. Losing their leaves in winter allows buildings to benefit from the sun's heat (Akbari, 2002).

Research shows that the original optimal productive temperatures of 21.6°C does not have to be set in stone. People are comfortable in a much wider temperature range, and if they are in control of systems they will tolerate a further higher and lower band. Gardens could also have calming benefits, relaxing guests, and could generate additional income from food and beverage concepts.

The use of plants can provide wonderful natural shade and create cool fresh air overnight.

Creatively adapting design of indoor spaces

History tells us that dwelling rooms have in the past been used creatively to maximise cooler spaces, where occupants would move between basement and roof to find lower temperatures.

In line with this concept, three properties in Australia were tested to see if energy consumption could be reduced during extreme hot weather, by creating 'cool retreat' spaces whose sole focus was to maintain healthy/lower temperatures. The cool retreat designs were found to save 85% to 94% of the cooling load. Modern designs could make better use of lower levels by using sunlight from light wells, where there is minimal exposure to the sun. This could dramatically cut energy use to keep comfortable (Palmer et al., 2014).

This approach is now applied at my own business where we give guests detailed guidance on how to keep cool/warm on days of extreme weather. This has helped to reduce our electricity load, making us less vulnerable to blackouts.

Designing ways to cut food waste

The plate size you give guests is a direct guide to how much they can consume (and waste). Chinese buffet diners were found to serve themselves 52% more, and wasted 135% more food than those guests with smaller plates. Even health warnings do not change consumption.

A further experiment showed attendees at a health conference who watched a 60-minute interactive health warnings on the dangers of using large plates still overconsumed, with 209 attendees, who were given larger plates, serving themselves twice as much food. Researchers believe people have a visual plate-fill line of 70% when serving themselves (Wansink & van Ittersum, 2013).

Fourteen chain hotels were involved in two research treatments to cut food waste. The first treatment used smaller plates and the second used a sign at the buffet reminding people that they could return as often as they wanted (so not urged to take too much in the first visit). The smaller plate size was found to save food waste by 19.5% while the sign cut food waste by 20.5%. Following 45,000 observations, there was no determinable difference in guest satisfaction (Kallbekken & Saelen, 2013).

4. Testing

We need to get far more scientific about sustainability. We need to meet clear legislative carbon and energy goals, demonstrate progress to stakeholders, and know the right places to invest capital. Testing, therefore, is essential to the creation and validation of new experiences.

Now you have assessed your audit, defined objectives, researched guests, staff and developed concepts, it is time for testing. Be sure to set up measurable parameters. If the design change is significant, (for example requiring capital or hitting a specific reduction target) compare with the previous standard over the same duration, climate conditions, occupancy, staff and time of day. Better still, run a test where you compare with current operations, running two streams, the new concept and the current simultaneously, and measure the performance.

When considering the findings seek to understand and empathise with guests and staff to help identify what, how, and when you need to make design adjustments to ensure your innovative solutions achieve their sustainability aim.

An important approach is to test a prototype using concept boards (more on these below) to show guests and staff. You will be developing a participatory guest experience so they should be involved in helping create that design. Likewise, you will want the project to create a transformation culture where staff enthusiastically participate to maximise your new idea.

You might have come up with ideas about sourcing food with a lower footprint and now need to test a new restaurant theme. Or to eliminate minibar fridges altogether and create a lively, relaxed lounge that guests prefer to be in than their rooms (Citizen M achieves this very well, though they still disappointingly have the fridges in guest rooms). Or use tech to reduce the friction of monitoring guests' carbon footprint. Guests and staff will provide you with valuable input to help create a competitive advantage for your sustainability initiative.

Concept boards

A concept board is usually a picture of the intended idea with a headline that summarises what the benefits will be. You can use smaller text to expand on key points. Then either personally speak with guests and staff for a response or use a survey where the questions are open (not simply 'yes' or 'no').

My colleague Creenagh Lodge introduced the idea of concept boards for her innovative 'projection techniques' when researching new products at Craton Lodge & Knight. She always encouraged the creative team not to use images of people in the board's pictures because she found it led research participants to focus on the people rather than the idea presented. Be careful to leave the people out of the image, imply them through props. This allows you to ask questions about whom the product would be used by, which gives more telling insights. With modern graph software or even PowerPoint and images, you can create concept boards easily. I use the plural because it is best to create a number of concepts and show them to your participants to get feedback.

Before introducing them, ask a couple of general questions to put people at their ease. Then without asking leading questions, focus the interview on the concepts, showing them one at a time. Display them together at the end for a final overview response. For genuine feedback, ask questions like "How would you describe this service?" "Who do you think would find it appealing/not appealing?" "If you could tell the inventor how to improve, what would you say?" You can also use probe questions like "why do you say this?"

It can also be very helpful to conduct interviews with two participants so that you can see how they share and compare their thoughts. If you are talking with staff consider their professional experiences and how this relates to the topic you are studying (Morgan et al., 2016).

5. Refine and implement

Collecting all the input now allows you to refine your concept, determining how it will work financially, environmentally, and what means are needed for implementation.

What evidence do you have that the innovation will conserve resources? How can you refine further? Ensure you have kept all your audit data, refer back to the objectives, and identify how much resource/waste you are proposing to save.

In preparing to implement your innovation, have you sufficiently considered the interconnection between Materials, Skills, and Meaning? What need(s) does it meet for staff and guests? How will you train and motivate staff? How will you explain the concept to guests and encourage them? How can this be improved?

There can be multiple refinement stages with product development. Each should build on previous innovations you have introduced. That is what happened at our business Crystal Creek Meadows*. Being small we introduced new ideas in stages, building on each so that in the end we had a holistic solution which created a compelling business result.

With each stage of refinement you build up a stronger body of knowledge that will then enable you to plan your marketing and be aware of future trends which could help your still further.

Story: Integrated result

We renovated and reconditioned the Materials in our self-contained cottages to design a more energy-conserving place using radiant temperature, air movement and ambience. This achieved a 20% increase in occupancy and top guest ratings in online review sites. Some of the little touches are fun to use and overall we are seeking guests to be joyful through their stay.

By modifying wall and furniture colours, guest comfort was improved by ambience so they *felt* more comfortable in cold or hot weather. Peoples' comfort is also affected by radiant temperature (the hot or cold surfaces around you), so seasonal material covers

---

*I sold the business in November 2021 to invest in My Green Butler and offer sustainability assistance to the hospitality sector.

were introduced. New technologies like solar fibre optic cable lighting and DC ceiling fans provided no/low carbon lighting and superior air movement.

This was not a 'buy all new' approach. More than 50% of items were restyled (so we eliminated the embedded energy and water use to make new furniture), all picture frames and glass were reused. Where possible, items such as cushion covers were made within a 35 km radius, and sofas manufactured using sustainable timber sources. We repainted the walls. Only eight items went to landfill, eight were resold, 61 items were purchased. Sixty five percent of expenditure was local.

Change by design, where you apply Integrated Thinking, can deliver savings, greater comfort, and good community results. This story describes the Materials of comfort, Skills and Meaning also should also be tackled to deliver conserving results that create a competitive advantage.

Summary

Transforming your guests' experience is a creative process which requires structure and free-wheeling ingenuity. From the beginning it is essential that you are aware of what savings you are actually trying to achieve so that you can measure the results. If you do not do this, then the whole project might cost you more, as so many supposedly green projects do. Remember the factors of escalating consumption, rebound, and backfire. The trials will help you identify this.

Having said that, it is not always possible to do this with very small changes, but you can survey guests to compare before and after behaviours. However, the purpose of this book is not to help you make small incremental changes, but to guide you towards the big opportunity of applying an Integrated Thinking approach. This will lead to experiences that make guests participants in your sustainability goals and, in doing so, build your reputation.

This chapter provides the structure needed to start planning. Next I provide more specific advice for implementing conserving innovations. Remember above all, your design solutions should be fun and uplifting.

Next steps

1. Assess your audits and define your objectives. Write this up.
2. Conduct research to understand what guests' needs are, how and why they currently do the things they do with fixtures and resources. Write this up.
3. Consider running workshops to develop new guest experiences which seek to easily enable guests to conserve.

References

Accor (2016). Responsible Guests are looking for sustainable hotels. Guest habits and expectations of hotels in terms of sustainable development: international report.

Akbari, H. (2002) Shade trees reduce building energy use and CO2 emissions from power plants. *Environmental Pollution*, 116, S119-S126.

Ambrose, M., James, M., Law, A., Osman, P., & White, S., (2013). *The Evaluation of the 5-Star Energy Efficiency Standard for Residential Buildings*. CSIRO, Australia.

Baker, M. & Schaltegger, S. (2015). Pragmatism and new directions in social and environmental accountability research. *Accounting, Auditing & Accountability Journal*, 28(2), 263-294

Brager, G., Paliaga, G, & de Dear R. (2004). Openable windows, personal control, and occupant comfort. *ASHRAE Transactions*, 110 (2)17-35, p32.

Brown, T. (2009). *Change by Design*. HarperCollins, New York.

Bundesministerium fur Umwelt (2021) Reusable is possible in the to-go area. https://www.bmu.de/pressemitteilung/mehrweg-wird-moeglich-im-to-go-bereich/ [Accessed 7 November 2021]

Chrisafis, A. (2016). French law forbids food waste supermarkets. *The Guardian*, 5 February. www.theguardian.com/world/2016/feb/04/french-law-forbids-food-waste-by-supermarkets [Accessed 7 November 2021]

Coles, T., Dinan, C. & Warren, N. (2016) Energy practices among small and medium sized tourism enterprises. A case of misdirected effort. *Journal of Cleaner Production*, 111, 399-408

Cooper, G. (2008) Escaping the house: comfort and the California garden. *Building Research & Information*, 36(4), 373-380.

Cozzio, C., Volgger, M., Taplin, R. & Woodside, A.(2020). Nurturing tourists' ethical food consumption: Testing the persuasive strengths of alternative messages in a natural hotel setting. *Journal of Business Research*, 117, 268-279.

Dawood, S., Crosbie, T., Dawood, N. & Lord, R. (2013). Designing low carbon buildings: A framework to reduce energy consumption and embed the use of renewables. *Sustainable Cities and Society*, 8, 63-71

De Dear, R., Braager, G. & Cooper, D. (1997) *Developing and Adaptive Model of Thermal Comfort and Preference*. Macquarie University and Centre for Environmental Design Research, University of California.

De Oliveira, S. & Nisbett, R. (2017) Culture changes how we think about thinking: From "human inference" to "geography of thought". *Perspectives on Psychological Science*, 12(5), 782-790

Dolnicar, S. (2020), Designing for more environmentally friendly tourism. *Annals of Tourism Research*, 84, 102933

Dolnicar, S., Cvelbar, L. & Grun, B. (2017). Do pro-environmental appeals trigger pro-environmental behavior in hotel guests? *Journal of Travel Research*, 56(8),988-997

Heikkila, L., Reinikainen, A., Katajajuuri, J., Silvennoinen, K. & Hartikainen, H. (2016) Elements affecting food waste in the food service sector. *Waste Management*, 56, 446-453

Horng, J. S., Hu, M. L., Teng, C. C., Hsiao, H. L., & Liu, C.-H. (2013). Development and validation of the low-carbon literacy scale among practitioners in the Taiwanese tourism industry. *Tourism Management*, 35, 255–262.

Kallbekken, S. & Saelen, H. (2013) 'Nudging' hotel guests to reduced food waste as a win-win environmental measure. *Economic Letters*, 119, 325-327.

6

Lane, L (2021) Hotel industry releases their top 5 requriements to avoid Coronavirus: Leasers express commitment to travel safe. Forbes, 21 July. www.forbes.com/sites/lealane/2020/07/21/hotel-industry-releases-their-top-5-requirements-to-avoid-coronavirus-leaders-express-commitment-to-travel-safety [Accessed 16th may 2021]

Lomas, K. & Kane, T. (2013) Summertime temperatures and thermal comfort in UK homes. *Building Research and Information*, 41(3), 259-280.

Martin, R. (2007). How successful leaders think. *Harvard Business Review*, June. https://hbr.org/2007/06/how-successful-leaders-think

Martin, R (2009). *The Opposable Mind*. Harvard Business Press, Boston.

Morgan, D., Elliot, S., Lowe, R & Gorman, P. (2016) Dyadicinterviews as a tool for qualitative evaluation. *American Journal of Evaluation*, 37(1), 109-117

Moseley, C. (2000). Teaching for environmental literacy. *The Clearing House*, 74(1), 23–24.

Nicol, J. (2011) Adaptive comfort. *Building Research & Information*, 39(2), 105-107

Pallesen, S., Larsen, S. & Bjorvatn, B (2015). "I wish I'd slept better in the hotel" – Guests' self-reported sleep patterns in hotels. *Scandinavian Journal of Hospitality and Tourism*, 16(3), 243-253

Palmer, J., Bennetts, H., Pullen, S., Zuo, J., Ma, T. & Chileshe, N. (2014) The effect of dwelling occupants on energy consumptions: the case of heat waves in Australia. *Architectural Engineering and Design Management*, 10 (1-2), 40-59.

Peffer, T., Pritoni, M., Meier, A., Aragon, C. & Perry, D. (2011), How people use thermostats in homes: A review. *Building and Environment* 46, 2529-2541.

Purtill, J. (2021). Heatwaves may mean Sydney is too hot for people to live in 'within decades'. ABC News, 25 January. www.abc.net.au/news/science/2021-01-24/heatwaves-sydney-uninhabitable-climate-change-urban-planning/12993580 Accessed [8 November 2021]

Robert, A. & Kummert, M. (2012) Designing net-zero energy buildings for the future climate, not for the past. *Building and Environment*, 55, 150-158.

Sakaguchi, L., Pak, N. & Potts, M. (2018). Tackling the issue of food waste in restaurants: Options for measurement method, reduction and behaviour change. *Journal of Cleaner Production*, 180, 430-436

Sheffield, H. (2016). How the humble doggy bag reduced food waste in Scotland by 40 per cent. *Independent*, 19 September. www.independent.co.uk/news/uk/home-news/hundreds-of-scottish-restaurants-sign-up-to-offer-customers-doggy-bags-to-reduce-food-waste-a7316731.html [Accessed 7 November 2021]

Silver, K. (2017). Check in, help out: Socially conscious hotels give back to the community. *Washington Post*, 30 November. www.washingtonpost.com/lifestyle/travel/socially-conscious-hotels-give-back-to-the-community-when-you-check-in/2017/11/30/1e8ce6f8-cbe3-11e7-8321-481fd63f174d_story.html [Accessed 16 May 2021]

Sommet Education (2019) Top trends in hospitality for 2019. www.sommet-education.com/wp-content/uploads/Sommet-Education-Top-Hospitality-Trends-2019.pdf

Starostinetskaya, A. (2019). Hilton Hotel unveils its first all-vegan suite. https://vegnews.com/2019/1/hilton-hotel-unveils-its-first-all-vegan-suite [Accessed: 16 May 2021]

Teng, C., Horng, J., Hu, M. & Chen, P. (2014) Exploring the energy and carbon literacy structure for hospitality and tourism practitioners: Evidence from hotel employees in Taiwan. *Asia Pacific Journal of Tourism Research*, 19, 451 - 468.

Tweed, C., Dixon, D., Hinton, E. & Bickerstaff, K. (2014). Thermal comfort practices in the home and their impact on energy consumption. *Architectural Engineering and Design Management,* 10(1-2), 1-24

United Nations Environmental Programme (2020). *One Planet Network 2019* annual magazine. UNEP, Paris

Vondrasek, D. (2011). *The future of smart grid technology in the US lodging industry.* Adelphi Study. University of Delaware, USA.

Wansink, B. & van Ittersum, K. (2013). Portion size me: Plate-size induced consumption norms and win-win solutions for reducing food intake and waste. *Journal of Experimental Psychology: Applied,* 19(4), 320-332.

Warren, C. & Coghlan, A. (2016) Can the hospitality sector ask customers to help them become more sustainable? *Progress in Responsible Tourism,*5(1), 98-102.

Warren, C., Becken, S., Nguyen, K. & Stewart, R. (2018). Transitioning to smart sustainable tourist accommodation: Service innovation results. *Journal of Cleaner Production,* 201, 599-608.

Westley, F., Olsson, P., Folke, C., Homer-Dixon, T., Vredenburg, H., Loorbach, Thompson, J., Nilsson, M., Lambin, E., Sendzmir, J., Banerjee, B., Galaz, V, & van der Leeuw, S. (2011) Tipping toward sustainability: Emerging pathways of Transformation. *AMBIO,* 40, 762-780

Whitmarsh, L., O'Neill, S., Seyfang, G. & Lorenzoni, I. (2009) Carbon Capability: what does it mean, how to prevalent is it, and how can we promote it? in A Stibbe (ed.), *The Handbook of Sustainability Literacy: Skills for a Changing World.* John Elford, Green Books, Totnes.

WWF (2021). More reusable, less packaging waste. www.wwf.de/2021/januar/mehr-mehrweg-weniger-verpackungsmuell [Accessed 7 November 2021]

6

7 Step 3: Teaching guests how to participate (Skills)

Introduction

The most beautifully designed green plan won't be much use if you can't convince your guests to participate. This chapter outlines the importance of having staff who can react to the unique backgrounds of different guests and encourage them to adapt their behaviour.

Some key points:

- **People are the core of your offering**. However sophisticated tech gets, there is no replacement for knowledgeable, supportive staff who can communicate the values of your business.

- **Guests bring their habits with them**. In unfamiliar settings, those habits are what they'll default to. It is the job of you and your staff to give your guests the information, skills, and resources needed to conserve.

- **Travellers want green solutions**. Do not by shy about your green initiatives. Share them! Communicate what they are and the difference they make to the local community. You'll be surprised how many guests want to participate.

- **Make the benefits clear and transparent**. 'Save the planet' is well-intentioned but vague messaging. 'Conserve resources and raise money for the local animal sanctuary at the same time' is concrete and exciting – something to feel proud of.

- **Sustainable hospitality requires shared interests and passions**. Guests and staff being on the same wavelength is essential to conserving, and done right it actually improves the hospitality experience.

When you visit a friend's house and help prepare a meal, how many times will you say, "Where do I find that?", or, "How do you turn this on?" If your friend is an economic cook and avoids waste, you might need more practical guidance. In exactly the same way we might invite our guests to act eco-friendly, but they will be receiving advice in a new environment where things are unfamiliar. If we want to offer eco-friendly accommodation we should teach our guests how.

Helping guests to be more eco-friendly is now being applied at multiple touch points of leading brands (disposal of packaging, reuse of parts, choice of products, etc.). For hospitality, responsible messaging should be at its core because helping guests to have a perfect stay is what hospitality is about. And the best method to date is using interpersonal communication. This is because people are more likely to respond to the persuasive suggestions of other people, particularly when they view them as an expert, or in charge, or likely to make a positive difference to their situation.

Interpersonal communication essentially means holding a two way dialogue. I will come to the 'contactless' and 'guest-facing-tech' later in this book with messaging examples, but the importance of your staff should not be ignored. They ought to be the framework of your sustainable hospitality drive.

Years ago I was fortunate enough to interview Bill Marriott Jr when he opened the Ledra Marriott hotel in Athens. To this young and impressionable travel journalist he appeared a very approachable man and easy to talk with. I was impressed with his personal interest and respectful attitude towards his staff, which as a young reporter I did not expect to see in a leader of a corporation. It was something I never forget after almost forty years! But much later I learnt that he was caring for his most precious asset – putting people first. It helped him build the world's largest hospitality company.

Marriott knew the power of people when it came to crafting delightful guest experiences:

> "This is what it's all about. Taking care of people, making them feel good when they're away from home, making them feel that they're appreciated and recognizing them. You can't do that with a computer. You can only do that with personal contact and that's what we talk about all the time — the importance of personal contact".
> (Eisen, 2017).

In the same spirit, we can use our staff to better engage guests with sustainability practices and ask them to participate. Central to the principle of offering hospitality is to guide guests so that they can have an exceptional stay, comfortable and well looked after, enjoying the delights of your destination. Why can this not include advice that helps them conserve if it makes for a better stay experience?

The focus of staff is held by others too, among them Swiss hospitality academics, Demen Meier and Marie-France Derderian:

> "Human interaction remains core to the hospitality industry. In the luxury industry, this human service is vital for brands to deliver a bespoke experience, in which guests

7

can feel both at ease and pleasantly surprised by service that surpasses expectations… these shared moments of personal service may turn out to be the real luxury that guests most value." (Sommet Education, 2019).

This chapter focuses on *Skill*, the second element that equips people to conduct their holiday routines and leisure activities in an effective manner. Your new design experience should consider how your staff make this as enjoyable and friction-less as possible.

Sharing skill becomes a strategy to help both differentiate your hospitality's customer service and improve guest satisfaction through greater personalisation and comfort. Sharing skill becomes a method for better communicating the value proposition of your business, something hotel CEOs often feel is lacking.

Lost in translation

When I arrive at a new place, I go to find amenities and then assess how they work. I feel a little lost and want to get my bearings. This inevitably involves some time in the kitchen, opening and closing windows to how I like them, and fighting with the a/c controls. If you are on a business trip, you want to function as efficiently as possible and prepare for meetings (where's the ironing board?). With the kids it means settling into the new home (finding and understanding the washing machine).

Have you ever felt like this too? This is the time when we need our newly designed conserving services to work smoothly.

Remember, there are three essentials that can instigate transitions: Materials, Skills and Meaning. You might have installed more eco-friendly Materials but guests still need the Skills to use them (we'll cover meaning in the next chapter). Applying integrated thinking means rather than avoiding guest involvement in conserving, we partner with them.

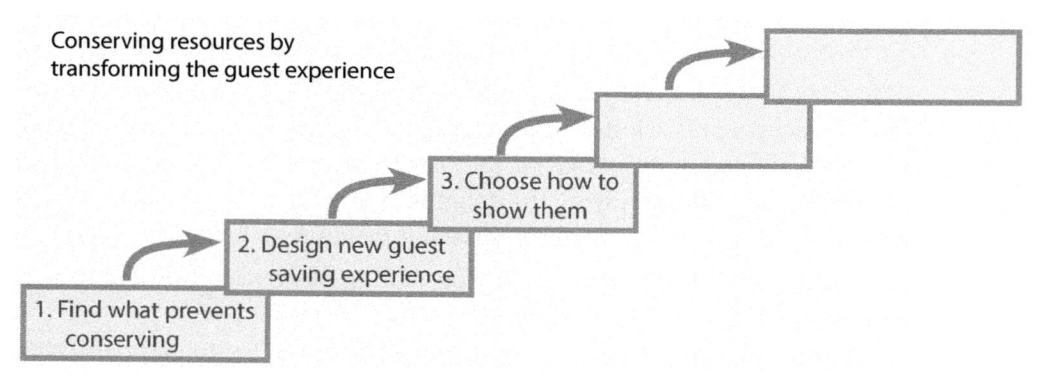

Figure 7.1: The 5 Step Method to create transformative guest participation

Unfamiliar

Hospitality could better acknowledge that our guests quite often come to stay in an unfamiliar place, with an unfamiliar climate, unfamiliar room controls, and unfamiliar food. Although many chain hotels and motels have an almost identical layout, for those of us who offer individual concepts this unfamiliarity is further heightened.

Like me, you might feel a bit stupid sometimes if you have to call reception and ask them how something 'everyday' works. I tend to avoid that call and try to work it out… often getting a bit stressed and frustrated when I haven't got the room temperature right or worked out the coffee maker. It's at this point I mourn the loss of the bell boy/concierge who would give you some instruction when you entered the room. My hat's off to those who continue this tradition. Isn't that what hospitality is about, helping people settle in? The usability of new technology might be fabulous, but not everyone is familiar with such systems. Understanding unfamiliar knobs, cupboards, windows, weather, and accommodation facilities may also be delayed when you are tired, have children running about, or need to make an urgent phone call.

Leaving guests to fend for themselves, hoping tent cards do the trick, could well be the reason some hotels only have a 2% involvement rate in the linen and towel reuse programme. We haven't engaged with guests, we haven't explained the systems clearly. Overall, we haven't persuaded them. Yet we know guests want to learn about the greener experience, which underlines the fact that many are unfamiliar with their new temporary surroundings.

7

Appearances are deceptive

Hospitality often makes assumptions about guests and standardise their saving approach. Guests might look similar with the clothes they wear and the gadgets they carry, and this can make us prone to think all guests have the same daily routines, and the know-how to conserve. This is a dangerous way of looking at conserving opportunities.

I have been fortunate enough to live and work in many countries across four continents, some poor, some immensely wealthy, some guided through religious cultures, and others new nations building their identities. They have all very different ways of life. Just because there is a retail brand available around the world in similar shopping environments doesn't mean people use these materials in exactly the same way. A couple from a modern city may be living completely different lives to their parents, who were nomadic herdsmen, but may still hold true to some of their traditions and consumption habits.

The world's wonderfully varied cultures mean that guests can actually spend their time on holiday in as many varied ways as there are places to stay. What are everyday leisure activities for me are mostly likely different for you. This subjectivity can result in vastly different levels of consumption. This is compounded by your unfamiliarity of where you are staying, facilities, and the climate.

We pack our habits with us

As we have seen, there is no such thing as a Mr & Mrs Average. Everyone's consumption and waste is different, so their conserving solutions will be too. In an unfamiliar place these skills have to be acquired, just like they would have been in the past.

When guests travel they pack their own routines with them. The knowledge of their a/c at home or the way to achieve a warm shower are carried in their minds. How often they shower and wash their cloths are normal activities conducted at a normal frequency. What they do at home they will likely do at your accommodation. From personal experience I know clothes can be washed and ironed twice a day in some countries, washed using hot water in front loading machines in the UK and a resounding preference for top loaders and cold wash in Australia. Is your laundry service typical of what's expected in your country?

The mis-match between your amenities and your guests' skills might be wider if they come from other countries with different cultural traditions, e.g. a day of rest on Friday, or Saturday, or Sunday. Their government might be encouraging easy green initiatives (change shower heads) so they have peace of mind. This still leaves us with the question of how long and how often one should shower.

In the past, travelers adapted to local community resource availability. If you stayed in my village, and I saw that you went down to the well a few times a day – not good for our village! – I would politely remind you that we have limited water and so are a 'one bucket a day' community. As a visitor you would comply because we can see each other's level of consumption and want to fit in to enjoy the security of our community.

People have different ways of keeping cool

The CSIRO monitored four homes in Melbourne over three months (end of summer-autumn) using sensors on windows, doors, energy use, and recorded inside and outside temperature/humidity. While experiencing the same weather conditions the occupants of the four homes showed a wide range of different behaviours (Ambrose & James, 2014):

- Windows open between 2.2% to 38.7% of the time
- Average inside temperatures while a/c running between 22.5 - 29.8°C

- Number of hours a/c was running, over three months, lowest 1.5 hrs to highest 76.5hrs

People have different comfort expectations and different levels of knowledge about being eco-friendly (or saving costs) and knowing how to use the systems well in their own home. This means you should be direct about what to use and when, so that you are able to guide people in the most energy efficient way that delivers the best possible levels of comfort. This is why I invented My Green Butler.

What you know dictates what you use

From my own business I can confirm that there are huge behavioural differences based on where people come from. My guests from Canberra (a city susceptible to droughts) use almost half the water of guests from Sydney (a coastal city that has the mirage of plenty of rainfall), while travellers from Malaysia and Singapore can use six times more water than Canberrians. Where you live affects how you live and what you use.

Guests' energy use differs by nationality

North American and European guests used 49-56% more energy than Taiwanese and Chinese guests when staying in Taiwan. Seventy-three hotels' electricity use and guest origins were monitored in Taiwan for one year. It showed significant differences in energy use by guest origin, with guests from Asia (excluding Japan and China), Australia and Japan using more than the domestic travellers.

Energy use was found to almost double during the warmer summer periods. Average hotel revenues and room rates did not change dramatically despite the higher energy use (Wang & Huang, 2013).

Guests' food waste differs by country and age

Researchers monitored food waste at a coastal Slovenian hotel buffet for 92 days and found that Austrian guests wasted less food per person. Next were German visitors, whilst Russian guests wasted significantly more. Food waste was much higher when there were a large number of young children eating breakfast in the restaurant (Juvan et al., 2018).

Guests' towel reuse differs by country

Studies on towel use show just as much variety. At a USA hotel, 44% of guests were persuaded to reuse their towels (Goldstein et al., 2008) In two hotels in Germany towel reuse was promoted, with guests achieving reuse rates of 82.3% (Bohner & Schluter, 2014). Meanwhile in Australia, 87.5% of motel guests were found to reuse their towels without this even being promoted (Mair & Bergin-Seers, 2010).

Applying our skills (and not)

Just as we can acknowledge that guests will bring their daily routines with them, so we should also note that they will apply existing skills, their cultural ways, and be influenced by their emotions even if they have competency to be less wasteful. Leisure holidays change our routines and may also encourage us to relax how we do them. If we spend much time at home preparing meals for others, then focusing on food waste might not be a top priority. Likewise making beds at homes becomes the opportunity of a little luxury of a prepared bed while away.

We don't possess the knowledge to understand the consequences of these routines. We have little comparative data of their true impacts when we use the accommodation's heating, cooker, shower, and three TVs. Just fitting more efficient equipment doesn't change people's level of skill or their behaviours. One common factor most people don't understand is the relationship between appliances and the amount of energy/water they use, so they won't know this at your accommodation either. This contributes to the gap between buildings' predicted energy use and actual – sometimes +300% (Delzendeh et al., 2017).

The science-based targets discussed in Chapter 2 clearly point out that efficiency and renewables will not be sufficient in the face of population growth, depleted resources, and business expansion. With a cut-off date to reduce emissions (66% by 2030 and 100% before 2050), changing shower heads and similar is not going to be enough. However, luckily, guests are interested in new innovations.

Tourists want to see green innovations

The majority of visitors believe it very important to see innovative environmental initiatives at tourism businesses. With landscaping with native planets (45.6%), energy efficient systems (41.5%), recycling (40.8%), renewable energy (38.7%), greywater systems (37.4%), and architecture that fits with the local landscape (36.3%) being considered as "extremely valuable".

However, only 29.3% think water use reduction programmes were "extremely valuable". The research was conducted in Arizona, which is a particularly dry part of North America. The public could only make subjective responses because they did not have any way of identifying what the overall impact would be to any specific innovation. Although visiting a dry place, water did not appear to them to be as important as natural landscaping and energy efficiency (Andereck, 2009).

Attitudes and interest in green technological solutions

Green customers are not necessarily the ones most interested in green innovations. People are oriented to different solutions based on their level of interest and skills. Different green solutions appeal to different people based on their lifestyles and what they value, i.e. how open minded they are to new ideas, or whether they enjoy technology, or avoid technology. As individuals we respond to what we understand and like. This means that some people with green values won't want to research electric cars (preferring to enjoy nature and the outdoors) while non-green people can be interested in the cost saving of solar panels (Axsen et al., 2012).

Stop and think

When you go to make a cup of coffee in the morning, it is instinctive. You get out of bed, put your robe on, move into the kitchen on a familiar route, fill the kettle with water, pop the coffee in and turn on, placing a cup at the ready…. all without really thinking about it. You could have been on the phone, calling out to the kids or chatting with friends who have come to visit. The activity of putting on the coffee is almost remote control. Daniel Kahneman, the acclaimed Nobel Prize winner, calls this System 1 thinking – the fast, instinctive ways we do things throughout the day.

Kahneman points out we also apply System 2 thinking in our day, where we slow down, think a lot more about what we are doing, evaluate, apply common sense to our intentions, decisions and actions. It could be stopping to read the dial and judging how much longer you need to cook the spaghetti. It could be giving your partner directions to the restaurant, or checking your mobile for your energy consumption and working out what to turn off.

Encouraging guests to conserve requires us to move guests from autopilot System 1 thinking to applying System 2 thinking. People in developed economies have lost the need to apply any mathematical juggling to work out which would be a more effective way to do things to save energy – something our ancestors had to do all the time. This means we aren't very good at comprehending the environmental impact of our decisions. Here is where you can help using your newly designed experiences which ask guests to apply System 2 thinking first.

Loss or gain?

When encouraging guests to recycle at a hotel, researchers found that people were more likely to participate if there was a clear message about what exactly they were supposed to do (i.e. not a vague 'save the planet message') and what were the consequences (loss) if they did not apply this responsible action.

The researchers concluded that the combination of a 'concrete' message and explanation of what would be lost, gave guests a higher level of self-efficacy – the ability to apply themselves successfully to the task at hand; "As sustainability becomes an ever more important part of tourism companies' strategies, an effective communication of green initiatives to consumers is of paramount importance to reduce costs and preserving natural resources."

The message combination was more effective because guests choose to apply System 2 thinking. This was because the messaging offered a clear cause of action with clear loss framing, which made them able to process the advantages of changing behaviours and apply them successfully which reaffirmed the benefits of that decision (Grazzini et al., 2018).

Sharing skills

First and foremost, you want to convey that the System 2 ways of doing something will benefit the guest. This will be the case if you have identified their needs correctly and reduced friction when designing the experience, thus enabling guests to more easily follow your advice. If you don't have a clear guest benefit you need to return to Chapter 5 and evolve your ideas further, showing and discussing your ideas with your guests.

People have preferences in the way they learn. You can share skills,

- by making your explanation verbal;
- by letting the guest practice applying the activity themselves;
- or read about the approach first.

Try to combine these three ways visual, auditory, and kinesthetic (hands-on) using a combination of communication approaches. That way guests can select the option they prefer. Think about how you currently communicate information to guests. Do you use all three, or are they restricted to text in the compendium? The key is to *not* leave vague approaches that may annoy guests and may backfire.

Stories are common on how guests resent being told about eco-friendly features, thinking the overture as preachy and irrelevent to them. This has tended to make some hospitality managers turn away from directly engaging with guests beyond discreet notes. The reason some guests do respond with frustration is the way in which we have approached them in the first place. I'll cover this in the next chapter on persuasion.

Ways to share skills

1. Be empathetic and tell them the benefit

Guests want to know why you are giving them advice. Make them aware that by providing information you are going to make them more comfortable, save them time washing clothes, or cook food perfectly in the microwave (these examples will of course differ according to your guest, and room types). If you think this will be banal, then that may be because the experience you have designed (Chapter 6) has not created a sufficiently frictionless, enticing benefit.

2. Show them

Think of the time it takes to get used to a new phone, or learn how to use a new washing machine. Wouldn't you have liked a friend to point out the short cuts?

When you introduce your newly designed guest experience ensure that guests see the positive reasons, understand how to use the amenities and achieve great results. The best way for people to pick up skills is through demonstration. It gives them the opportunity to ask questions without feeling awkward. When we freely guide people, by giving them new ideas and tips, they are appreciative as you've given them a new skill and helped them master it. They might even want to apply this new skill at home.

3. Let guests do it themselves

If they see that it is a solution and they can apply to their everyday lives, they'll be self-motivated. So, aim to show that they can save (time, money, less waste).

4. Don't write a book!

Provide written information in easy-to-read format, with steps shown in bite-sized pieces, whether it's in text and visual form, on the phone or through voice activation. Too much information in one go overloads people.

5. The guest is king/queen

Don't force the sharing skills. If the guest doesn't want to know then that's fine, you have provided the information. They can choose if they want your help. Applying the persuasive techniques in the next chapter will enable you to involve a higher number of your guests.

6. Let guests build the skills

Let guests see for themselves the benefits they achieve from applying the skills you have offered. This motivates them to continue. I explain further the value of feedback in Chapter 10.

Partners in creating solutions

Social innovation can involve the synchronisation of staff and guests to apply more eco-friendly behaviours. This form of innovation is much less expensive than corresponding hard technology to deliver similar results (Warren, 2018). It is possible to use autominius technology to replace hosts. However, it is important from a persuasion perspective that the technology is humanised so that the sense of hospitality is maintained and that the information is structured to assist guests as an educational service. Chat bots and self service apps can be 'cold' and frustrating and not carry the warmth of human interaction. That is why I invented My Green Butler. Technology does give you the opportunity of providng more information that a host can do in person if you integrate with multi-channel options e.g. video, manuals, communicate in easy to follow steps.

7

People like picking up new skills when they can see the common sense benefit, can follow progress, and are not embarrassed trying it in front of others. So, staff should be trained to apply plenty of reassurance and empathy. You see this regularly when visiting your DIY store and helpful staff make recommendations. You've likely noticed the growing trend to offer stimulating retail experiences in stores to build loyalty where, for example, customers can learn to cook new recipes, learn about kitchen appliances or apply makeup ideas. Going beyond the supply of services can create valuable opportunities to offer customer service that helps guests enjoy better experiences than they have applied themselves at home.

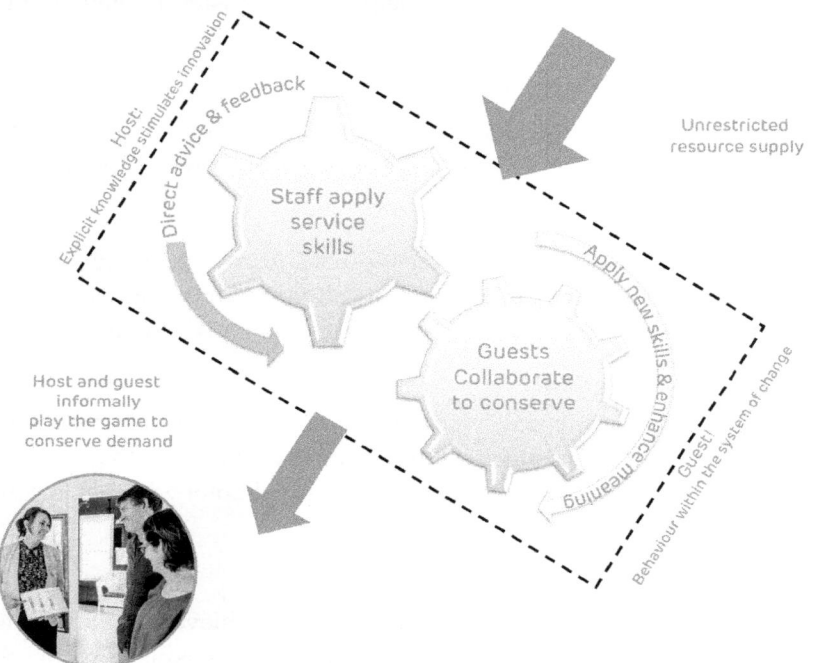

Figure 7.2: You are creating a social technology

Today we are all so much more informed. You tell friends you're going to do some DIY and someone might freely give you advice on a new, more effective way to paint or repair. The very act of DIY is an example of how we have moved to a co-created consumption experience where we can enjoy learning new skills and customising exactly what we want. Still not sure? In our busy lives we often don't have time to learn and try new things. That's what holidays and leisure can be all about. Think about those breaks you've had when there has been time to learn a neat new skill, when the chef has shown you how to cook a local dish, or when you've watched the locals and learnt a new dance.

Making the world a better place is a key skill we all need to learn right now. Holidays catch people when they can stop and apply System 2 opportunities more easily. I've been amazed at the response from our guests, and our guest reviews illustrate this.

Innovations can evolve through communities

Those who share a similar passion will often share ideas and help each other. In sports and leisure, people can often develop an innovative idea for skateboarding or gaming and get help from within their community to evolve it as a prototype.

As sociable creatures we have a natural desire to belonging. Something Facebook found from its research is why the communities feature was pushed forefront and central in their last update. Generally, people are happy to learn from one another when they have complementary skills. People like to help one another as quite often their primary motivation is the joy of working with others.

As the public are aware of environmental challenges, they are happy to receive advice which is of practical assistance to them. By the same token, I have received further questions from guests to learn more, or they offer their advice to help us. It can become a symbiotic relationship, which only enhances your brand values (Franke & Shah, 2003).

Innovations outside the world of manufacturing can occur through the collaboration of people who share an interest in the same activity. Those who have come up with new ideas can get help and advice from others. This can be seen in DIY and in outdoor activities, like the new phenomenon Nordic Walking. The innovative way of doing the activity evolves through the introduction of new materials or applied skills of others, or different skills and the meaning we give them. These can start a 'chain reaction' as new ideas are applied in new ways by others (Pantzar & Shove, 2010).

The City of Sydney's Sustainable Destination Partnership is an example of individuals working at competitor hotel groups coming together to plan and benefit from the advice of others. In the same way that staff can share innovative ideas with guests and benefit from their insights, the programme is an example of organisational innovation, and has driven progress. Why not stimulate the same thinking in your destination and benefit from ideas others share with you?

Green initiatives exclude guests at their peril

Guests are generally not involved in green accommodation projects. Analysis of three major hotel chains' green or social practices marketing did not consider any guest engagement. This means missed opportunities before guests arrive, during their stay, and after departure (Weiss & Straub, 2018).

When analysing over 30,000 guest reviews from 53 German hotels, only 10% carried some guest feedback on green or social good initiatives. Perhaps this is because many of the eco-friendly initiatives are invisible to guests and they don't really experience them personally (Gerdt et al., 2019).

When I introduced My Green Butler at my own business we found our reviews didn't just talk about our green issues – guests also talked about the greater level of comfort. Isn't this the competitive edge you want?

Adapting, not changing behaviour

Adapting, not changing, is an important distinction. Quite often people will challenge me by saying you can't *change* guests' behaviour. To be clear, I have no intention of changing their needs so they behave very differently. People interpret the words 'behaviour change' as though we are proposing to stop guests washing and eating. What we are striving for are experiences where guests adapt their behaviour to conserve resources.

People adapt all the time. You might be sitting reading a book when the sun becomes too strong, so you move your chair or pull the blind down, rather than turn on the a/c. That's only possible if we have designed the experience with a movable chair and blind. You can tell guests that "this is a lovely warm room with the afternoon sunshine and if it gets too warm you can move the blind or it's easy to move the chair". Showing guests how to adapt, using the materials you provide, increases your chances of conserving, it also demonstrates courtesy and empathy. You can show guests how to enjoy the aspect of your accommodation by highlighting the materials you have. That way they have the tools to adapt.

Showing guests 'how' doubles their efforts to conserve

We conducted an experiment where half the guests received the My Green Butler service and the other half continued to enjoy the regular experience. The experiment ran for over a year so that all seasonality factors could be assessed.

We found that guests who received My Green Butler took twice as many actions (12 on average) to conserve, compared to the regular guests (6). The saving actions included those listed below:

Heating/cooling

- chose not to use the a/c
- chose opening windows for cooler air
- closed curtains earlier to keep warmth in
- did not use electric blanket
- chose wood fire instead of a/c
- was mindful in use of wood for fire
- chose ceiling fans to have cooler air
- used draught excluder to prevent cold air coming in
- closed curtains in the day to keep cooler

- chose extra blanket instead of fire or a/c
- used draught excluder to stop hot air coming in
- chose extra blanket instead of electric blanket
- chose ceiling fans to circulate warm air

Lighting

- turned off lights when not in a room
- used less lighting

Standby/recharging

- used green 'eco' switch by TV

Kitchen

- mindful use of gas cooktop/oven
- washed dishes in sink instead of dishwasher
- used gas kettle instead of electric
- only ran dishwasher when full
- selected dishwasher 'eco' setting
- opened window in kitchen instead of cooker fan
- showered less frequently during stay
- used water measuring jug for kettle

Bathroom

- chose not to use the bath
- used less hot water in the bath
- took fewer baths
- used the bathroom clock to time shower

Figure 7.3: Guest actions to reduce resource use

We also found that the My Green Butler Guests were more comfortable, i.e. being not as uncomfortable in winter with higher temperature inside, and likewise feeling cooler in summer. The use of natural ventilation helps them adapt to a temperature they personally preferred. We examined their inside temperatures records and found that the My Green Butler guests tolerated a 1 °C higher temperature in warmer seasons and 1°C lower in cooler seasons. By showing guests how to adapt, their overall experience was more comfortable (Warren et al., 2018).

Involving guests enhances the service

Directly involving your staff is the best way to show guests how to conserve. While hospitality increasingly favours using the internet, people still like to talk with other people. These shared moments of personal interaction are highly appreciated. That is why customer service is still the primary guest satisfaction measure (Chapter 3) that discerns a market leading property. The time spent with guests can lead to increased satisfaction, justifying a price premium above other commodified services.

In the last chapter I encouraged you to include staff as part of the new guest experience journey to conserve. They should be integrated within the holistic solution to make it easier for guests to save by showing them how.

When staff talk with guests they use Interpersonal Communications, which I consider one of the most effective methods to persuade people (Chapter 8). When offering practical advice it should be your primary method to help guests. This is because staff can moderate their delivery based on the type of guest and accommodation arrangement. They can adjust the way they explain using verbal or written information, or by showing guests. In other words, they can tailor their delivery to have a far greater level of success.

Excellent customer service is when a member of staff doesn't point the way to a hotel facility, but takes you to where you want to go. You feel special and looked after. The same principle applies to conserving. Showing guests how, means you will out-service your competitors whilst reducing wastage.

Case study: Reciprocating with tangible results when they know how

My Green Butler was introduced at a property in France with a large number of self-contained cabins. We ran an experiment where 16 cabins were offered My Green Butler. This entailed training the 32 staff to introduce the service to guests at check-in and persuading them to frequently use the service during their stay.

Our technology also include multiple levels of advice on how to operate the cabins using no or low carbon methods. A further eight cabins were monitored and were a control so that we could compare if our sustainability technology made a difference.

The results showed the My Green Butler guests achieved a 24% decrease in electricity and 15% decrease in water use (we also identified considerable saving opportunities that housekeeping and maintenance could apply).

Other pilot sites also achieved similar results and My Green Butler became the United Nations Environment Programme's sustainable tourism case study two years running (United Nations, 2019).

Guests will reciprocate when they receive specific advice and understand the consequences of their actions. They also need to be motivated, and if they know what happens to the savings, they know their co-operation is going to a worthwhile cause rather than corporate profits.

Cost-benefit analysis

Well before the COVID crisis, one hospitality role was already fast disappearing. Remember that pleasant and helpful well-dressed person who could be the first individual you came across at the property: Yes, whatever happened to bell boys? Now guests have luggage with wheels we've seen this as an opportunity to save… but having staff who welcome guests to their rooms can itself lead to savings. The welcome guests are given is a critical opportunity and one we should invest in.

However, events have played into the hands of technology. Hygiene regulations and health fears have led the industry to fast-track contactless alternatives to helpful staff, with 'guest-facing-tech' offering automated check-ins/checkout, activity suggestions, and cross-selling room service and spa services. These have been seen as both a labour-saving and profit-generating opportunity with a wide range of providers focusing on software technology replacing human contact (Hospitalitynet, 2020). However, what we require for sustainable hospitality is persuasive technology, which until recently was not available to managers.

Your staff should already be selling other hospitality services to guests, solving complex guest concerns, and helping to create a great stay experience that generates more positive reviews. This leads to higher occupancy that enables you to sell at a premium price.

From my experience, with adequate training, the same staff members can also provide advice to guests on how to conserve. This saves costs and cuts carbon. Staff are a fundamental communication channel for hospitality. If you are considering moving to a higher level of contactless guest solution, then it must replicate your excellent staff communications. It has to go beyond the binary steps of a simple digitised compendium or online transaction. It has to be persuasive to adapt guest behaviours and help you conserve.

7

If your bell boy/guest relations/service team can be trained to answer key questions and at the same time guide the guest to better-conserving behaviours, then this same level of persuasiveness must be transmittable through an advanced digital assistant, otherwise you weaken your interaction and can exacerbate wasteful behaviour.

Summary

It is essential to show your guests how to conserve. Frequently guests are unfamiliar with the accommodation they book, the local climate, and how things work at your property. This can lead to energy and water waste. To compound matters, every guest's party is unique in the way they know how to use heating/cooling systems, laundry, and kitchen appliances. They bring their habits from home and will use things in they way they understand, but that does not mean they know how to save.

If you have designed changes at your accommodation to be guest-centred then you must also introduce these new concepts to guests so they can comply with your goals.

Will guests be interested in learning new green skills? Research shows that people are interested in green innovations and like to try new things that appeal to them. But their personal awareness, cultural habits, and routines means we have to be flexible in the way we explain conserving skills.

What can help is to encourage guests to think 'slow'. That is to not automatically apply regular routines, but pause and consider an alternative approach. This requires concentration on the part of the guest as they apply a new skill – or refine an existing one. It is at this precise point that you affect the amount of resource a guest may use. The result is the guest learns to apply a new and more effective action, and saves.

Showing the guests how to conserve is part of the integrated social technology approach you will be developing. Staff are a core resource because they can share information with guests in various ways, modifying their approach to their guests' needs and attitudes. By working together, you will benefit from guest feedback, which will in turn allow you to refine and improve your approaches.

When and how to introduce skills are described in the following three chapters.

Next steps

1. Assess your guest types and where they have travelled from. Write this up
2. Monitor your resource use and compare with the guest profiles. Write this up
3. Review your workshop output (Chapter 6) and assess staff involvement. Can it be improved upon?
4. Review your job descriptions, roles and responsibilities. Consider how you need to evolve these so that staff can become motivated to play a greater role. How can your new experience design help you improve staff loyalty?

References

Ambrose, M. & James, M. (2014) *Natural Ventilation and Air Conditioning Use*. CSIRO, Australia

Andereck, K. (2009). Tourists' perceptions of environmentally responsible innovations at tourism businesses. *Journal of Sustainable Tourism*, 17(4), 489-499.

Axsen, J., TyreeHageman, J. & Lentz, A. (2012) Lifestyle practices and pro-environmental technology. *Ecological Economics*, 82, 64-74.

Bohner, G. & Schluter, L. (2014) A room with a Viewpoint revisited: Descriptive norms and hotel guests' towel reuse behaviour. *Plos One*, 9(8), 1-7

Delzendeh, E., Wu, S., Lee, A. & Zhou, Y. (2017) The impact of occupants' behaviours on buildings energy analysis. A research review. *Renewable and Sustainable Energy Reviews*, 80, 1061-1071

Eisen, D. (2017). We got 18 minutes with Bill Marriott. Here's what he said. *Hotel Management*, 2 June. www.hotelmanagement.net/development/bill-marriott-his-past-future-hospitality-and-wisest-choice-he-ever-made [Accessed 24th May 2021]

Sommet Education (2019). Top Trends in Hospitality for 2019, www.hotelnewsresource.com/pdf19/Sommet-Education-Top-Hospitality-Trends-2019.pdf.

Franke, N. & Shah, S. (2003) How communities support innovative activities: an exploration of assistance and sharing among end-user. *Research Policy*, 32, 157-178.

Gerdt, S., Wagner, E. & Schewe, G. (2019) The relationship between sustainability and customer satisfaction in hospitality: An explorative investigation using eWOM as a data source. *Tourism Management*, 74, 155-172

Goldstein, N. J., R. B. Cialdini, & V. Griskevicius. 2008. Room with a viewpoint: using social norms to motivate environmental conservation in hotels. *Journal of Consumer Research* 35 (3), 472–82.

Grazzini, L., Rodrigo, P., Aiello, G. & Viglia, G. (2018) Loss or gain? The role of message framing in hotel guests' recycling behaviour. *Journal of Sustainable Tourism*, 26(11), 1944-1966.

Hospitalitynet (2020). Special Series: Visioning a Post-COVID era in guest-facing tech. https://www.hospitalitynet.org/panel/125000071.html. [Assessed 23 may 2021]

Juvan, E., Grun, B. & Dolnicar, S. (2018) Biting off more than they can chew: Food waste at hotel breakfast buffets. *Journal of Travel Research*, 57(2), 232-242.

Mair, J. & Bergin-Seers, S. (2010) The effect of interventions on the environmental behaviour of Australian motel guests. *Tourism and Hospitality Research*, 10(4), 255-268.

Pantzar, M. & Shove, E. (2010) Understanding innovation in practice: a discussion of the production and reproduction of Nordic Walking. *Technology Analysis & Strategic Management*, 22(4), 447-461.

United Nations (2019) One Planet network 2019 Annual Magazine. Internet: https://www.one-planetnetwork.org/knowledge-centre/resources/one-planet-network-2019-annual-magazine

Wang, J. & Huang, K. (2013) Energy consumption characteristics of hotel's marketing preference for guests from regions perspective. *Energy*, 52, 173-184.

Warren, C. (2018) *Encouraging pro-environmental behaviour change at tourist accommodation*. Griffith University, Gold Coast, Queensland, Australia

Warren, C., Becken, S., Nguyen, K. & Stewart R. (2018) Transitioning to smart sustainable tourist accommodation: Service innovation results. *Journal of Cleaner Production*, 201, 599-608.

Weiss, A. & Straub, M. (2018). Sustainable experience: Innovative sustainable communication methods in the hotel industry. Best EN Think Tank XVII. The Institute of Tourism at Lucerne University of Applied Sciences and Arts.

7

8 Step 4: Interpersonal communication (Meaning)

Introduction

Earlier, we explored Materials used to save resources and the reasons why guests need to be shown Skills to conserve. Now in this chapter, I discuss Meaning, the third element that integrates with Materials and Skills. It considers the psychological factors involved in persuading guests to participate. Meaning is the essential element to master for businesses wishing to involve guests in resource conservation.

This chapter sets out how to persuade your guests to actively participate in conserving. This approach must be interwoven with your guest-centred designed experience (Chapter 6) so that you can make significant savings. Doing it right means increased guest satisfaction by exceeding expectations. It also means more positive reviews heralding your innovative hospitality. Is that not a breath of fresh air in a world full of commercial challenges?

Some hosts are sceptical about persuading guests, preferring to continue with the tangled web of materials. They fall back on unobtrusive signs and merely monitoring guests' consumption. This doesn't provide guests with know-how, nor does it persuade them. Monitoring results is not meaningful unless translated into tangible action. Your new design needs to be a purposeful, positive, core feature of the guest's stay. What you will discover from this chapter is that persuading guests is a joyful experience that delivers wide-reaching dividends.

This chapter is not a general review of what persuasion is, but a specific interpretation that can be applied in commercial service contexts like hospitality. It is based on my research conducted in several countries at different properties. You might think that this is all very well but in times of staffing issues and evolving accommodation services does not technology have a role here? Rest assured at the end of the chapter you will find a technology approach. Technology does have a role but it must be humanised if we are to maintain the thrust of offering hospitality rather than a mere service.

Some key points

- **Motivation is essential to sustainable hospitality.** For guests and staff to adjust their behaviours, they need to believe in the cause. Deliver sincere, sustained, thoughtful communication and your customers will reciprocate.

- **Don't force guests; persuade them.** No-one likes being bossed about at the best of time, let alone while on holiday. Recognise your guests as partners who are free to decide their own level of participation

- **Show integrity and credibility.** You and your staff must know your sustainability policies and house rules intimately if guests are to take them seriously. Don't just know the whats, but the whys too

- **Keep it personal.** When introducing guests to your sustainability practices, start with what affects them directly. Chemical-free bathroom products and locally sourced food makes it easier to get them onboard

- **Adjust to cultural contexts.** There is no one-size-fits-all approach to guest communication. Treat them as the individuals they are, adapting your messaging to their culture, background, and priorities

All this helps foster a culture of reciprocation, with staff and guests influencing each other to make the hospitality experience as delightful as possible. When properly nurtured, these relationships actually improve satisfaction, all while conserving resources and supporting the local community.

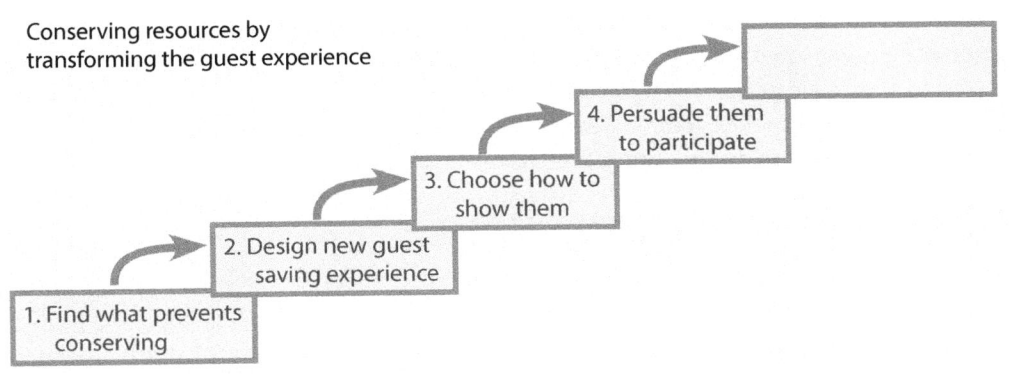

Figure 8.1: 5 Step Method to create transformational guest engagement

We must do better than 'guest engagement'

Many hospitality firms leave the role of eco-friendly persuasion to tent cards, signs, websites, and in-room tablet communication. They use messages inviting guests to help, often with bold statements of 'Saving the Planet' or broad requests to 'Help us save water'. These advertising approaches are far less persuasive. One-sided communication often backfires because it can appear superficial – an afterthought leaving guests and staff alike unconvinced, unable to relate, or dismissing the messages as greenwashing. (For contactless communication, I cover the best way to create written persuasive messages in the following chapters.)

Sustainability should be deeply embedded within the business. The request for guests to participate must be clearly and fundamentally integrated into the service experience. If you want to be convincing, you will need to offer a dialogue that persuades guests to participate. Simplistic messages can seem meaningless. To be persuasive, your communication must be meaningful.

Figure 8.2: You can provide evidence of your sustainability commitments. This is often of great interest to guests and persuasive. If you cannot afford the time, make sure guests can see and read this in their own time in their accommodation. Technology can replace this host-guest interaction provided it is humanised and you apply a multi-channel approach.

Beyond engagement to persuasion

Remember, we are asking guests to conserve by using less, cutting wastage or avoiding resource use. That may very well mean adapting their behaviour and breaking from routine actions. It should involve using your improved experience design. Text messages aren't enough to encourage the guest to reassess their efforts sufficiently.

Persuasion is a more sophisticated communication method than the one-way approach of advertising. It involves delivering messages to change attitudes in an atmosphere where guests and staff feel they are free to choose. You may use multiple communication contacts using verbal, non-verbal, visual, and written approaches. Persuasion influences how someone thinks through steps that change attitudes, which then lead to adapting or even changing behaviour. It is essential that people adopt of their own free will rather than being cajoled into complying.

Compliance makes people do things without necessarily changing attitudes. When guests complain of preachy messages, rules, and 'notices everywhere', it is likely because they feel a sense of enforcement, which paying customers react negatively to. This is also an internal challenge. When your green team sends out an information sheet explaining a new procedure, staff can simply perceive the change as more work.

What's required for successful persuasion

My research found three critical factors that make a host persuasive in the eyes of their guests and staff.

- First, you must be seen as credible and trustworthy in order to attain guests' goodwill (McCroskey & Teven, 1999), so they listen further and participate. This requires you to know your subject and be able to answer questions well. Involve all your staff in this. Train them so they can explain your environmental, social, and governance programmes and most relevant sustainability initiatives. This is a must, but sadly lacking at most properties as key staff are often in the dark. Instead they will say things like, "I'm not sure actually what we are doing beyond removing plastic water bottles for events and conferences, you will have to speak directly to the event team". Not very convincing.

- Second, treat each guest party as an individual. Be flexible in delivering your communication so it is genuinely relevant. For example, when a young family arrives, focus your delivery on the children. Increasingly, school children are learning about sustainability from an early age and recognise the importance of saving resources and not wasting them (reading water meters is now an activity in primary schools in New South Wales). This way, you turn the sharing of your sustainability programme into a fun and exciting service that will mean something to your guests.

- Third, recognise the context of your exchange with guests – which is first and foremost a commercial transaction – while always remaining polite. You can apply several different techniques to adapt your friendly manner to encourage guests.

Addressing these three factors can secure a high level (+80%) of guest commitment to conserving (Warren et al., 2017).

Story: Flexibility works to your advantage

Our policy is that when we meet with young families, we tend first to greet the kids, bending down to their height and saying, "Hi". When we do a tour of the accommodation, we direct the introduction presentation to the children and ask them direct questions. By getting the kids involved, you take the pressure off the parents who now don't need to keep the excited children quiet. By involving the kids, they then become your little helpers and, on occasion, remind the adults to conserve. This way, the children see applying new actions as a fun activity.

On one occasion, a father enthusiastically pointed out to me that his daughter had just made a video at school about sustainability. Then she explained it to me. Her dad was more than just proud of her; he wanted to demonstrate a sharing of values and convey his family's commitment. Had I just applied a standard hospitality check-in introduction, this scenario likely would not have occurred, and an opportunity would have been missed.

For those who can not afford the time to show guests around their accommodation, there are other ways to reach out. Disney theme park and hotel staff communicate with families to create a genuinely different experience (Kinni, 2011). Here they actually have special stairs for children to climb up and talk directly to the concierge team or join mum and dad during the check-in. They are treated equally, if not specially. The aim at a Disneyland accommodation stay is like another of their theme park rides: for the staff to tell a story that sprinkles magic on the experience. The 'cast' adjust their delivery to their audience. They do this on a massive scale, daily, around the world. Being flexible will help you to build a bond with your customer and becomes an advantage in persuasion.

Making the message meaningful

Meanings are the values we hold for habits, routines, or special activities. Meanings can cover the humdrum of brushing teeth to the intricacies and excitement of organising a wedding proposal.

Meanings give us the reasons why we do things in our particular way, how often we do them, and their level of importance. How we feel about the environment can be very high. How we feel about our personal health can be higher still. COVID has shown that people became concerned about both their health and the environment (Latham, 2021). Thus, Meanings are fixed with the way we consume. To encourage more sustainable consumption, our messages should be targeting meanings that have a direct personal link rather than broad aspirations.

Meanings can change priorities. Once a glass of tap water was an accepted beverage. Today consumers prefer to trust bottled water (Doria, 2006) because of health fears and perceptions of bad flavour (Harvey et al., 2016; Scherzeret al.,

2020) even though bottled water has environmental impacts. A person's health can come before the planet's environment.

We, therefore, need to frame such paradoxes differently to reduce environmental impacts. It is the person's health that is the main driver. If you frame your sustainability practices by first acknowledging your guest's health, like using zero chemicals in bathroom cleaning, then it becomes easier to persuade guests to consider saving water. Because you have directly empathised with the importance of their needs first, you can then share your policy of saving water (house rules) and ask them to reciprocate (more on this below).

Similarly, guests might like great healthy food. You can link this driver to your decision to remove single-use-plastic, which helps reduce microscope plastic fibres entering the food chain. This can again be evidence to persuade guests to take other prescribed responsible action. You are transferring the meaningfulness of one key driver to influence another desired behaviour.

Insight: Cultural context

Meaningful messages can be presented differently to different cultures. The examples in this book tend to focus on Western culture, which leans on the individualist side. There are, however, many societies where collectivism is a stronger value. This is important if you are appealing to a member of staff or guests' altruistic motivations. In a Western country, they can be more about self, people, and plant, in that order, whereas in Asian countries, for example, the appeal can be focused on the wider population or community first, as self is viewed according to Singles *et al.* "as part of the collective" (Munroe, 2017). In some cultures, people have a oneness with their community leading to a higher level of altruism, so your communication should be directed to appeal to that sense of oneness.

In collectivist societies, research indicates that it is better to focus messages on self-efficacy (information that helps people understand what to do, when and how, building their capabilities to apply the action) rather than talking about attitudes to encourage more sustainable behaviours. Persuasion is even more effective when self-actualisation messaging is coupled with altruistic society gains of taking pro-sustainability behaviour, as opposed to the individualistic Western messaging approach (Shahzalal & Font, 2017).

When living in the Middle East, I have witnessed people's strong sense of moral responsibility and collective behaviour through religious festivals like Ramandam, where giving (*zakat*) is a key pillar of Islam. Communities will sit together and celebrate as one, breaking their fasting (*iftar*) at sunset after many hours, often during high temperatures — repeating this daily for a month. It is an example of how humans can change behaviour from 'normal' everyday life and, in so doing, gain a solid spiritual benefit. Successful persuasive communication is therefore strongly influenced by cultural context.

8

Creating successful partnerships

Using action research, I found that applying a set series of persuasive steps saw the host-guest relationship evolve into a successful partnership that saved considerable resources. Not only that, but as the relationship evolved, a greater level of trust was reached, and guest satisfaction rose. Discussing the findings with Professor Susanne Becken and Associate Professor Alexandra Coghlan, colleagues from Griffith University, led to mapping the changing nature of the host and guest relationship whilst staff deliberately applied persuasion. This I've called Spiralling Influence and is shown in Figure 8.2.

Generally, many hospitality staff go through 'procedures' communicating a commercial transaction, informing guests about services, answering queries or resolving maintenance requests. The dialogue is often seen by staff and managers as linear, maintained at a similar level of connection between the customer and the service provider.

However, when you show staff that the guest relationship can and does evolve, they recognise opportunities to persuade at different stages in that relationship. Reflecting on this evolution can help you and your staff be more confident in delivering persuasive messaging to guests. Making your communication meaningful and sustained, building over the duration of the guest stay, can increase guests' efforts to adapt their behaviour to save.

Each successive step reinforces the previous persuasive encounter. It convinces guests that the host is serious about conserving. We found that guests are willing to apply new shared Skills, and they can enjoy the process in a game-like manner. Our research showed feedback stimulates guests to self-improve by altering the meaning of their consumption (which was verified using our mixed methods research design). In other words, guests changed priorities, and therefore the Meaning of using energy or water changed for them. None of this took away from their overall holiday experience. In fact, it added to it, as I explain in Chapter 10.

The Spiralling Influence that sustains conservation

Figure 8.3 captures the concept of Spiralling Influence in a hospitality context. Read the chart from bottom to top. On the left, the host applies a series of sequential influencing steps. On the right, the guests' mood changes over time. The combination of your involved steps and the guests' mood creates a transition for each phase.

I will now explain these phases. Further details of the results and the repercussions for a business are given in our papers in the *Journal of Sustainable Tourism* (Warren et al., 2017, 2018). The next chapter describes proprietary persuasive techniques used as part of the My Green Butler service.

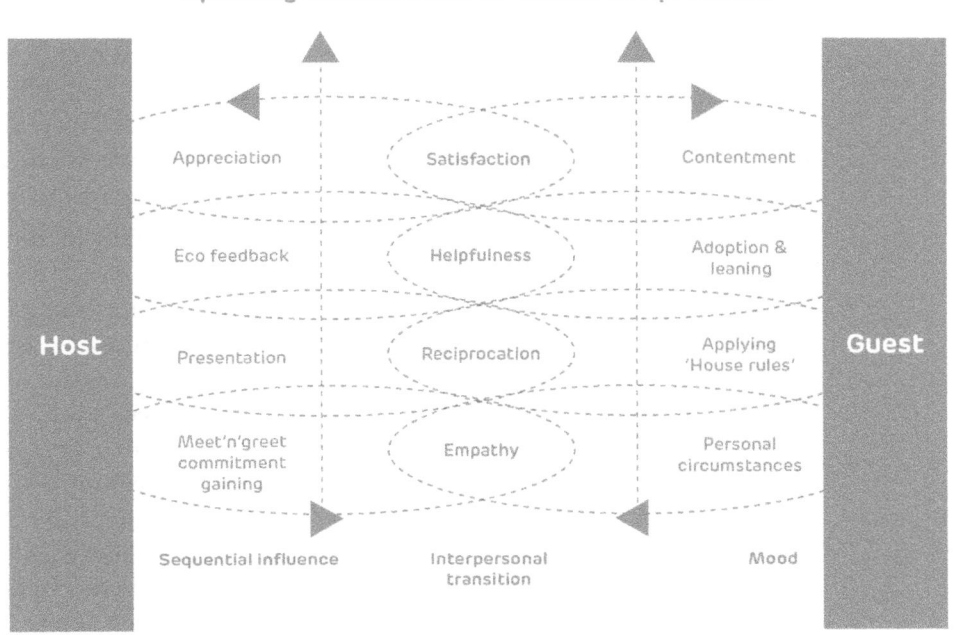

Figure 8.3: How host – guest interpersonal communication builds over the stay duration. Source: Warren et al., 2018.

The diagram illustrates four interpersonal transitions during the course of a guest's stay:

- **Empathy**: From check-in, the host uses empathy to reassure the guest that they have bought a quality service that will meet their expectations. The aim is to put the guest at ease, understanding their personal arrival circumstances. The guests might be tired from their journey or excited to begin their holiday. If applied correctly, the guest should be more at ease. There are a number of techniques (discussed in the next chapter) to reassure the guest at this point and permit you to politely move to a new step the guests will not have experienced before.

- **Reciprocation**: The host addresses primary guest concerns (health, nutrition, comfort, etc.) first and then explains sustainability aims and policies, inviting the guest to participate of their own free will. To be persuasive, the host should convey credibility and trust. If you demonstrate ways to conserve, it shows expertise. It also increases guests' commitment to participate when they learn new skills. Guests, in turn, interpret the policies as quality standards, meaning you are credible. Your invitation to participate are seen as 'house rules', a tradition within the broader concept of hospitality for which they become more likely to commit.

- **Helpfulness:** Offering feedback enables guests to see their results from adopting your recommended actions and learn. Providing regular feedback reconfirms your integrity to guests, ensuring information is taken as helpful advice. Here you must be careful not to cross boundaries of privacy or spotlight a person's inability to operate your systems well. It is our responsibility to enable guests to apply conserving behaviours easily. Special attention should be given to those with physical or mental disadvantages, pregnancy, old age, newly born infants, or terminally ill. They appreciate that extra level of care and respond positively.

- **Satisfaction:** As the relationship spirals upwards, your ability to persuade increases. Your demonstrations and eco-feedback build trust as guests see and feel the difference from your advice. Guests' experiences are heightened when they see the positive results. Often, they are keen to share their success, which increases their satisfaction. Importantly, this emotionally rewards you and your staff. Guest appreciation of your experience sustains staff motivation to share it; it becomes a self-sustaining cycle. The changes in your experience design can be used to pinpoint moments that will delight the guest, e.g. remove plastic single service items and create fun, attractive alternatives that convey a more homemade and personalised delivery.

There is a sound business case

The more we retract from actual guest interaction with staff, the harder it becomes to boost commercial performance. If your business model is to provide hospitality, then you need opportunities to interact, so you can upsell, cross-promote, encourage an extended stay, and most of all ensure that the experience is optimal. All these things ensure guest satisfaction and return visits. They also affect the bottom line.

The bottom line is your bottom line. Staff are there to make an immediate difference. The size of your payroll is not as important as how your payroll is well integrated into delivering profit. If you do not recognise Spiralling Influence, this could be the reason you view cutting payroll costs as necessary, because revenues per guest are not as substantial as they should be for you to deliver a quality product. This is an economic sustainability argument.

To attract good staff and keep them, they need to be given opportunities to make a difference. Offer access to career progression through scaled training, and encourage them to view the importance of their role in generating change within their environment and community. They are not order-takers or merely cleaning a room; they are setting the stage for an outstanding guest stay experience. That is our profession. Even if you run a 1,000-room resort, the guest is an individual, We must integrate staff and technology solutions to ensure guests are treated like the individuals they are and not part of a 'factory' experience.

Guests keep quiet if they are not completely happy with their stay experience. It can be "too much hassle" to keep contacting staff to fix problems. Many problems exist because guests are unfamiliar with the workings of your systems. They are not warm enough, cool enough, able to find what they want. Don't let these gaps exist; they waste resources, cost you money, and lose you business.

The status quo is always thought the easier option. But consider your 'pains' running the business now: the need to keep great staff, retain customers, boost business performance, and significantly cut carbon. If you do not engage your staff and guests, if you do not synchronise their behaviours to conserve, if you do not maximise the use of your improved, more sustainable guest experience, then you will continue to leak cost and still have to work uphill to maximise demand and revenue. You already have to retrain staff and casuals, why not introduce in this training ways that maximise the guest relationship?

Adjust to the length of guest stay

I recognise that you might think the concept is too complex for your business and time consuming for your staff. Or you might feel it is hard to see if there are worthwhile cost savings. Or that your guests don't have time and are in a rush to get to their room. But let me reassure you, Spiralling Influence at different degrees is what occurs naturally at your property. You can make adjustments for the accommodation service and guest profile you offer.

The length of time a guest stays with you presents different communication opportunities. Solve this by providing a holistic approach to your persuasive communication; guests learn of your commitments and receive an invitation to join from the moment they book and throughout their stay. At every touchpoint, your message should interest, entice, inform, and persuade. Tech can play a part here, but it should be humanised rather than cold displays on a tablet besides the bed. It should be part of the brand character and stay experience to be novel and enjoyable.

Sometimes guests who have worked hard all day and want to get to their room quickly think the check-in will be just the same old process they have done a hundred times. Work with that, surprise them with a different approach, feed information in easy steps.

Equally, if you have long-staying guests, then you can build strong relationships using less tech. You have time to focus on host-guest interaction at all staff levels where greater trust and relaxed conversation can flourish. By better understanding the phenomenon of Spiralling Influence, you can introduce service innovations that improve productivity.

If you are applying an autominous system, then from a technology perspective you can see that many systems do not permit the evolution of the relationship. It is the same level of communication throughout the user experience. This is a

8

weakness, because in persuasion there are usually multiple steps and the free-will choice made by the guests. With My Green Butler we evolve the relationship just as you would find in 'real life'.

You are maximising what should already exist

As Spiralling Influence is naturally occurring, it isn't too complex for the business or staff. We just need to recognise it more clearly. You might already be carefully measuring and monitoring resources, but can you see those saving potentials that easily? To recognise them, you have to take apart what is already assumed to be 'normal'. Likewise, guests make time for things that have meaning to them such as advice on how to be more comfortable in their room, to learning about the carbon footprint of items on your menu.

If you want to improve your guest satisfaction and cut resource use, design service delivery around the concept of Spiralling Influence. Use the flourishing relationship you create to your and your guests' benefit. Identify moments and interactions where your sustainable hospitality solutions can delight guests. It is by delighting the guest that the business can justify a premium price in its category and avoid the commodification of the marketplace.

I have used this framework to introduce multiple persuasive communication steps at both large and small firms. Despite them being very different types of accommodation, they share common qualities. They are all commercially sound enterprises, leaders in their field who can see the marketing benefits. They recognise more must be done to cut carbon and save water and want to take responsibility. And most interestingly, they all pride themselves on providing quality customer service. The Meaning for these firms is that they clearly see how they can create happier guest stays that exceed expectations. This then boosts demand and revenues.

Pre-suasion and pre-giving

Importantly, interpersonal persuasion should include what you do before you make a request, pre-suasion (Caildini, 2016). This means setting a sequence of multiple steps (Perloff, 2010) that make the guest more receptive to your invitation to conserve resources, by extending good hospitality from the word go, before and during check-in and before they reach their room. One such technique is pre-giving – providing a gift followed by requesting their participation (Gass & Seiter, 2014). The pre-giving approach encourages the guests or staff to comply with your request by stimulating positive emotions like gratitude for the favour or a desire to reciprocate and repay the host (Burger et al., 2009). In our context of tourist accommodation it is an established practice for hosts to use initial guest contact to convey the House Rules (McIntosh et al., 2010) within the exchange. This is when pre-giving like "breaking the ice" can stimulate the guests' commitment (Gueguen et al., 2013), for example, through light physical touch such as shaking hands (Hornik, 1992) or smiling (Vrugt, & Vet, 2009).

You can also consider asking guests to sign a voluntary commitment, which has been shown to be a compelling way of increasing participation (Baca-Motes et al., 2013; Joule et al., 2008). I did this for 16 months with every guest party and found that putting the proposal to them after I have won their trust became a pivotal moment. It is not essential, but if you run a business in a world heritage conservation area, ecolodge or in a rural region where tourism can be a strong focus for good, and you can demonstrate this, commitment gaining could well enhance outcomes. I only had three refusals. One of those was from a man I later found out was testing me because he did not believe we were seriously going to offer a greener experience. But because we had designed a greener experience, he quickly was convinced and commented how impressed he was. He wrote a great review, so you should not make assumptions.

Example: You open the door to your accommodation and are greeted with this afternoon tea of home made scones and jam. The display exceeds the guest's expectations, not because it is grand, but because it is authentic and generous with personal touches like cakes for kids. It is a guest benefit straight away. It is pre-suasion as it signals "your needs come first", and it is now not hard to invite them to participate in conserving. Cost $15, paid by the customer, yet this simple feature ranked one of the highest features of guest review satisfaction…along with their appreciation of our eco-friendly tips.

Message approach

Pre-giving is an extremely valuable tool to help you achieve strong guest participation. You and your guests have already entered into a commercial exchange. By designing the guest experience well, you can introduce tactical service delivery features from before and during arrival that puts them at ease and places your invitation to conserve into a context that guests can appreciate and consider. Guests are more likely to accept your invitation to conserve if you have made them feel comfortable and trust you.

As an opener, to focus the mind of the guest and enable me to introduce a more persuasive appeal, I would use this introduction line when showing them to their accommodation: *"Have you ever stayed in an eco-friendly cottage before?"* While this was successful in focusing their attention, it did make most look surprised because they had not. A few did tell me they had, to which I would respond, *"excellent; then you will know the reasons why we have designed this experience in a particular way…."*

But, I could have done even better if I had started by sharing values and achieving what I call the 'nodding factor", saying something that people would agree with so they were more likely to agree with the real essence of my conversation-conserving. What I should have said was: *"I know we are all concerned about the environment these days, and none of us likes to be wasteful; that is why we have created this more comfortable eco-friendly experience for you."* When I applied this approach I got nods of agreement, smiles and interest, not doubts.

Very few people would want to think of themselves as wasteful, and today few people will want to believe they are unfriendly to the environment. Whether they are or not is another point. Most people do not know their footprint or their negative impacts exactly. But we like to think of ourselves as good citizens and want to comply with reasonable suggestions that do less harm and, in fact, in the case of using My Green Butler, can deliver positive environmental and social benefits.

Before introducing your new, greener guest experience, set the stage by focusing the guests' minds on what is essential to you. Then emphasis the benefits to them. I always stress their greater comfort. You could choose a different guest benefit depending on what experience you have designed. If your staff set the stage with a well-crafted opener, the guest will be focused on the subject about which you want to persuade them. So rather than talking about the amenities and where everything is on the property, with the guests trying to remember and contain their excitement about their stay, reframe these features into a sustainability message they can agree on and then entice them with a better experience message.

Recipe for success

From the advice above and the next chapters, you will find ingredients to create a recipe for delivering effective interpersonal communications. Remember there is not just one feature or strategy alone that will convince guests and staff to conserve more to consume less. It must be an orchestrated flow that not only persuades guests to participate but maintains their motivation and turns them into loyal customers who will refer your business – the most potent form of selling. You will find these tactics come together as a recipe for success. An example can be found in the My Green Butler website (www.mygreenbutler.com/resources). Use it to formulate your own unique recipe for successs, persuading guests and staff to help your business become more sustainable.

A technology case example

Can technology replace interpersonal communication when you have low staff levels or low guest-to-host contact? As the name implies My Green Butler provides guests with a fun interactive service when hosts are not available or you want to provide a deeper level of sustainability storytelling.

Despite the majority of tourists (85%) wanting to go on vacation to 'get away from it all', 92.5% feel compelled to bring their mobile phones, and 55.5% check their phones up to five times an hour (Turner, 2022). COVID-19 has led to the rise of online check-in, digital documents, and re-emergence of QR codes – we are ever more willing to use new services and tools on mobile devices. This presents hospitality with an exceptionally widespread medium to communicate and engage guests with. Technology has given hospitality the means to make informative, gamified, live services which are customisable and familiar to guests (Souza et al., 2020).

My Green Butler uses a variety of elements to help motivate guests to continuously take sustainability actions throughout their stay. Extrinsic motivators are used alongside the 'RAMP' framework, which targets key needs on Maslow's Hierarchy of Relatedness, Autonomy, Mastery, and Purpose (Marczewski, 2013). In this way the guest becomes 'king' of their sustainability contribution. These four areas are incredibly powerful at engaging people for long durations of time, focusing on psychological needs and satisfaction, unlike extrinsic prizes – which if unsupported by deeper motivations are short lived and can make the user lose interest (Marczewski, 2018).

With My Green Butler, gamification is present throughout the guest's experience, targeting different needs. Gamification in this context means the use of game-like elements and principles used in a non-game situation to motivate individuals to adjust behaviours and become self motivated to achieve goals (Walter, 2022).

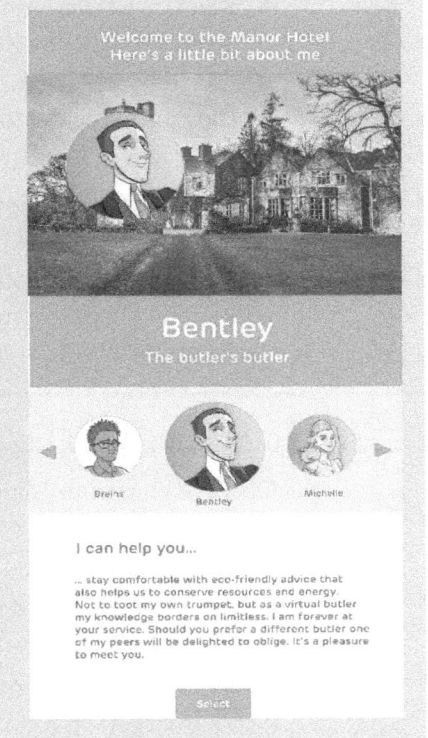

Using the bulter theme helps the experience stand out and feel more enjoyable. Social elements help guests feel relatable and part of a community of engaged and eco-conscious guests, and also provides a score from the most resource saving guest to compare to. Choice is given to guests in the form of lists of personalised itineraries they can select from, or their choice of butler companion throughout their stay – both helping deliver a sense of autonomy and personalisation. Targets and goals provide a sense of challenge, intrinsically and extrinsically motivating users to save resources. Extrinsic rewards include badges, freebies, and tips on how to be comfortable; and a sense of mastery and accomplishment forms part of the intrinsic motivation.

Guests communciate with a humanised social system that advises them on ways to keep comfortable with personalised feedback that extends the concept of hospitality.

Summary

Guests must make their own free-will decision to support your conservation requests. Your job is not to compel, but persuade. Delivering the right message at the right time means you should understand the spiralling relationship between host and guest. To achieve significant savings, you must go further than 'guest engagement'; you want guests to actively participate. By giving your team quality training, they can apply persuasive communications approaches and other multiple channels to influence how guests behave of their own free will.

Show guests how to save, and you move things still further forward. Guests will reciprocate provided you have shown them empathy, the firm is credible in asking guests, you have sufficient expertise in helping them conserve, and the result is used effectively.

The Spiralling Influence Model builds relationships with guests. You may currently apply many of these steps or leave some to technology. Make sure you have covered them all if you want to maximise your persuasive communication and achieve outstanding results. Each stage has a purpose, and through my research, I've found them to be highly effective when applied in combination.

These steps are:

- Meet 'n' Greet your guests to seek their commitment to participate in your sustainability programme
- Present your efforts to improve the guest experience, show them how they can conserve. Tell them what you and your staff do too.
- Provide eco-feedback on progress
- Thank them for their stay and enjoy their positive feedback, which will self-sustain your staff to continue the process

Technology can be a substitute or enhancement to the interpersonal communications, but it must be humanised, evolve the conversation during the guest stay and can use gamification to stimulate guests' motivation to achieve desired outcomes.

Next steps

1. Observe your guest's journey from booking to departure against the Spiralling Influence steps to see where there are opportunities to integrate. Write this up.

2. Consider your workshop output for a new guest experience design (Chapter 6) and consider where you will be able to tell your back story about what the firm is doing. How can guests see this? Write them up.

3. Collect all your current staff training on guest engagement and integrate the use of interpersonal communications.

References

Baca-Motes, K., Brown, A., Gneezy, A., Keenan, E., & Nelson, L. (2013). Commitment and behaviour change: Evidence from the field. *Journal of Consumer Research*, 39(5), 1070–1084.

Burger, J., Sanchez, J., Imberi, J., & Grande, L. (2009). The norm of reciprocity as an internalized social norm: Returning favors even when no one finds out. *Social Influence*, 4(1), 11–17.

Caildini, R. (2016) *Pre-suasion. A revolutionary way to influence and persuade*. Penguin, London.

Doria, M. (2006). Bottled water versus tap water: understanding consumer' preferences. *Journal of Water and Health*, 4(2), 271-276

Gass, R., & Seiter, S. (2014). *Persuasion: Social influence and compliance gaining* (Vol. 5). Abingdon: Routledge.

Gueguen, N., Joule, R., Halimi-Falkowicz, S., Pascual, A., Fischer-Lokou, J., & Dufourcq-Brana, M. (2013). I'm free but I'll comply with your request: Generalization and multidimensional effects of the "evoking freedom" technique. *Journal of Applied Social Psychology*, 43, 116–137.

Harvey, P., Handley, H. & Tayulor, M. (2016). Widespread copper and lead contamination of household drinking water, New South Wales, Australia. *Environmental Research*, 151, 272-285.

Hornik, J. (1992). Tactile stimulation and consumer response. *Journal of Consumer Research*, 19(3), 449–458.

Joule, R., Bernard, F., & Halimi-Falkowicz, S. (2008). Promoting ecocitizenship: In favour of binding communications. *International Scientific Journal for Alternative Energy and Ecology*, 6(62), 214–218.

Kinni, T. (2011). *Be our guest. Perfecting the art of customer service*. Disney Institute, California.

Latham, K. (2021). Has coronavirus made us more ethical consumers? BBC News, 14 January. / www.bbc.com/news/business-55630144 [Accessed 17 July 2021]

Marczewski, A. (2013). Understanding Intrinsic Motivation with RAMP. www.gamification. co/2013/05/01/understanding-intrinsic-motivation-with-ramp/ [Accessed 31st May 2022].

Marczewski, A. (2018). *Even Ninja Monkeys Like to Play: Unicorn Edition*. Gamified UK. Pg. 77

McCroskey, J. & Teven, J. (1999). Goodwill: a reexamination of the construct and its measurement. *Communication Monographs*, 66(1), 90-103

McIntosh, A., Lynch, P. & Sweeney, M. (2010). "My Home Is My Castle": Defiance of the commercial homestay host in tourism. *Journal of Travel Research*, 50(5), 509–519.

Munroe, R. (2017). Altruism and Collectivism: An exploratory study in four cultures. *Cross-Cultural Research*, 52(3), 334-345, p240

Perloff, R. (2010). *The Dynamics of Persuasion* (Vol. 4). New York, NY: Routledge.

Scherzer, T., Barker, J., Pollick, H. & Weintraub, J. (2020). Water consumption beliefs and practices in a rural Latino community: Implications for fluoridation. *Journal of Public Health Dentistry*, 70(4), 337-343

Shahzalal, M & Font, X. (2017). Influencing altruistic tourist behaviour: Persuasive communication to affect attitudes and self-efficacy beliefs. *International Journal of Tourism Research*, 20(3), 326-334

Souza, V., Marques, S. & Verissimo, M. (2020). How can gamification contribute to achieve SDG's? *Journal of Hospitality and Tourism Technology*, 11(2), 255-276.

8

Turner, A. (2022). Digital detox on vacation: Tourists aren't ready to unplug their Android and IOS smartphones. https://www.bankmycell.com/blog/digital-detox-phone-use-on-vacation

Vrugt, A., & Vet, C. (2009). Effects of a smile on mood and helping behaviour. *Social Behaviour and Personality*, 37(9), 1251–1258.

Walter, Z. (2022). What is gamification? Gamify. www.gamify.com/what-is-gamification [Accessed 8 October 2022]

Warren, C., Becken, S. & Coghlan, A. (2017). Using persuasive communication to co-create behavioural change – engaging with guests to save resources at tourist accommodation facilities. *Journal of Sustainable Tourism*, 25(7), 935-954

Warren, C., Becken, S. & Coghlan, A. (2018). Sustainability-oriented service innovation: Fourteen-year longitudinal case study of a tourist accommodation provider. *Journal of Sustainable Tourism*, 26 (10), 1784-1803

9 Step 4: Persuasion (Meaning)

Introduction

How is it that some tourist accommodations are able to persuade guests to happily participate in their responsible tourism actions while other properties are not? Messages on their own do not always deliver the response you want, right? Often this is because we fail to recognise the importance of interpersonal persuasion. This could be by ignoring pre-suasion (gaining staff and guest support before requesting a specific action), or allowing a mismatch between messaging directed at guests and the reality they perceive in business operations and management. All these factors have to be aligned.

Managers have asked me, is it the type of accommodation that matters or is it the type of guests? If your accommodation has no contact with guests, then the relationship can be purely an economic transaction. People also behave differently due to cultural reasons, or acclimatisation where it is a business or leisure-based property. So how can you maximise your persuasive potential despite these factors so that they do not hinder you, but actively support your sustainability initiatives?

This chapter covers three golden features of interpersonal communication that make it the most powerful form of persuasion in hospitality. Interpersonal communication can encourage guests to choose of their own free will to behave in ways that support your sustainability programme.

- **Apply Politeness.** Politeness is a skill that can and should be developed. Being courteous and empathetic with your guests, yet also knowing when to be serious, gives your green initiatives a much better chance of being embraced.
- **Leverage 'House Rules'.** Even in hospitality, there is an understanding that the host's way of doing things deserve respect. Share your green behaviour rules expertly and with pride, showing guests that you live by them too.

- ■ **Maximise reciprocity**. It is human nature to want to return a favour. Go the extra mile for your guests and they will meet you halfway, respecting your House Rules and trying out new ways of behaving.

By using interpersonal persuasion, you can introduce your requests in ways that encourage positive responses. It can help you direct the guest's consciousness to make better decisions for their holiday, the environment and the community.

Why move from a purely commercial exchange to one of reciprocation exchange? You can encourage guests and staff, for that matter, to recognise the wisdom of making that decision to participate.

Communication must integrate with the *Materials*, the accommodation, amenities, and facilities, and the *Competency*, the guidance guests are given on how to save. Without creating a service experience that is greener you cannot expect your guests to act more responsibly.

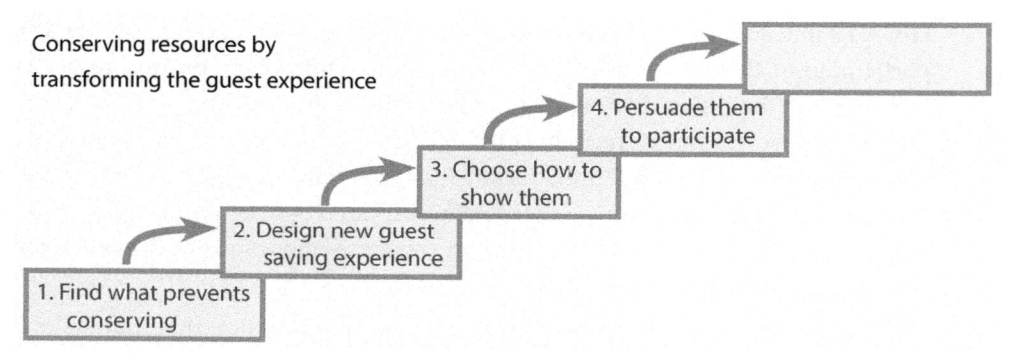

Figure 9.1: 5 Step Method to create transformational guest engagement

Down to details

1. Applying politeness

Guests should be greeted with empathy. Knowing how to apply the right touch of politeness to handle a situation is a valuable skill that enhances persuasion. It is the way the steward asks you if another passenger could swap seats, or sales assistant tells you they don't have that specific model you requested, or at the accommodation reception desk the guest relations manager explains your original choice of apartment is not available, but they have an alternative which is a better match for your needs.

There's a science to politeness, and if mastered well it can add to your persuasive communications. It is more than being subservient or simply smiling. You want to use politeness to encourage people to adapt their behaviours and use facilities that may be new to them. You want to use it to manage their responses and guide them to apply System 2 slow thinking to adopt what you have said.

Politeness tactics are an essential first step to persuading guests to commit to your sustainability programme.

How to manage guests through politeness

Politeness theory is a rich cultural field with strong links to hospitality services. Politeness is demonstrated through our facial expressions, language, and actions. Studies found we each have two 'faces'. There is the positive face – when we want to be socially accepted. Then there is our negative face – when we want the freedom to assess and make up our own mind. (Brown & Levinson, 1987)

| Guests displaying negative face – this can mean they are assessing what the staff member is explaining. It does not mean they are rejecting their approach. | Guests displaying positive face – this can mean they are not accepting the staff members' suggestions but smile to defuse any embarrassment or conflict. |

Figure 9.2: Taking responsibility for the impacts of your holiday is a new social interaction. Do not be surprised if guests keep a straight 'negative' face. Likewise, smiling guests do not signify that they have accepted and will comply with your requests. Smiling is sometimes used to defuse social tensions.

Staff apply the positive face when guests arrive and are welcomed, which is to be expected. But are staff trained to better interpret facial expressions of the guests? When you deliver your sustainability communication, guests most often show a negative face. That is keeping a straight face with no expression. This does not mean they are rejecting your proposal. Far from it. This is when they are assessing what you are saying and considering it. If staff do not recognise this they can feel hesitant, as we are often taught something is wrong when people do not smile.

Staff can use the negative face too. If they communicate solely using their positive face then guests may interpret it as insincerity, i.e. you are simply going through the process and there is no real meaning. Smiling does not emphasise the importance of what you are saying. If you smile it can suggest that you are not convinced by the sustainability message yourself. If you are not convinced, why should guests be? Instead staff can at the right times use a negative face to explain your programme if you want guests to take the information seriously.

9

I have often used a negative face in front of a larger guest party where some are getting a little too excited about our programme and risk trivialising the topic. If I smiled with them then it might weaken perceptions of how serious we are about cutting resources and conserving nature. This would undermine my persuasiveness and consequently reduce their commitment.

Train your staff to apply both positive and negative face (My Green Butler, n.d).

Polite language

How we express a persuasive message shows how perceptive we are about the conversation's context. If we do not pitch our message correctly it can be taken the wrong way and backfire. Fear can make a manager believe their staff cannot approach guests and ask them to save resources, but it is actually all the more reason to train them to apply the right types of politeness. Doing so has wide customer service benefits.

Something we instinctively know but seldom discuss is that there are also two forms of language politeness. Positive politeness is used when we cannot say what we want, and a friendly approach is applied:

"It also took me forever to figure out how to use this shower effectively, but I eventually found the secret by..."

"We really appreciate the way the community is saving water so at the hotel we've worked hard to improve things here..."

Negative politeness is a more formal approach and can be used by hosts to not appear to coerce the guests. If your guests have shown only formal negative face and are keeping a distance then one should recognise that they are still assessing and do not want to feel they are being forced to comply. As we want to persuade guests, it is their free will decision to support us, not the hospitality provider trying to enforce a policy. You are not going to convince everyone, and nor should you try. In these situations, you want to convey to guests that you are merely making a request and they can choose to ignore it:

"It's a small thing to ask but if possible could you..."

Or claim 'common ground':

"I realise this air conditioning control panel is complicated at first to understand well, let me show you how to get the best results...."

Or you can convey that your request is normal, and the consensus from guests has been to support it.

"It's generally done this way by most of our guests..."

These subtleties demonstrate why a standard script for staff has flaws. They need to be professionally guided to express positive and negative politeness through language.

Broaden your staff's politeness skills

Hosts should be able to apply both positive and negative politeness using facial expressions and language. This requires training. It should be designed to elevate your customer service standards beyond the regular meet'n'greet or handling complaints scenarios, to a more advanced delivery of using specific hotel brand language. Politeness techniques should be introduced to have wider reaching benefits across all host-guest interaction.

Training should include ways to ensure that guests do not feel embarrassed or humiliated, which is a significant social concern in many countries. To avoid guests 'losing face' staff need to be trained in adjusting their delivery. For example:

1. The staff's verbal interaction must not be construed as a directive; they can use positive face and positive language to invite guests to try something different as part of the fun holiday experience.

2. When interacting with guests, staff have a clearly defined role as 'host' with a clear level of perceived authority using a predefined title.

3. Staff should demonstrate they are fully aware of the guest's stay details so feel welcome and not as a stranger.

4. Don't discuss matters which would be seen as inappropriate, such as personal hygiene.

When shown empathy from the time of their arrival, guests are considerably less likely to feel threatened and are more likely to comply with your requests.

Conversely, the greater the level of automation or absence of hosts in peer to peer accommodation, the less staff contact. This leads to lower ability to apply politeness and an increased reliance on signs, which reduce persuasion. If you are applying a high level of contactless guest interaction, then there are alternative solutions, including video. We are now all familiar with contactless travel check-ins, but they can still provide warm engagement rather than cold functionality. This has been our most recent area of innovation at My Green Butler. Game-like features build a relationship using politeness in a similar way to human interaction.

Everyone likes to fit in

A further strategy is to apply *social norms* – accepted ways of behaviour in society. They can suggest what is perceived to be the regular way most people behave in a given situation. You can talk about the way most guests choose to behave at your property. for example:

> *"80% of our guests have tried using our waterless shower* and highly rated the experience…"*

* The waterless shower is actually a real invention! https://drybathgel.com/

No longer active

9

You might be operating in a country with strong religious or cultural traditions. In such situations, and where appropriate, you can refer to the country's heritage as a way to support your approach

> *"Water is precious and sacred in our culture, we have always celebrated it through water saving inventions. Why not try the innovation of this a waterless shower?"*

You don't want to raise feelings of guilt, so it is important to not overstress your point. How far you should go depends on your culture and how engaging your story is, but you always want to extend the offer of warm hospitality.

Remember, guests have free will to choose. You are simply making available to your guests alternative ways of staying at your accommodation, and informing them that the majority of guests approve and enjoy this experience.

A host who understands the guest party will seek to frame the technical resource message in a way that guests value.

> *"Winter is here and you want a lovely warm apartment, that is why we recommend closing the curtains early - around 4:30 pm - to keep the cold air out, then turning on your ceiling fan when you turn the heater on to medium only, as our guests tell us this way you circulate the warmth faster using less energy."*

And here's a more extreme invitation, perhaps for desert eco-lodges:

> *"I realise you have travelled a long way and have a busy schedule, so I recommend our new waterless shower, it saves time, and our guests tell us its eucalyptus scent invigorates the mind..."*

Everyone likes to fit in, even by wanting to be seen to comply with new trends (Chapter 9).

2. Leveraging 'House Rules'

What are 'House Rules'?

A second helpful factor in aiding your persuasion is the concept of 'house rules'. This is a particularly strong characteristic of smaller accommodation, eco-lodges, and independent properties. It is rarer at international chain hotels. House rules is a hospitality custom passed through the centuries and can still be observed in the way we visit friends' homes – and we of course also apply it to our home life (Focus on the Family, 2018).

There is an understanding that guests must follow the rules of your house, e.g. leaving shoes outside. For accommodation, house rules could be bar closing time, serving preserves from jars and not individually wrapped containers, or pool use policy. One of ours is to provide food scraps buckets to guests, which they fill and then feed to our chickens.

While a commercial transaction has occurred, paying guests are buying a service that can have socially accepted house rules attached. This has been well documented by Sara Dolnicar, who points out that house rules are a key element of a host's terms when booking peer-to-peer accommodation (Dolnicar, 2018), and by Tucker at B&Bs (Tucker, 2003). Both demonstrate that rules become part of the stay experience in Airbnb and B&B accommodation, a category which is also perceived by travellers to be more environmentally friendly than commercial hotels and holiday apartments.

Is this because those rules are more transparent? It certainly has not put travellers off using peer-to-peer accommodation at Air B&B! They use house rules as a way to educate and show a distinctive style of your property (Airbnb, 2021).

Why should this be left to only the shared economy?

A key aspect of the successful deployment of house rules is scale. The visitor is more acutely aware that they are staying in someone else's place, especially in the cases of peer-to-peer and B&B. The owner is present or is felt to be present. There is a sense of not transgressing the way things are done.

Why can we not transfer this sense of guest obligation and respect to larger establishments? It is partly due to volume, the sheer number of guests who overwhelm the smaller number paid staff whose place it is not. We again need to adjust the experience design to help us create a better sense of intimacy, respect, and commitment to follow the rules.

Deliver the rules proudly, expertly

Rules are part of Meaning. They are the social practice fabric of complying with a set of standards that allow you to perform a routine or activity in a socially accepted manner. When you enter a larger scale accommodation, the rules are almost invisible. They are assumed. If you are a guest staying in your own country many social practices are clear to you. Stay in another culture and you adjust to their ways of having no alcohol served (Saudi Arabia), or going to dinner at 10 pm (Spain), or being greeted with a massive TV playing Rugby League (Australia).

What hospitality is not good at, is introducing house rules that reflect environmentally sustainable requirements. These are small examples. If we want our guests to partner with us and conserve resources, avoid waste, and act responsibly in our destination, we need to gain the guests' compliance. Research tells us that interpersonal communication is much more likely to be effective.

9

Case study: Vegetarian only

Making a commitment to carbon reduction, the Ovolo Nishi Hotel in Canberra (68 rooms) has proudly stuck to its rule of no meat for a year – a policy applied to the whole chain (Ovolo Hotels, n.d.).

Perhaps considered a brave move initially, the restaurant has become more popular. With so many restaurants close to the property, it was more challenging for the hotel's food and beverage to stand out. The decision to go veggie actually helped increase visitation by setting it apart. Guests who want to eat meat are directed to other eateries.

The house rule strongly reinforces the property's commitment to be more sustainable, which can also be seen through building materials, such as restored vintage furniture. What could be improved is to directly involve guests in conserving resources.

Persuading through 'reasons to believe'

When I was running my agency years ago, a well-known washing detergent manufacturer wanted to introduce a 'new improved' product; it washed whiter. Difficult to persuasively claim if the powder still looks exactly the same... very white. They had a scientific message to explain the technical advancement, but the consumer could not see the difference.

So, the newly added ingredient (bleach) was coloured blue. Inside the box of the familiar white power appeared specs of blue. The packaging explained this new active ingredient, which you could see. The blue specs were a 'reason to believe' the manufacturer's claim. It was important because otherwise the claim was taken on faith only. How could you really see the difference between the old and new? The point of my story is that if you are going to say you are greener and promise sustainability, you have to remember that guests cannot see all the inner workings of your business. They need 'reasons to believe' that they can see.

Story: A 'reason to believe.'

We use lemon-scented tea tree oil as an antibacterial cleaner. It is 100 times more powerful than caustic soda but does not harm humans. We explain its Aboriginal use, which demonstrates safety, and invite guests to smell the air when they enter their accommodation (a scent similar to lemon sherbets). They sniff and smile. This is a 'reason to believe' moment. Then we highlight our own aromatherapy spa products in pump dispensers, all-natural. The guests are delighted their dreams of indulgence are being met. So now we can ask them to save water because we harvest only rainwater.

Figure 9.3: It is hard to believe an alpine hotel that makes environmental claims when their gas log fire is burning all day while everyone is outside (in temperatures of +5°C) on the slopes enjoying the last snow of the season. For five hours, this lounge was empty. Here there is 'no reason to believe'.

Applying house rules

Reasons to believe must be applied across the guest experience. You cannot have gaps. You cannot ask your staff and guests to conserve if you miss fundamental operational inconsistencies, because then they doubt you. Your staff and guests are far more savvy about what is good practice now than they were five years ago. For example, the excellent campaign to remove single-serve plastic waste in hospitality 'Travel Without Plastic', founded by my friend Jo Hendrikx, has been quickly taken up by many and pushed through peer groups (We are travel girls, 2021). Importantly, in this example, Travel Without Plastic helps you apply the practice comprehensively (Travel Without Plastic, 2021).

Rules are not just administrative procurement decisions. You are applying a rule for a genuine reason, because you understand the negative impacts. There is substance behind the decision. Procurement decisions can change. Rules are group commitments for order and common good. Defining your house rules and substantiating them are demonstrable examples of greener practices. They:

- Help guests appreciate your endeavours
- Let you record the difference you are making (before and after figures)
- Act as signals of other practices you are claiming that are invisible to guests

Remember, we are seeking to step beyond the sharing of green values with our guests. We are asking them to conserve and apply new skills of conserving resources, and for some it might be the first time they have considered it. Having house rules and explaining their reasons provide credibility, which in turn makes you more persuasive.

Applying house rules therefore requires:

- **Comprehensiveness**. Do not focus on vegetarian food only and ignore that your property leaves all the lights on day and night.
- **Evidence for your rules**. "We do not sell bottled water because it takes 5 litres of water to make each bottle…but we do refill your used bottle for free!"
- **Demonstrations of success**. "By separating your waste we have saved 10 tonnes of methane from landfill every year."
- **Adaptability.** Do not enforce your rules to the point of creating negative moments with guests or staff, persuade people by saying "All our guests love our approach to sustainability, see our guest reviews, join us!"

Managing expectations

Many guests and staff will be curious and enjoy doing something new, while others will be happy to be applying practices they already do at home. There will be some who do not want to join the party. Depending on the scale of the issues, do not get disappointed. There will always be that 2-20% who do not comply. Do not get disheartened because you achieve 80% support! They are the people who supported you and will write good reviews.

The majority know the planet faces challenges and for most it is simply human nature to do the right thing. When guests learn that you apply house rules yourselves they are much more likely to do likewise. Tell them your staff house rules are to turn off all computers and lights, that your chef selects ingredients that create no preparation waste. Be seen measuring water tank status, opening and closing windows, and pulling out shading. These are reasons to believe that there must be real value in the other rules.

The idea of using house rules might seem contradictory as you, as you might feel that they are paying guests and can consume as they wish. The picture I seek to paint is not one to deny guests 'normal' experiences, but to offer them better, fun alternatives. By inviting to try, you subtly reinforce the old adage to visitors that they should behave as a guest and consider house rules.

Do not penalise those who do not comply, but reward those that do. Rewarding here means praise and thanks, you do not have to keep giving away a cocktail every time someone chooses to keep their sheets for a night longer. It is common sense. If you do want to reward them materially, do so by sharing. For example, offer some antipasti at the bar that comes for a local grower, tell guests they can visit the property and buy some local ingredients. You could negotiate some sample product from that supplier in return for stimulating visitation. Be creative!

When it comes to managing guest expectations, remember the closer the level of human contact the more likely understanding prevails and compliance is achieved. The more impersonal the hospitality is, the less the human bond, the weaker the compliance.

3. Maximising reciprocity

What is reciprocation?

While there are a range of ways people can influence others, I have found reciprocity one of the most powerful in responsible sustainable tourism. The offer of helping guests with their luggage, the suggestion of making a restaurant booking or the unprompted action of selecting a more suitable room is regularly applied in hospitality.

At my business, when we found out that it's a guest's birthday or anniversary, we provided a special cake or a display of flowers with bottle of wine, and our best wishes. My wife delighted in making these little gifts to unsuspecting guests. It always surprised them and made her happy to see their joy. In hospitality we generally do not link what is assumed to be good service to encouraging participation in behaviours that help us achieve sustainability goals. What are we missing?

Reciprocation is a social behaviour that is familiar across cultures. If someone does you a favour, you may respond and do one in return (Cialdini, 2009). I noticed that the effort we made prompted our guests to reciprocate and comply strongly with our house rules. Just as politeness is a helpful strategy to persuade guests, social exchanges like those described above are powerful persuasive communication opportunities (Perloff, 2010). They can encourage reciprocation where individuals feel obliged to repay favours, gifts, or helpfulness.

Insight: The science of persuasion

Robert Cialdini and Steve Martin clearly demonstrate the power of reciprocity through experiments they did at a restaurant. Waiters who gave a mint to guests at the end of their meal saw tips increase by 3%, and giving two mints saw tips rise by 14%. If the waiter gives just one mint turns and walks away and then returns saying " for you nice people here is an extra mint" tips rise by 23%. It was not the mint that made the real difference, but how the waiter gave the mint. The waiter's return to the table and the compliment was the key. To stimulate reciprocation you therefore should be the first to give. Make it personal and unexpected (Cialdini & Martin, 2017).

9

My wife's cakes and flowers were seen as soon as the guests entered, the message was personalised by her directly to the guest and the experience was a delightful surprise. Such occasions help persuade guests comply with our house rules.

The science behind reciprocation

Reciprocation in a commercial situation fits into what we call 'exchange'. An exchange relies on the potency of exchangeable items that individuals might possess and the value of these items for others (Callaghan & Shaw, 2002). Social structures enable individuals to employ persuasion as either reciprocal or nego-tiated exchanges (Cook & Rice, 2006). Reciprocation is "one of the most potent weapons of influence" (Cialdini, 2009), as the process of reciprocation generates emotions that can then contribute to sustained reciprocation.

People's feelings of trust can evolve as the exchange continues, increasing the positive affect between the buy/seller or guest/waiter. This can perpetuate the persuasive communication thereafter. This is why in the context of behaviour change, reciprocation is an important consequence of social exchange.

Earlier research has identified the importance of negotiated exchange within a hospitality context as a method of control (Lynch et el., 2011), for example, in the context of house rules of a smaller accommodation (Tucker, 2003) where you pay an amount of money but comply with the owner's request to use facilities in a specific way. The owner is present on site, knows the traveller who feels they should comply with the rules of the house. How well the house rules message is conveyed determines the level of compliance versus reciprocation, i.e. the travel-ler *wants* to respond rather than feeling they *must*.

The question then arises can reciprocal exchange be a persuasive method for encouraging guests to save resources? Dolnicar and Greun concluded the best way to encourage visitors to take pro-environmental action was for hosts to ask them to behave as 'guests', implying the accepted social protocol of following rules in unfamiliar places. The host–guest relationship offers an "intense social exchange" that could be a focus for tackling sustainability in tourism (Selwyn, 2000).

The negotiated exchange may therefore be the first step in what could be a positively reinforcing communication beyond passively opting into corporate social responsibility programmes (Levy & Park, 2011).

Figure 9.4: Housekeeping can contribute to pre-suasion with personal touches that signal extra care and attention, making the staff 'liked', which persuades guests to reciprocate with your requests.

Why guests will reciprocate

Guests will reciprocate provided they feel there is genuine credibility to your invitation. If you are making an effort to influence them, they want to know and feel that what you say has credibility and integrity, shows goodwill and is trustworthy.

Demonstrating goodwill is to show empathy. The more you can customise your guest booking details and reasons for their stay, the easier it is for you to apply empathy and understand their needs better. Guests might need respite, have a physical disability, or have a dietary requirement such as being vegan. When the guest appreciates your genuine interest in their needs, they will feel obliged to repay the favour.

You cannot ask people to conserve if you do not have a strong environmental story of your own. This makes you credible.

- If you explain how you have sustained progress and show guests (or staff) examples they can apply, you are demonstrating your expertise, which is persuasive.
- Awards, certifications and proof that you contribute positively to your local community can build a sense of trust, which is also persuasive.
- Even if you are just starting out on your sustainability path, you can begin simply by sharing your intention. People will be willing to help.
- But you need to introduce the subject by giving something to these guests first that is personalised and unexpected.

Maintain the commitment to assist the guests when they need advice. Be seen to help others, and displaying examples of the results of efforts will show guests your business has integrity. Guests will reciprocate if they can see a genuine concerted effort. Each time you will be reinforcing your persuasive communication which in return helps to sustain the guests' reciprocation.

Story: Example of encouraging reciprocation

Reciprocation can be a very powerful persuasive tactic. It encourages your guests and staff to adapt their behaviours to help you cut costs and reduce carbon, but the outcomes can also greatly increase their satisfaction and loyalty.

Reciprocation has become a foundation of My Green Butler's success. Tourism could do well if it better understood the dynamics of reciprocation. It is one of the most powerful tactics to persuade others to choose of their own free will to help you. Returning a favour is a natural human tendency. If you ask me to conserve, tell me how well your staff are doing, and then give me the tools so I can minimise waste, I am much more likely to support you and return the favour.

9

What we found is that people did not know how to save. While they might agree with your request to conserve, they do not always have the competency. So at the heart of My Green Butler is the guest's personal butler giving them advice to keep cool or warm by recommending how better to use the facilities. People reciprocated and used less energy. This led to significantly higher levels of saving. Guests in spring time who received My Green Butler we were using 83.83 Wh per guest per hour compared to regular guests who consumed 117.46 Wh per guest per hour. That is a 40.12% saving.

In winter time guests can have long hot baths to keep warm as well as relax. We found the advice from My Green Butler cut water use by 34%. My Green Butler guests individually used 1.9 litres less water per hour than the other guests. This is because 26.39% of the guests who were advised about the environmental impacts chose to use few baths. And three times the number said they chose to use less hot water in their baths to conserve.

The reciprocation stretched across other responsible actions My Green Butler had not directly requested. An impressive 93.1% of My Green Butler users said they recycled their waste while only 88.3% of the other guests chose to do this.

Is it worth the effort?

Undoubtedly, yes.

Understanding and fuelling the Spiralling Influence becomes your guiding light. For my own business, we were able to increase our guest reviews significantly (multiple winners of the TripAdvisor certificate of excellence, for example). It led us to be ranked highly nationally (Reviewpro) and to command a price premium over competitors, proving that guests are happy to pay for a quality thoughtful experience delivered by a committed team.

If you simply tell your staff not to waste and exclude them from your sustainability progress, it means they will be far less motivated to save in their own duties, let alone promote what you are doing. Your most powerful weapon to persuade guests is therefore blunt. Involve your team, reward them on progress, educate them, then they can become shining ambassadors who will take pleasure in share your property's journey. Each and every positive guest feedback boosts their confidence.

There is a double benefit here. After our sector has been hit so hard by Covid-19 and we have lost so many good employees, you need to be able to attract the best talent and keep them. Second, happy guests, who enjoy your new, improved green guest experience, will be a pleasure to serve. It then becomes more than a job to your staff as they celebrate working as a team that makes a difference. Your team then becomes a discernible component of your competitive advantage, which in turn boosts demand and revenues.

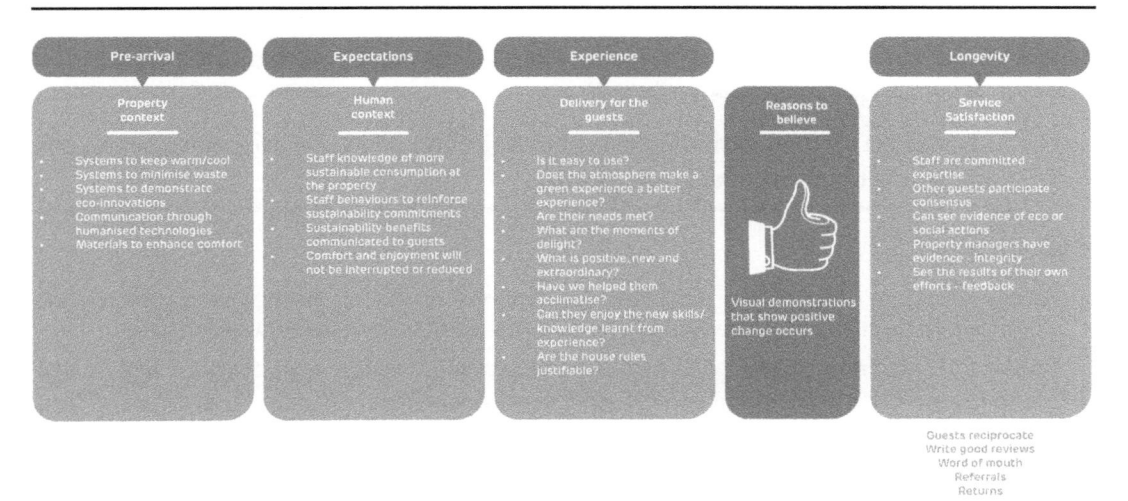

Figure 9.5: Guest Service Experience – integration of property amenities/features with service delivery to create outstanding sustainable hospitality experiences. The questions and issues you need to address.

Summary

We often dismiss politeness as a smile and a 'thank you', but there is a science to politeness. When applied correctly it can be a valuable tactic to help hosts persuade guests.

Your team are essential to delivering persuasive communication. While many parts can be left to AI, digital technology and written text, human persuasiveness is hard to beat. In hospitality it should be the core of your delivery. Training your staff will help you build a valuable and loyal team.

The power of persuasion is that it can let you create a deeper relationship with your guest. Advertising, in-room signs, and websites are passive one-way communication methods. Persuasive communication is a two-way approach where you try to influence the other person in an atmosphere of respect and free choice. Guests must feel they are at liberty to choose – no coercion at all. Persuasive communication can involve talking, non-verbal or visual methods. You are seeking to appeal to emotions that change what people think and do.

The impact is stronger when you apply persuasion in the right place. Simply flagging an eco-friendly symbol or stating 'no single-use-plastic' will be less effective than showing people how the integration of green solutions enhance the accommodation experience. From my own work I have found almost all guests are prepared to listen, and the vast majority contribute.

9

Next steps

1. Collect all your current guest communication which asks for green action and assess the tone used. Write this up.

References

Airbnb (2021). Writing helpful House Rules. Airbnb Resource Centre, www.airbnb.com.au/resources/hosting-homes/a/writing-helpful-house-rules-21. Accessed 1 August 2021]

Brown, P., & Levinson, S. (1987). *Politeness. Some universals in language usage, Studies in International Sociolinguistics*, Vol. 19). Cambridge: Cambridge University Press.

Callaghan, M., & Shaw, R. (2002). A theoretical application of exchange theory to online purchase decisions. In *Proceedings of the Australian and New Zealand Marketing Academy Conference 2002* (pp. 3241–3249). Melbourne: ANZMAC.

Cialdini, R. (2009). *Influence. Science and Practice* (Vol. 5). Boston, MA: Pearson.

Cialdini, R. & Martin S. (2017) Science of persuasion www.youtube.com/watch?v=kv0sOX6Alrk [Accessed 2nd August 2021]

Cook, K., & Rice, E. (2006). Social exchange theory. In J. Delamater (Ed.), *Handbook of Social Psychology*, pp. 53–76. New York, NY: Springer.

Dolnicar, S. (2018) *Peer-To-Peer Accommodation Networks*. Oxford: Goodfellow.

Focus on the Family (2018). Why do House Rules strengthen my family. Focus on the Family Singapore. www.family.org.sg/fotfs/Blog/Parenting/Why_Do_House_Rules_Strengthen_My_Family.aspx. [Accessed 1 August 2021]

Levy, S., & Park, S. (2011). Analysis of CSR activities in the lodging industry. *Journal of Hospitality and Tourism Management*, 18(1), 147–154

Lynch, P., Molz, J., McIntosh, A., Lugosi, P., & Lashley, C. (2011). Theorizing hospitality. *Hospitality & Society*, 1(1), 3–24.

My Green Butler (n.d.) Information video. www.mygreen butler.com/resources.

Ovolo Hotels (n.d.). Celebrating Year of the Veg. Ovolo Hotels. https://ovolohotels.com/eat/ {Accessed 1 August 2021]

Perloff, R. (2010). *The Dynamics of Persuasion: Communication and attitudes in the twenty first century*. Routledge.

Selwyn, T. (2000). An anthropology of hospitality. In C. Lashley & A. Morrison (Eds.), *In Search of Hospitality: Theoretical perspectives and debates* (pp. 18–37). Oxford: Butterworth-Heinemann.

Travel Without Plastic (2021) Let's reduce single-use, the plastics guide for hotels, https://www.travelwithoutplastic.com/product-page/shop [Accessed 1 August, 2021]

Tucker, H. (2003). The host-guest relationship and its implications for rural tourism. In Hall, D., Roberts, L. & Mitchell, M. (eds). *New Directions in Rural Tourism*, pp 80-89. Aldershot Publishing, UK

We are travel girls (2021). 10 easy ways to avoid single-use plastics when travelling. https://wearetravelgirls.com/ways-to-avoid-single-use-plastics-when-traveling/ [Accessed 1 August, 2021]

10 Step 5: The eco-feedback loop (Skill)

Introduction

Much of this book focuses on the steps needed to reach sustainable hospitality, but there is a final, essential step that takes you back to the start: feedback. This chapter will cover why it is so important and how to do it in ways that enrich your hospitality offering.

For scanners and return readers, below are the key points.

- **Feedback is all around us**. Be it through apps, fitness bracelets, websites, or bills, your guests are already used to live, granular feedback. Many may even expect it. Who are you to let them down?

- **Guests like being trusted**. There is a hesitancy about giving guests and staff eco-feedback, but done artfully the process actually enriches the hospitality experience. It can give even the most casual getaway a sense of meaning and purpose.

- **Embrace responsible technology**. The most useful, actionable feedback is delivered quickly. Energy monitoring systems are vital tools, allowing you to identify areas for improvement quickly.

- **Gamify!** Feedback can and should be fun. Gamification – the tangible sense of progress and accomplishment – hugely boosts guest engagement with your conservation efforts.

- **Put feedback in context**. There is no one-size-fits-all answer to feedback. There are so many variables at play that you have to be able to step back and separate correlation from causation.

The sustainable hospitality process is incomplete without feedback. It's that simple. No-one gets it perfect first time, but if we're willing to learn then the second will be a whole lot better, and the third time even better still. Conserving is a continuous process.

Resources are often invisible to the public, making it hard to compare one activity with another. When you turn on the light, you can not see how much electricity is being used. When using an oven or putting on central heating, you cannot see the gas being burned. Do you know how much water is used when running the taps or when the dishwasher is on? Of course, you can see the food you waste, but that does not translate into a precise carbon equivalent, for you also do not know the wastage and transport involved in bringing that food to your plate in the first place.

Energy and water seem a limitless supply. We often forget the complexity of pipes and cables involved in bringing such essentials to a building. We do not have much idea about the energy and water embedded in the food and beverages either. The invisibility of power and embedded water makes it hard to make greener choices even if we want to. We just cannot compare.

So far we have discussed the designing change that enables guests and staff to consume less (Chapter 6), why it is essential to explain how to conserve (Chapter 7), and how to persuade them to participate (Chapter 8). Now we will focus on feedback and why it is the essential step to sustain change.

Feedback, of course, is two-way communication, and we will look at both offering guests eco-feedback and using that feedback to improve the guest experience. This will be equally true for staff, giving them feedback on their resource use and hearing from them so that operations are more effective. Feedback is only valuable if you use it. Start a continuous process of improvement and identify what prevents conserving behaviours. Also, recognise that feedback is helpful in preparing and surviving extreme weather events.

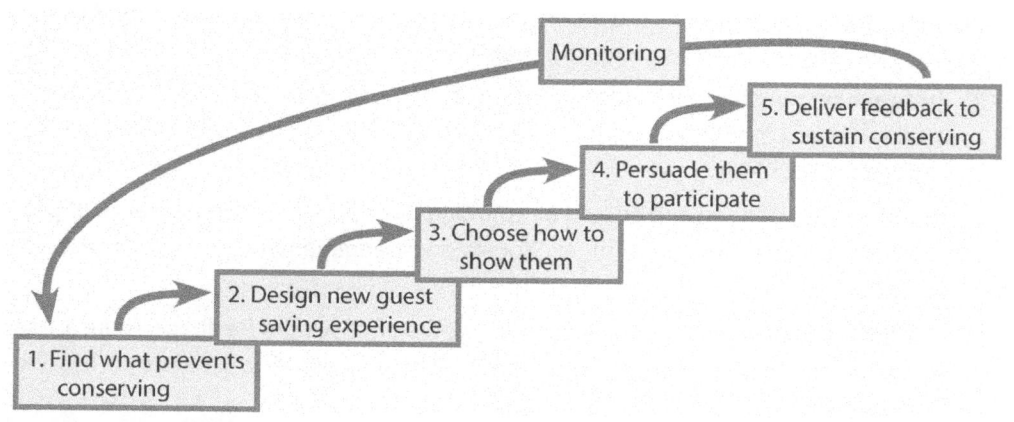

Figure 10.1: 5 Step Method to create transformational guest engagement

Changing our ways

After moving to Australia, I found we can go without real rain for more than six months. Despite owning a white car, I did not wash it. Before living in a desert I seldom thought about the need to conserve water because it was 'on tap'. My car, therefore, was washed weekly. I'm not proud of this now, but I was too busy with work to stop, think, and assess what I was doing.

What changed? In our home and business in Australia, we harvested rainfall for all our water needs. Noting the landscape's dryness made me self-aware. Monitoring the depth of our water tank revealed the ever-decreasing supply. This regular observation comparing our demand to supply was feedback. Feedback changed my behaviour because it made common sense to be water wise*. This feedback helped me endure the observations of others as I would arrive in my car looking less than pristine.

The water storage feedback motivated my family's behaviour to reduce or avoid showers. The weather forecast showing no sign of rain gave us feedback on what was available, so we collected shower water and spread it on the gardens. Rainfall (or lack of it) gave us feedback on taking careful precautions for bush fires. It was not simply one source of input but multiple layers and the nexus of these facts that changed our lifestyle. Many Australians adapted their behaviour in similar ways (Barbour, 2019). This is critical learning. Just like map reading, you need multiple trig points to navigate your course, to improve your skills, change the meaning of those daily practices, and understand which are truly important when materials are running out.

My example here has been water, but what I am describing is equally true of renewable energy (I have worked with renewable suppliers who must adjust a community's consumption based on the changes to the wind and waves). It is also true of changing consumption to meet different energy tariff rates, or changing menu items to avoid preparation waste. Feedback is your key card to sustainable hospitality and continuous improvement.

What feedback is

Feedback turns the invisible use of resources into something visible that can be responded to.

The level of activity is the key. We all have received utility bills, which are a form of feedback. You see your monthly or quarterly bill arrive and scratch your head as to why it was so much more than before. This is known as *indirect* feedback (Serrenho et al., 2015). It is a statement of what you have used and covers a very

---

*Now I note many car washes in Australia recycle their water.

long period, so you can not correct behaviours. One bill groups total consumption as a block over a month, making it very difficult, if not impossible, to work out what caused the consumption specifically.

In tourist accommodation, I have held countless meetings where data is presented in monthly columns. The problem with this is it does not tell us who is using these resources and how. It also makes it hard to see if eco-technologies have actually saved resources or caused backfire.

In some cases, indirect feedback comes with advice on how to save, comparing your consumption year-on-year or month-by-month. It might be useful for benchmarking one property with another, but it does not take into consideration the unique building characteristics. This is a particular problem for chain hospitality brands. Even when you reduce consumption down per square meter it does not account for age of the building, age of equipment, aspect to the sun, climate, and so forth.

Direct feedback is more refined, the principle being that consumption is reported quickly. Just how fast is elastic. Some utility providers will send you consumption every 24 hours and compare against a seven day average (e.g. Isata Minute View for bioenergy or Jemena for gas).

Increasingly there is direct feedback available to us that is updated every hour – or even every minute. An example of this is the building management systems or SMART monitoring equipment. This is mainly driven around energy use and, to be more specific, electricity and its relationship with heating and cooling, lifts, power distribution, and power usage during different tariff periods for more precise coordination. This requires experienced technicians. In some cases, on-site engineers do not have the time or expertise to maintain these systems. I have found examples where building management systems are run by independent companies thousands of kilometres away from the actual site. The difference with My Green Butler is that we record on-site staff and guests' behaviours around the clock so the AI constantly responds to the real environment not a virtual model.

There are several weaknesses of feedback like this. It is very selective on who actually sees it, the data is very dull to look at, and anyone who does not enjoy spreadsheets and graphs would find it hard to be motivated. Above all, there are vital factors often excluded like occupancy, climate, age of equipment, different work cultures, or profiles of the guests — all factors which can affect consumption.

The eco-feedback ladder

By ranking feedback, we can better assess the degree of persuasiveness. Sherry Arnstein's Ladder of Citizen Participation (Arnstein, 1969) inspired me to display the feedback below in order of degree of participation . This is because to achieve real change one has to give real power, so that people can have greater control and be motivated by their empowerment.

The more instant the feedback and the more relevant the comparisons, the greater the level of empowerment. To tip people into greater and sustained action, one needs gamified experiences which are self-rewarding. In the business of everyday life, we need to know which actions are best and learn how to conserve. This must be done quickly and often so that our Skills improve and it becomes System 1 thinking over time.

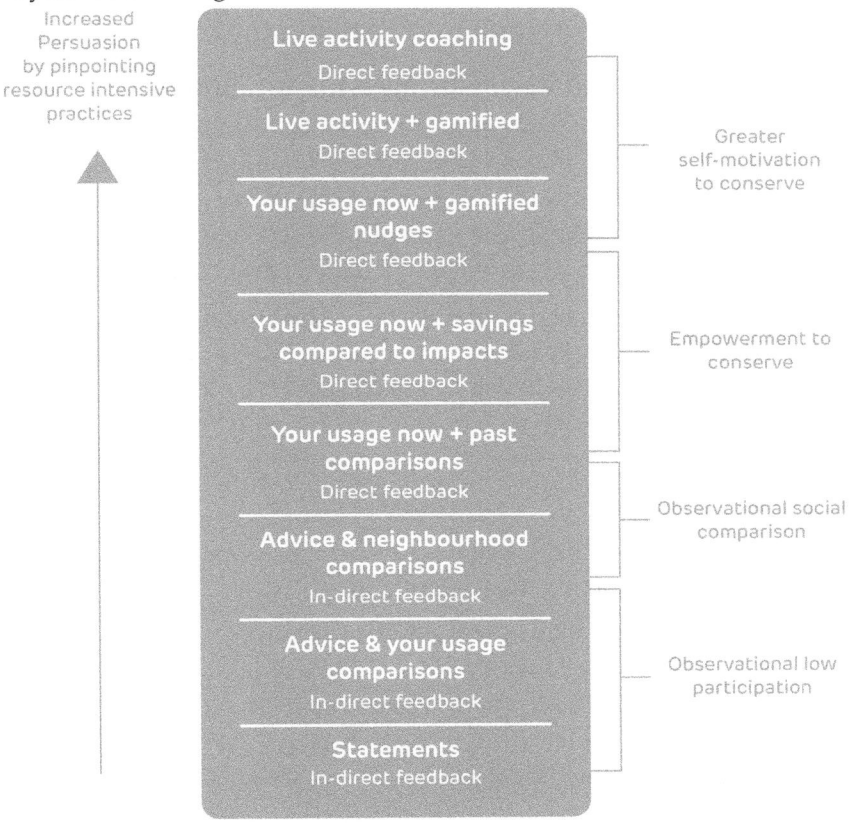

Figure 10.2: The Eco-feedback Ladder shows the degrees of persuasiveness with the increase in immediacy and personalised advice and fun.

Case studies

1. Advanced direct feedback

The advent of renewable energy has been a wonderful example of progress, but with its own complications. When the sun does not shine, we see supply drop. When the wind does not blow, we see turbines stop and waves flatten. One company, FlexiGrid, provides a solution by monitoring production and demand, then using this direct feedback, automatically turning off/on systems like batteries and electric car recharge. This is a form of conserving focused only on equipment (SMS, 2021). Why not people too?

10

2. Motivating many

During the droughts in Australia, the local government erected digital displays which showed exactly how much water was left in the reservoir. A researcher investigating how to persuade people to limit their water use said that "everyone could relate [to the digital displays], and it showed what it would mean if they ran out of water". So feedback can also be supply focused (Patterson, 2015) and has the potential to influence consumption. What happens if we offer this to guests?

3. Renewable energy and water supply and rationing

At one of our Australian properties, My Green Butler provided supply details such as solar generation, an allocation for each cottage, how much guests have used of that allocation, and how much was purchased from the grid to meet demand. Guests can see the impact cloudy days have. We also provide details of their water tank level – whether the site is in drought conditions or not and their daily consumption.

In short, we offer feedback that offers details of rationing guest usage. We have never had any negative feedback, but we have seen significant water and energy reductions. In this example, we have demand, supply, and the concept of rationing. This helps people gauge precisely by how much they should be conserving.

What's in it for me...

An experiment was run at a hotel to test the most compelling way to encourage guests to opt out of having their room cleaned.

Guests were told if they opted out, they received a free drink voucher. They were told that as the hotel saved costs so the guest should benefit from a free perk. The result was a 42% reduction in hotel room cleans. Just asking guests to care for the environment is not sufficiently persuasive. What happens to the savings is a critical factor in persuading more guests to participate. Every time a room was not cleaned, the hotel saved 1.5kWh of electricity, 25 litres of water, and 100 ml chemicals (Dolnicar et al., 2017).

Research also showed that using signs that directly encourage conserving behaviours does reduce waste. A sign saying "Welcome back! Again! And again! Visit our buffet many times. That's better than taking a lot once" helped cut food waste by 20.5% at seven hotels (Kallbekken & Saelen, 2013).

Feedback is all around us

Feedback exists in many forms in our everyday lives and is becoming a whole lot more common. You might argue that loyalty points and air miles are a form of feedback. They update you on your amount, tell you the benefits of making a booking, and algorithms assess your performance and send you customised incentives. Currently, some hotels offer guests a carbon audit message on check-out with an offset (Hospitalitynet, 2021).

Your electricity bill, which shares resource use and off-peak rates, help you to reschedule activities to fit in lower price ranges – remember the Danish homes laundry behaviour (Khalid et al., 2019). These are forms of indirect feedback where you read and think about how you are performing.

Hybrid cars share your energy-saving performance and compare your journeys and battery level (Toyota, 2011). When you're in your car travelling down the motorway, you've got a speedometer, speed signs, and police radar to help you keep to a speed safe. There are cycle riding apps that celebrate and share your fastest result on a specific route (Strava, 2021). There's feedback on calories used and number of steps taken. Even the lift in the GAP clothing store in Piccadilly Circus, London, shows you the energy used to descend and rise. Examples of direct feedback are growing are all around us. Hospitality and sustainable tourism should surely be part of that. It is now expected.

When there are water shortages, people are told to comply with hosepipe bans, which are supported by government fines. People then apply different behaviours like collecting shower water to water their gardens.

So why can't hospitality use feedback to deliver exceptional guest service that helps guests conserve? I have found that well-designed feedback can save over 30% of guest use and be enjoyed for its educational value.

In this chapter, we are focusing on feedback that prompts conserving behaviours. In the example of providing an estimated carbon consumption for a meeting and then an offset solution, there is no conserving, only a perception that it is carbon neutral. This still does not reduce consumption, and of course, we still have to wait for the trees to pump out the oxygen, which takes many years.

Figure 10.3: Energy consumption displayed real-time at the Al Ain Museum in the UAE

10

Figure 10 4: Financial confidence data displayed by lifts in Sydney

Feedback works is not just for those who opt in

There have been many studies into how feedback achieves savings. However, concern was voiced that the research sample was an opt-in group of individuals who are not reflective of the actual real-world consumer or were tempted by incentives to reward their actions (Tiefenbeck et al., 2019). A study at six hotels (totalling 265 rooms) in Europe placed smart shower displays in bathrooms which showed real-time feedback between the showerhead and the shower hose, showing water use and energy use. Savings were calculated from 19,596 observations and reported an 11.4% or 0.215kWh saving per shower. The researchers point out that even though the guests were not informed about the smart system and were not pre-selected, because the feedback was activity-based and in real-time people could apply conserving behaviours with ease.

Insight: Location affects saving potential

A European Union examination of 118 feedback studies conducted in 16 countries showed that up to 20% of energy could be saved. However, there are strong variations by region. For heating, 14% saved in Northern EU and19% in North America. For electricity North EU up to 20% and South EU up to 18%. Immediate feedback was considered the best method when people are learning how to save (Serrenho et al., 2015).

Adapting behaviour

Today smart meters are normal in the US, Europe, Australia, and many other countries. It has become an everyday reality. Likewise, people are responding to the ideas of feedback. A study of 105 Finnish homes found when households had feedback, 54% reduced energy consumption by turning off the lights, 27% had lower winter room temperature, 27% dressed more warmly, and 23% paid more attention to their thermostat (Haakana et al, 1997).

Case study: **Eating by numbers**

Another example of eco feedback is guiding guests on more sustainable menu items to select. At the Sticklebarn Inn in Langdale Cumbria, guests can see the carbon footprint information for each individual dish on the menu (Sticklebarn Inn, n.d.) so they can calculate their meal's footprint. It is a fascinating way to bring the realities of a low carbon future to the dinner table and create conservation and choice making. Which has a bigger footprint – the Halloumi & Mushroom Burger or the Sweet Potato and Black Bean Curry (National Trust, 2019)?

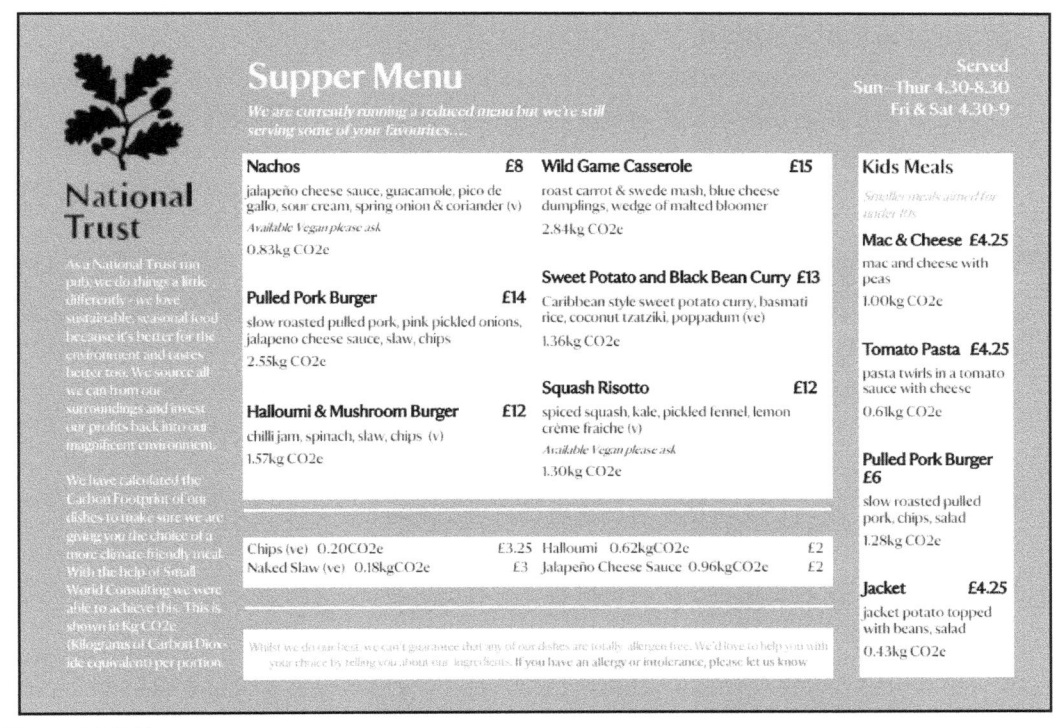

Figure 10 5: The menu

Adapting to climate change using feedback

We need our staff and guests to take adaptive behaviours, particular during periods of intense heat, cold, heavy rains, and wind, to protect them from the extremes and avoid using high levels of energy to prevent blackouts. In worst-case scenarios, we need to inform and protect people during bushfires, flooding, and sea surges. Feedback is also important in prewarning people of extreme weather events, minimising risks of excessive resource use, and guiding staff and guests to take emergency steps. Use these occurrences to provide them with further feedback on how they did. This becomes a learning exercise for staff; it shows your guests that you care for their well-being and helps you keep a lid on costs.

10

Already normal

Monitoring systems not only monitor your solar energy production and battery storage, but also tell you which appliances you are running in the home. Fitted with smart plugs, you can therefore run your home without being there. Such Internet of Things systems are low cost and provide a web app so you can view from anywhere in the world. Many community energy groups and social media blogs are building market acceptance (WECA, 2019). Is your accommodation ready for the new wave of tech-savvy guests who already receive daily feedback and like it?

Smart Global Growth

The rollout of various SMART meter programmes worldwide will lead to production reaching 285 million smart electricity meters by 2025. Three-quarters of the market will be domestic metering offering various public forms of feedback to help users reduce consumption. Increasing renewable generation is also informing households of their solar generation (Grand View Research, 2018).

Foresight: Feedback to take a holiday

Very soon, we could be linking our health indicators to taking holidays. Using the health indicators from your smartwatch, your energy and stress levels suggest you need an urgent holiday. Algorithms study your previous feedback and identify that you prefer the wilderness of Norway to a beach in Hawaii. The trip is automatically booked for Sweden (you have stayed in Norway and it is a similar experience), and off you go. A vision from the World Economic Forum (2017).

Monitoring for feedback

Managing feedback is essential for green business success. You will want to use it to improve your service, inform guests, and compare goals. There are three types of monitoring, which need not be laboursome or time consuming:

- **Resource use monitoring**: Record energy, water, waste, and laundry. The more granular (sub metered and recorded by the minute compared to daily totals), the greater the level of insight and the more persuasive the feedback.
- **Observation**: When coaching guests, note your observations, separated for either immediate corrective action or as part of regular reviews to improve the service. Pay particular attention to seasonality, age, guest type, and room type. This will help you adjust your feedback to better match situations.
- **Guest feedback**: What did they find delightful, good/poor or hard/impossible to apply? Take immediate corrective action or assist in future planning.

Those niggling maintenance issues of windows not closing or dripping bathroom taps will be quickly spotted by guests who want to do well. Comments on the ease of use of materials will also help you replace ineffective items that you might not otherwise have learnt about. This way effective monitoring enables you to continuously improve the guest experience in areas of comfort, customer service, and cleanliness.

Electronic monitoring using SMART equipment has different strengths. Remember the actual details of how much guests are using will be positively revolutionary for them.

Together, resources use, observation, and guest feedback will help you out-service your competitors. Essential to this is that you feed back into your sustainability programme to find out what prevents conserving. This way you re-start the refining process through my five-step programme to create transformative guest engagement (see diagram at the beginning of the chapter).

Responsible technology

Technology can be an excellent enhancement to our lives, but it can also hamper us and lead to unexpected consequences (such as rebound and backfire). This is often because we become further removed from applying self-control and minimising impacts.

Feedback should emanate from Responsible technology. Responsible technology transparently aids us to reduce the consequences of our consumption, help us adapt to changing climates and extreme conditions, and enable us to protect biodiversity and rejuvenate nature. Responsible Technology offers a fabulous opportunity. Central is that its output must translate data into relevant and actionable behaviours. It must go further than reporting. It must be instructive.

Start by auditing what metering and recording systems you have. You can read meters regularly, or link to your SMART meters and assess your building management system. How you present the information to staff and guests though, is critical. The eco-feedback ladder shows that the more immediate the feedback is to the actions, the greater the opportunity to conserve. The more comprehensive the resource range you must measure, the more complex the process can be. That is why I invented My Green Butler. It takes time and regular routines to monitor consumption, and even more time to translate this into meaningful advice.

Responsible technology can also be used to target adaptive behaviours for extreme weather events to help save lives.

When responsible technology feedback works

An example of responsible technology at work is via in-room TV channels that display guest consumption, carbon emission and trends in real-time. I have successfully set this up for clients such as the significant 37-storey Amora Hotel Jamison in Sydney, or the modest 600-year-old Thorney How in Cumbria. The

10

very fact that you share such details with everyone makes people aware of continuous consumption. It turns the invisible into motivating visible evidence. It also provides projections and advice to take preemptive action. By integrating advice and gamification, my technology motivates like a seat belt, clicking everyone into the driver's consumption seat, making them aware and in control — a great way to to make change happen day and night at the push of a button.

Having your own personalised coach

Eco-feedback as coaching has been found to have substantial benefits over automated systems, which can confuse people or lead to the unexpected backfire of increased resource use. Responsible technology that coaches individuals – i.e. empowering them to take control – make it easier to save. It increases people's involvement, enables them to compare saving strategies, and will build their confidence. Personalised coaching is about understanding the individual's needs and guiding them to the best solution for them.

Figure 10.6: My Green Butler delivers multi-channel feedback through paper reports, mobile phone and in-room tv channel. Like all good advertising you should consider a multi media approach with feedback and not rely on one medium alone.

Eco-coaching is giving personalised suggestions for people to take specific conserving actions, to go further than just feedback as it attempts to reduce wastage in the future. Yang and her colleagues, who have done multiple experiments with intelligent systems, found that providing eco-coaching using technology was more effective in saving than manual programming and even more effective than automation. This is because eco-feedback technology on its own might raise awareness but does not actually instigate action that saves. What people want is advice that enables them to take pre-emptive action. When they received 'eco-feed-forward' messaging, individuals saw where they could make greater savings. In addition, when they are shown historic evidence that the advice works, people were motivated to change because their confidence grew (Yang et al., 2016).

Story: Adapting to a brave new world

Eight out of ten households in a Danish study of photovoltaic owners with hourly metering at home, admitted to time-shifting some of their electricity-use practices. This meant they synchronised activities to match solar generation. Their motivations are less to do with environmental reasons than economic reasons.

This change in timing of routines involved households postponing laundry activities when the weather was cloudy (less solar energy) to benefit from the following day's sun when drying outside is also better.

The research found that balancing energy supply with a flexible demand approach helped people feel more independent and self-reliant with energy (Khalid et al., 2019). In addition, this demonstration of adaptive skills appeared to make the homeowners happier.

Story: Blending technology with human delivered customer service

The Upper House Hong Kong integrates both technology and human delivered service. They do not see the integration of technology as disturbing their luxury hotel values. When asked if technology changed the balance of delivering a hands-on customer service led experience, the general manager, Marcel Goma, said, "I think they are equally important and complement each other, and the definition of what 'classic' is, may no longer apply in today's hospitality industry. It is still vital for us to engage with our guests face to face, gather information and receive feedback".

Using data is critical to enhance the experience as it allows this hotel to introduce a very high level of personalisation while still "having that human connection". In the same way, eco-feedback enables a closer relationship between the tourist accommodation, staff and, guests by providing consumption, carbon updates, and advice whilst also receiving feedback that enables management to refine services. Guest feedback is constructive.

10

The challenges the property has to reduce can be improved upon through the responses guests give. They can reveal matters you were unaware of and might have been an impediment to reducing wastage for a long time. Responsible technology and classic face to face engagement generate a two-way dialogue that helps you ever improve your sustainable hospitality experience.

When direct coaching works

This leads me to cover live activity coaching feedback, where you show or assist guests. It will sound obvious, but I want to emphasise how important it is to manage feedback from guests. If we are inviting them to conserve, we must have conserving methods available, working, and understandable.

If guests ask for assistance, ensure protocols exist so that someone responds promptly. For contactless response, ensure your messaging system is directed to the relevant support and that it is not simply a chatbot but an actual member of staff. Remember to be persuasive; you must demonstrate expertise and integrity. Bland and generalised responses, therefore, do not cut it.

Your response will be successful if you show that expertise in ways that are instructive and practical. Be flexible to adjust your politeness approach so guests feel supported, not patronised. Reassure them by explaining either:

- "Our set up is designed like this because most of our guests want to conserve and they like to apply these steps to help us. Let me assist you"; or,
- "I quite understand, many guests find they need help with this as it is unfamiliar, and we are delighted to assist"; or,
- "Yes, I found this unusual and a bit different when I tried it first too, let me help you."

These types of responses show empathy and integrity.

Overall be gracious. Your guests are asking for help because they are trying to help you. In doing so your guests feel they have mastered a new system or learnt a more eco-friendly way to consume.

Remember not everyone understands your amenities

At our hospitality property we installed instantaneous gas water heating (this is an example for smaller accommodation businesses), so there was no hot water tank. Also, because of saving energy and being able to use systems in a power cut, the pumps we used were small. This saved us gas, electricity, and water.

If guests turned on the cold tap and then only gently added hot, there might, on occasion, not be sufficient water pressure to ignite the gas, resulting in no warm water available. Sometimes newly arrived guests who were used to their hot water tank system from home thought the hot water was not working. After

I explained the system and showed them piping hot water by turning on the hot tap first, they were relieved. Note I choose to explain the story in full to them, so they did not feel embarrassed, and by so doing, created proof of our sustainability commitment, which became a strong positive for them. This contributed to our reduction in gas (20%) and water use (21%).

Your prompt, helpful personal responses are essential. Before you leave with a smile, check if they have any other feedback. If they do, note it down immediately and report back to improve experience design. In my example of hot water, we integrated the advice when introducing guests to the accommodation, and this helped to cement our commitment and gain their participation. It goes without saying if the facilities are operating poorly, then be sure to fix them immediately!

No longer a guessing game

We gave eco-feedback to two sets of guests staying at four accommodations sites where we monitor energy and water. Half the guests received eco-feedback and half did not. Using a survey at check-out, we asked the guests if they had "tried to save" during their stay.

Interestingly, 84.85% of guests who received eco-feedback from My Green Butler said they had tried to save, while 59.49% of the other guests who had not been invited to conserve said they also had tried to save. When we examined the data, we found that the benefit of eco-feedback had enabled the My Green Butler guests to use just 88.53 Wh and 5.72 litres of water per guest per hour compared to the other guests who used 122.55 Wh and 7.09 litres per guest per hour. Those guests with feedback used 38% less electricity and a 24% less water (Warren, 2018).

With the supply of specific information, guests do not have to guess. They can see their results and improve upon them. Just as if you show similar feedback to staff. We cannot easily save if we can not see what we are consuming. Consumption is invisible to most; feedback makes the invisible visible.

When feedback doesn't work

There is an art to feedback. Just telling guests consumption is high does not help them reduce; they need to understand what was the cause and how to address it. People do not know how to compare one activity with another.

If there is a significant time lag between when feedback is produced and then delivered to guests, there will be a drop in intention and action to save. Telling me how much plate waste there was at breakfast time at 4pm is not helpful. Telling me at the time helps me take responsible action.

Providing general information is not helpful either. Beyond the obvious, people are confused about how to save, especially in unfamiliar places. Providing information that does not spell out actions to help them progress only makes

10

people feel downhearted... which is not persuasive at all. When feedback does not give power to the people, it renders them passive observers. If you do not let them adapt that can lead to despondency (Brown et al., 2009).

Remember, guests not only have different levels of knowledge, they also have varied consumption levels (Mr & Mrs Average does not exist). If you tell everyone the average amount consumed, you are in danger of creating rebounds or backfires as low-level consumers see they can consume more as they already use minimal amounts, while others use more. One UK study found that while high and medium energy users tried to save, low users actually increased their consumption by over 10%! (Brandon & Lewis, 1999)

Sometimes we can get too smart using graphics that can lose people. If you start comparing usage and time with fancy graphs that show big spikes in electricity use over a few minutes, people get lost and look at the drama of the spike and not the incremental usage.

People are on holiday, relaxed and happy. Harsh, clipped feedback is not going to be welcomed. Providing it frequently can be invasive. It is a fine balance that should be targeted at relevant times.

Let's be honest, the reason many people save at home is for economic reasons. Feedback doesn't work if you do not close the loop in savings. Guests will not be motivated to save simply to make you, in their eyes, richer. It is your job to show them your "why"! That you consider this the right thing to do, for your staff, local community and the planet.

Case study: Carbon footprint – timing and meaning

Researchers conducted a study at two hotels in Benelux to determine if notifying guests of their carbon footprint would reduce energy use. A sample of selected guests at either property was notified that they would receive a statement at check-out. At one hotel, there was no difference in consumption of electricity between the control and sample guests. At the other hotel, guests who were told they would receive a carbon receipt actually used more electricity than the control group (not given). The carbon receipt was delivered too late after guests had consumed it, and a carbon figure is complex for guests to relate to.

All taken care of... not

Another example of weak feedback is not being in control. A research team studied the effectiveness of an intelligent thermostat that offered both saving energy and improved heating/cooling comfort. Their findings revealed that it left occupants with a false sense that they were saving as the system appeared to manage everything on its own. Their involvement dropped off over time, resulting in extra energy being consumed and no savings achieved at some properties. Systems need to focus on energy saving and let the person choose to adjust the temperature. Feedback needs to involve the person, with the suggestion of push notifications, so they can take action rather than sit back (Yang et al., 2014).

Golden rules about how to make eco-feedback work

1 Integrate methods

Combining direct (real-time), indirect (over time) feedback with coaching are the most effective methods to achieve guest (and staff) participation. Your solution should be built into your newly designed guest experience so it truly becomes guest centred.

2 In-person

Verbal feedback providing advice to guests enables flexible and polite delivery and is highly personalised. If guests give you feedback, note it down immediately and input it into your internal review process, so you continuously refine the guest experience and smooth out any confusion or complications.

3 Timing is important

Maintain frequent feedback; otherwise, guests will go back to old habits.

4 Set yourself a target

Provide feedback that helps guests work towards what you want. Keep focused on what you are trying to do and keep it simple

5 Avoid rebound or backfire

Be warned if you show 'average' figures that may not help them or you and lead to more significant usage as some below-average users can feel excused to consume more.

6 Avoid being too SMART

Advanced intelligence can leave people dazed, use the most intelligent device in the room – the human being. Keep AI intelligence levels to ones of helping guests adapt their behaviour, providing information by sensing what occurs and learning.

7 Concentrate on delivering good customer service

This is where guests are shown how to get the best results. These results, first and foremost, make the guest happier. They must enjoy a better experience like being more comfortable and then conserve. What I mean by 'better' occurs in a variety of ways – do not make assumptions that only eco-warriors want to get involved.

8 Transparency is 'good'

Note the importance of economic truths. People want to know what happens to the savings. Plan responsible use of the savings so you can demonstrate investment into eco-innovations or to nature conservation (note My green Butler's 'Noble Cause' feature).

Above all, eco-feedback can work!

10

Story – How my guests responded to water scarcity

After setting up our business, we went through a couple of dry summers, and I became aware of the shortage in water as we collected 100% of our water needs. During these periods, I regularly measured water levels in all our eight tanks, and staff would notify guests when they arrived that we were dependent on our own water storage and times were dry. To our surprise, we receive plenty of knowing nods and no complaints. I felt at the time we should be able to reduce consumption but could not be specific as I was unable to actually know what behaviours accounted for the most water consumption and so could not explain this to guests. Our request was very general.

Once I started using electronic sensors, I was able to confirm that guests responded to our gentle nudge to be mindful as water usage went down. I also knew which behaviours accounted for the greatest water usage. Now our guest engagement programme offers daily feedback with hourly updates targeting specific behaviours.

Guest will respond to shortages when they can see you have applied best practices in water efficiency and give them practical advice. Drought events did not affect our guests' high satisfaction ratings (in fact, as I have previously said, it has increased). Experiences like this have taught me, that in fact, consumption is not linked to guest happiness. As one guest told me

"I don't believe knowing such information (feedback) would change the experience of the holiday".

So Margaret never actually needed to hide the bathroom taps!

Rationing... it works!

David Attenborough has talked of the plague from human overpopulation to urge us to do something. It is another way of approaching the planet's state of affairs rather than only talking about the Climate Emergency (Javelosa, 2016). It reframes consumption. If you want to encourage rapid resource-saving, my research has found implying the need to share resources with others can be very effective. Sharing what we have is a more tangible proposition than flagging indirect causes of greenhouse gasses, even if the guests don't know who the other people are. They choose to apply civic responsibility.

I proposed rationing every day to our guests at a 4½ star award-winning accommodation for people seeking romantic tranquillity or escape from the city. Guests learn their share of water resources, the drought conditions, and how much they are using. Likewise, they learn of our solar generation, their share, and what we buy from the grid. We never received any complaints about this feedback. It is a form of civic persuasion where everyone at the property was encouraged to consider consuming within what was available.

Do you measure resources to a level that convincingly explains what is sustainably available to each person? If not, you are missing one of the most cost-effective sustainability initiatives you could apply. There are different ways to present this. I chose what was available on my property. If you are an ecolodge, for example, you might want to show precisely how much people in a developed country actually use compared to your location with more frugal means. It is not simply overpopulation that is the problem but how much first world populations consume and waste (Pont, 2021).

Story – Cape Town water usage

Cape Town's water shortage is a good example of combining several methods to change behaviour. The government gave feedback on dam levels, set rationing limits, and told of the consequences of using more than your share. Residents were asked to cut their use by half; farmers donated their water for the city folk and the mayor's office named and shamed the top 100 worst offenders, some of whom were consuming more than 50,000 litres per month. Visitors were asked to "save like a local" (Chutel, 2017).

Making feedback fun – gamify!

There have been occasions when people ask me, "but how can you get guests interested in saving when they are on holiday?" The question is a good one. Naturally, holidays are about having fun, relaxing, enjoying a hedonistic time (Malone et al., 2014); resources saving might be furthermost from your mind. After all, you deserve that break (Barr et al., 2010).

As I have mentioned earlier, holidays are also a time of trying new things. Through this book, we have covered creating an experience that is more sustainable, introducing it to guests by showing them how to save, persuading them to participate, and now providing eco feedback. Another factor can help build and maintain involvement, something that has been with us all the while, but now with the advent of computer games, we call it gamification.

My son and business partner, Maxwell, has helped integrate gamification into My Green Butler. You might remember BCG (before computer games) companies applied techniques to motivate staff. "The salesperson with the best result this week gets a prize". We even apply the same thinking with our children "if you do all your homework, then you can have a chocolate sundae". These are incentives rather than gamification.

A gamified version would be if your sales staff were invited into the game (optional). A picture of their character or a description of themselves is included on the board. They then earn points for weekly great client sales feedback, as well as gaining points for early sales or for being the 'best teammate' of the week for

10

example. While sales are the goal, you increase the engagement and motivation of those around you to participate. It becomes gamelike, and most of us like games. In fact, most mid-aged adults love computer games; the average age is, in fact, 34 years old (Yanev, 2021). As we have found with My Green Butler, gamifying eco-feedback strongly increases participation.

Gamifying to improve skills

We generally learn better when the experience is enjoyable, and gamification is a very effective way to persuade guests and staff to maintain – if not increase – their participation. Gamification is applying 'gamelike' features into the user experience, increasing engagement and motivation. It holds stronger meaning, provides fun feedback, and builds the momentum of use (Abdi, 2016). Applying gamification to your feedback, enhances your customer experience by being informative, rewarding, and fun.

You can achieve this by designing feedback to help people learn and set personal goals. Integrate your new guest experience design so that the gamification works with the new amenities. Use the opportunity to enhance guest communication and build strong shared values, so the experience is far superior to no feedback at all.

The higher the frequency of feedback, the greater guests can act, though too much can become invasive. You need to get the balance right. To do that, present it as part of your accommodation's style, e.g. an ecolodge might display it all the time, while a luxury apartment could integrate it into their nature conservation experience of individual appliances and the Internet of Things (IoT) demonstration of the future. This is what Maxwell does at My Green Butler; he applies gamification strategies found in successful computer games to self-propel guest participation as they enjoy learning new skills and viewing the results (Warren, 2020).

Everyone's performance should be private (unless you wish to gamify a group booking or conference) so guests are not under pressure. Be careful not to make it competitive unless, of course, the guests enjoy a sense of competition. Even then I would not recommend disclosing performance to other guests (unless it is the group/conference audience). However, we have found that sharing best practice examples of previous (anonymous) guests who stayed in the same property/ accommodation/room encouraged the current guest to do as good or better.

You can link gamification to marketing loyalty, but its overriding function should be to increase guest involvement to drive your goal to improve and maintain conserving efforts. Applying gamification requires you to consider the motivation of your staff and guests. Just as people like different genres of film, food types, or video games, people like different things within games and gamification. It is not "one size fits all" in gamification, but there will be a style to captivate and motivate everyone. Gamification's purpose is to *increase engagement* – helping guests improve their skills is a goal, but not the purpose.

Maxwell's take on gamification for sustainability solutions

Information alone won't get all people to read on, or take certain tasks, or be more energy conscious. There has to be some motivation behind the information and actions, something to drive the engagement. Self Determination Theory and the RAMP model (Relatedness, Autonomy, Mastery, Purpose) show us that we all have different motives, and gamification can help us play into these core psychological needs, turning numbers and words into a raison d'être for a moment, of sorts.

Gamification can greatly increase user engagement with eco-feedback and tips by motivating all types of users, targeting what drives them. When using the right tools, gamification will bring out the competitive streak in us (to beat a target), or give a sense of a shared community or goal for those who desire relatedness (being part of a property and shared guest experience). It can give us a sense of autonomy as we power through tasks and tools (clicking off tasks, learning more and feeling empowered from success), and it can bring out the philanthropist in us as we see the greater goal and vision (contributing to tackling climate change).

Gamification can emphasise to users what drives them, whether it be for climate action, to have the best score, receive a reward, or to be part of a community. Regardless of the users' motives, if they engage with your eco-feedback and system and use less resources, it is a success to your property and the environment (Warren, 2021).

Case study: Guests can rise to the challenge

The award-winning Chepu Ecolodge in Chile introduced the water and energy monitoring of guests rooms and are pioneers of the concept. I was fortunate enough to interview Fernando and Amory after they won the WTTC awards. What struck me was how they had turned the monitoring of water into an informal game; it was a pretty natural step of the host-guest relationship to progress this way (Chepu Ecolodge, 2016).

Question: What are the positive guest responses?

Fernando: "We ask the guests how much water they think they have consumed after the first night at breakfast. They are often surprised by how much they have used. We tell them how much each item uses water like the toilet uses 7 litres and the shower is regulated at 7 litres per minute. Some guests can be quite accurate about how much they have used by calculating it in their head the next morning."

10

Question: What are the negative responses?

Fernando: "They play the game of sustainable tourism. There are certain rules which they accept to play" "It is like the police radar trap. People see the sign and slow down when they know they are on the radar!"

Note: Chepu Ecolodge was a very distinctive property, where 98% of its guests come from Europe.

Feedback adds value

I tested if guests liked the idea of feedback. I gave half the guests the My Green Butler experience, including resource use feedback, and the other half just received our regular service. In the My Green Butler group, 71% said they "strongly agreed/tend to agree" and 24% were "neutral" to the idea of feedback. The guests who had not seen the eco-feedback were less enthusiastic, with only 37% "strongly agree/tend to agree" and 48% "neutral". As this latter group of guests had never experienced feedback, they were more cautious, as perhaps you would be too, right? I then asked both groups why they had given this response. These are comments from guests who received the My Green Butler experience:

"I've never done that before, and it was exciting" Guest 23 (My Green Butler)

"It would be good to know how much energy we used and associated impact" Guest 56 (Regular)

"It's a great way of discovering what activities carry the most amount of energy and usage" Guest 262 (My Green Butler)

Meanwhile, those regular guests who were "neutral" about the idea of feedback felt they were already efficient, but of course, they had no way of telling this. This is what a regular guest said who had not experienced the MGB service

"I'm already mindful of my consumption" Guest 169 (Regular)

The experience of receiving feedback was positive and reduced caution. By making the feedback part of the experience, guests do not feel it was invasive (Warren, 2017).

Accept flexibility with feedback results

Be aware that guests might be trying to achieve your goals and are applying their skills but can't reach the targets. There can be several reasons for this:

- **Guest needs**. Some guests might be physically disadvantaged and not have a high level of mobility or require extra warmth or coolness.

- **Guest values**. You might not share the same values as your guests, and you don't want to impose yours. Do not try to convince everyone. You are applying persuasions that require free will compliance, not enforcement.

But you can moderate how you introduce feedback so that it appeals to people's holiday motivation.

- **Time limitations**. Guests might be staying a single night and arrived late, so accept you will have had less opportunity to apply persuasive messages.

- **Guest practicalities**. The party size and make-up do affect response to feedback. You may have a booking with many young children or three generations together (grandparents, parents, children), the primary person who booked has to look after the needs of their party first. But do not forget that My Green Butler also presents an opportunity for connecting with young children about the topic which they enjoy

- **The weather.** If you have very cold, very hot, or rainy weather, guests might be staying in their accommodation longer or using the resources at a high rate, so feedback should be sensitive to this. Though My Green Butler's comfort and activity suggestions have been found to mitigate this as much as possible

These examples do not prevent conserving behaviours but do remind us not to apply a one size fits all approach to feedback. These factors actually offer you opportunities to out-service your competition by tailoring your messages more effectively. The types of guests (e.g. they have booked an accessible room) gives you clues as to their likely challenges. My Green Butler provides guidance to follow, but as you become more comfortable with the service, you will develop your own flexible approach to feedback which can enhance politeness and credibility.

At my accommodation, when we had families with young children, we addressed feedback to the kids as they get absorbed in learning, and parents are pleased to have a helping hand. Consider offering kids' activities and hand out rewards. Make sure you have proposed actions as diversions that help to reduce resource use in extreme weather.

Imagine if people travelled back from 2050 after we had achieved Net Zero Emissions. What would they be showcasing as the turning point in your firm that enabled you to accomplish this goal?

Summary

Feedback is a valuable way to make the invisible visible. Most people are not aware of their consumption, and if you are going to ask them to save, they need some idea of how. Feedback is all around us in our everyday lives, and with the introduction of new technologies like smart metering in homes, our resource use will become apparent.

10

To be effective, feedback must be delivered promptly, be available in multiple forms, and be helpful. It fails to deliver when it is too smart, too confusing, or makes people feel guilty. Gamifying the experience is one way to turn feedback into an integrated part of your hospitality experience using your brand values and imagery.

To deliver feedback, you will need to install monitoring systems for your resources and establish good procedural systems so that you can act swiftly and continuously.

Some hosts worry about guests being unhappy about receiving feedback. You don't want to force it on paying guests, and you must ensure that no message can be seen as preachy. You should test how you approach it and make sure it is a positive step forward before introducing it. Test it on staff and friends first, then after refinement test with a sample of guests for their views – you can start gently and modify as you listen to their responses. Feedback must account for personal circumstances which could prevent what appears to be conserving behaviour.

There is no getting away from it: feedback is the deciding factor in saving resources. It is also critical to taking preemptive actions in advance of extreme weather events, protecting your staff and guests.

Above all, feedback must be an integrated feature within an experience design that provides the materials to save and offer the skills to conserve, as a positive experience.

Next steps

1. Assess your metering systems. Will you manually read or apply SMART technologies?
2. Assess what guest feedback systems you have in place and procedures for handling guests' feedback that requires immediate responses.
3. Set up procedures to collect and review observations from guests' requests for assistance.
4. Analyse resource usage regularly to give you ideas about how to modify your design and future planning. You can do this hourly or daily, depending on the Responsible Technology solution you choose.

References

Abdi, A.(2016). *Process of Gamification*. Bachelor's Thesis, Tampere University of Applied Sciences.

Arnstein, S. (1969). A Ladder of Citizen Participation. *Journal of American Institute of Planners*, 35(4), 216-224

Barbour, L. (2019). Country towns close to reaching 'day zero' as water supplies dry up in the drought. ABC News, 23 July www.abc.net.au/news/2019-07-14/day-zero-approaching-as-towns-run-out-of-water/11271430 [Accessed 22 August, 2021]

Barr, S., Shaw, G., Coles, T. & Prillwitz, J. (2010). A holiday is a holiday: practising sustainability, home and away. *Journal of Transport Geography*, 18, 474-481.

Brown, Z. Dowlatabadi, H. & Cole, R. (2009). Feedback and adaptive behaviour in green buildings. *Intelligent Buildlngs International*, 1, 296-315.

Brandon, G. & Lewis, A. (1999). Rescuing household energy consumption: A qualitative and quantitative field study. *Journal of Environmental Psychology*, 19, 75-85

Chepu Ecolodge (2016) Personal communication

Chutel, L. (2017). Africa's favourite tourist city is about to run out of water. Quartz Africa. https://qz.com/africa/1147081/cape-town-drought-as-day-zero-approaches-the-city-needs-to-learn-to-talk-about-climate-change-not-spread-fear/ [Accessed 30 August 2021]

Dolnicar, S., Cvelbar, L. & Grun, B. (2017) Making hotel guests voluntarily waive daily room cleaning. BEST, Think Tank XVII. www.besteducationnetwork.org/Papers_Presentations/15562

Grand View Research (2018) Smart electricity meter market size, share & trends analysis. https://www.grandviewresearch.com/industry-analysis/smart-meters-market

Haakana M., Sillanpää L. & Talsi M. (1997) The Effect of Feedback and Focused Advice on Household Energy Consumption. In: *Printed Proceedings of the 1997 ECEEE Summer Study,1997*.

Hospitalitynet (2021). Hilton launches carbon neutral business meetings in Europe. www.hospitalitynet.org/news/4104707.html [Accessed: 22 August 2021]

Javelosa, J. (2016). David Attenborough: If we don't limit our population growth, the natural world will. https://futurism.com/david-attenborough-if-we-dont-limit-our-population-growth-the-natural-world-will [Acessed 30 August 2021]

Kallbekken, S. & Saelen, H. (2013) 'Nudging' hotel guests to reduced food waste as a win-win environmental measure. *Economic Letters*, 119, 325-327.

Khalid, R., Christensen, T., Gam-Hanssen, K. & Friis, F. (2019) Time-shifting laundry practices in a smart grid perspective: a cross-cultural analysis of Pakistani and Danish middle-class households. *Energy Efficiency* 12, 1691–1706.

Malone, S., McCabe, S., & Smith, A. P. (2014). The role of hedonism in ethical tourism. *Annals of Tourism Research*, 44, 241–254.

National Trust (2019). National Trust pub among first to list items according to their carbon footprint. www.nationaltrust.org.uk/press-release/national-trust-pub-among-first-to-list-items-according-to-their-carbon-footprint [Accessed 30 August 2021]

Patterson, B. (2015). What Australia can teach the World about surviving drought. *Scientific America*, 28 May. www.scientificamerican.com/article/what-australia-can-teach-the-world-about-surviving-drought [Accessed 22nd August 2021]

Pont, E. (2021). Population and climate change. *Enquêtes écosophiques*, https://medium.com/enquetes-ecosophiques/population-and-climate-change-88d43e23941a [Accessed 22 August 2021]

10

Serrenho, T., Zangheri, P. & Bertoldi, B. (2015). Energy Feedback Systems: Evaluation of Meta-studies on energy savings through feedback; EUR 27992 EN; doi:10.2790/565532

SMS (2021). Flexigrid. www.sms-plc.com/our-services/energy-management/flexigrid/ [Accessed 22 August 2021]

Sticklebarn Inn (n.d.) Menu, https://nt.global.ssl.fastly.net/sticklebarn-and-the-langdales/documents/our-current-menu.pdf [Accessed 30 August 2021]

Strava (2021) www.strava.com/mobile [Accessed 22 August 2021]

Tiefenbeck, V., Wörner, A., Schöb, S., Fleisch, E. & Staake, T. (2019). Real-time feedback promotes energy conservation in the absence of volunteer selection bias and monetary incentives. *Nature Energy* 4, 35-41.

Toyota (2011) Camry Hybrid How-To: Energy Monitor. www.youtube.com/watch?v=TESb-19vWOYQ [Accessed 22 August 2021]

Warren, C. (2017). Check-out survey conducted over 16 months. Griffith University.

Warren, C. (2018). *Encouraging pro-environmental behaviour change at tourist accommodation.* Thesis. Griffith University.

Warren, M. (2020). Tailor made is always best: Knowing what gamification work for you and why. My Green Butler. https://mygreenbutler.com/tailor-made-is-always-best-knowing-what-gamification-works-for-you-and-why/ [Accessed 31 August 2021]

Warren, M. (2021) Personal communication, 1 September.

WECA (2022). Energy assistance. www.weca.coop/energy-assistance

Yanev, V. (2021). Video game demographics – Who plays games in 2021. Techjury. https://techjury.net/blog/video-game-demographics/#gref [Accessed 1 September 2021]

Yang. R., Newman, M. & Forlizzi, J. (2014) Making sustainability sustainable: Challenges in the design of eco-interaction technologies. *CHI*, April 26-May 1, Toronto, Canada.

Yang, R., Pisharoty, D., Montazeri, S., Whitehouse, K. & Newman, M. (2016). How does eco-coaching help save energy? Assessing a recommendation system for energy-efficient thermostat Scheduling. *UBICOMP 16* (12-16 September) Heidelberg, Germany.

11 The Guest R/Evolution (Meaning)

Introduction

Hospitality is about winning over people through not being judgemental, applying empathy, generosity, and kindness. A sustainable future is only possible with the buy-in of guests, staff, and suppliers. Believe me, when you empower people to act positively by extending hospitality you will get that buy-in, and the power that unleashes is incredible.

The key points of this chapter:

- **Utilise character strengths**. Each and every one of us has strengths. From bravery to inquisitiveness, these qualities can be given room to express themselves through conserving behaviours.

- **Health and wellbeing have never been more important to guests**. People the world over are paying more attention to their physical health, mental health, and the health of the planet. Hospitality experiences that cater to good health have a competitive advantage.

- **Seek flow.** Aim always for sustainable hospitality offerings that facilitate moments of flow – of total commitment to and immersion in a given task. It should be rewarding for all involved.

- **Involve everyone**. When you look for allies you will be amazed by the number out there. Guests, staff, and suppliers are key to a sustainable future, but so too are NGOs, community groups, and local governments.

Conserving behaviours can make people happy. It can enrich holiday experiences, build loyalty, and be the centrepiece of beautiful memories for guests and staff alike. It can transform the industry and have a knock on effect on the lives of your guests too. In this chapter, I reveal why guests like to participate in conserving and can find adapting their behaviours makes them happy. Using real-world evidence from projects undertaken with my academic colleagues, I explore the motivation to participate in pro-environmental activities and sustain them, even if an individual does not hold a high level of affinity with nature.

Understanding what is at the heart of the guest's motivation to conserve will help you generate a more positive guest review, increase staff retention, reduce costs and carbon, and better support your efforts to regenerate your community. In addition, you will discover that it is not so much about whether people are environmentally minded, but the pleasure and positivity they gain from participating in conserving behaviours.

This last chapter is not the 'icing on the cake' that you add at the end of your sustainability initiative. It should be at the heart of the solution. Guest participation must be seen as an enhancement to a person's stay as it rewards them emotionally, besides assisting you to reduce impacts.

This chapter also challenges an accepted norm that guests will only comply with eco-friendly tourism provided it does not compromise their comfort and quality expectations. What that means is often poorly defined. Comfort can mean peace after a busy week, not being cold, or reconnecting with loved ones. Likewise, quality is a very unspecific term. Do we mean luxury? If so, we frequently get great pleasure from life's little luxuries that don't require ostentatious living.

As far back as Socrates (and before that, no doubt), we knew that pleasure was best when accompanied by intelligence so that we could appreciate something's value (Pursuit of Happiness, 2021). Earlier in this book, we discussed research that has applied theories that assess people's green intentions, but as we learnt, that is not necessarily an accurate measure of whether they will make green choices. If we consider the problem from another perspective, what motivates and drives people, we see the wealth of other opportunities. As I have explained, guests will happily adapt their behaviours once you persuaded them with the right combination of Materials and Skills, enabling them to apply their Meaning. Your guest experience solution should be transparent so that guests can appreciate their benefits (e.g. better food choices, healthier environment, greater comfort, authentic activities, knowing they have made a good choice) and see environmental and social results.

Tap into character traits

Tourism research often focuses on a narrow lens to assess our motivations to take eco-friendly actions, either a) by being incentivised or disincentivised, or b) by being altruistic. That is limited because we ignore that people also are motivated through drawing on their character strengths. To expand on this we are going to dive a little into psychology and philosophy. Not something you might expect, but it is necessary to think more deeply about guest and staff participation than simple incentives.

We as humans have virtues – moral values that affect the way we behave in society and help us grow, building our resilience and contributing to our wisdom (Emmons & Crumpler, 2000; Emmons & Paloutzian, 2003). Virtues affect our character, which we display in the way we conduct ourselves. There are a debated number of virtues as they can be strongly affected by culture and religion.

What has all this to do with tourism? People perform better and are more successful if they can build upon their strengths, rather than focusing on their weaknesses (Buckingham & Coffman, 1999). If you tap into people's character strengths – which stem from their virtues – you can persuade them more effectively and, by so doing, stimulate them to sustain those behaviours. That is the important part. They might do an action once, but you want them to keep going.

The approach is similar to the psychology of influence but uses *positive* psychology, which focuses on people's mental health, rather than the application of psychology which in the past focused a great deal on peoples' mental illness (Seligman & Csikszentmihalyi, 2000). What we are seeking is commitment to your idea of sustainable hospitality and the guest experience. People are only going to be genuinely committed when they like and are part of the solution. We do not want nodding heads and polite positive faces that change as soon as contact ends, so we must strive for commitment. We can do this by reaching out to people's own happiness using positive psychology.

How is this relevant to tourism?

When we value something, our actions to achieve those goals make us feel good. These values can sustain our effort to reach them. Some people think that it is vital that the world's rich biodiversity survives, and this sustains their efforts to work as a volunteer on an African holiday. Equally, they can feel it is good to celebrate their marriage anniversary, which sustains their saving for their escape to Fiji. We tend to use hedonism as a sort of shorthand for all tourists' desires for holidays. That's a danger because it devalues the pleasure we all get from nature, love, truth, freedom, adventure… This shorthand of hedonism camouflages the true values many of our guests actually have, which can hold back hospitality evolution.

Guests, like us, are motivated by self-interest. We are motivated by things we value, to take care of ourselves and our ability to perform. This is not the same thing as selfishness, where you waste without concern. This can be directed to ourselves and the world around us. So if we frame conserving resources, cutting waste, cutting carbon emissions, and promoting environmental benefits in a manner in which guests value themselves, we are more likely to appeal to their

11

character strengths, which in turn gains their commitment to applying better actions.

We all have traits that define us – interest in learning, wanting to be efficient, giving love, or applying great bravery or zestfulness. These traits stem from our character strengths and give us our own authentic way of thinking and living life to our optimum. They can drive us. They can drive your staff and guests' conserving actions.

Thinking more about building on your staff's individual strengths, rather than looking only at their weaknesses, is the way to go. We need our staff's commitment to sustainable hospitality. Being positive, enabling them, and working on their strengths is far more likely to build traction than rules, policies, and negative speak. Likewise, asking guests to apply System 2 thinking is not giving them a preachy message but enabling them to choose to stop, think more deeply, and draw on their strengths to apply the suggested action.

We are a service industry run by people for people 24/7/52. It is a happiness business. We offer hospitality to people who seek their well deserved holiday, or enjoy a successful event, or achieve a rewarding business trip. Taking a positive psychology approach lets us focus on connecting with people in a way that stimulates their own drive whilst moderating consumption and waste. It can also be applied to encourage our staff and guests to take adaptive behaviours in preparation for and during extreme weather events to minimise our resource use and fortify them to stay safe.

Drawing on an individual's character strengths is the lever that makes sustainability fun.

The variety of character strengths

We found that when guests apply their character strengths they become self-motivated and more satisfied when they accomplish tasks well. Nansook Park and colleagues identified 24-character strengths split between the virtues (Park et al., 2004). Using this criteria Associate Professor Alexandra Coghlan and I refined them to reflect pro-environmental behaviour strengths (Warren & Coghlan, 2016). These are displayed below.

We then conducted research to determine which were the most applied when it came to conserving on holiday. Our thinking was that if we better understand how to tap into people's strengths, then our experience design will benefit, and our persuasive communications could be refined.

Table 9.1: Pro-environmental character strengths

Character strength	Applied to pro-environmental behaviour
WISDOM & KNOWLEDGE	
Creativity [originality, ingenuity]:	Coming up with/putting into practice novel, different ways of living/consuming to minimise impacts on the environment
Curiosity [interest, novelty-seeking, openness to experience]:	Taking an interest in all of an ongoing environmental experience; exploring and discovering about one's impact on the environment; interested in new ways of living which minimise negative environmental impacts and might be positive impacts
Judgment [open–mindedness, critical thinking]:	Thinking environmental things through and examining them from all sides; not jumping to conclusions; judging environmental claims, defining environmental problems; changing one's mind in light of information; weighing all evidence (environmental, societal, social norms) fairly
Love of learning:	Mastering new pro-environmental skills, topics and bodies of knowledge, whether on one's own or formally; beyond curiosity to describe the tendency to add systematically to what one knows
Perspective [wisdom]:	Looking at the bigger picture, placing pro-environmental behaviours within a larger context.
COURAGE	
Bravery [valour]:	Not shrinking from a natural environmental threat, difficulty, or pain, speaking up for what is right for the environment even if there is opposition; acting on convictions even if unpopular and/or costly; includes physical bravery but not limited to it
Persistence [perseverance, industriousness]:	Finishing what one starts; persisting in pro-environmental action in spite of obstacles (internal and external); "getting it out the door"; taking pleasure in completing pro-environmental tasks.
Integrity [authenticity, honesty]:	Speaking the truth about one's pro-environmental behaviour and practices, presenting oneself in a genuine way; being without pretence; taking responsibility for one's feelings and actions towards nature and the environment
Zest [vitality, enthusiasm, vigour, energy]:	Describing a passion for the environment that translates into pro-environmental behaviours; not doing pro-environmental practices or behaviour halfway or half-heartedly; feeling alive and activated to enjoy the environment
HUMANITY	
Love:	Valuing a close relationship with nature (animals and planets); being close to animals and plants; valuing 'mother earth'
Kindness [generosity, nurturance, care, compassion, altruistic love, "niceness"]:	Undertaking an action because we feel a sense of care for nature. Doing favours and good environmental deeds for nature and natural resources; positively improving nature
Social intelligence [emotional intelligence, personal intelligence]:	Being aware of the motives and feelings of other people and oneself and how they conflict with the desire for pro-environmental behaviour; knowing what to do to be more pro-environmental; knowing one's own limitations.

11

JUSTICE	
Fairness:	Treating the environment according to notions of fairness and justice; not letting personal feelings bias decisions about nature; moderating behaviour to give nature a chance
Leadership:	Encouraging a group of which one is an member to get things done such as: encouraging pro-environmental change in a public-sphere; trying to see pro-environmental actions happen
Citizenship [social responsibility, loyalty, teamwork]:	Working well as a member of a group which cares for the environment; recognising that everyone has a role to play in protecting the environment, wanting to do one's bit, being loyal to the group; signing a petition, making a donation; belonging to an environmental group
TEMPERANCE	
Forgiveness and mercy:	Being understanding of how we as a species impact the environment, and wanting to do better. Forgiving those (including oneself) who have done harm to the environment; giving people a second chance; not being vengeful
Modesty and humility:	Letting one's pro-environmental accomplishments speak for themselves: not seeking the spotlight for one's actions; not regarding oneself as more special than one is
Prudence:	Being careful about one's choices; not taking undue risks; not saying or doing things that might later be regretted for the environment; weighing up alternatives and taking the one that is the least damaging.
Self–regulation [self–control]:	Formally regulating one's consumption to not waste natural resources, pollute nor harm habitats; to choose alternatives even when they do not offer financial benefits
TRANSCENDENCE	
Appreciation of beauty & excellence [awe, wonder]	Noticing and appreciating the beauty of the natural world and its symmetry
Gratitude:	Expressing an appreciation of nature. Being aware of and thankful for the good environmental things that happen in society by a company, community, institutions or individual; taking time to express thanks
Hope [optimism, future–mindedness, future orientation]:	Expecting the best from society for environmental care in the future; believing that a good future for nature and the environment is something that can be brought about by themselves, and others

Do travellers apply character strengths to choosing more sustainable holidays

To find out if people did apply their character strengths to pro-environmental holidays, I interviewed travellers using a set of survey questions, and then asked them why they had given that response (Warren, 2012a). Their answer to my 'why' question was then analysed using a technique called signature spotting. It is a method used by positive psychologists adopting strength-based approaches (Niemiec, 2013).

The results were analysed separately by Alexandra Coghlan and myself by coding responses to one of the 24 pro-environmental character strengths. We went on to compare our coding, and 98% agreement was achieved. Then a further independent researcher carried out a reliability check; at the end, 100% agreement was reached. We then compared the character strengths to the response to the research questions. Here's what we found.

An incredible 81% of participants who displayed a character strength said they "agree/strongly agree" with "I take environmentally friendly tourism considerations into account when choosing a holiday", whilst the same was noted for only 30% of participants who did not record a character strength. Similar responses were noted with my other questions.

In one example, they were asked to respond to the questions "I don't want to be told what the accommodation is doing to minimise its environmental impacts as long they are taking action". I found the majority of people did want to know. I asked them to explain their reasons. The way they replied revealed a range of character strengths, including curiosity, judgement, citizenship, hope, integrity, as well as five others. They said:

"It's always interesting to find out how others are acting & if anything can be improved" - Curiosity (Male, 45–64 years old)

"I'd like to know specifically what makes them 'eco-friendly' so I know I'm not being greenwashed" – Judgement (Female, 24–44 years old)

Interestingly people who applied their character strengths to my survey questions also were prepared to buy eco-friendly cleaning products, donate to charity, purchase green energy, participate in conservation activities on holiday, donate to wildlife causes, were interested in receiving carbon emissions information, preferred fresh local foods, and wanted to learn about the accommodation's green power (Warren, 2012b).

There was no difference between those who displayed these character strengths and the other travellers when it came to their holiday priorities like weather, destination choice, cost, indulgence, comfort, or to impress their fellow traveller.

These findings got me thinking. If you could tap into their character strengths, then would guests be happier to conserve, be prepared to take more eco-friendly adaptive actions in extreme weather, and save accommodation costs and carbon?

Guests apply character strengths to feedback

With these learnings in tow I then conducted several research studies to see if my idea was right, that pro-environmental character strengths would help create more sustainable hospitality. My first study was to see if the effect of eco-feedback was welcomed and why.

11

Two groups of guests were asked if they would like feedback whilst on holi-day. For those who did not see the feedback, only a third said yes they agreed it should be provided. The second group, who received multiple feedback reports during their stay, responded much stronger. 70.2% said they agreed/strongly agreed feedback should be provided — more than double. When I asked both sets of guests why had they given their answers, there were great similarities in the range and weight of pro-environmental character strengths. There was not one strength that was applied consistently, but both groups applied a similarly wide range of strengths.

The findings revealed two points. First, that people respond to feedback using different strengths. This is important to share with your staff so that they learn to understand why guests are willing to participate. It is definitely not the "'one size fits all" approach to "saving the planet."

Second, that seeing the eco-feedback convinced more than double the number of people who thought feedback was a good idea,because the evidence convinced them, leading them to draw on their strengths.

The benefits of drawing on character strengths

This tells us that before we need to even consider offsetting our carbon emissions, we can actually ask our customers to help us reduce. Character strengths are present in our staff too. so collectively, significant savings can be reached without major cost. It is achieved without having to rely on offsetting like tree panting (which takes 80 years to balance our CO2). And it is achieved without having to make a capital investment in large size renewables when we might need a considerably smaller and less expensive system.

Therefore first, consider how much you can save by drawing on people's strengths to help you conserve. This is freely given by guests. Providing feed-back can cost very little, and the payback can be in a few days, weeks or months, depending on the original baseline.

We need to turn to our strengths when coping with extended heatwaves and extreme events that require adaptive behaviours. If we only sit back and rely on energy to keep us cool and safe and ignore what we could do to pre-empt the need for high energy use, then we continue to put pressure on the environment. And so the cycle of high resource use, pollution and extreme weather events accelerates. Humans can adapt, we are very adaptable. Human can live in the Sahara and the North Pole. Offsetting is no solution for the here and now. Design your guests experience to enable your staff and guests to adapt, take pre-emptive measures to focus resources on areas that matter most. Plan ahead.

Strengths for feedback

What are the pro-environmental character strengths that guests apply to eco-feedback? When I asked guests whether they agreed or disagreed with the idea of accommodation providing eco-feedback, the most popular character strengths were curiosity (discovering one's environmental footprint) and judgement (assessing options fairly).

Table 9.2: Pro-environmental character strengths found in positive response to feedback

		My Green Butler %	Control %	Weighted %
Wisdom & Knowledge	Creativity	0	0	58.6
	Curiosity	25.7	28.6	
	Judgement	20.3	21.4	
	Love of learning	5.4	7.1	
	Perspective	5.4	4.8	
Courage	Bravery	1.4	2.4	13
	Persistence	0	2.4	
	Integrity	6.8	14.3	
	Zest	1.4	0	
Humanity	Love	1.4	4.8	12.9
	Kindness	2.7	0	
	Social Intelligence	10.8	4.8	
Justice	Fairness	4.1	2.4	6.9
	Leadership	1.4	0	
	Citizenship	2.7	2.4	
Temperance	Forgiveness and mercy	0	0	7.7
	Modesty and humility	0	0	
	Prudence	0	4.8	
	Self-regulation	9.5	0	
Transcendence	Appreciation of beauty	0	0	0
	Gratitude	0	0	
	Hope	0	0	

In total, there were 16 strengths recorded – see Table 9.2. This shows people respond differently to the idea of eco-feedback. It is not 'love' or kindness' to nature that people are motivated by, but the application of their wisdom and gaining knowledge (combined 58.6%) through the strengths of curiosity and judgement. They want to learn about their environmental footprint and make better choices. Guests were also motivated by courage (13%), in particular integrity, and being honest about one's footprint. Humanity (12.9%) was also valuable,

11

caring for nature and holding social intelligence to know that one's behaviour is in conflict with caring for the environment.

Guests also displayed the virtue of temperance. Here guests who had experienced My Green Butler were applying self-regulation to know exactly where and when to conserve, because they had seen feedback. Meanwhile guests who had a regular stay experience drew on their strength of prudence, to be careful. There were some guests who applied their virtue of justice (6.9%), believing they wanted eco-feedback because it was pro-environmentally fair and offered the opportunity to work with others as good citizens (Warren, 2018).

Not surprisingly, as my question had focused on eco-feedback, guests did not draw on transcendence, appreciating nature's beauty, being thankful for nature and hoping humans would be more pro-environmental. Yet this seems to be an underlying image from those message cards you see, "save xxx to save the planet".

In what ways can guests save?

People will consider applying themselves to new forms of behaviour if the experience design and persuasion are effective. Have a look at Table 9.3 to see the result from hundreds of guests to my questions of what actions they took following a stay using My Green Butler. It is important to remember that some of these actions are only relevant to certain times of day, season and weather conditions, so they will not be applied 100% of the time.

The list also reflects a self contained accommodation perspective, i.e. having kitchen facilities and windows that open. It also reflects a method to manage food waste on site ... having chickens. No doubt you can think of ways to replicate some of these factors in your own accommodation situation, whether resort, hotel, camp site, or B&B.

The take away point is just how much guests are actually prepared to adapt to the experience design. As they were prompted to conserve, turning lights off when not in their room was almost universal, as was recycling. Using features like a draught stopper for hot air prevention (35.3%) and cold air (22.5%), and choosing an extra blanket rather than using an electric blanket (29.3%), showed how people will adapt during cold and hot occasions. They are also prepared to conserve by timing their shower (41.3%), filling the kettle with the correct amount of water using a jug provided (46.7%), with 40.8% avoiding a bath and 30.4% using less hot water.

Many of these features were not available in the guests' own home, e.g. wood fire, ceiling fans, managing food scraps. They choose to participate in applying new Materials and Skills because it held relevant meanings to them: love of nature, self regulation, hope. They also responded due to persuasion wishing to comply, reciprocate, and follow advice.

Table 9.3: Pro-environmental action by My Green Butler guests

	actions applied throughout stay/sometimes
Turned off lights when not in a room	100
Recycled waste	93.1
Placed food scraps in chicken feed bucket	88.4
Showered less frequently during stay	52.3
Fed chickens with food scraps	50.4
Used water measuring jug for kettle	46.7
Used the bathroom clock to time your shower	41.3
Chose not to use the bath	40.8
Chose ceiling fans to circulate warm air	37.5
Took fewer baths	37.3
Opened window in kitchen instead of cooker fan	36.7
Used draught dog to stop hot air coming in	35.3
Used less hot water in the bath	30.4
Chose extra blanket instead of electric blanket	29.3
Chose ceiling fans to have cooler air	28.1
Chose extra blanket instead of fire or a/c	27.7
Used draught dog to prevent cold air coming in	22.5
Used gas kettle instead of electric	20.2
Selected dishwasher 'eco' setting	20
Closed curtains in the day to keep cooler	19
Made donation to local nature conservation	17.8
Only ran dishwasher when full	14.5
Was mindful in use of wood for the fire	14.3
Did not use an electric blanket	12.7
Rode bicycles	12.4
Washed dishes in the sink instead of dishwasher	12.1
Planted a tree for conservation	10.1
Closed curtains earlier to keep warmth in	7.1
Chose woodfire instead of a/c	6.7
Mindful use of gas cooktop/oven	6.3
Used green eco switch by TV	6.3
Chose opening windows for cooler air	6.1
Used less lighting in an occupied room	3.7
Chose not to use the a/c	3

11

Do people do what they say?

The recognition that guests draw on their strengths for eco-feedback does not automatically mean they apply them. So what did the research actually reveal?

These same guests had their resources monitored and were asked to record the pro-environmental actions they had taken. What we found was that 76.5% of guests who had received My Green Butler feedback had taken at least one pro-environmental action during their stay, compared to 48.6% of regular guests who said they had taken one action or more (Chart 11.1). These weren't one-off occurrences either. The My Green Butler guests chose to apply many multiple actions at a higher level of intensity than regular guests.

Looking more deeply (Chart 11.2), we found the butler technology stimulated pro-environmental actions across the year, particularly during seasonal change from summer to spring (March – April) and winter to spring (August to September). For context, this data is Southern Hemisphere. These peaks of activities during seasonal change demonstrate how guests were responding to the advice to take low- and no-carbon actions to advantage, or preempt big changes in temperature/conditions during seasonal fluctuations.

This emphasises how important it is to include a good range of Materials that empower guests to take pre-emptive actions. The different levels of action between the two groups led regular guests to have a higher inside temperature (Chart 11.3), most notably in Spring and Winter. The number of actions did not mean guests were uncomfortable as we compared the average annual temperature and found them similar (20.85C – 21.25C). In other words, the advice to take pre-emptive actions and use natural ventilation had kept them at a similar level of comfort.

I was interested to learn if family groups applied less pro-environmental behaviours? The My Green Butler group applied more actions overall, especially when they had one child (Chart 11.4). Overall though, both groups did see a decline in actions as the booking party size grew. Nevertheless families of three children who received the My Green Butler still applied three times the number of actions compared to regular guests.

The research was done at a site with four cabins with either a single guest room or two rooms. There were differences in aspect to the sun as the accommodation was scattered across the property. Statistically the number of bedrooms did not make a significant difference between how guests responded. Both sets of guests applied actions similarly (Chart 11.5), though there was a significant difference between the groups as expected.

Overall, guests who had been encouraged to conserve using the butler technology had taken an average of 11.9 pro-environmental actions compared to 6.06 for regular guests, a significant increase.

Did the guests really do what they said? Overall the My Green Butler group used 38.4% less electricity, 24% less water and 20.4% less gas than the regular guests. Comparing this data with the self-assessed actions and responses to feedback (Table 9.2), I found a strong case for guest participation. If people are encouraged to participate and conserve, are shown how to do so, and are given eco-feedback that enables them to reflect and refine their actions, my research shows you can encourage guests to apply their strengths and create a self-propelling saving system.

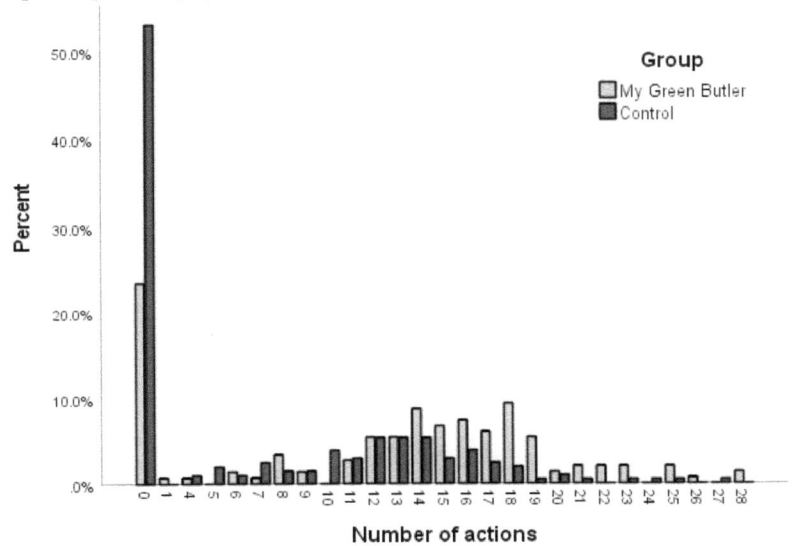

Chart 11.1: How many pro-environmental actions did guests take

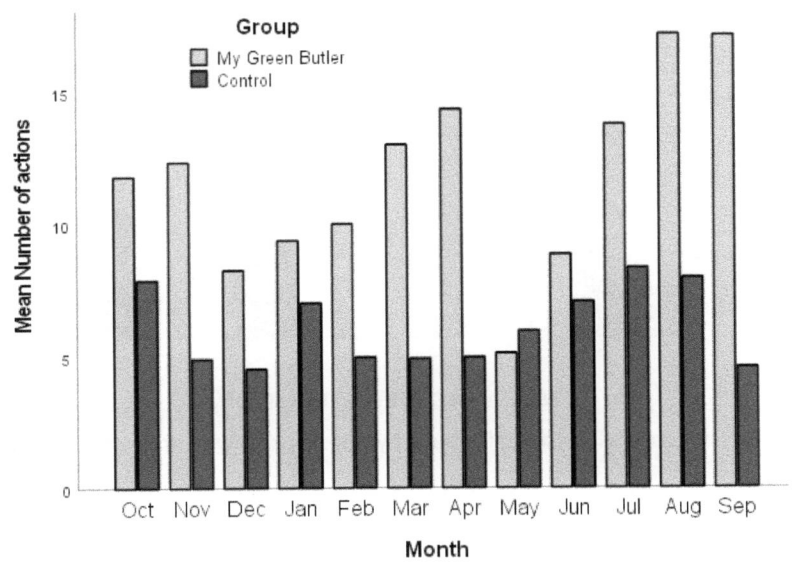

Chart 11.2: How many pro-environmental actions did guests apply, by month

11

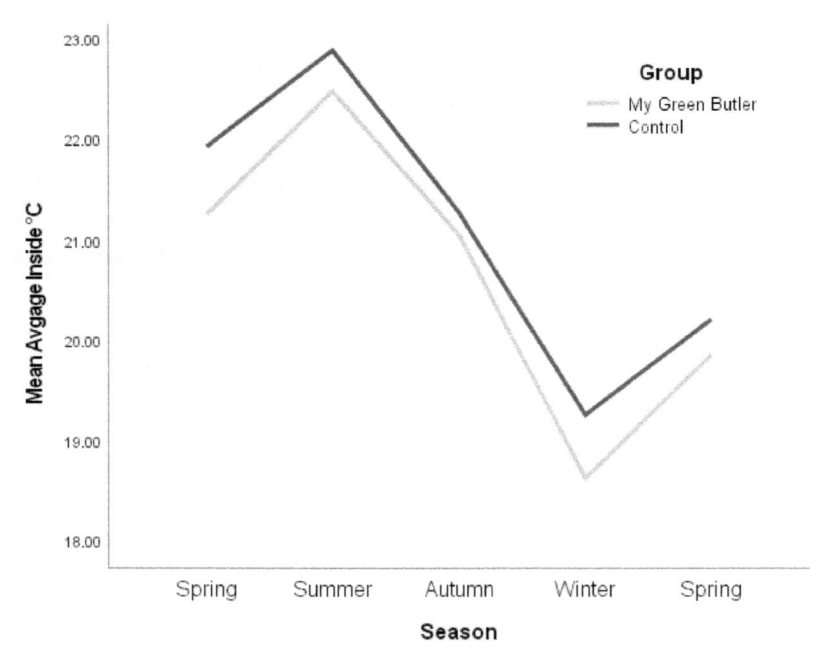

Chart 11.3: The average inside temperature of guest accommodation

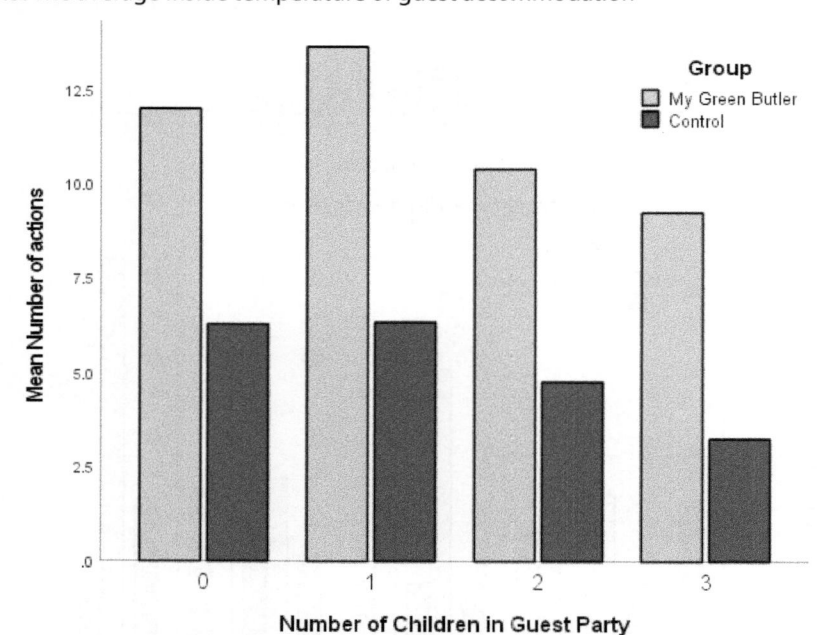

Chart 11.4: Number of pro-environmental actions by guests party with and without children

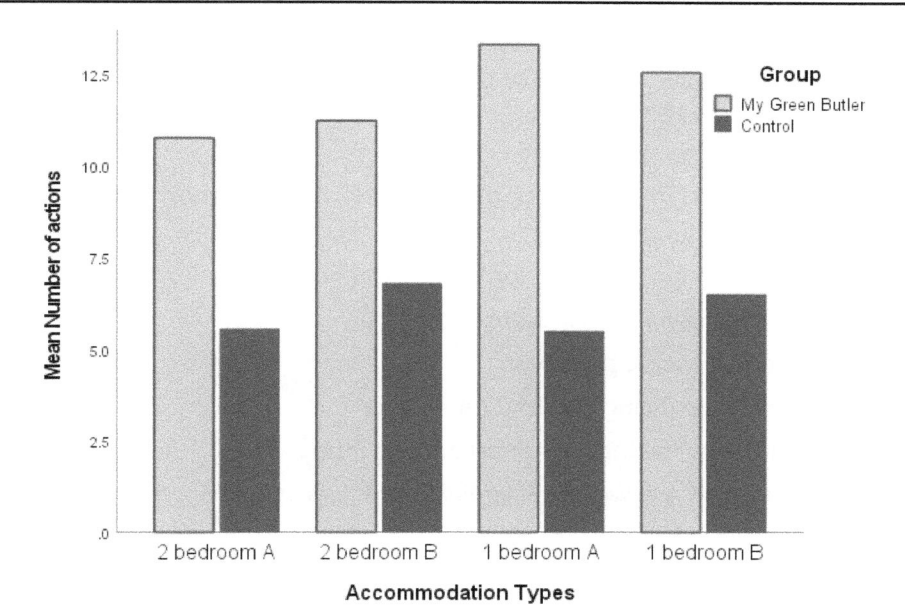

Chart 11.5: Number of pro-environmental actions by accommodation size

Table 9.4: Comparison in behaviours and resource saving

	My Green Butler Guests	Control Guests	Savings
Did you try to reduce (Yes %)	75.2	43.9	
Number of pro-environmental actions	11.99	6.06	
Average inside temperature C	20.85	21.25	
Average outside temperature	16.2	16.6	
Average Wh per guest per hour	88.52	122.54	38.4%
Average litre water per guest per hour	5.71	7.08	24%
Average m3 gas per guest per hour	0.00613	0.00738	20.4%

Health and well-being have never been more significant to our guests

Higher levels of education, longer life spans, and increased personal income is leading many to look after their health, arguably to higher levels than previously in history. Expenditure on online wellness courses is growing significantly in both developed and developing economies.

The pandemic has pushed the concept of wellness hotels to the forefront as we see hoteliers considering how to offer facilities that meet the needs of guests who have been working out at home for months, installing technology that can stream

11

workouts and adding specific spaces for yoga or other health orientated concepts. People are increasing aware of their diets and often prefer to pay higher prices for organic foods. The health of our planet is perhaps the ultimate indicator of everyone's future wellness.

Research has found five specific character strengths most linked to high well-being (Park et al., 2004):

- Zest, having a passion for the environment
- Love, closeness with nature
- Hope, expecting the best
- Gratitude, being thankful for nature
- Curiosity, taking an interest and exploring

The definitions here reflect pro-environmental values, not the original paper's.

Creating happiness

It is when you are applying character strengths that you feel positive emotions, which is a wellness benefit. Suppose we could encourage this further when guests were conserving resources. In that case, we could restore some of the magic that tourism had when numbers were smaller and tourism was a more individual expression of one's interests and desires. I am not suggesting that you turn your hospitality business into a niche wellness service (unless you want to), but to draw from your guests' self-interested motivations and link to the new service you offer them. It is certainly in their self interest to adapt to extreme weather. It is certainly in their self interest that you support local nature conservation they can see, or enjoy your recommendations of authentic and more sustainable places to visit.

Sweeten your approach

Psychologists reviewed nine studies from around the world and found that when people conserved resources, they get enjoyment from:

- Participation, when you see you have a role and feel your efforts matter
- Skills, applying them to solve problems well
- Frugal, being good at making things last

They don't feel it is contradictory to simultaneously value and enjoy luxury – and remember that luxury doesn't mean opulence (De Young, 2000).

Therefore, the more you focus on facilitating guests' enjoyment from conserving (skilful at being frugal), the more they will be able to participate. And it's not contradictory to offer guests some of life's little luxuries and encourage them to care for the environment. It might persuade them more as each guest has a very individual balance of these values.

Case studies

Guests enjoy memorable and meaningful experiences when applying their character strengths and personal interests. This can be nurtured by increasing advice to guests, giving them time to reflect on those experiences, and inviting them to support goals that align with their strengths (Wan, 2018). Here are two examples:

Montague Island (New South Wales) is a tiny island managed by the National Parks and Wildlife Service, which has reused the empty lighthouse keeper's quarters for short stay holiday lets with guided diving activities to observe sea lions and learn about the heritage of the island. A key part of the stay involves visitors actively participating in conservation work, which can involve a day inspecting baby penguins burrows, or removing weeds to restore their habitat. It is not light work and involves plenty of bending and physical exertion. Visitors appear to love donating time to this worthy cause. They get joy from knowing what they do benefits the wildlife, and they feel good about themselves giving something back (Westwood, 2008). It is also a fascinating activity that children appear to enjoy (which can be confirmed by the author's family responses to their holiday) as they may sense the authentic connection between their actions to improve the 'cute' wildlife's habitat.

Echidna Walkabout (Victoria) is a Responsible Tourism Award-winning wildlife guided tour based in Australia. Tours are mostly filled with international visitors from Europe, North America, and Asia. After viewing koalas in their native habitat with personalised interpretation, the guide will then invite members of the party to remove weeds in the surrounding area. This was tentatively done to start with as the company expected only a mild response and didn't want to annoy paying customers. To the operator's surprise, visitors enthusiastically participated. Some put a great deal of effort and time into the process of removing harmful weeds. Their work is self-sustaining. For example, when some visitors see larger weeds, it becomes a positive challenge, and then they like to admire the results of their work. The duration of this volunteer behaviour ranges from ten minutes to an hour (Duffey, 2016).

Reasons why leisure time adds to life satisfaction

We can maximise the benefits of our conserving experiences for guests if we better understand how leisure activities increase peoples' sense of well-being and life satisfaction, i.e. we make our guests happier.

Research has found that people's motivations for choosing leisure pursuits, beyond the initial simplification that they like having fun, is because they feel more autonomous, enjoy acquiring new knowledge, and like the time with other people (Kabanoff, 1982; Crandall et al. 1980). Think about focusing your requests

11

to conserve with benefit-led suggestions for pampering yourself, learning something new, and doing something as a group.

We can heighten this happiness by savouring the moment. Psychologists William Compton and Edward Hoffman suggest this savouring process starts with a person being absorbed in what they are doing, being encouraged to focus on the sensation from the activity, being able to record that occasion to memory, then sharing it with others and allow themselves to feel good about the experience (Compton & Hoffman, 2013). Sounds very much the recipe for all those holiday tales one tells and hears from friends, right? In creating new, more sustainable guest experiences, we could do well to think how we can nurture those steps.

The leisure activities that stand out are therefore more meaningful, enable that 'me time', build skills, are a break from routines, and help us build positive relationships with others. We encourage guests to borrow bikes, pay for a picnic, and take time to paddle in the stream at their destinations. This goes hand in hand with other conserving messages.

Likewise, one of my clients supports a bee foundation. Guests can view a hive at their hotel (from a safe distance) and read information about the effort involved in making honey – a worker bee only makes ½ teaspoon in its lifetime (Complete Beehives, 2019). This message works well with my service's feedback that does not just tell guests the amount of food waste saved; it reports that by so doing, they have not wasted the production efforts to grow that food, the fuel to deliver it, energy and water to cook it, and that food not wasted can be given to others. Their straightforward decision to avoided waste has a wealth of positive benefits repercussions. Watching the beehive lets them savour the strengths they applied to conserve.

Flow - how we feel when applying character strengths

If you are planning to create a new experience from scratch, consider the benefit of absorption. When you enjoy doing something you love, time can feel like it has taken on another dimension. You can quite literally feel you are immersed very deeply and lose all sense of time. Have you ever felt this? Psychologists call this *flow*, where you lose self-awareness and are absorbed completely, no matter how important or humdrum. In the end, you feel contented, satisfied. It is the sort of satisfaction that can be calming or an elation.

The psychologist Mihaly Csikszentmihalyi was interested in what happened to people when they seemed absorbed in artistic production. He found that people gained positive emotions as they made happiness occur through voluntarily accomplishing something difficult (Csikszentmihalyi, 1990).

The elements I have been talking about should be staged. You want to encourage this flow and the time for reflecting and sharing. You do not want to destroy the moment with eco-feedback that interrupts the magic. It must be a balance of skills, challenge, and immersion. For this reason, I do not necessarily prescribe constant digital display feedback when you have asked guests to apply new skills if you want them to feel good about something. Such feedback could interrupt their flow as the pressure to comply supersedes the learning of the skills.

Consider an earlier example of the eco-lodge where guests' flow was the balance of applying skills and the challenge to save energy and water in their bathroom. It was only later they discussed feedback over breakfast with their host. It was a social activity that allowed them to savour what they had achieved. The danger with instant feedback in a hospitality situation is that it can feel pressurising rather than emotionally rewarding for making the right decision. They might think, "Sure, I am happy to save, but I didn't enjoy the experience."

Likewise, eco-feedback recording exactly how many weeds visitors removed during *Echidna Walkabout's* tour is not provided during the experience. Instead, they allow guests to be immersed in the activity and savour their results. Feedback comes in the form of thanks and congratulations later. Likewise, for your staff, first advise them on new practices, coach them, let them savour what they achieved, then provide eco-feedback and suggest ways to improve skills. This helps build people's emotional satisfaction through the flow experience and enables reflection whilst savouring the results.

Guests as 'craft consumer'

We have witnessed major changes in society and tourism in recent years. Guests seek more individualistic holidays (my example of a French gite holiday in Chapter 2), and the power of the internet has given them the ability to easily and quickly self-select different types of places to stay.

Social scientists have noted that people are increasingly confident in pursuing their self-interests to apply greater creativity in how they spend their money and time, something accelerated for some during the Covid pandemic (Suri, 2020; Baxter et al, 2020; Brignall, 2020). Individuals may now seek to design, produce, and consume without as much regard to their perceived image, unlike in previous decades, because they are clear about who they are. An example would be the growth of Airbnb and Uber – we design, produce, and consume our holiday package.

Greater market fragmentation:

- Craft production (ensemble activity) where people design and build what they want (DIY), e.g. booking self-contained accommodation, bedding arrangement, choosing selected services and 'living' in the destination.

11

- Customised experiences where the mass-produced items are adjusted for your needs, e.g. long-haul flights where you can choose class, seat, menu, films, transport to terminal.
- Personalising what are essentially mass-produced things, e.g. the welcome card in the hotel room.
- Craft consumption where people appreciate individualistic things that are made, e.g. choosing to eat at that special little bistro which hand makes all its pies, using lamb from the family farm.

Craft production and consumption is a process where people want to make things more unique, meaningful, and 'beyond price', so they become precious. They can be driven to counter standardisation and search to express their individuality, cultural, and spiritual values (Campbell, 2005).

A factory-like production of hospitality experience might be leading to a reaction for greater personalisation and customisation. As I have explained earlier, giving guests' greater control over materials and providing the Skills and Meaning allows them to participate and save resources through their own self-expression of applied strengths. There is, therefore, an increasing danger that the more we automate, the less humans learn and are in control. Lack of control will lead to wastage. Let guests and staff craft solutions by humanising technologies.

Maximise guest motivations to help save

Applying your character strengths to activities that really matter can increase your sense of what psychologists call *flourishing*, the highest good people can reach (Ethics Centre, 2016). A simple example could be that apple pie you love to bake. You create that apple pie following the steps closely, cutting the fruit perfectly, making your own pastry, adding a zest of lemon. It is something you love to do, and you devote time to make it perfect. Taking it out of the oven makes you proud of the result and gives your a little boost to your day. Pursuing activities which reward you like this can increase your happiness.

If we design guest experiences that enable people to apply themselves as best as they can, and they see the positive results from eco-feedback, this can give them a little boost. It also builds their confidence in the advice you offer. Think of my example of guests taking their food waste to feed chickens. It might seem non-descript, but when you read our guest book reviews you'll see that such moments of connection can be important for some people's wellness.

We also need to persuade guests to adapt when there are extreme weather events like heatwaves. We need to persuade them to take pre-emptive adaptive actions before they get too hot and use high levels of energy. We need to guide them to keep cool and safe. If they apply this advice, remain comfortable, and see their energy use has still been modest, they are more confident to repeat the actions the next day. Success breeds success, and what was horrid hot weather transforms from being a disabler to an enabler, building people's resilience.

Remember, when I discussed politeness, smiling isn't necessarily the end result you seek from a guest. For example, in some occasions people can smile to get rid of unwanted approaches from sales people. The negative face, when you are considering something, can be far more important. When I see guests feeding the chickens with their own food waste some are considering the life of a free-range hen, enabled by judgement.

So, the gem is to incorporate opportunities for guests to improve their wellness within the core of your eco-friendly experience design. When guests apply their character strengths and enjoy the flow of the moment, they can create memorable holiday experiences that improve their sense of wellness. Enjoying more memorable holiday experiences is more likely to encourage them to be a returning guest and a guest who posts a positive review and recommends you to friends.

Consider the guest experience design (Chapter 6). How can you integrate opportunities for guests to craft their stay and in so doing have a more enriched sustainable hospitality experience?

Story: Creating special times

Holidays are about those special times when we can reflect and savour. We tend to slow down to absorb the moment – a System 2 opportunity to share meanings, when guests can reconsider their actions.

In Arabia, I stayed at a hotel where there was a wonderful Arabic cardamom coffee display with seating arranged in the traditional way as though in a tent. Preparation and drinking of the coffee is a ceremony that involves pouring the water into a *dallah* (coffee pot) then decanting the coffee into *finjan* (small brightly coloured cups). You are then offered local dates that are amazingly soft, sweet and creamy in texture. Coffee continues to flow till you wiggle your cup as a sign of contentment.

The moment naturally leads you to ask questions to your new Bedouin friend. You might start to learn about the traditions of the Bedouin people, how precious water is (hence the small cups), and the two-thousand-year-old irrigation systems (now a world heritage site) that waters date palms. You might even learn about the old mosque where the names of the local farmers are listed on the outside wall indicating their water-sharing schedule (Solaiman Al Rifia, 2017). You discover there is an order about sharing resources in the harsh desert environment.

If we can encourage people to stop and think, whilst enjoying a special moment, we can help them assimilate System 2 thinking to memory as a positive experience. The Special Time for drinking coffee could, for example, easily convey a message of water conserving at the hotel and we might apply our strength of 'citizenship' and 'self control' in a respectful manner.

11

These are my thoughts, but Guliz Ger and Olga Kravets beautifully described the process of tea drinking as a ritual and an important social exchange in Turkey. The time it takes to make and drink tea is part of the fabric of Turkish culture (Ger & Kravets, 2009). We might initially think such moments as unimportant yet they can become moving and memorable events for our guests which help tell your sustainability story. We feature Special Times in My Green Butler through wellness and mindfulness messaging as it has become increasingly valued by the public.

Happily consuming less

What could be some of the alternative conserving behaviours you encourage your guests to do? Here are two examples, take time to come up with ideas more relevant to your own location and property type.

- Taking a glorious bike ride through the countryside ... avoids carbon emissions from driving.
- A brisk walk through the park, gardens ... gets you warm, so less need for heating.

The joy of riding through your beautiful local place and seeing the sights the accommodation has recommended could be a joyful break for someone living in a city. This might draw on their 'zest' or 'love' of nature. Feeling the soft breeze on their skin, smelling fresh scents as they glide past lovely views. They may not have ridden a bike for a long time, and as their skills improve, they can have a wonderful sense of achievement, making them feel happy. Offer them the reward of a tasty homemade snack at a stall on the route. The trip becomes more special.

The pleasure of a brisk walk in the morning gets the mind going. Tell the guests what to see in the park and lead them to view some conservation work through the efforts of local volunteers. What they discover can trigger hope and gratitude for what is being achieved. You did not give them just a map or leave them to an app; you gave a personal recommendation. You could fuel this by introducing a game element of distance, time, and calories.

Our job often is to create diversions. Left to their own device, guests can sometimes be lost with too many choices and high expectations for their well-earned break. They are not necessarily very good at enjoying leisure time. When there are several members in the group, there tend to be the petty stresses of agreeing on itineraries and pressure of planning, which get in the way of the holiday dream.

Spend more time thinking about the activities you recommend that introduce authentic, more sustainable experiences close to their accommodation, so they spend less time travelling about, and so reduce their carbon emissions. Lace the recommendations with stories that can draw on guests' character strengths to delight. They might repay you with great reviews because their sense of happiness has been heightened. Building this relationship can influence guests' level of free will reciprocation to help you conserve.

Story: Planting Trees – Planting ideas

We offered guests the opportunity to plant trees on our property. They can book the service online or when they arrive. For a small fee we provide a small seedling native to our area. They sign their certificate with details about the tree and its habitat benefits to local birds, and then sign an audit sheet which we keep to tally the numbers. Then we head across the grounds and discuss a suitable location. We may then talk in a relaxed way; most often, they like to know how the property has changed since we arrived.

I bring a spade, but they are encouraged to dig. For some, it's the first time they have dug up soil or planted a tree in the garden (increasingly less so for young children as preschools and primary schools are embracing gardening and land care). They water the tree and put a guard around it. Many request we take a picture of them beside their tree. If you ask them the reason for choosing this activity, inevitably, it has some deeper meaning, often very personal. Guests could well be applying strengths of 'love' and 'kindness'.

Figure 11.6: The tree planting experience.

Kids will name the tree. Parents will talk about return visits. Both want to remember exactly where it is located. The barriers are down, and they will want to chat to understand our efforts to conserve. They may well share their ideas for refinements on our experience design or ways to apply our suggested adaptive behaviours at home. Tree planting is what we are physically doing, but planting ideas is what occurs during flow and savouring. The ceremony reinforces our other efforts and creates a holistic experience.

You might not have space or time for tree planting, but develop an experience that enables your guests to apply their strengths, and you will sow the seeds of new thinking and guest loyalty. It is particularly relevant to staff who find the exchange self-rewarding and helps them to see their role as much more than a job but providing sustainable hospitality.

11

Guests repeating skills

There is an overriding guest benefit from applying your conservation suggestions. When they apply them multiple times, their skills improve.

Here's another example from my own business. Rather than have guests use the reverse cycling a/c for heating, we focused on getting guests to use slow-burning combustion stoves that use sustainably sourced wood from the property. When I explain how to set a fire, guests watch with curiosity. Recognising the logic of first starting with paper, then twigs to sticks and small logs. They memorise the amount of material and the size and shape of the final arrangement. It is much more complex and time-consuming than flicking a switch. After they have lit the fire, they have to continuously feed it, unlike a reverse cycle air conditioning working on a thermostat. Each day they set the fire and repeat, their skills improving.

Rather than seeing this as irksome task, guests apply their curiosity to learn how to set the fire. They repeat the process in flow. They savour the experience they have created by sitting back and admiring their work. Our eco-feedback guides them on when to start the first fires and report how much wood they have used. Just keeping warm becomes a stay experience. The thrill of seeing their self-improvement elevates an activity into a rewarding accomplishment. Our guest books are full of remarks about the "lovely wood fires".

From my monitoring, I know guests who have been shown how to use the wood fires hardly use the electricity for heating. They are quite prepared to spend time and effort to make and enjoy the fire rather than the a/c's immediate response to the touch of a button. Over time many get better and better and more efficient, and they revel in telling us how over their stay, they honed their skills. We help those who need more coaching, and they apply gratitude and still enjoy the fire.

You are right to assume that not all guests like this, sometimes a few guests have chosen the convenience of the electric heating on their last morning. But in total, we have cut electricity use in winter by more than 30%. That's a result!

Is that effort from our side worth it? As I have said earlier, winter became busier for us than the original peak at summer holidays. Guests come back to repeat those skills, apply their character strengths, and as a result use less electricity. They see it as a positive end result of their experience and skills development. Does that mean we used more firewood? On the contrary, we have cut our bioenergy by 38% thanks to advice and monitoring (Warren et al., 2018).

Advice allows people to repeat behaviours and build their skills. Similar to the wood fire, you could illustrate the carbon footprint of your menu items so they can choose a low carbon meal or provide a carbon comparison of riding to an attraction rather than driving their car. To sustain these actions, guests must be able to recognise the value of their choices. Show them the results each time. When they pay the bill for the meal, show them the carbon footprint of that meal compared to the average. When they return the bikes, show them the carbon difference they have made and how, if sustained over a 14 day holiday, it makes a huge difference. They will become better at learning to choose less impactful ways, seeing their progress, and enjoying something different that might otherwise have been mundane.

Increased staff Skills and Meaning

Our profession is about people – staff delivering a service and guests consuming it – but it can be so much more if we surpass everyone's expectations. What can be missing in this exchange is a sense of value that distinguishes the experience. Most staff want more than a job, and most guests want more than a stay. If you have worked hard and won converted awards or achieved high review rankings, then you recognise that this extra effort brings smiles to everyone and gives them a stronger sense of value from working or staying at your accommodation. This, too, can be achieved by introducing approaches to conserve.

By grasping the opportunity to teach people how to save, you are doing social good – sharing the consequences of wasting and demonstrating practical solutions which people can apply every day. The beauty is that helping people improve their skills can cost very little, a lot less than equipment, and the payback can be significant. It can also take less time because there is less infrastructure to maintain.

By taking strong action to conserve, you add meaning to working and staying at your accommodation. People take you more seriously because you are going beyond their expectations and see the greater good you strive for, to help them learn practical skills, however small.

Surpassing the standard commercial exchange between staff and guests exceeds guest expectations. This has an automatic knock-on benefit of building better reviews, increasing demand and revenue.

Character strengths are also relevant for staff

Some managers confide that retaining staff and motivating them is their top priority. Its importance should not be underestimated because staff are an essential factor in becoming more sustainable.

Sourcing and retaining staff takes time and money. As a manager, you can build loyalty not simply through salary adjustments, but by supporting the staff, building up close working relationships, and strengthening employees' identification with your property (Ineson et al., 2013; Gable, 2021). Applying character strengths is also true for staff. We each individually have different strengths.

11

What I have described above about your guests can also be applied to motivating your team, building their positive emotions, and feeling part of something they can believe in. Follow the principles I have described above to retain and inspire your colleagues.

As an example, imagine you have explained to staff the best way to take preemptive actions in advance of a heatwave. This means additional duties like shading the building's windows, closing off underused sections so energy and your cooling system is concentrated on areas of most importance, and keeping doors closed to avoid loss of cooler air. The staff might find this frustrating at first because it can seem to get in the way of their other duties. Providing a list of the actions you want them to take is not sufficient. Just as the guests might need coaching, so do staff.

Step one, give them:

- The big picture vision – the pre-suasion.
- Examples of how important their role is.
- Demonstration of what you want.

Now let them apply their actions, with a moment to savour the result.

Step two, report to them:

- Eco-feedback – what were the effects of their actions.
- Feedback from guests and other staff members
- And ask them, what could we have done better?

Step three is:

- Refinement of the goals
- Agreement and repeat

Completing the information loop using evidence enables the staff members to realise the broader impacts and benefits of their actions. Before the monitoring of resources, temperatures and other conditions, feedback was often one dimensional and therefore lacked full meaning.

Staff might have been unconvinced at first, perhaps a bit annoyed to do extra duties, but with the debriefing you are drawing out their curiosity. Positive results will fuel their persistence as they see they are making a difference.

Case study: **Even sceptics join in**

Joan is a member of our housekeeping team. She was not bothered about saving energy and thought the idea of taking pre-emptive action to keep the accommodation cool for guests would be worthless. "Why bother? The guests just change everything and whack on the a/c!"

Joan saw that we introduced the My Green Butler smart technology and recorded what happened in the accommodation. This became the evidence. We demonstrated how setting up the cottage reduced the inside temperature on hot days. She could see the figures. Over time my wife showed her the benefits of pre-setting the room. She also heard the guest gratitude for entering a cool room and not having to hear the a/c. The mere fact that we had taken pre-emptive action convinced the guests to conserve. She saw savings. Soon Joan came around and was telling us she had applied those measures before we had even asked her. She had started to recognise the outside weather conditions and changes, then chose to help, applying 'leadership' and to the guests 'kindness' so that they were in a cooler safer room without using lots of energy. Joan now applies pre-emptive measures at home.

Involving everyone

Synchronise all behaviours to conserve. It maximises savings and increases people's happiness. Involve everyone in your revolutionary hospitality experience – staff, suppliers, and guests. They can all participate. Share your problems, agree on solutions, receive and reflect on feedback refine goals. This stimulates people's strengths.

Use guest participation as a strategy to improve staff participation – not only through the experience design but by sharing guest performance with staff. Help staff connect with values they prize. I note that another member of our team loves the chickens and spends extra time ensuring all food scraps are given to them and conscientiously watching out for their welfare. When guests walk by, she introduces them to the chickens. This is all over and above her duties to deliver excellent customer service.

As staff apply new conserving skills, let them see monitored feedback and enjoy their self-improvement. Give them more meaning by letting them share in good causes to support and be involved in the guest experience designs that encourage conserving.

I have been amazed by the genuine support we receive from our community, interested parties in government, NGOs, and suppliers of technology, when I share knowledge about conserving. Even OTAs now want to progress greener agendas – notice how Booking.com (Booking.com, 2021) reports sustainability, how MEWS offers advice (MEWS, 2021), but perhaps the biggest game changer is Google's spotlighting sustainable hotels (Google, 2021) which many feel is a game changer. You will see much more from them in the future as they better understand how to present and promote greener solutions. Involve everyone to make this revolutionary transition.

11

Draw on your character strengths

While hospitality is deep within our cultures as professions, we urgently need to become more scientific in the way we design and optimise our service. I have talked about guests and staff, but what about you? You have read this far, so you've already applied strength of character. Keep tapping into what really matters to you. Is it leadership, bravery, integrity, or any of the other 24 strengths? Shape your overall programme around those strengths, use them to help create a company culture that progresses sustainable hospitality. Company culture matters more than strategy, and if you build it around sustainability, you will have a double-edged advantage.

If you really want to stand out as a business, benefit the environment, support your local community, then follow the steps explained in this book. Go back to Chapter 5 now and make a start. Use the tools in the resources to help you further.

Read about the results from some of my case studies at www.mygreenbutler. com. Learn how owners and managers in hospitality are revving up to embrace their next evolutionary step forward to interact with guests — involving them in conserving production and co-creating consumption of their experience.

Innovative interlinking steps

Your property's evolution journey to become more sustainable will most likely be in stages that grow and reinforce each other as you apply more solutions. This is what happened at our business. Being small, we introduced new ideas in stages, building on each so that, in the end, we had a holistic solution that created a really powerful business result. With each stage of refinement, you build up an even stronger body of knowledge about your property, its characteristics, the behaviour of staff and guests, and how to persuade them.

My journey of applying sustainability over 14 years was most strongly influenced by gaining knowledge. Some of the most influential triggers that enabled me to take progress steps were complying with certification programmes (Ecotourism Australia), entering state and national tourism awards programmes (their criteria gave me focus), and undertaking and maintaining our carbon audit (since 2006). The conceptual knowledge from certification and awards was helpful, but the audits showed me where to focus.

The adage, monitor, measure, and manage is helpful to a point. But the word 'manage' is vague. Manage against what criteria? What are your goals? To stimulate the innovation our industry requires, I prefer to interpret this advice differently, to measure, monitor and then *image, inspire*, and *improve*. It is more specific and reflects that we have to be creative to evolve our guest experience, involving everyone in conserving and continuously improve as new technologies and social trends enable us to take steps forward.

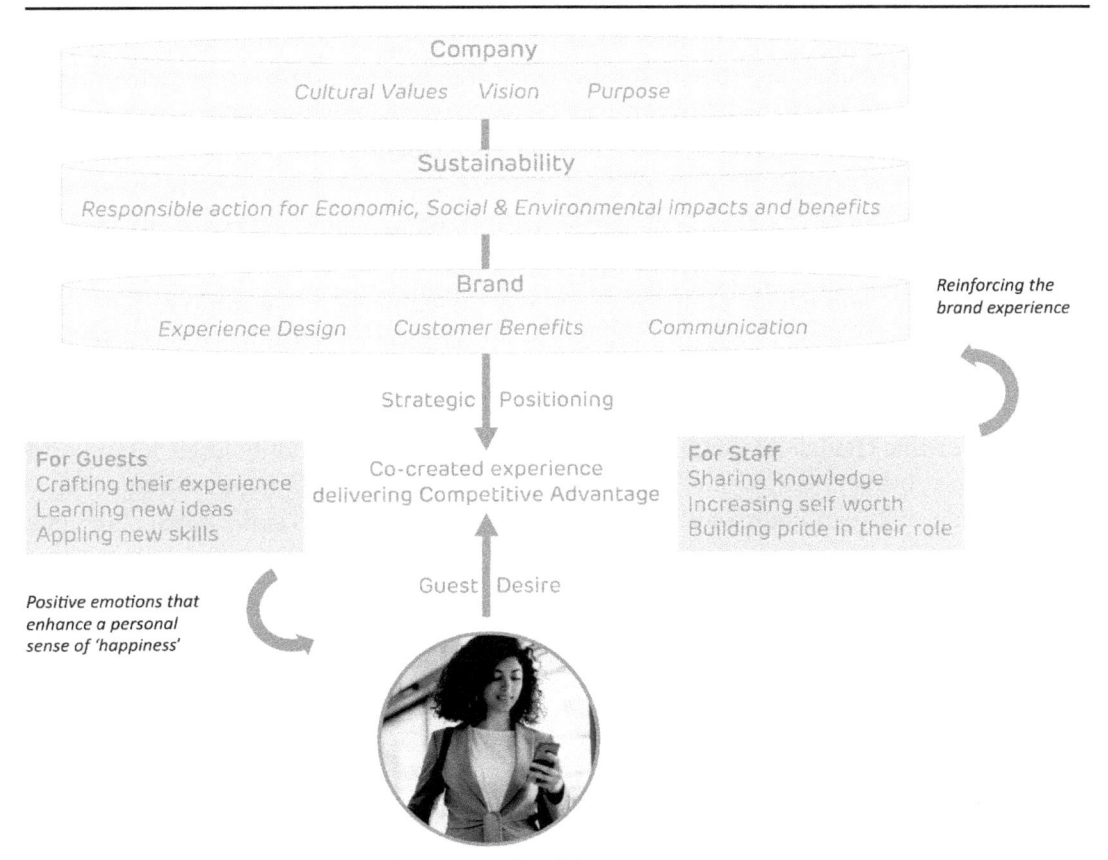

Figure 11.7: The route to *sustainable* Competitive Advantage

Innovation is like piecing together Lego bricks. Each brick in itself is not an innovation. It might be new to you, but it is not a radical change. It is the combination of multiple different types of bricks that enables us to create a holistic result. Simply adding a more efficient cooler, food waste technology, or movement sensor are not game-changers. But they are the bricks of change. How will the business look when all these features and more are integrated?

This becomes sustainability-oriented service innovation that tackles process, organisation, service and marketing as an integrated whole for a service industry, rather than the technology focus of manufacturing (Warren et al., 2018). Technology is a great enabler, but company culture will drive your innovation because conserving is all about people, not machines.

Involving your staff and guests in creating hospitality makes good business sense. Your staff can reinforce, re-invigorate and sustain the magic of the stay experience by demonstrating your strategic positioning in everything they do. Your guests co-create their experience, sometimes crafting it and through this enjoy positive emotions and feelings of happiness. They really enjoy their stay.

11

This is simply good business sense when at the same time you are able to reduce your sustainability liabilities and grow your assets, as I have shown through this book. Taking responsibility to shape your business through a guest-centred strategy that targets conserving behaviours enables you to improve the equity for everyone.

The consumer is way ahead of the hospitality industry. The majority have accepted that change is inevitable. They are making daily changes to their routines and habits, bit by bit. They want good news and want to to be part of progress. Seize this opportunity. Make sustainability the flame that burns powerfully at the heart of your business, build your company culture around it, invite your guests to participate. There is a massive business opportunity by embracing positive change and offering sustainable hospitality. Do not hold back but build your transformation surely, step by step, and you, your staff, guests and destination will reap the rewards. I wish you all the very best to enjoy advancing your business.

Please do use the freely available resources and videos to help on that journey: www.mygreenbutler.com/resources.

Summary

In this chapter, we have covered why guests can find participating in sustainable hospitality enjoyable. Positive emotions grow as guests apply their character strengths and become more immersed in the experience. Encouraging people to apply their character strengths can be applied to create a positive company culture that stimulates sustainability-oriented service innovation.

Focusing on positive psychology and character strengths offers an alternative approach to guest participation in eco-friendly actions. My practical experience running our successful 4 ½ star accommodation family business and my academic research over three continents shows taking responsibility is not necessarily about how strong staff/guests' pro-environmental attitudes are. Instead, it is much more about designing experiences that have sustainability built-in, using people's character strengths to minimises impacts and maximise benefits at the accommodation and beyond.

Through this book, I have shared much of that research and the debate has focused on measuring levels of people's commitment to turn their care for the environment into real-life action (see Chapter 2). If you present your new guest experience in a manner that elicits people's character strengths, significant carbon reduction and resource savings can be achieved. By providing eco-feedback, eco-coaching, cultural and nature immersion, you can enable people to reflect on their actions, savour their progress, and motivate them to repeat those responsible actions. Repetition of these newly learnt adaptive behaviours builds guests' skills, and provide a self-reward to sustain conserving results.

Eco-feedback significantly increases guests' application of their character strengths, stimulating greater adaptive behaviours to make significant resources savings like cutting electricity by 38%. Guests accept feedback because they are reciprocating the efforts the host has made. They apply themselves to accept and use eco-feedback through their traits of judgement, curiosity, social intelligence, and self-regulation.

Guests reciprocate if they know you are an expert and your brand has integrity. Asking guests to conserve is less about making pleas to be good to nature, and more about targeting guest benefits, explaining how your more sustainable solutions help them have a better stay. You can have an 'epic meaning' (gamification term for features like My Green Butler's Noble Cause) that further stimulates reciprocation, enabling guests to saves resources.

Your design should also help people adapt to extreme weather events and reduce dissatisfaction. It is also suggested that by including experiences that increase understanding of cultural routines and nature's systems, you can improve guest participation as they enjoy a holistically sustainable hospitality experience that is consistently applied and lets them enjoy the flow of applying skills and savouring the results.

Guest participation should be deeply woven into service delivery from the outset of your planning. Interconnect all the guest touchpoints at your property (from guest rooms, restaurant, leisure activities and immersion into culture and nature) so that your sustainability practices and messaging are consistent. Motivate guests to reciprocate through choices that have clear benefits to the guest, the environment, and the community.

Drawing on character strengths is a strategy that should also be introduced to motivate staff to accept new routines. Positive company culture is essential for innovation to stick, as it is built brick by brick, requiring multiple stages that will gel together.

Recognising and stimulating people's character strengths to create sustainable hospitality experiences, therefore, will help you receive more positive guest reviews, increase staff satisfaction and retention, reduce costs and carbon, help you support your local community and create a healthy organisational culture. It is great for business success!

11

References

Baxter, J., Budinski, M., Carroll, M. & Hand, K. (2020). *Families in Australia Survey: Life during COVID-19.* Australian Institute of Family Studies.

Booking.com (2021) Sustainable Travel Report. https://news.booking.com/download/1039986/booking.com-sustainabletravelreport-us.pdf [Accessed 154 September 2021]

Brignall, M. (2020). Hobbycraft reports 200% boom in online sales since start of pandemic. *The Guardian,* 3 August. www.theguardian.com/business/2020/aug/03/hobbycraft-reports-boom-in-online-sales-since-start-of-pandemic-crafts-coronavirus [Accessed 3 September, 2021]

Buckingham, M. & Coffman, C. (1999). *First, break all the rules: What the world's greatest managers do differently.* Simon & Schuster, New York

Campbell, C. (2005). The craft consumer. *Journal of Consumer Culture,*5(1), 23-42

Carayol, R. (2012). Why culture is more important than strategy. Management Issues. www.management-issues.com/opinion/6576/why-culture-is-more-important-than-strategy/ [Accessed 14 September 2021]

Compton, W. & Hoffman, E. (2013). *Positive Psychology,*Wadsworth Cengage Learning (2nd ed.)

Complete Beehives (2019). http://completebeehives.com/how-much-honey-does-a-bee-make/ [Access 12 September 2021]

Crandall, Nolan & Morgan (1980) cited in Compton, W. & Hoffman, E. (2013). *Positive Psychology,*Wadsworth Cengage Learning.

Csikszentmihalyi, M. (1990). *Flow: The Psychology of Optimal Experience.* New York: Harper and Row.

De Young, R. (2000) Expanding and evaluating motivates for environmentally responsible behaviour. *Journal of Social Issues,* 56(3), 509-526.

Duffey, J. (2016). Personal communication, Conducted 1st March 2016. First published in *Progress in Responsible Tourism* 5(1),99

Emmons, R. & Crumpler, C. (2000). Gratitude as a human strength: Appraising the evidence. *Journal of Social and Clinical Psychology,* 19(1), 56-69

Emmons, R. & Paloutzian, R. (2003).The psychology of religion. *Annual Review of Psychology,* 54, 377-402

Ethics Centre (2016). Ethics Explainer: Eudaimonia. https://ethics.org.au/ethics-explainer-eudaimonia/ [Accessed 17 September 2021]

Gable, S. (2021). The benefits of positive emotions at work. Corporate Wellness Magazine.com

Ger, G. & Kravets, O. (2009) Special and ordinary times. In: Shove, E., Trentmann, F. & Wilk, R. (Eds.) *Time, Consumption and Everyday Life,* pp 189-202

Google (2021): Sustainable hotels: https://support.google.com/travel/answer/10976106?p=hotel_sustainability [Accessed 9th November 2021]

Ineson, E., Bente, E. & Laszlo, J. (2013). Employee loyalty in Hungarian hotels, *International Journal of Hospitality Management,* 32, 31-39

Kabanoff, B. (1982) Occupational and sex differences in leisure needs and leisure satisfaction. *Journal of Organizational Behavior,* 3, 233-245, cited in Argyle, M. (1987). *The Psychology of Happiness.* London, Methuen.

MEWS. (2021). The Green Hotel of the Future, www.mews.com/en/resources/research/green-hotel-future [Accessed 14 September 2021]

Park, N., Peterson, C., & Seligman, M. (2004). Strengths of character and well-being. *Journal of Social and Clinical Psychology, 23*, 603–619. doi:10.1521/jscp.23.5.603.50748

Pursuit of Happiness (2021). Socrates. www.pursuit-of-happiness.org/history-of-happiness/socrates/ [Accessed 1 September 2021]

Seligman, M. & Csikszentmihalyi, M. (2000). Positive Psychology: An introduction. *American Psychologist*, 55(1), 5-14

Solaiman Al Rifia (2017) Hatta Mosque heritage, personal communication, Dubai, UAE

Suri, C. (2020). Not a crafter? Here's why you should consider becoming one during the pandemic. *Washington Post*, 20 May. www.washingtonpost.com/lifestyle/wellness/home-crafts-coronavirus-pandemic-calm/2020/05/19/9785e11e-9a11-11ea-89fd-28fb313d1886_story.html [Accessed : 3 September, 2021]

Wan, B. (2018). Flourishing through smart tourism: experience patterns for co-design technology-mediated traveller experiences. *The Design Journal*, 21(1), 163-172

Westwood, M. (2008). Personal communication, Conducted 5th November 2008. First published in *Progress in Responsible Tourism* 5(1),99

Warren, M. (2018). *Get Smart with the 'Human Touch': Guest conserving resources use.* Working Paper Griffith University.

Warren, C. (2012a). Masters Thesis. Leeds Beckett University

Niemiec, R. (2013). *Mindfulness & Character Strengths: A practical guide to flourishing.* Boston: Hogriefe Publishing.

Warren, C. (2012b). Positive Connectedness: Encouraging pro-environmental behaviour change in responsible accommodation. *Progress in Responsible Tourism*, 2, 40-66

Warren, C. & Coghlan, A. (2016) Using character strength-based activities to design pro-environmental behaviours into the tourist experience. *Anatolia*, 27(4), 480-492

Warren, C., Becken, S. & Coghlan, A. (2018). Sustainability-oriented service innovation: fourteen-year longitudinal case study of a tourist accommodation provider. *Journal of Sustainable Tourism* 26,1784 - 1803.

Warren, C., Becken, S., Nguyen, K. & Stewart, R. (2018). Transitioning to smart sustainable tourist accommodation: Service innovation results. *Journal of Cleaner Production*, 201, 599-608

11

Index

Milton Keynes UK
Ingram Content Group UK Ltd.
UKHW011528311024
450488UK00016B/126